The lunette above the altar of First Lutheran Church

"It needs to be pondered in the heart
what it means to be the mother of God."

— Martin Luther, *The Magnificat* (1521)

Last on Grant

The History of the
First English Evangelical Lutheran Church
in the City of Pittsburgh

Philip H. Pfatteicher

*for Sister Teresa Irene
and the Episcopal Carmel of St Teresa
May peace ever abide in this house.*

*Philip H. Pfatteicher +
Corpus Christi
6 June 2010*

Lutheran University Press
Minneapolis, Minnesota

Last on Grant

The History of the First English Evangelical Lutheran
Church in the City of Pittsburgh
by Philip H. Pfatteicher

Library of Congress Cataloging-in-Publication Data

Pfatteicher, Philip H.
  Last on Grant : the history of the First English Evangelical Lutheran
Church in the city of Pittsburgh / Philip H. Pfatteicher.
       p. cm.
  Includes bibliographical references and index.
  ISBN-13: 978-1-933794-22-8 (alk. paper)
  ISBN-10: 1-933794-22-4 (alk. paper)
  1. First English Evangelical Lutheran Church (Pittsburgh, Pa.)—
Church history. 2. Pittsburgh (Pa.)—Church history. I. Title.
  BX8076.P6E5 2010
  284.1'74886—dc22
                                        2010001243

ENDPAPER: The lunette above the altar of First Lutheran Church
"It needs to be pondered in the heart what it means to be the mother of
God." — Martin Luther, *The Magnificat* (1521)

Lutheran University Press, PO Box 390759, Minneapolis, MN 55439
Manufactured in the United States of America

To the people of the First English Lutheran Church
in gratitude for giving me the extraordinary privilege
of serving among them in this remarkable parish

Contents

Illustrations

Preface

It is a great pleasure, as well as a relief, to have completed this new history of the First English Evangelical Lutheran Church in the City of Pittsburgh during the centennial year of the completion and publication of the original history by George J. Gongaware. That volume has been invaluable in the preparation of the present book. Moreover, I am pleased to note, the date of the publication of this new history, 2010, marks the fiftieth anniversary of my ordination.

This book is a history of the parish rather than a guide to the building and its ornamentation. The principle governing the selection of the photographs and illustrations therefore is that photographs of pastors and events not easily accessible showing what went on in the past are included to help readers visualize and understand the historical record. Photographs of objects in the present building (altar, cross, tabernacle, stations of the cross, columbarium) have been omitted. One can walk into the church and see them for oneself, one hopes for many years to come. Moreover, photographs of these are accessible on the parish website on the internet.

Several people have contributed to the work on this history, and their names deserve to be recorded. About 2005 a person whose name is unrecorded came to the church office to present to the First Church an envelope containing a priceless gift. It was a photograph of the chancel as it appeared when the church was consecrated November 4, 1888. Until then the congregation did not possess a representation of what the original altar and chancel looked like. Since the Ladies' Sewing Society a half-dozen years later sought permission to renovate the chancel "in keeping with our Lutheran tradition," the assumption was that the original altar was somehow embarrassingly unworthy. The faded photograph proved that such was not the case. Paul Meyer digitalized the precious photo to preserve it for future generations. Janet

King digitalized all the other photographs and drawings that are an essential part of the book. John C. Harmon, remarkably knowledgeable in the history of the Lutheran Church and particularly of the Church in Western Pennsylvania, who has visited all the sites mentioned in the book, read the manuscript and made useful comments throughout. Beatrice B. Weimer, who has long served the parish in many ways, most of all as administrative secretary, has gone over the manuscript with her accustomed care and precision and caught errors that escaped other readers. David P. Gleason, the present pastor of the parish, has also read these pages and has made helpful suggestions.

Although he is mentioned briefly in the following pages, André Bierman, tenor soloist and the longest-serving member of the present staff, who for a quarter-century has enriched the worship of the congregation by his piety and devotion and the perfection of his singing, deserves recognition here.

Most of all, the gratitude of the whole congregation must gladly be extended to Glen and LaVonne Johnson, extraordinary benefactors of First Church, for yet another contribution that has made possible the publication of this history.

Finally, I must record my gratitude to my wife, Lois Sharpless Pfatteicher, who, in September 1998, learning that First Church did not then have a second pastor, urged me to offer my services, temporarily, until the search committee found a suitable person. The temporary service lasted twelve years.

Philip H. Pfatteicher
Pittsburgh
The Commemoration of J. C. F. Heyer
7 November 2009

Introduction

From very early in its life the congregation of First English Lutheran Church was aware that remarkable things were happening in its midst and that its story was worth telling and preserving. As early as 1846, just nine years after the congregation had been founded, the congregation explored the possibility of a brief history. "Even this early in the congregation's history we find a record of January 13, 1846, that a committee was appointed to ascertain how many copies of a history of the Church could be disposed of, if prepared and printed in pamphlet form, and later it was resolved to print one thousand copies."[1] The interest in recording the story continued. "November 3, 1884, the Council requested Mr. [Thomas] Lane, in view of the approaching semi-centennial of the congregation [1887], to collect all material accessible for a history of the congregation from its organization."[2] This having been done, the actual writing of the history was entrusted to the pastor of the parish, David Harrison Geissinger: "January 7, 1896, at the regular congregational meeting, the pastor was requested, upon the suggestion of Mr. Lane, to prepare a history of the congregation from its founding to the present."[3] The council minutes include the note "at his convenience."

The publication of that history was delayed by the illness and death of Pastor Geissinger. His successor, George Gongaware, completed the writing with the significant assistance of Luther Dotterer Reed (1873-1972), then pastor of Emanuel's Church in Manchester on the North Side and later Professor of Liturgics and President of the Lutheran Theological Seminary at Philadelphia.[4] The history recounted in the following pages is a continuation of the past efforts to preserve for future generations the story of this remarkable parish. The present book leans heavily on that 1909 history and indeed shamelessly borrows much of the very language of that history as a way of paying homage to those learned predecessors who originally compiled and shaped the history.

The intrepid founders and benefactors of the parish were aware of the significance of what they were doing and were eager to record the story so it would not be forgotten, but the urgency seemed to fade in their successors as the twentieth century unfolded. Not many continued to sense the excitement of what was happening on Grant Street. An historical booklet was compiled for the centennial of the congregation in 1937, but there was no movement toward the preparation of a larger book. Confidence, vision, and hope had been eclipsed as the congregation struggled through changing circumstances and surroundings to find its mission and to understand its purpose. The importance of history in shaping self-understanding was recognized at least by one woman. In December 1973 Mathilda Ittel gave the church $675 toward the publication of a history of the parish. She died June 5, 1984 without seeing the fruition of her hope. Now, more than a quarter-century later, her desire is perhaps fulfilled.

The title of this account, "Last on Grant," implies that it is the story of a survivor. First Church is indeed the last surviving church on the street. The Roman Catholic Cathedral of St. Paul used to be at Fifth Avenue and Grant Street, across from the Allegheny County Court House; next to it was the lovely Gothic brownstone St. Peter's Episcopal Church. Both churches left downtown for the Oakland section of the city at the beginning of the twentieth century. The Roman Catholic cathedral flourishes; St. Peter's declined and was closed and demolished in 1990. There was a Reformed Presbyterian church next to First Lutheran Church, built *ca.* 1880; in 1908 it relocated to Frankstown Road in Homewood and again in 1958 to Penn Hills. First German Lutheran Church had erected its first building on the northwest corner of Sixth and Grant Streets; it later built a new house on High Street (now Sixth Avenue) near Wylie Avenue, just off Grant Street, and then it too moved to Oakland in 1925. Only First Church remains—the church called First is now also the last. Its uninspired name, merely a number, stands nonetheless as a living testimony to the truth of both sides of Jesus' declaration, "So the last will be first, and the first will be last" [Matthew 20:16]. Moreover, First Lutheran Church shares with Henry Hobson Richardson's famed Allegheny County Courthouse the dignity of being the two oldest buildings on Pittsburgh's principal thorough-fare, both completed and dedicated in the fall of 1888.

Two other parts of the full title of the church require comment. It is "English" because it was founded by those who wanted to worship not in the language of their forebears, German, but in the language of their adopted and eventually their native land. It is "Evangelical" because it is based on the Gospel of our Lord Jesus Christ. ("Gospel" in Greek is *Evangel.*) "Evangelical" is commonly used throughout the world as part of the title of Lutheran churches and organizations.

A further note on usage may be helpful in the interests of accuracy. The charter of the congregation calls the governing body of the congregation "the vestry," a common name in the Episcopal Church and a not uncommon name in Lutheran churches of the time. Vestry remained the legal name of the body, although members of the congregation and of the vestry itself as well as the careful 1909 *History of the First English Evangelical Lutheran Church in Pittsburgh* use the more common name among Lutherans, "church council." "Vestry" was proper until 1958 when the formation of the Lutheran Church in America required the revision of the constitution. Then the name of the body became "church council." With the formation of the Evangelical Lutheran Church in America in 1980, the name "church council" was appropriated by the governing body of the national church and the local body was called the "congregation council." For simplicity and clarity, "church council" is used throughout this book, as it was in the previous history.

The original history was compiled for the members and friends of the parish. This book seeks to expand that audience and has in view many beyond this congregation, not only those in the Lutheran tradition, who find themselves in situations similar to those through which First Lutheran Church has made its way through the almost two centuries of its life.

The story presented here may be of interest and, perhaps, of help to many beyond this parish as an encouragement to remain faithful to the tradition that has formed them in their own spiritual life, even as it has shaped the lives of generations before them. Such faithfulness is always difficult. It runs counter to the prevailing spirit of the age; it opposes the way of the world. But fidelity to the tradition, to those who understand and with eyes to see, is not a lonely struggle. It keeps faith with the Church of all times and all places and is part of that large communion of those who preserve and maintain community with the Church through the ages. In these pages the reader will see the context in which and not infrequently against which First Lutheran Church has struggled to identify and to preserve its identity and its heritage. It is a context that keeps recurring in various guises as the centuries pass, but at its core the issues are remarkably similar.

Through its history, First Lutheran Church in Pittsburgh has influenced the larger Church in many ways. It was the first English-speaking Lutheran church west of the Allegheny Mountains. The first American Lutheran deaconess was consecrated in its first building. The first Protestant hospital in America was founded in Pittsburgh by the pastor of First Church, William Passavant. The Lutheran Liturgical Association (a counterpart to the Tractarian movement in the Church of England) was founded and met regularly in the chapel of the present church. Harry G. Archer, organist of the congregation, collaborated with the renowned liturgical scholar Luther D. Reed in setting the Lutheran Liturgy (The Service with its propers, also Matins, Vespers, and the Litany) and the complete King James' Psalter to plainsong chant. One of the earliest radio broadcasts of church services began in the church.

The careful reader will notice in this account how intertwined is the history of a relatively small number of parishes and pastors, whose names keep recurring and who continually support and refresh each other: First Lutheran Church and the Ministerium of Pennsylvania and the Lutheran Theological Seminary at Philadelphia and St. John's Church, Easton, Pennsylvania.

Attention has been lavished on the building during the past two decades as it had been in the early years of the building. Then it was the installation of the marble altar and chancel and the glorious lunette of the Holy Virgin. A century later it was the free-standing altar, the tabernacle, the columbarium and oratory, the stations of the cross, a carefully thought-out repainting of the chancel and nave. Both then and now the improvements and enhancements were understood to be part of the mission of the congregation, to make the building inviting and attractive and rich with traditional aspects of Christian worship through the ages.

Outside the building, the Resurrection sculpture attracts attention to the church, the cross on the spire proclaims the center of the Christian faith, especially to those whose upper-story office windows look out on it, the tower bells announce to the city that the church is going about its daily business and invite all who are so inclined to come and see what is going on and perhaps become part of the story.

The First Church is "a serious house on serious earth."[5] In its unassuming presence it still stands on Grant Street ready to surprise those who may not yet recognize a hunger in themselves to be more serious and who, sharing its life, can grow wise within its walls. The nineteenth-century church, surrounded by twentieth-century skyscrapers speaks to twenty-first century workers and visitors of continuity amid change, of stability amid turmoil, of the longer perspective of the eternal God and the ever-new power of the everlasting Gospel.

Interest in the building and its significance is a result of the Christian understanding of the Incarnation. God took on human flesh and uses the things of this world to make himself known, chiefly in the sacraments by which God's grace comes to us through the earthly elements of water and of bread and wine. The places where these actions happen, the font and the altar, are rightly honored, as is the house in which they are located. It is from the building and the actions accomplished in it that Christians are strengthened and encouraged to carry the work of the Church out into the city.

CHAPTER ONE

The Pivotal Decision

In 1987 the pastorate of the longest-serving pastor in the history of First English Evangelical Lutheran Church was coming to a close. The senior pastor had announced his intention to retire in 1988; the assistant pastor had recently resigned, as had also the director of music. The congregation, in examining itself with a view to identifying desirable characteristics of their next pastor, saw itself in numerical decline and in search of a clear sense of direction and purpose as it looked to the future. The decline in membership had continued for half a century and was experienced by all the downtown churches. Pittsburgh itself, with the collapse of the steel industry in the decades following the Second World War, seemed to be in a downward spiral. Through several pastorates the congregation had been searching, sometimes with a hint of desperation and always in vain, for some way to reverse the decline. It was difficult to be optimistic about the church or the city.

Nonetheless, a notable strength of the congregation was the members' remarkable and long-standing devotion to the parish. Clear evidence of that commitment is seen in the capital fund campaign for the restoration and renovation of the church building conducted in the early 1980s that raised more than $240,000, double the amount predicted by fund-raising professionals. (The annual budget for 1982 was $240,104.)

A twelve-member Research and Assessment Committee, chosen to represent virtually all the points of view within the congregation[6], was appointed by the church council to lay the groundwork for the selection of the next pastor. The committee made a detailed survey of the congregation's priorities and ideas and on the basis of that came to a number of conclusions, none of which was surprising. There was agreement, reflecting the character of the congregation as the members had known it through several pastorates, that "preaching is of primary importance to our future. Dynamic preaching is probably the single most important method of outreach and ministry in a downtown congregation." Worship, the committee reported, closely followed the importance of preaching. By "worship" at least some members of the committee seemed not to mean the formative strength of the full historic liturgy but simply the setting in which preaching took place, and an important part of the setting was music. Christian education and pastoral care were the next priorities. One pastor, the committee recognized, could not be expected to fulfill these four requirements, and therefore the senior pastor, whose primary responsibilities were to be preaching and worship, must be supported with a second pastor or a lay professional to be sought immediately upon the calling of the senior pastor.

After sorting through seventeen candidates, the call committee (most of whom had been members of the Research and Assessment Committee) presented the Reverend David Paul Gleason, D.Min., then pastor of Palm Lutheran Church in Palmyra, Pennsylvania, as the seventeenth pastor of the First English Evangelical Lutheran Church in the City of Pittsburgh.

In 1990 the new pastor of First Lutheran Church inquired of the office of Mayor Sophie Masloff concerning the impossibility of legal parking for deliveries to the church. Her office dismissed the inquiry with the declaration, "There is no church on Grant Street."

In the intervening decades, officials of the city and county have come to learn that there is indeed a church on Grant Street, one that is healthy and vibrant and in daily service to the city. The developing respect for the congregation and its work was the result of a vision that Pastor Gleason had instilled in the congregation.

First, the congregation was invited to look at the churches in their immediate area. Around the corner on Sixth Avenue, First Presbyterian Church, long renowned for its vigorous Calvinist preaching, was strong and vibrant. Directly behind the Lutheran church, Smithfield United Church had brought together several traditions, Reformed, Congregational, and Methodist. Trinity Episcopal Cathedral, next door to the Presbyterian Church, maintained the Anglican cathedral tradition of a large professional choir with daily services. The Lutheran congregation was brought to realize that downtown Pittsburgh did not need another generic Protestant church. Good and popular preaching, together with strength in sacred music, alone would not revive the congregation.

Second, looking back across their own history as a parish, the congregation understood that the years when the congregation was strongest and most influential were the closing decades of the nineteenth century and the early twentieth century. Those years of numerical and financial strength and wide influence were characterized by Confessional clarity and liturgical richness.

Third, the congregation therefore concluded, the way ahead was to look to the strongest period in its history and emulate those strengths. The congregation needed to be clearly and distinctively Lutheran, proud of its noble heritage, led in the past by many of the great names in Lutheran history in North America, figures whose work will be described in the pages that follow. The emphasis of the work of the new pastor was to be sacramental, focusing on the centrality of the Eucharist in the life of the congregation together with a clear sense of the community established by Holy Baptism, a communion with the Church through the centuries. And this vision and understanding had to be taught patiently and clearly and convincingly to the congregation so that they would understand that their mandate, under the leadership of their new pastor, was to restore the liturgical and Confessional strength of the congregation to give it a distinctive identity and a clear purpose for its existence.

CHAPTER TWO

Establishing Christianity at the Forks of the Ohio

Each of the major denominations in Pittsburgh has been eager to show how early its representatives brought their brand of Christianity to the area that was to become Pittsburgh.[7]

Pittsburgh in 1817

In August 1748, the same month and year when Henry Melchior Muhlenberg and five other Lutheran pastors organized the venerable Evangelical Lutheran Ministerium of Pennsylvania,[8] the first Lutheran synod in America, Muhlenberg's father-in-law, Conrad Weiser, the trusted Indian agent for the descendents of William Penn, led a small party to Logstown on the banks of the Ohio River to meet with the Native Americans. Twenty years later, November 1768, in the Treaty of Fort Stanwix, the lands east of the Allegheny River were purchased by the Penns.

These lands were opened to sale and settlement April 3, 1769, and German settlers from eastern Pennsylvania, Maryland, and Virginia, and also from Germany itself found themselves side by side with the Scotch-Irish pioneers in taking up the lands. Indeed, some of the stouter-hearted pioneers had settled in the region in advance of the Land Office.

The first Christian religious services in the region were, without much doubt, Masses celebrated by the chaplains of the French expeditions in the area in 1729 and 1749. The first Mass at Fort Duquesne, at the confluence of the three rivers (where the Allegheny and the Monongahela combine at Pittsburgh to form the Ohio), was celebrated April 16, 1754 by the Reverend Denys Baron, a Recollect Friar[9], chaplain to the French forces there. A chapel was built at the fort, dedicated under the title of "The Assumption of the Blessed Virgin of the Beautiful River" (La Chapelle de l'Assomption de la Ste. Vierge a la belle rivière). In November 1758 the small military outpost was burned by its builders and abandoned just before a large force of British and Colonial soldiers commanded by General John Forbes reached the Point. The first resident Roman Catholic priest in Pittsburgh, Father William F. X. O'Brien, did not arrive until 1808; the first Roman Catholic church, Old St. Patrick's, was dedicated in 1811.

The Presbyterians in Pittsburgh trace their history from 1762 when a "school-church" was established with religious services conducted by a Presbyterian school master. In 1773, under the Donegal Presbytery, the congregation of First Presbyterian Church was established. Formal organization occurred in 1784, when the Reverend Joseph Smith was chosen as the first pastor. Services were held in members' homes until their first building, made of logs, appropriately located on Wood Street, was constructed in 1787. The present building (1905), the congregation's fourth house, is on Sixth Avenue.

The first regular preaching place for the Methodist Episcopal Church, which had been organized in Baltimore in 1784, was the historic block house at the Point. In 1810 a brick chapel was built at Smithfield and Front Streets; in 1818 a new church was built on Smithfield Street at Seventh Avenue, which, from the character of the preaching in the building, soon bore the nickname "Brimstone Corner." That church was replaced with another in 1848; it stood until 1968.

The "African Church" was organized in a home on Front Street in 1808. Ten years later Bethel African Methodist Episcopal Church received its charter. In 1827 the congregation purchased a church building on Strawberry Way that had been vacated by the Methodists; in 1830 a church was purchased on Front Street. The pastor, the Reverend Lewis Woodson, was involved with the Underground Railroad. The great fire of 1845 destroyed the church building, and the congregation purchased property at Wylie Avenue and Elm Street in the Hill District and erected a church in 1906.

The English forces and their chaplains at Fort Pitt doubtless held Church of England religious services there; the fort was abandoned in 1772 and was dismantled about 1792. The 1764 block house alone survives.

What was to become Trinity Episcopal Church has its origins about 1790.[10] Services were held intermittently. In 1797 parishioners called the Reverend John Taylor to serve as their priest and rector. Services were held in private homes and in the courthouse in Market Square until 1805 when Trinity Church was incorporated and a church of sophisticated octagonal design in Georgian style was built, not on the land granted by the descendents of William Penn but on a triangular plot of land bounded by Liberty Avenue, Sixth Avenue, and Wood Street. The growth of the congregation encouraged the building of a new church, this time in a Gothic style designed by the rector, John Henry Hopkins,[11] in 1825 on the larger plot of land that had been granted to the congregation by Penn's descendents in 1787. The church was consecrated by Bishop William White, the first Bishop of Pennsylvania, on his only visit to Pittsburgh, June 12, 1825. At that visitation, showing the growth of the city, the rector presented to the bishop a confirmation class of one hundred thirty-seven.

The history directly related to First Lutheran Church begins in 1782, when the population of the small village of Pittsburgh was about two hundred-fifty people living in some sixty houses, most made of logs, clustered around the old Fort Pitt site. In that year the German Lutherans and Reformed in and about Pittsburgh called a Reformed minister, the Reverend Johann Wilhelm Weber, to be their pastor. He was born in Germany in 1735 and came to America with his young wife in 1764 at the age of twenty-nine. After teaching school for several years, he decided to enter the ministry and was ordained by the German Reformed Synod. In May 1782 the Synod sent him to visit Western Pennsylvania, giving him a permit to be their pastor if the congregations there should call him. It took him a month to cross the state on horseback. He preached in Pittsburgh and in other German-speaking communities in the area, and was called to be their pastor. In June 1783 he crossed the Allegheny Mountains again, this time in a wagon with his wife and their six children. He organized and served the German church in Pittsburgh, the first organized congregation in the city, in connection with three congregations in Westmoreland County: Salem in Brush Creek, Old Zion in Harolds, and St. Paul's in Mt. Pleasant Township. Although the Pittsburgh church was his chief appointment, he lived in his log cabin home in Westmoreland County with his second wife (his first wife had died in childbirth) and their eighteen children. His salary was fixed at "eighty pounds sterling in money, one hundred bushels of wheat, a free dwelling house and yearly fire-wood."[12] He apparently provided the dwelling house and cut the fire-wood himself. Pittsburgh was thirty miles from his home and other churches; he rode his horse at least eighty miles each week. Travel was difficult over poor roads, through woods, and across often swollen streams and rivers. It was also dangerous. He carried a gun, a knife, and a hatchet in case of an attack by native people. There was as yet no church building in Pittsburgh. One Arthur Lee, a visitor to western Pennsylvania recorded in his diary, "Pittsburgh is inhabited almost entirely by Scots and Irish, who live in paltry log houses, and are as dirty as the north of Ireland or even Scotland. . . . There are in the town four attorneys, two doctors, and not a priest of any persuasion, nor church nor chapel."[13] In 1783 the German Evangelical Church rented a log building at Wood Street and Forbes Avenue.

In 1787 the grandson and great-grandson of William Penn, for the purpose of "encouraging and promoting Morality, Piety and Religion in general, and more especially in the town of Pittsburgh," deeded three lots, then cornfields outside the city proper, for churches and graveyards. One was granted to the First Presbyterian congregation on Wood Street, a second to the German Evangelical Protestant Church on Smithfield Street, and the third to certain trustees to hold in trust for an Episcopal congregation to be organized in the future.

The property of the Smithfield Street church was deeded jointly to "the two German religious societies or congregations," one of which "adheres to the Unaltered Augsburg Confession" [the Lutherans] and the other known as the "Protestant Reformed Church."

The German congregation did not immediately build on the land because it was then so far out of town, but in 1791, four years after the grant of land, the united congregation began to erect on that land its first church building, of brick, at the corner of Smithfield Street and Sixth Avenue (then called Sixth Street) with an adjoining graveyard stretching along Smithfield Street to Strawberry Alley (now Strawberry Way). J. W. Weber served the congregation until 1794, the year following the completion of the church building, probably feeling that once the meetinghouse was completed, he could reduce his travel. He was fifty-nine years old and continued to serve his other three congregations near Greensburg until his death at age eighty-one. The German Church in Pittsburgh had no synodical connection, and for many years its pastors were drawn from the ranks of Reformed or Lutheran clergy. The primary adhesive was the exclusive use of the German language.

A Lutheran, John Michael Steck (1755-1830)[14], visited occasionally from Greensburg between1791 and 1796 but found himself unwelcome. The Reformed side of the congregation was determinedly unionistic and anti-confessional, opposing all efforts by the Lutherans to have a distinctive identity and services. In 1806 the Lutherans withdrew to form a separate and distinctive congregation, but after six years they reunited with the Reformed congregation. The reunited congregation adopted the name *Deutsche Evangelische Protestantische Kirche*: "Evangelical" because it is based on the Gospel, the word commonly used in Germany to designate non-Roman Catholic churches; and "Protestant," the word used in Britain and America to express the same thing. Noteworthy is the use of *Kirche,* church, rather than the more Protestant *Gemeinde,* congregation, probably indicating the influence of the Lutherans.[15] A Lutheran pastor of the Ministerium of Pennsylvania, Jacob Schnee, was called as pastor; he served the German Evangelical Protestant Church from 1813 to 1818.

Pittsburgh was growing from a small village to an industrial town. By the end of the eighteenth century a constant stream of homesteaders passed through Pittsburgh, "the gateway to the West," on their way to find a new life in the Ohio River settlements of Ohio, Kentucky, Indiana, and Illinois. They stopped in Pittsburgh to buy boats, farm equipment, clothing, and supplies. Shipbuilding became a major industry. The town had iron and brass foundries, a textile mill, glass works, tool and nail manufacturing, and factories making household items such as candles and soap. In 1816, when Pittsburgh was incorporated as a city, it had a population of 6,000.

Pittsburgh seemed promising for an English Lutheran church, and in 1817 the Ministerium of Pennsylvania proposed a candidate for the ministry by the name of Stecker [or Stecher] for work in Pittsburgh, but ultimately he was sent to Macungie, in northeastern Pennsylvania instead.[16] In 1821 the church was incorporated under the title the German Evangelical Protestant Church, and the pastor from 1821 to 1822 was a Lutheran, Heinrich Geisenhainer. He was succeeded by Heinrich Kurtz (1823-1826), the last Lutheran pastor to serve the congregation. The church continues today as Smithfield United Church of Christ, on Smithfield Street at Strawberry Way. The congregation is now in its fifth house, designed by Pittsburgh architect Henry Hornbostel, built in 1926.

Third building of the German Evangelical Protestant Church, 1833-1875

As the corporate name of the united congregation makes clear, the German settlers in the New World clung stubbornly to their accustomed language. It was more than a deep conservatism embedded in the settlers of western Pennsylvania. The continued use of the *Muttersprache,* the mother tongue, was a way of maintaining contact with the *Vaterland,* the fatherland. The use of German persisted for a remarkably long time. The first bi-lingual morning services in the German Evangelical Protestant Church (established in 1782) were not conducted until 1917; English did not become the language of the congregation until 1928.[17] The Roman Catholic Church faced similar ethnic and linguistic divisions. Old St. Patrick's Church became a German-speaking parish in 1834 when St. Paul's church at Fifth Avenue and Grant Street was completed; it reverted to English in 1839 when St. Philomena's was established for the German Catholic community.

Since the Germans were surrounded by neighbors who spoke only English, it is to be expected that the use of German in daily life eventually declined. For business to be carried on with those beyond the German fold, the use of English was required. After a few generations, the Germans, like those around them, spoke English, the language of law and of commerce. The one exception was the worship of God. The last things one learns to do in a new language are to count and to pray, and so German continued to be the language of worship. It preserved the connection with the old country and was a significant part of the practice of the faith. One German pastor summed it up, "English für Gescheft aber Deutsch für Gottesdienst" [English for business, but German for worship]. Another pastor, Dr. Hacke, a cultured German with a deep love for the German language and literature and German services, who eventually concluded that the use of English in worship was a necessity, was dismissed with the remark, "Hacke will become an Irishman too."[18]

The use of German, which was understood to be a nearly essential aspect of the character of the Lutheran Church, was stubbornly persistent. In 1815 the sixty-eighth convention of the Ministerium of Pennsylvania received "a memorial from Mr. Cook, an English preacher, who belongs to the Episcopal Church, in which he states that he is convinced of the purity of the principles of the Evangelical Lutheran Church, and that he has a great desire to be received into the same, and also expresses the hope that he may be located as a preacher in Huntingdon."[19] The synod referred the matter to the Ministerium. Two days later, the pastors formulated their reply. "Concerning the request of the English Episcopal preacher, Mr. Cook (*vide* No. 21), it was resolved, that as our Ministerium is a German-speaking Ministerium, we cannot have anything to do with him, according to our present principles; but as soon as he, according to the declaration of his letter, has acquired the German language, so that he can also preach in the same, he may apply to us again and expect prefer-ment."[20] The synod did not hear again from Mr. Cook.

In 1816 a group was actually tried in court in Philadelphia for conspiring to prevent the introduction of the English language into the services of St. Michael's and Zion churches (two churches with one organization).[21]

The preservation of the German language at least in wor-ship was further encouraged by the suspicion on the part of many that the use of English led to accommodation with the sects and the loss of the authentic Lutheran tradition. The German language was seen to be an essential part of the whole tradition. When in the middle of the nineteenth century certain Lutheran leaders sought to abandon or dilute their confessional heritage in order to become part of a general American Protestantism, it was ob-served that all of them were English-speaking. The preservation of the German language seemed to be a bastion against betrayal of the heritage.

Nonetheless, the language of the land made inroads into Lutheran worship. In 1796 the first entirely English Lutheran con-gregation organized in the United States, Zion's, was established in New York City. In response, the New York Ministerium de-clared in a resolution, "Since a close connection exists between the Episcopal and the Lutheran Church and on account of the similarity of doctrine and close relationship in church discipline, the Ministerium will never acknowledge a newly established Lutheran church that uses only the English language in a place where members may participate in the Episcopal service."[22] In 1805 its pastor, the Reverend George Strebeck and a large num-ber of its members joined the Episcopal Church, and in 1810 the remaining portion along with their pastor Ralph Williston, who had originally been a Methodist, also entered the same commun-ion. This was in keeping with the prevailing view of many. An untold number of Lutherans, desiring to use English in all their activities, including worship, had left the Lutheran fold, often for the Episcopal Church which in doctrine and in usage they found comparable to the church of their forebears. The New York Ministerium had even declared the Protestant Episcopal Church, as it was then called, to be the English Lutheran Church, to which all Lutherans preferring English to German should be directed.[23] The Swedish Lutheran congregations in and around Philadelphia, having long abandoned the use of Swedish, one by one all became parishes of the Episcopal Diocese of Pennsylvania. In 1806 the first permanent English Lutheran congregation in America, St. John's in Philadelphia, had been established after a most bitter controversy over the question of the language appropriate for worship, by a party which under the leadership of General Peter Muhlenberg, son of the patriarch Henry Melchior Muhlenberg, had left Zion Church.

Even the Ministerium of Pennsylvania, which in 1815 had insisted to Mr. Cook, the Episcopalian who wanted to become a Lutheran pastor, that it was "a German speaking Ministerium," resolved in 1818 "That the Synod, however, from time to time, is becoming more and more convinced that the saving doctrine of our Lord, according to the principles of our Evangelical Church, should be brought and preached to the younger portion of the Philadelphia congregation [St. Michael's and Zion] in the English language," and "That the Synod issue to the congregation and Church Council in Philadelphia an urgent and earnest request, that they should seriously see to it that, without injury to the German service, the instruction and edification of the younger portion of the congregation, in the English language, be introduced, without causing a still greater separation of the congregation by continued refusal."[24]

What distressed even those who were open to the use of English was that many of the Lutheran churches which adopted the English language were abandoning the distinctive Lutheran doctrines and usages and were becoming almost indistinguishable from the various Protestant churches around them. Charles Porterfield Krauth told his Philadelphia congregation in 1860, "The inevitable substitution of the language of our land for the German and other foreign tongues, first inclines and finally compels them [those who have been Anglicized] to seek a home in English churches. But if our English congregations show no sympathy with the life and usages of the Lutheran Church, they will not come to us. They will be carried off in directions in which there is more seeming conformity with what they have been trained in, than they find in our congregations; and a class of persons, not second in value to any in this nation, are thus lost to us."[25] He issued the warning, "The diversity of usage, moreover, tends to foment party spirit. . . . . It tends to divide our house against itself. . . . It plays into the hands of those who would rather rule in some little fragment of a torn Church than work on the broad and equal ground of fraternity in an undivided Church; it encourages those who would widen the breaches, would have Old and New School Lutherans, and would aggravate our differences until they ceased to be the mere necessary variations of a free and healthy life, and became the sources of party feuds and sectarian divisions. We should aim at having such uniformity throughout our whole land, that wherever our people enter a Lutheran Church they will feel that they are at home."[26]

William Passavant accepted and passed on an account, reported in the 1909 congregational history, that George Weyman, traveling eastward on a canal packet, discovered that Dr. Peter Schoenberger was also a passenger, bound for the iron furnaces of Huntingdon County. They discussed the movement for a Lutheran congregation in Pittsburgh, and came to a tacit understanding together to seek a suitable property and guarantee the payments. Dr. Schoenberger, although a member of Trinity Episcopal Church, held a pew in the Seventh Avenue church and communed occasionally.[27]

In 1806 an itinerant missionary effort was begun by the Ministerium of Pennsylvania, and in 1814 the first attempt was made to labor among the scattered Lutherans in Western Pennsylvania. One of these missionaries was John Frederick Christian Heyer, who in 1817 was ministering in Crawford and Erie counties. At the request of some settlers who could not understand the German language, in that year in French Creek, near Meadville, he preached what were perhaps the first English Lutheran sermons in Western Pennsylvania.

The General Synod, organized in 1820, sent some missionaries into this territory, and it may be surmised that they visited Pittsburgh, met the English-speaking Lutherans, and did preliminary missionary work. In 1825 the pastors of the Ministerium of Pennsylvania west of the Susquehanna River organized the Evangelical Lutheran Synod of West Pennsylvania, and for a time continued the itinerant missionary system. "In 1833 . . . Mr. T. Lape of Johnstown, N.Y., was employed to work for the establishment of an English Lutheran congregation in Pittsburgh. His missionary zeal found field for service not only in this western city of the State of Pennsylvania, but took him as far as Cincinnati and Louisville, and brought from him the report of promising opportunities in both of these places for the organization of Lutheran congregations."[28]

At the 1835 meeting of the West Pennsylvania Synod the Central Missionary Society was organized to encourage foreign missions, but until opportunity presented itself its activity was to be directed to home mission work on the American frontier. In 1836 the Synod in session at Lewistown received a letter from the Reverend D. P. Rosenmiller of Perrysburg, Ohio, in which he wished "to know, whether, and to what extent, the Synod would aid him in the attempt to organize an English Lutheran congregation in Pittsburgh." The Synod referred the proposal to the executive committee of the missionary society with the recommendation that likewise Nicholas G. Sharretts, who had been ordained in 1827, and Jacob Martin, who had been ordained in 1829, would also be suitable persons for the Pittsburgh mission.[29]

The pastor who was to organize the first English Lutheran Church in Pittsburgh, however, was John Christian Frederick Heyer[30], a notably zealous and restless missionary and president of the Central Missionary Society. (His name was pronounced in the German manner, "HIGH-er.") He reports in his autobiography, "Efforts had been made at various times to establish an English Lutheran congregation in Pittsburgh; but so far unsuccessfully. The Synod of West Pennsylvania at its meeting held in October [1836] had resolved to make another attempt, and appointed three of its members to preach in Pittsburgh in rotation. Those thus commissioned were N. Scharretts [sic], J. Martin, and C. F. Heyer."[31] Heyer had visited Sharretts in Indiana, Pennsylvania and found that "he was unwell, but able to be up, and we had no fear at that time that this promising and gifted young fellow-laborer would in a few weeks be called from our midst." Sharretts had announced a service for Pittsburgh for the following Sunday; Jacob Martin was scheduled to administer the Lord's

John Christian Frederick Heyer

Supper elsewhere on that Sunday. Martin therefore told Heyer, "It comes to your turn, if the undertaking in Pittsburgh is not to fail in the very beginning."[32] And so the task of establishing an English Lutheran Church fell to Heyer.

The renowned missionary was born in Helmstedt, Germany, July 10, 1793, the third child and second son of a master furrier, Johann Heinrich Gottlieb Heyer and his wife Fredericke Sophie Johanne Wagener Heyer. After his confirmation, when he was fourteen years of age, Europe being disrupted by the Napoleonic wars, he was sent to America to his mother's brother in Philadelphia. He sailed on a ship with the prophetic name, *Pittsburgh*. In Philadelphia he practiced the furrier's trade under the supervision of his uncle and became a member of Zion Church. In 1810 the illustrious pastor of Zion, Dr. Justus Heinrich Christian Helmuth agreed to take Heyer on as a theological apprentice, there being as yet no Lutheran seminaries in America.[33] Dr. Helmuth suggested in 1815 that his able student spend some time in Europe. It was a bold suggestion. Europe was still disrupted by the Napoleonic wars, and European clergy were distrusted in America because of the rationalistic turn that German theology had taken. It was Heyer's intention to attend the famed University of Halle, an important center of Pietism from which Henry Melchior Muhlenberg, "the patriarch of the Lutheran Church in America," had been sent out in the eighteenth century, but the university was closed because of the war. He therefore attended Göttingen, the most fashionable university in the land. There he adopted the shoulder-length hair style of the students, which was his distinctive mark throughout the rest of his long life. At the university, his brother Heinrich was influenced by the popular rationalistic spirit, but J. C. F. Heyer remained in the orthodox fold.

In 1816 he returned to Philadelphia. There he married Mary Webb Gash, a thirty year-old widow with two children, Caroline age 8 and Basil age 4. The place and the date of the marriage are not known. Through the years she perfected his English so that he was equally comfortable praying and preaching in German or in English, speaking the latter, it is reported, without a trace of an accent. The couple had six children, four girls and two boys. Sophie, named for her grandmother Heyer, was born in Philadelphia in 1818; Carl Henry was born in Cumberland, Maryland in

1820. Their third child, Mary Ann, died of malaria in Cumberland, a year and a half old; Henrietta was born in 1823 two months after the death of her sister. Their fifth child, Juliann Eliza, born in Somerset, lived but three months (September 25, 1825 to January 1, 1826). The last child, Theophilus Luther, was born in Somerset in 1827.

In 1817, the year after he returned to Philadelphia, Heyer was sent by the Ministerium of Pennsylvania to Crawford and Erie Counties in the northwestern corner of the commonwealth; he was stationed at Meadville. On his way to Meadville, he had an opportunity to preach a sermon at a vacant parish in Macungie, Lehigh County. He thought he had a fair chance to begin his ministry in an established congregation instead of out on the home mission frontier. His hope was dashed. A friend told him later, "You failed on three counts. First, the people did not want a preacher who had been educated in Germany; they had been taught to fear the new thought of Rationalism. You failed in the second place because you did not follow the usual custom of announcing your text at the beginning, so the people thought you had forgotten it because you saved it until the middle of the sermon. And most of all, they were shocked at the way you wear your hair, long and parted in the middle, like the students at Göttingen." In his autobiography Heyer reflected, "What trifling circumstances can give our lives a different course."[34]

He was pastor in Cumberland, Maryland, 1818-1824, spending time in 1820 prospecting for Lutherans in Kentucky and Indiana, where he encountered Methodist revivals for the first time. In the same year he was ordained by the Ministerium of Pennsylvania, who had found his work praiseworthy.

Heyer was pastor in Somerset only from 1824 to 1827, but this became his permanent home to which he would return periodically from his far-ranging travels and missionary activity. Somerset was where his wife and children made their home from 1825 on, and when she died, January 13, 1839, at the age of fifty-two, she was buried in Friedens Cemetery there. Heyer spent three years in Carlisle, Pennsylvania (1827-1830), and then for two years was the itinerant Sunday School missionary for the Ministerium, establishing Sunday Schools far and wide. (The Sunday School movement was begun in England by Robert Raikes [1735-1811], a layman, in 1780 and was brought to America in 1790.) In 1832

Heyer resumed work at his Somerset parish. He became secretary of the West Pennsylvania Synod in 1828 and served as its president 1831-1834. Because in that office it was his responsibility to preside at ordinations and because the ordination rite of the Ministerium of Pennsylvania was in German, Heyer, together with Nicholas Sharretts translated the order into English.

In this review of his exhaustingly active life, his restless spirit is evident. Heyer could never stay long in one place, but was ever moving on, energetically accepting new challenges and opportunities. He was ready to embrace new approaches—the use of English in Lutheran worship, the introduction of Sunday Schools, even experimenting with revivals a few times —but he always maintained loyalty to Lutheran orthodoxy. In 1831 he laid the cornerstone of the new building of Gettysburg Seminary. In the stone were placed a German Bible, a Lutheran hymnal, the Small Catechism, the minutes of the sessions of the General Synod, the constitution and by-laws of the seminary, and a list of the names of the directors and professors of the seminary. Heyer some years later recognized the significance of the omission of the Augsburg Confession: it was characteristic of the era of "American Lutheranism", a much diluted and adulterated version of the inherited faith which Heyer and others championed.[35]

So this restless and energetic German-American, only five and a half feet tall, with his shoulder-length hair, came to Pittsburgh. Bold and forward-looking, he was the right person to carry out the intention of the West Pennsylvania Synod and, despite the predominately rural character of Lutheranism in America, to establish a church in the city of Pittsburgh and, despite the predominately German character of the Lutheranism in Pennsylvania, to organize an English-speaking Lutheran church.

Pittsburgh at the time had a population of about twenty thousand, thirty-five thousand when the immediate environs were included. There were four or five daily stage lines to and from the east, and others to the west, north, and south, whose large covered six-horse wagons carried great quantities of the city's freight. Steamboats plied the rivers, and the canals afforded important facilities for transportation of freight and passengers. Two daily packet lines maintained communication with the east; other lines operated in other directions. Pittsburgh was a growing center of industry as well as the junction of wagon traffic from the east and river cargoes from the west. The smoke for which the city would be known a century later was already rising from the coal and lumber mills. By 1836 there were eighteen churches in Pittsburgh. "An unmistakable Calvinistic piety pervaded the life of the city, which came into its own especially with a strict code of Sunday observance. Laymen were active in religious affairs, and the clergy took a leading hand in education."[36]

The title "Father" by which J.C.F. Heyer is universally known was in common use as an expression of respect for older clergy of many denominations[37] down to the twentieth century. "Father" also indicated a tutorial relationship as instructor, counselor, teacher, leader. (See Genesis 45:8; Judges 17:10; 2 Kings 2:12; Jeremiah 31:9.) Younger clergy in the nineteenth century were usually referred to as "brother"; the plural was "brethren." Franklin Clark Fry, President of the United Lutheran Church in America in the latter twentieth century (1944-1970), regularly addressed his monthly pastoral letters to his clergy, "Fathers and Brethren."

Before Father Heyer arrived in the city, careful and thorough preparation had been accomplished by a remarkable layman, George Weyman (the pronunciation of his surname was anglicized to WAY-man instead of the German WHY-man). He had grown up in Philadelphia and was a member of Zion (German) Church there. Perhaps because he remembered the ugly controversy surrounding the separation of the English-speaking members to form St. John's in 1806, he was determined to establish an English Lutheran church in the western frontier town to which he had come in 1822 as a bold entrepreneur and where he had established a flourishing tobacco business. He invented a way to make moist snuff, giving what he called "Copenhagen"[38] a bold distinctive taste, making the tobacco in his factory and, instead of packaging it and sending it out, would age it in oak barrels for several years. The symbol "WC" adorned each can: Weyman's Copenhagen. By mid-century Copenhagen brought in $30,000 annually.[39] The 1837 *Harris Business Directory* contains a drawing of George Weyman's four-story factory.

In 1857 his son Benjamin Franklin Weyman[40], known as B. Frank Weyman, entered the business, and the firm was known as Weyman and Son. In 1867 the second son, William P., became affiliated with the business and it took the name of Weyman and Brother. By 1879 the firm had increased the worth of its annual product to $68,075. William died in 1877, but the firm continued its growth under Frank Weyman to the point that by the end of 1879 it had increased the worth of its annual product to $68,075 and employed thousands at a factory at the corner of Liberty and Union Streets. The factory and warehouse moved to Duquesne Way in 1866, and a branch was opened in New York City. Today Copenhagen is manufactured by U. S. Smokeless Tobacco.

Weyman's Tobacco Factory and Store

In Pittsburgh George Weyman had associated with the Smithfield Street German Protestant Church, but was unhappy with its insistence on German and with its by then Reformed doctrine. He had corresponded with the Lutheran clergy in Philadelphia concerning his desire to establish a congregation in Pittsburgh, and "this undoubtedly prepared the way for the final action of the West Pennsylvania Synod and the appointment of Father Heyer as the missionary to organize the congregation."[41] George Weyman worked tirelessly toward the creation of an English Lutheran church. The name of this devout and extraordinarily generous man deserves to be linked with that of John Christian Frederick Heyer as founders of the First English Lutheran Church in the City of Pittsburgh. Indeed, it is the judgment of the 1909 history of First English Lutheran Church that "we may truly say that the congregation was founded by a layman."[42] A century later, that assessment remains accurate.

Heyer arrived in Pittsburgh on Saturday and preached the next morning and

George Weyman

evening to the Lutherans whom Weyman had gathered in space he had found in the Cumberland Presbyterian Church. The work had begun. The following Tuesday "seven or eight heads of families came together to discuss what further could and should be done to attain our purpose," the pastor recorded in his autobiography. "Among other things it was resolved to accept with thanks the promised assistance of the West Pennsylvania Synod. Further, a committee was appointed to look for a suitable building where meetings could be held in the future. All were urged to hunt up English-speaking members of our Church in and around Pittsburgh, and to encourage them to take part in the establishment of an English Lutheran Church.

"Some weeks after this beginning had been made Bro. J[acob] Martin went to Pittsburgh and preached very acceptably in the Cumberland Presbyterian Church. When I came to Pittsburgh the second time, the Unitarian Church, on Smithfield Street, had been rented for our use for six months. At the first meeting in this building a Constitution was proposed, adopted and signed by eleven or twelve heads of families. Soon after this I received instructions from the Missionary Society to remain in Pittsburgh, to carry on the work which had been begun."[43]

The date was January 15, 1837. The Unitarian Church, built in 1823, was at the corner of Smithfield Street and Virgin Alley[44] (now called Oliver Avenue) and its use was allowed by Benjamin

The Unitarian Church in which First Church was organized

Bakewell, the owner of the building. The formula annexed to the hymnbook of the General Synod was adopted for the government of the congregation; George Weyman and F. A. Heisely were elected elders, and Jeremiah Ritz and W. J. Anschutz deacons. At eight o'clock that evening, "after religious exercises and a sermon," the four officers were installed as the church council of the congregation by Father Heyer. The church was then declared duly organized with the name of the First English Evangelical Lutheran Church in Pittsburgh. The service concluded with a hymn and the benediction. The record concludes, "The meetings were interesting, and the Divine Presence was manifested to some good degree in our midst."

The new-elected church council met for the first time on January 18 at George Weyman's residence. F. A. Heisely was elected secretary and George Weyman treasurer. The regular meeting time was set as the first Monday of each month. At the next meeting, February 6, the council recommended the election of two additional deacons and also that the meetings be opened with "singing and prayer" and that the members kneel for prayer. The custom of kneeling for prayer continued well into the twentieth century, and even when the council members no longer actually knelt for the opening prayer at their meetings, the minutes continued to refer to it as "the kneeling prayer." The first celebration of the Holy Communion was set for Easter Day, March 26, with the stipulation "in the evening, at candlelight." Such was a not uncommon designation of time. The church council minutes for January 1842 record, "It was decided to discontinue the afternoon meetings and to hold them in the evening at candlelight."[45]

By the end of June the struggling Unitarian Church had its own pastor and occupied their church on Sunday morning, but the Lutheran congregation was permitted to conduct its services there on Sunday afternoons. The Lutherans apparently wanted to worship at the accustomed morning hour, and so a schoolhouse was secured on Smithfield Street between First Avenue and what is now Fort Pitt Boulevard. (In 1839-1840 the Monongahela House, Pittsburgh's premier hotel, was built on the site; it was razed in the 1920s.) For the celebration of the Lord's Supper in the schoolhouse in the absence of an altar Father Heyer is reported to have taken blackboards from the walls and improvised a table. In November 1837 the peripatetic congregation secured the old Court House for regular services and continued to worship there until April 1839, despite its being "a dark and gloomy place." This building, a two-story structure with one-story wings built of brick about 1789, stood on the west side of Market Street, opposite the semicircular market house.

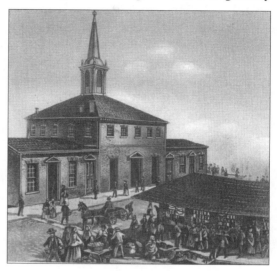

The Old Court House where the Lutherans worshipped

Father Heyer's restless energy would not let him rest content with the establishment of an English Lutheran Church in Pittsburgh. With equal energy and denominational zeal, in addition to the English Lutherans, Heyer gathered the German Lutherans as well. Since 1827 the Reverend David Kaemmerer of the Reformed Classis (Synod) had been pastor of the Smithfield union church. Most of the members of that church apparently were Lutherans, and Heyer considered it no more than fair that they occasionally hear a pastor of their own denomination. He applied to the pastor for permission to preach and was referred to the church council who told him in no uncertain terms that only the regularly installed pastor of the congregation might preach from their pulpit. Heyer promptly put up notices announcing that "next Sunday afternoon, January 22, 1837, German Lutheran service will be held in the rented Unitarian church." There was a good response, and after the service it was resolved to establish a German Lutheran congregation. January 23, 1837, a week after he organized the English church, he organized the First German Evangelical Lutheran Church of Pittsburgh, and those who had been worshipping with the Reformed now had their own church. The names of 172 people were recorded. Two weeks later a constitution was adopted and officers elected.[46]

On Christmas Day 1837 the German Lutheran congregation was given the use of the Court House in the morning of every fourth Sunday; the English congregation held its service in the afternoon on those days.

As if the two congregations he had established in January were not enough to keep one pastor busy, Father Heyer late in the same year, 1837, established St. John's German Lutheran Church across the river in Allegheny City (now the North Side of Pittsburgh), and by January 1, 1839 the congregation had erected a small church building. Father Heyer is indeed the father of Lutheranism in Pittsburgh. In time, First German Lutheran Church, having added the name Trinity to its title, joined the Missouri Synod; St. John's joined the Joint Synod of Ohio, which later was part of the American Lutheran Church; and First English eventually became part of the third principal denomination of Lutherans on the continent in the twentieth century, the United Lutheran Church in America.

The Sunday School began with the establishment of the English and German congregations and was a joint effort of the two congregations. The third Sunday in January, 1837, twelve persons, five teachers and seven scholars, met in the Unitarian Church and organized the school. The following Sunday Father Heyer, acting as superintendent, began the session of the school. For several years growth was slow, and the early minutes frankly say that the enterprise was looked upon as "doubt-

ful". Part of the reason for the slow growth was surely the lack of a fixed location. The Sunday School followed the congregation in its wanderings, in June to the schoolhouse, a few weeks later to the Court House, and on November 25 back to the Unitarian Church. In March, 1838, the school was again in "its uncomfortable old quarters" in the Court House where it remained for two years.

The work of three congregations was clearly too much for one person, and Father Heyer, the builder of foundations

Father Heyer

and always being restless for new challenges, within a year relinquished the pastorate of the English church, although remaining pastor of the two German congregations somewhat longer. In 1839 he accepted a call from the Society for Foreign Missions to become a missionary in India. He appealed to the Ministerium of Pennsylvania to undertake a distinctively Lutheran foreign mission and offered himself for the work. October 15, 1841 he was sent to begin mission work in India, the first missionary sent out by the American Church. After three successful years, he returned to the United States and organized St. John's Church in Baltimore, Maryland, and earned an M.D. degree from what was to become Johns Hopkins University. In 1848 he was back in India. In 1857 he came back to America and set about missionary activity in Minnesota. He organized the Minnesota Synod and served as its president for eight years. In the summer of 1868, seventy-five years old, he sailed with his granddaughter to Germany where he expected to live out the remaining years of his life. He had been in Germany less than a year when he received word that the Foreign Mission Society contemplated transferring the Lutheran mission station in India to the [Anglican] Church Mission Society in England. He hastened back to America and presented himself to the annual synod of the Ministerium of Pennsylvania as willing to return to India and reorganize the work.[47] Throughout his life Father Heyer valued a distinctive Lutheran approach and understanding and opposed co-operative efforts that would obscure or swallow up that distinctive contribution to the work of the Church.

In the spring of 1871 he left India for the last time and returned to the city where he began his ministry, Philadelphia. He became chaplain and housefather at the new Lutheran Theological Seminary, where his extraordinary life ended November 7, 1873. He was buried next to his wife in the cemetery in Friedensburg, Somerset County, Pennsylvania. His gravestone bears the inscription he himself suggested: "Justified by Faith—Saved through Grace—Resurgam [I will rise again]."

Father Heyer is remembered on the calendar in the *Lutheran Book of Worship* and the calendar in *Evangelical Lutheran Worship* on November 7.

CHAPTER 3

Years of Uncertainty

I t quickly became obvious that serving as pastor of two German parishes in addition to the English congregation was too much for one man, even for someone of Father Heyer's prodigious energy. Within a year he had relinquished the English church. Such deprivation of pastoral leadership might well have ended the life of another struggling congregation, but First English Church was not just another struggling congregation. The lay leadership was undeterred. As Father Heyer was concluding his service, the church council at a meeting January 12, 1838, at the residence of Mr. Weyman, at which Father Heyer was present, Father Heyer and Michael Egolf were appointed to ascertain whether a suitable pastor could be obtained. It was further decided that a salary of three hundred dollars be added to the two hundred which the Missionary Society gave. Moreover, as evidence of the optimism and commitment of the council, George Weyman, Jeremiah Fritz, and F. A. Heisely were appointed to look for a lot or a building to be leased or purchased.

On February 5, at the home of Michael Egolf, the property committee reported that they had examined two lots, one on Irwin Street, between Penn Street and the Allegheny River, and the other on Grant Street, between Sixth and Seventh Streets, almost surely the lot on which the present church is built, which the owner would not sell at that time. The search continued. A lot at the corner of Fourth Street and Cherry Alley could be obtained for seventy-five hundred dollars; a building on Marbury Street and a property on Coal Lane were also considered. None of those available seemed suitable.

In February, 1838, the congregation received a letter from Samuel Simon Schmucker, president of the Missionary Society, announcing that the executive committee had appointed the Reverend H. Haverstick of Somerset to serve the English congregation. A month later Mr. Haverstick wrote that it would be impossible for him to visit the congregation before the end of April. Father Heyer was asked, when he visited his family in Somerset, to meet with him concerning the needy state of the congregation. Shortly afterward, the congregation was obliged to write to Dr. Schmucker informing him of Mr. Haverstick's failure to accept the appointment. The congregation continued without a pastor.

On October 2, still without a pastor, the church council, meeting at the residence of George Weyman, with the Reverend John N. Hoffman, of Chambersburg, Pennsylvania, in attendance, passed this resolution:

> That relying on Divine aid, we forthwith commence operations in view of the erection of an English Evangelical Lutheran Church, and that every member of the Council, and such other members [of the congregation] as are so disposed, furnish themselves with subscription books and without further delay call upon friends and citizens for their contributions; and that a united and general and vigorous effort be made to collect a sufficient sum to authorize the purchase of a lot at the first opportunity.
>
> Resolved that the Rev. John N. Hoffman is hereby requested to call upon the Church generally, through the Lutheran Observer and otherwise, in aid of the First English Evangelical Lutheran Church in Pittsburgh.

Father Heyer reports in his autobiography that the German and English congregations worshiped in the same building, but that it was not a helpful arrangement. "[W]e felt that if each congregation was to continue and grow, it must have services every Sunday, and in the forenoon. To make this possible, the Missionary Society appointed one of our most able young preachers, Candidate E. Frey, to take charge of the English congregation." It was encouraging news.

November 14, 1838, Emanuel Frey met with the council at a special meeting where he was introduced as the officiating minister for the coming year. His commission and instructions from the Missionary Society were submitted five days later, November 19, at a meeting at Mr. Weyman's house, and by a unanimous resolution he was accepted and cordially welcomed as the pastor for the term of twelve months mentioned in his commission. In less than five weeks, Christmas Eve, December 24, 1838, the council reported "that we regret that the Rev. Emanuel Frey, our pastor, was compelled on account of his health to leave Pittsburgh, and that a committee be appointed to address a letter to the Executive Committee of the Missionary Society at Gettysburg to ascertain whether we can be supplied again shortly."

Mr. Frey, suffering from rheumatic gout, caused by "the sulphurous gas or thick smoke of the coal,"[48] returned to his home in Somerset. Instead of an improvement in his health, he became a confirmed invalid, and "was disabled from active labors in the ministry during the remainder of his life."[49] He finally "lost the use of his limbs entirely, and for years has had to spend most of his time in a wheel-chair."[50] The *History of the West Pennsylvania Synod*[51] indicates that "E. Frey" was licensed in 1838, presumably for his service at First Church, and that he was ordained in 1840, indicating some further service to the Church elsewhere. According to the practice of that time ordination followed a period of successful ministry and the approval of documents that the candidate supplied. There is a genealogical record that Anna Witmer, who was born November 14, 1831 in Lancaster County, the fourth of ten children of Jacob Witmer and his wife Mary Rohrer Witmer, married an Emanuel Frey in 1863; he may be the same as the Reverend Emanuel Frey. In that year, 1863, the History of the West Pennsylvania Synod finds Frey in York, Pennsylvania, and notes that he died there in 1871.

Before Pastor Frey arrived in Pittsburgh, the teachers of the struggling Sunday School had met, October 24, 1838, at the home of Michael Egolf to form a "Sabbath School Society." A constitution and by-laws were adopted, their host, Michael Egolf, was elected president, John R. Hersh secretary, and George Hubley treasurer. They had high expectations of both teachers and students. Teachers were required "frequently to hold close and searching conversation with their scholars on the principles of our most holy religion." A few months later the treasurer reported that his class had committed to memory 491 verses of Scripture and hymns in two months. For many years the sessions of the school were held twice on Sunday, at nine o'clock in the morning and again at one in the afternoon. Education was taken with laudable seriousness and was surely a significant part of the increasing strength of the congregation.

The congregation had no pastor, but nonetheless remarkable steps were being taken to establish a visible presence in the city. March 13, 1839, George Weyman announced that he had bought three lots of ground, each 22 by 75 feet, on the corner of Seventh Street and Miltenberger Alley (now Seventh Avenue and Montour Way). There was another lot, 25 by 66 feet, running crosswise in the rear of the other three, which would be advisable

Pittsburgh in 1843

to purchase, thus making one lot of 66 by 100 feet, and at a total of $8400. The council asked Mr. Weyman to purchase the fourth lot on as favorable terms as possible. The young congregation was prepared to take its place among the other churches of the city. Smithfield Street Methodist Church was across the alley; a Presbyterian church was across Seventh Street from the new property.

It was announced that a man by the name of Ewing offered to the congregation a loan of four hundred dollars. It was resolved to accept the loan and to appropriate the borrowed money and also all that was in the treasury to the first payment on the lot. An attorney was employed to prepare the deeds.

"So this handful of people, without a pastor, subscribed three hundred dollars a year to supplement the missionary appropriation [for a pastor] and obligated themselves for $8400 for a lot. Here was earnestness and courage indeed!"[52]

After an interval of four months, a new pastor arrived. The council met at the home of George Weyman on May 9, 1839, to meet the Reverend John McCron and to receive his credentials as "resident missionary." It was Mr. McCron's first parish. He was born in Manchester, England, October 23, 1807, of an English father and an Irish mother, had studied at Gettysburg Seminary, and in 1839 was licensed to preach and sent as missionary to Pittsburgh, although he was not ordained until after the meeting of the West Pennsylvania Synod late in 1840. He is described as tall and dignified in his bearing "with engaging social gifts." He was a popular preacher, noted for his oratorical abilities ("possessing a sonorous voice, a fluent delivery and a style animated and at times even excessively florid."[53]) He was especially admired and befriended by the Methodists for whom he repeatedly preached and who were very kind to the feeble congregation.

The congregation still did not have a home. The Methodist church was rented for services on Sunday afternoons, but the Sunday School could find no better terms than those paid to the dismal Court House and so it continued to meet in that unpleasant place.

A committee was appointed to secure a charter to incorporate the congregation. It was granted not by the local courts but by the Commonwealth of Pennsylvania, March 11, 1840. "Charter. An Act to Incorporate the English Evangelical Lutheran Church in the City of Pittsburgh. Section I. *Be it enacted by the Senate and House of Representatives of the Commonwealth of Pennsylvania in General Assembly met, and it is hereby enacted by authority of the same,* That the First English Evangelical Lutheran Church in the City of Pittsburgh, is hereby erected into one body corporate and politic, in deed and in law, by the same name, style, and title. . . .

Section II. That no person shall be considered a member of said Church, so as to be entitled to vote at any election for Pastor, for Trustees, Elders, or Wardens, except such as shall have paid one year's pew rent or rent for part of a pew, sufficient for one person at least, and shall not be in arrears for such rent for more than one year, and shall be in full communion with the Evangelical Lutheran Church. . . .

Section III. That the Vestry of said Church shall be thirteen in number, consisting of the Pastor, three Trustees, three Elders, and six Wardens [later called Deacons]. . . .

Section IV. That the said Vestry shall have full power to enact and enforce such By-laws and ordinances as they may deem proper for the regulation and transaction of the business of said corporation. . . ." The charter was signed by the secretary of the commonwealth, Francis R. Shunk.[54] Sixty people were listed as charter members. Although the governing body of the corporation is called the Vestry by the charter, throughout the history of the congregation the vestry was usually referred to as the church council.

The presence of a pastor and the granting of a charter encouraged the plans for building a church in order to give the congregation a clear identity and presence in the city and to free it of continually moving from rented space to rented space, most of which was unsuitable for worship. The church council moved toward making definite arrangements for a building. Each member of the council was requested to "inquire of a carpenter the probable expense of putting up a building about the size desired." No time was to be wasted. A draftsman was employed to make a design and to make a report at the next meeting of the council. The pastor was asked to plead at the meeting of the General Synod at Chambersburg, June 1, for financial assistance in building the church. The synod's response was cautious. Mr. McCron reported that there was no prospect of aid until a beginning had been made in building, after which the clergy had promised to assist an agent of the congregation in appealing for funds in their congregations. Loans were sought from the Theological Seminary Fund and from several banks in the city, but to no avail. Mr. McCron suggested that a floor plan of the proposed church be drawn up and that pews be offered to the congregation for rent, the value to be determined by their location.

John McCron

Finances remained a serious problem that continued to threaten the existence of the congregation. On August 8, 1839, a special meeting of the council was called to find a means to provide for the payment of a note for $1025 due the next day. There were no funds in the treasury. George Weyman, the extraordinarily generous leader was asked to pay the note and the officers of the council agreed to make every effort to collect the money by the next meeting. At a meeting on September 9, money not having been found, a motion was made to sell one lot on Seventh Street, 20 [actually 22] by 75 feet, on which the new church was to be built, together with the lot on Miltenberger Alley 25 by 66 feet on or before November 1. Consideration of the motion was deferred to September 16 and then was tabled indefinitely. Still with no money, the council at that meeting nonetheless went ahead with the building. The Building Committee was instructed to receive proposals for building a church, 60 by 70 feet, of brick, having a basement story and a gallery at one end of the nave, to be completed before January 1. A committee was appointed to write a letter describing the progress and asking for funds to be presented to the West Pennsylvania Synod at its next meeting, October 3, in York. The minutes of the synod report receiving this "letter from a committee of the First English Lutheran congregation of Pittsburgh, in which they testify their entire satisfaction with Mr. McCron, and pray that Synod may soon ordain him. The same committee expresses the desire that the members of this Synod might aid the Rev. J. McCron in his projected visit in behalf of their new church. They also invite Synod to hold its next annual meeting among them." The synod recommended the congregation to the generosity of its members and accepted the invitation to meet in Pittsburgh the following year. The remarkably optimistic congregation, entirely without funds and dependent on the generosity of others, had such irrepressible confidence in their success that they fully expected to have a finished building in which the synod could meet within a year.

March 8, 1840, George Weyman reported that the building committee had contracted for construction of the church building (carpenter work $3900, brick work four dollars per thousand, stone work two dollars per perch); the whole work to be completed before September 5. The West Pennsylvania Synod was to hold its next meeting in Pittsburgh October 1, and a committee was appointed to confer with First German Lutheran Church regarding hospitality. The German congregation offered to "find places for six preachers and fourteen horses." The excavation of the basement of the new church was quickly completed at a cost of $166.25.

Pastor McCron was furnished with credentials for use on his proposed collecting tour. In July he reported that he had visited and received contributions amounting to $519.05 ¼ less expenses of $71 from churches "in the East": York, Gettysburg, Oxford, Berlin, Emmettsburg, Woodsbury, Frederick, Jefferson, Winchester, Martinsburg, Shepherdstown, Hagerstown, Chambersburg, Shippensburg, Lewistown, and Williamsburg. He was given permission to preach at the Liberty Street Methodist Church, both morning and evening, and a collection was taken at the evening service for the benefit of the Lutheran congregation. Early in September Pastor McCron reported that a second trip to Blairsville, Somerset, Cumberland, Berlin, and Carlisle gathered $216.53.

The church building was completed well within the time specified in the contract. The Sunday School, eight teachers and sixty-four scholars, which had been meeting in the gallery of First German Lutheran Church (on the northwest corner of Sixth and Grant) since its dedication on the first Sunday in April, was the first to occupy its new home, and met in First Lutheran Church September 13, 1840. The council met in their new building for the first time the next day, September 14. At that meeting George Weyman reminded the council that a bond for $3000 would come due October 1 and asked the council to adopt measures to meet it. Two days later the council resolved "to beg or borrow" the funds necessary to pay the bond and to report to a meeting three days later. The first of October came, but the necessary funds had not been secured. The solution was all too familiar. "It was resolved that Mr. Weyman be requested to give his notes for the last payment on the lot drawn at sixty, ninety, and one hundred twenty days, or if possible, to extend the time six months, the councilmen pledging themselves to use every exertion possible with the members of the Synod and to try every other means to raise funds to meet said notes at their maturity."

The West Pennsylvania Synod, at its first convention held west of the Alleghenies, resolved to "sustain the mission in Pittsburgh under the care of Mr. McCron for another year," and also to "sustain to some extent a minister in the German Lutheran Church at Pittsburgh, provided that he be approved of by the committee."

"The fruition of hopes deferred, of anxieties and perplexities bravely endured, was happily realized when the congregation was able to occupy its own house of worship, and to solemnly dedicate it to Divine service on the first Sunday of October,"[55] October 4, 1840. The first service in the church was held in the evening of the preceding Friday in the lecture room. Holy Communion was celebrated, the ancient way of consecrating a church, doing in it what it was built to accommodate. The Reverend Augustus H. Lochman, pastor of Christ Church, York, Pennsylvania, was the preacher.

The building, typical of the time, similar in design to the Methodist church across Miltenberger Alley and much like the Unitarian church in which the congregation had met, was an unremarkable rectangle, with two doors providing entrance from Seventh Street. Stairs to each side led up to the upper story church. Even the second building of Trinity Episcopal Church (1825) "was a typical Protestant meeting house with Tudor Gothic components added to an exterior shell. The nave was a simple, central rectangular hall, flanked by raised side galleries, with the main entrance and chancel/pulpit niche at opposite ends"[56] In the gable of the Lutheran building was a cast iron plate with raised letters declaring, "First English Evangelical Lutheran Church, 1840." The plate was rescued from the building when it was demolished and preserved for a time in the present building. It has since disappeared.

The chancel recess projected beyond the rectangle and was furnished with an imposing pulpit desk, designed by Samuel Holman of Harrisburg, Pennsylvania, raised on three steps, behind which was a plush sofa in the American style. (When the accomplished pastor Adolph Spaeth built St. Johannis Church in Philadelphia in 1868, he lost control of the furnishing of the chancel. There his German congregants took over because the architect's drawing "was 'not American enough!' They demanded a pulpit in the centre of a great platform, filling up the entire altar niche, and back of it a 'real American' red plush-upholstered sofa must be placed!" The huge desk overshadowed the poor excuse for an altar that a carpenter had put together.[57] Similar arrangements were seen in St. Michaels's and Zion [German] Church and in St. John's [English] Church, both also in Philadelphia.) In front of the pulpit of the First Lutheran Church was an unobtrusive wooden communion table flanked by two Victorian chairs. Neither pulpit nor table was adorned with linens or paraments.

The space was a simple room designed for preaching in the Protestant style. There were no ornaments other than the imposing desk-pulpit from which the pastor would preside and preach. The rail seen in the existing photograph of the interior of the building was not original to the church. At its meeting in September 1849, the church council refused to consent to the placement of "a railing in front of the pulpit." The rail was installed sometime before Samuel Laird began his pastorate (1867). There seems to have been no provision for kneeling at the rail. Access to the chancel was through a gate on either side of the rail.

The Seventh Street church

There was a narrow center aisle and two side aisles, each leading from doors from the narthex. The pews were furnished with doors and the pew number was shown on the door. Pew rent was the principal source of income for the congregation, and collections were gathered only on special occasions. When offerings were gathered, closed boxes of black walnut with a slot in the top and provided with handles about three feet long were used.

A gallery extended across the rear of the church. The organ was in the center with three choir pews to either side. The pulpit and chancel recess were painted white. Green Venetian blinds (at a cost of $110) covered the windows, four on either side of the church. The building was heated by four round cast iron coal stoves, one in each corner of the Sunday School room in the lower level of the building. Each stove was surrounded by a sheet iron casing with a duct connecting it to a round cast iron register in the floor of the upper church. The Sunday School benches were segments of a circle and formed a semi-circle in front of a teacher.[58]

The chancel of the Seventh Street church

At the dedicatory service Sunday morning the church was crowded to capacity. Charles Philip Krauth, whose son was to be the sixth pastor of the congregation, and Samuel Simon Schmucker, both of Gettysburg, assisted Pastor John McCron. Dr. Schmucker presided at the formal act of dedication and preached a sermon which he afterwards published under the title "A Portraiture of American Lutheranism." He was soon to champion what came to be called "American Lutheranism", a much diluted version of European Confessional Lutheranism, that was virtually indistinguishable from general American Protestantism. The Mozart Musical Society, having offered their services, occupied the gallery and conducted the music with instrumental accompaniment.

Fifty years later, William Passavant, the fifth pastor of the parish, wrote, "The building consecrated was the first English Lutheran church in any city west of the Alleghanies [sic]. It was to bear an important part in the history of this Communion from the Atlantic to the Pacific. It was to become the seat and centre of doctrinal, educational, and merciful influences which will be felt to the end of time."[59]

The financial health of the congregation remained precarious. Pew rent was set at six to fifteen per cent of their assessed valuation. The council resolved "that Pews 67 and 69 be pre-

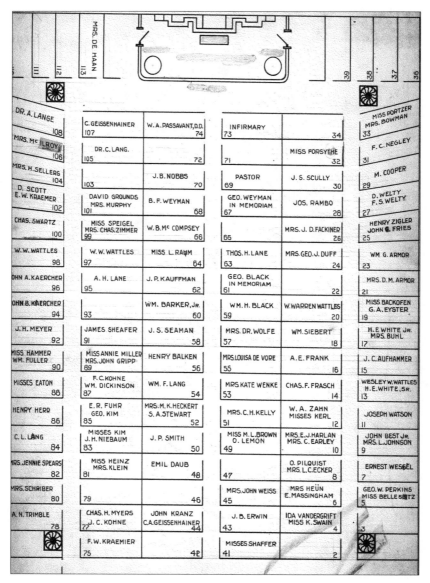

Pew plan of the Seventh Street church

sented to Mr. George Weyman, and that a regular deed be made to him, his heirs and assigns forever, as a small token of gratitude for what he has done for the congregation." He thanked the council but declined the offer and asked that the resolution conveying them be repealed. The council granted his request. Money from the rental of pews was not always forthcoming. In July, 1841 provision was made for the forfeiture of a pew by those who were more than six months in arrears. In February of 1841 C. S.

The gallery of the Seventh Street church

Passavant had examined the books for the preceding year and found them to be correct, but noted balances due to George Weyman ($9645.51), H. W. Caufman ($516.57), and Jeremiah Ritz ($432.94).

October 12, Pastor McCron was requested to make another visit to eastern churches to make collections. He gathered $464; his expenses were $70.49.

John McCron, together with the renowned Joseph A. Seiss and William Passavant, gathered a collection of hymns and tunes which they offered to the General Synod as a revised edition of its *Hymns, Selected and Original for Public and Private Worship* (1828). The synod did not accept the collection, and the editors published it themselves in 1860 under the title the *Evangelical Psalmist.*[60]

The religious character of the congregation and its building were carefully guarded. The Odean Singing Society was notified that they could no longer use the schoolroom, and it was decided that this room should be used only by the Sunday School and for other religious meetings of the congregation. Services preparatory to the celebration of Holy Communion were held on the preceding Saturday afternoon in the lecture room. A sermon was preached and "the formula of confession and absolution was read by the pastor." At the conclusion of the service, the secretary took his place at a table in front of the pulpit and recorded the names of those who announced to him their intention to commune. In March 1842 the Juvenile Total Abstinence Society of the Sunday School was given permission to use the Sunday School room once a week "so long as they conducted themselves in an orderly and quiet manner."[61]

Some of the work of the parish was languishing. For more than a year the Sunday School Teachers' Association had held no meeting. In May of 1842 a new superintendent was elected and an article in the society's constitution was changed to provide that the president of the society be a member in good standing of the congregation, "a zealous advocate of Sabbath Schools, a determined enemy of Sabbath breaking, and willing at all times to open or close the sessions of the School, our society business meetings, and our society social prayer-meetings by prayer."[62] American Protestantism had made inroads into the life and work of the congregation.

On March 14, 1842 the cash received to that point in the year was reported as $1439.74. But George Weyman presented a notice that a judgment in favor of Sharpless & Company had been procured which had to be satisfied on or before March 20 or the church would be offered for sale by the sheriff on April 25. Twelve days later the pastor offered his resignation. The council tabled action.

The situation was indeed gloomy and discouraging. The delegate to the synod which met in 1842 was instructed "to confer with that body on the subject of the missionary station in Pittsburgh, and enter into any arrangement which the expression of the Synod may warrant." The desperation of the congregation is apparent. David H. Geissinger later observed, "The First Church was also once a child that needed to be ministered to, even as she has now for many years in her maturity generously ministered to others. . . . How little, comparatively, we know of the difficulties and trials of our fathers in their faithful and noble efforts to maintain and promote the Faith."

November 9, 1842 John McCron, in earnest about leaving First Church and having accepted a call to First English Lutheran Church in New Lancaster, Ohio, on the east side of Columbus, requested a settlement of his account. In responding to his resignation, the Vestry, after praising his work in Pittsburgh, added, "We cannot, however, help our deep sorrow that we have to separate, and in doing so our sincere and fervent prayer is that the Great Head of the Church will abundantly reward him for his labors of love in our midst."

Pastor McCron was even more restless than Father Heyer. He never remained long in one parish. One imagines that there was something in his approach to ministry that would get him into some difficulty in a congregation and encourage him to move on to another. He was not one to give attention to the details of parish ministry. The 1909 congregational history of First Church Pittsburgh says of his successor, "Mr. Smith was in striking contrast with his predecessor in every respect. . . . [H]e lacked the oratorical abilities of Mr. McCron, but in practical efficiency was his superior."[63] After service in Ohio, Mr. McCron was pastor of St. James Church near Phillipsburg, New Jersey 1847-1851; he ministered in Pikeland, Still Valley, and Norristown, Pennsylvania; Rhinebeck, New York; Middletown, Maryland, 1853-1855; Baltimore at Third Lutheran Church 1855-1860, and then at First English until 1875; and Hagerstown, Maryland; Bloomsburg (St. Paul's 1875-1877), Pottsville, and Philadelphia. Roanoke College conferred on him the Doctor of Divinity degree in 1857. John McCron died in Philadelphia April 26, 1881, in the seventy-fourth year of his age.

The congregation sought the Reverend Samuel Sprecher of Martinsburg, Virginia as Pastor McCron's successor, but they were, fortunately for the unfolding history of First Church, unsuccessful. Dr. Sprecher, with Samuel S. Schmucker and Benjamin Kurtz, was a leader of the "American Lutheran" movement. He was trained by Dr. Samuel Schmucker at Gettysburg and adopted his teacher's views. He was a more profound thinker than either Schmucker or Kurtz, and served as president of Wittenberg University in Springfield, Ohio, for twenty-five years, where he exerted a far-reaching encouragement of "new measures" and a modified Lutheranism. The "new measures" of which proponents spoke were an adoption of the methods of frontier religion that emphasized the "religion of the spirit" as opposed to a "religion of forms". The Lutheran Confessions were largely abandoned as outdated and irrelevant to the New World. The Lutheran Church, these proponents contended, could flourish on American soil only if it adjusted to its environment and made broad concessions to become like the surrounding Protestant denominations. In 1838 Samuel S. Schmucker issued his "Fraternal Appeal to the American Churches calling for reunion on "the apostolic basis". The common enemy was Romanism and anything they thought resembled it. "All liturgical worship was denounced as formalism. Revival methods were zealously advocated, and personal piety was exalted above everything else."[64] Alcohol, card playing, and dancing were condemned. The Lord's Day, Sunday, was equated with the Sabbath and prohibition against work or entertainment on the Sabbath was enforced. All distinctive Lutheran teachings were repudiated.[65] A prominent feature of revivalism was the "anxious bench," usually a simple table which sinners, who wanted to be saved, would approach and there make a public accounting of their sins. John Williamson Nevin (1803-1886), a prominent Reformed minister, published *The Anxious Bench—A Tract for the Times,* an influential criticism of the revivalism and disregard of confessional traditions and the sacramental side of the Church by such evangelists as Charles Grandison Finney (1792-1875).

During the pastoral vacancy arrangements were made for supply preachers "at any salary not exceeding five dollars for each sermon."

The congregation's debt to George Weyman climbed to $13,504.30. Two members of the council were asked to solicit funds from churches in Harrisburg and Philadelphia while on a business trip to the East.

Despite its being without a pastor and despite the dire financial situation, the congregation invited the General Synod to hold its next session, in 1845, in Pittsburgh.

Early in April 1843, the announcement was made that the Reverend William H. Smith, assistant to the renowned John Bachman, pastor of St. John's Church, Charleston, South Carolina, had accepted the call as pastor at a salary of $600 per year and that he and his wife, a native of Charleston, were expected to arrive in a few days. "He was in striking contrast to his predecessor in every respect. Slight of build, with a quiet and pleasing address, he lacked the oratorical abilities of Mr. McCron, but in practical efficiency he was his superior. Not depending exclusively upon his efforts as a preacher, he labored zealously as a pastor to promote the interests of the congregation." [66] He served less than a year, but in that brief pastorate he had notable accomplishments. In his confirmation class were W. C. and Thomas H. Lane, the latter of whom will become prominent in later pages. Various improvements were made to the church building, the most welcome being the introduction of gas for illumination, although when this was done, an immense chandelier, constructed of iron tubing, was suspended from the center of the ceiling. This deformity was unattractive "and a failure in the diffusion of light, while it obstructed the view of the preacher from a considerable number of pews in the rear."[67]

To raise funds for these expenditures, it was proposed to hold a fair, and in order to attract public attention, the pastor, by a resolution of the council, was authorized to visit Washington, D.C., to attempt to obtain permission from the Custis family to bring George Washington's tent, which they owned and greatly prized, to Pittsburgh for exhibition. Pastor Smith, a native of Georgetown in the District of Columbia, was personally acquainted with the Custis family, and obtained their permission for the enterprise, "though never before or since did they permit the tent to go beyond their protection."[68] The tent, upon its arrival in Pittsburgh, was escorted by the Duquesne Greys. The fair was held July 4 in a storeroom on Wood Street a few doors from Diamond Street (now Forbes Avenue). The tent was set up on the second floor and was carefully guarded day and night. When the council returned the tent it sent with it grateful acknowledgement to the Honorable G. W. P. Custis and invited him to visit Pittsburgh.

Financial problems remained. On March 4, 1844 the council received a bill from the long-suffering and continually generous George Weyman for $810.25 interest on the church debt for one year. The council ordered the bill to be paid "as soon as the money could be secured."

At the same meeting William H. Smith tendered his resignation as pastor of the parish. He had been in Pittsburgh less than a year, but his health was weak and his physicians advised him that the atmosphere of Pittsburgh was not conducive to his recovery. His letter of resignation closes with a prayer in the fulsome and florid language of the time, that "the Great Shepherd and Bishop of Souls may continue to water your Zion with copious effusions of His rich and saving grace and that Christ may hold in His right hand the candlestick which now burns with its healthful and cheering glow in the midst of your devoted and faithful flock." If Pastor Smith "lacked the oratorical abilities" of John McCron, one can only wonder to what heights of oratory his predecessor soared.

William Smith had accomplished a number of things for the struggling congregation during his brief pastorate, but none was more significant than his recommendation of the one he selected to succeed him: William Alfred Passavant. Mr. Smith not only recommended Passavant, but submitted to the council a copy of a letter he had written to Mr. Passavant urging him to come to Pittsburgh, and he remained until Mr. Passavant had accepted the call. March 25 the council received a long letter from Passavant explaining his position in Baltimore and declining the call. Pastor Smith, and probably the leadership of the congregation as well, continued to press their case. April 22 Mr. Passavant was present at a special meeting of the council and was introduced by George Weyman. He said that if the call from First Church should be repeated, he would be willing to accept. The council unanimously agreed to extend the call again.

Pastor Smith's brief but significant work was brought to a fruitful conclusion, and his resignation was formally accepted on May 14, 1844 with a unanimous expression of deepest regret, their "sincere regard and love for his zeal and devotion to the interests of the Church which fully marked his short sojourn in our midst," and their prayer that "the Father of all Mercies may restore him to his wonted health."

He served in Barren Hill, Pennsylvania; St. Louis; and Baltimore. "He was much interested in scientific studies, especially chemistry and electricity, and developed a number of inventions. He is also said to have received the degree of M.D. He visited London in the interest of his inventions and died there."[69]

The First English Church was not alone in its succession of brief pastorates; First German Church had a similar early history.[70] But brighter days were about to dawn on the struggling English congregation.

CHAPTER 4

Stability: New Life and a New Course

W illiam Alfred Passavant, youthful, energetic, gracious in manner, put new courage and life into the disheartened and debt-burdened congregation. His family was among the early settlers of western Pennsylvania. Their home was in Zelienople, which took its name from Passavant's mother, Zelia (usually given as Zelie), but the family also had many acquaintances among prominent people in Pittsburgh. Pastor Passavant's presence attracted attention to the young congregation that had yet to make its presence known in the city. His broad view of Christian responsibility saw beyond the bounds of the congregation and sought out all in need: the poor, the neglected, the imprisoned. Such outgoing concern turned the view of the congregation from its precarious existence toward a new sense of service to others and gave the struggling congregation new vision and purpose and imbued it with life and hope.

He was twenty-two years old when his ministry at First Church began in June, 1844.[71] Vigorous new life in the parish began at once. At the June 10 meeting of the church council, on motion of the pastor, the celebration of the Lord's Supper was set on the last Sunday of every other month, thus providing for six communions a year. Every month saw another step forward. The Fourth of July Sunday

William Alfred Passavant

School outing in 1844 was held "in a beautiful grove on the banks of the Allegheny" where the new pastor made an earnest appeal for the cause of missionary activity. By the end of the year the "missionary boxes" returned sixty dollars, which were sent to Father Heyer in India. A month later the Teachers' Association resolved to begin a new Sunday School in the Fifth Ward (the Hill District) to be known as "The English Lutheran Sunday School No. 2". (No. 1 was at the church.) The first session was held September 1 with forty-seven scholars; by January 132 were enrolled. Also in the fall of 1844 another school was begun in Birmingham, on the South Side of Pittsburgh, "in the house of Mrs. Millinger." Yet another school was begun on Fourth Street and still another across the river in the city of Allegheny.

Passavant's ordination certificate

His evident success convinced the Synod of Maryland to ordain him at the convention in Middletown, Maryland, October

The new pastor encouraged the development of music in the young congregation. In November a committee was appointed to confer with a suitable person "on the subject of leading the singing in the church and instructing the choir;" the salary was to be $25 per year. In September 1847 authorization was given to "the young men who have offered to procure a leader of choir to lead the singing of the congregation" with permission to choose their own leader and that fifty dollars per annum be appropriated for this purpose.

The influence of the congregation began to be felt beyond the city. In September 1844 Pastor Passavant had preached at the consecration of a modest brick church in Zelienople, which was only the second English Lutheran church in the area. At that service he proposed to the pastor, the Reverend Gottlieb Bassler, the formation of a local synod. His "unceasing agitation on the subject" resulted in a meeting on January 15, 1845 at First Lutheran Church of eight clergy and six lay delegates. First Church took care of housing the delegates; George Weyman (of course) was the congregation's lay delegate. J. Michael Steck of Greensburg, representing seven congregations, was elected President; Gottlieb Bassler of Zelienople, representing five congregations, was elected secretary. Mr. Passavant was the only clerical delegate representing only one congregation.[72]

In the first ten years of the synod's history sixty new churches were built. During much of this time, in addition to all his other labors, Mr. Passavant served as Missionary President of the synod.

The new life encouraged the growth of the congregation. At the February 1845 meeting of the church council thirty-six new members were received, one of whom was Asa H. Waters, afterwards ordained to the ministry and long closely associated with William Passavant in his charitable work. Even the financial situation was improving. April 1, the treasurer's report for the year showed an income of $1205.29 and expenses of $1145.35.

Disaster struck Pittsburgh April 10, 1845. A large portion of the city was destroyed by a fire which began at Second and Ferry Streets and spread through warehouses on Water Street, the Monongahela bridge, along Wood Street to Diamond Alley and along Smithfield Street to George Weyman's building at the corner of Diamond Alley (now Forbes Avenue). Strenuous efforts saved the Weyman building, which had been recently rebuilt after a fire had destroyed the structure. Had his new premises burned again, it would have been a nearly irredeemable loss for him and therefore also for the struggling congregation. The salvation of his building was "recognized as a special Providence." Nonetheless, one-third of the city was left a smoking ruin. Eleven hundred houses, stores, and warehouses were burned in a district covering more than twenty squares. Two thousand families were made homeless. The legislature of the Commonwealth appropriated $50,000 for relief at once and remitted taxes. Further contributions of $200,000 were received from eighteen states of the Union. Many members of the congregation lost their homes and their stores, and some were forced into bankruptcy. Pastor Passavant labored indefatigably to relieve the distress of his people and of the community, and he even postponed for several weeks his marriage to Eliza Walter of Baltimore, which had been scheduled for May 1.

The congregation, already burdened with debt, found its suffering increased. George Weyman reminded the congregation that interest on its debt to him for two years ending January 1844, $1640, was still due him. He proposed to give the interest to the church if the church council would give him a note for $1000 to be paid when the debt was reduced to $500. His proposal was promptly accepted.

In November the net proceeds from a lecture by the pastor and a concert amounted to $103.54. One hundred dollars were applied to the interest on the church debt. One month later, the council, needing to raise $300 before January 1, resolved to hold a concert to assist in raising that amount.

In the summer of 1846, Pastor Passavant, "breaking down under the strain of labors, most of them self-imposed,"[73] sailed for Europe as a delegate of the Pittsburgh Synod to the World Convention of the Evangelical Alliance which gathered in London in August to form an Evangelical union of individual Christians to promote religious freedom, and to counteract Romanism. The principal American leader was S. S. Schmucker. This turned out to be a transforming trip for the exhausted pastor. He met representatives from Europe and was able to examine closely the philanthropic enterprises in England, France, and Germany. He found there a Lutheranism that was not ossified as its American detractors asserted but a church that was indisputably alive and of service in surprisingly impressive ways. He wrote to his parents:

"Again I am on the mystic Rhine at Kaiserswerth, an obscure village of two thousand inhabitants but celebrated all over Europe for the interesting institution of Protestant deaconesses which Pastor Fliedner, an unobtrusive Lutheran minister, has established there. As I had letters from Bremen and from the Sisters in the hospital in Frankfurt and London, Fliedner at once made me welcome and we were soon seated around a frugal but comfortable repast to which my long walk enabled me to do ample justice. During the afternoon, we went over the whole institution which, from nothing but a believing heart, has gradually increased to an ample establishment, consisting of a hospital, an orphan home, an infant school, a day school, an asylum for released female prisoners, an institute for the training of Evangelical teachers, and a mother house for deaconesses! Building after building goes up and, with nothing but faith for a capital, the necessary

Kaiserswerth Motherhouse
("F.N." is Florence Nightingale who entered training there in 1850)

means is always at hand. Though the institution is only a few years old, it has already sent forth two hundred and sixty female teachers and a large number of nursing sisters who are scattered over Europe in hospitals from St. Petersburg to Rome! It is interesting to see how the good and great from all lands make their pilgrimages to this obscure spot. Kings, queens, nobles, philanthropists, and others from all parts of Europe have seen, examined and approved of this institution. . . ."[74]

In a lengthy letter (ten closely printed pages) to the congregation from London, October 18-19, 1846, he summarized the significance of his European experiences. "Having visited Kaiserswerth on the Rhine, where the first Protestant institution of this kind was commenced from which all the others are copied, Both in Germany, Holland, France and Prussia, I shall on my return give myself the pleasure of giving the brethren an opportunity of learning more of this wonderful institution which is spreading its blessings so rapidly over the whole of Europe. In my whole course of observation, I saw nothing anywhere which so commends itself to the better feeling of the heart as the order just referred to. The King of Prussia has erected a large hospital and of his own funds in Berlin, which is to be a kind of training school for a large "central motherhouse' for all the Prussian dominions. In Frankfort and many of the principal towns I visited, I found that the Protestant hospitals and charitable institutions of a similar nature were wholly given over to the care of these sisters and so great and happy had been the change for the better under their management that the city authorities could find no language sufficiently expressive of their approbation. When once fully admitted and set apart by prayer for this holy work, they enter upon it with a self-sacrifice truly astonishing and many of them never leave the hospitals till removed by death! They make no vows for life, but can return to their friends if so disposed. And yet very few ever use this privilege, but live and die in the service. Why cannot we find among us a devotion and self-sacrifice similar to that manifested by our Lutheran sisters in France and Germany?"[75]

Fliedner's recovery of the ancient order of deaconesses impressed Passavant with the uses of historical tradition. He was also impressed with the spirit of reverence that obtained in worship. He wrote to his congregation, "We have some three or four French and German Lutheran congregations in Paris, but I did not succeed in finding any of them, so I attended the French Reformed Church in the 'Church of the Oratory', 'Rue St. Honore'. This large church was well-filled with a solemn and attentive congregation and the whole services were conducted with a propriety and order which made me feel it was God's house. Would that we had the admirable custom, which prevails in England and everywhere on the continent, for the congregation to remain a moment in silent prayer after the benediction, instead of rushing to the door as if in haste to escape from the house of God! I also observed here with great pleasure, what I have noticed in all churches in England and on the continent, that each of the Christian worshippers engaged in silent prayer on entering the church! May the example of others impress your minds, dear brethren, with the propriety of this duty which I have so often endeavored to set before you while in your midst."[76]

G. Gerberding observes of these transformative experiences in Europe, "There he came in contact with the leaders of Protestantism in its various forms. . . . Such men could not but greatly enlarge the horizon, sharpen the judgment and quicken the enthusiasm of a young man not yet twenty-five years old and hungry for knowledge and direction. Here he saw the difficulties that are a part of an indefinite and inconsistent faith. He saw the danger of liberalism. He saw the struggle after a foundation on which all could stand."[77]

From the time of his pastorate in Baltimore, Mr. Passavant had been influenced by the practices of Protestantism that were subsumed under the title "new measures." These included an avoidance of distinctive denominational doctrines and teaching and the use of revival methods that characterized the frontier religion. *The History of the First English Evangelical Lutheran Church in Pittsburgh* describes the impact of such "American" Christianity on the Lutheran Church:

"This was a period of great unrest and of great looseness of doctrine and practice in the Lutheran Church in this country. With practically no Lutheran literature of an historical or confessional character in the English language, and with a radical professor in the Seminary at Gettysburg and equally radical editors of the Church papers, it is not strange that many of the English pastors were swept off their feet by the widespread fanatical movements in the country and the 'new measure' practices of the denominations about them."[78]

In Gettysburg Seminary from which he graduated in 1842, in his parish in Baltimore, 1842-1844, and during his first years in the Pittsburgh parish, Pastor Passavant was under these influences. He had graduated from Jefferson College, a Presbyterian institution, in 1840. Many students of the Presbyterian seminary regularly attended his services in Pittsburgh. He participated in a series of what were called "protracted meetings" (revivals "of the most emotional type"[79]) held jointly with the pastor of the Cumberland Presbyterian Church, and he earnestly advocated in the columns of Benjamin Kurtz's paper, the *Lutheran Observer*[80], organic union of the Lutheran Church and the Cumberland Presbyterian Church. The Cumberland body commended itself to him because it was less narrowly Calvinistic than the Presbyterian Church and generally more liberal in doctrine and practice. It is also to be noted that Passavant was of Huguenot heritage, his father Philippe Passavant, his mother Zelie née Basse.

In line with such leanings, it is significant although not surprising that when Passavant left for his trip to Europe his place was taken not by a Lutheran but by a Presbyterian, the Reverend Eliot E. Swift, who had just completed his studies in the Western (Presbyterian) Theological Seminary. Mr. Swift afterward "served the leading Presbyterian church in Allegheny [now the North Side of Pittsburgh; then a separate city] with conspicuous ability."[81] Such was the state of affairs when Passavant sailed for Europe.

In Germany Passavant encountered a Lutheranism with which he was entirely unacquainted: distinctly confessional, historically liturgical, and oriented toward service of those in need. He returned to his parish having quite lost his enthusiasm for "new measures" and sought to introduce more conservative and authentically Lutheran methods.[82] Many of his colleagues in the ministry now distrusted him, and many in his congregation strenuously opposed even the simplest liturgy (the use of the Apostles' Creed and the Lord's Prayer was too much for some of them) and other conservative innovations. Nonetheless, at the end of the year his salary was raised one hundred dollars.

William Passavant had a remarkable ability in fund raising. Even while abroad he collected money for a church cemetery, and in April 1847 he reported to the church council that he had received a letter from a woman in Switzerland enclosing a draft for two hundred francs for this purpose. Thirteen lots were purchased in Allegheny Cemetery.

Passavant's dissatisfaction with the theology and the spirit of the *Lutheran Observer,* which was shared by the more conservative Lutheran clergy, led him to begin his own paper, *The Missionary,* which first appeared in January 1848, as a small four-leaved monthly. The title reflected Passavant's view of the work of the Church. It was not to sit by and make often acerbic, even vitriolic observations; it was to be an outgoing missionary enterprise, carrying the Gospel to those who did not know it or who did not believe it. The paper was devoted to the interests of inner, home, and foreign missions. (In the language of the time, "inner missions" meant the work of social ministry among the needy, "home missions" meant the establishment of new Sunday schools and new congregations; "foreign missions" meant carrying the Gospel into places beyond the shores of America.) *The Missionary* soon grew into a large family weekly and opened a new era in the Church's thought and activity. Through the columns of this and later a second paper, *The Workman,* he not only stimulated local missionary and philanthropic activity within the bounds of the Pittsburgh Synod, but he awakened the entire Lutheran Church to the opportunities and responsibilities of "the great Lutheran Diaspora in the West." "The cause of the Germans and the Scandinavians was unceasingly advocated, and the foundations were laid by his efforts for uncounted enterprises which have since developed into vigorous congregations and synods, colleges and seminaries, hospitals, homes, and religious and philanthropic institutions of every description."[83]

In 1850 he and W. M. Reynolds of Capital University in Columbus made a "missionary journey" among Norwegian and Swedish settlements of the West. Upon his return he published in *The Missionary* a ringing appeal for work among Scandinavian Lutherans. He proposed printing of information about their needs, missionary chaplains in New York and other seaports to distribute tracts and furnish guidance to the newcomers, a professorship to train pastors for Scandinavians, and the organization of a Scandinavian synod.

Mercy Hospital had been established in Pittsburgh in 1847 by the Roman Catholic Church. There was no Protestant hospital anywhere in the United States. This situation impelled Passavant to found a hospital and to introduce into America the deaconess movement which he had studied appreciatively in Kaiserswerth and elsewhere in Germany. He rented a building on Fleming Street in Allegheny City in the spring of 1848. The first patients were two discharged soldiers from the Mexican War. In the absence of nurses or doctors, Pastor Passavant cared for them with his own hands, assisted by his friend Asa Harris Walters, then a student. The hospital was not officially opened for patients until January 1848.

Pastor Theodor Fliedner of Kaiserswerth arrived in July bringing with him four deaconesses to inaugurate the new work, and the first Protestant hospital and the first deaconess work in the United States were launched on Sunday afternoon, July 22, 1849 at the service of dedication of a building Passavant found on Minersville Road in Lacyville (now the Hill District). Later the deaconess work was fully organized and the Institution of Protestant Deaconesses in the County of Allegheny, Pennsylvania, was legally incorporated.

Theodor Fliedner

In the following year,1850, in the Seventh Avenue church, Catherine Louisa Marthens, who had been catechized and confirmed by Pastor Passavant, was consecrated as a deaconess, the first American to be set apart for this ministry of mercy.

While he was in London attending the World Convention of the Evangelical Alliance, Pastor Passavant found shelter from a driving storm in the Jewish Orphan Asylum. The purpose of that institution percolated in his fertile mind, and he saw the

Sister Louisa   need for a home for orphans in Pittsburgh.

The growing work of his infirmary soon demanded a corresponding institution. In September 1851 he proposed such an institution; it was organized in April, 1852. Two years later it was moved into the country to Zelienople as an Orphans' Home and Farm School. Sister Louisa was the matron of the home. In March 1859, Sister Louisa went with four orphan children to the Germantown section of Philadelphia and established the Orphans' Home there. She returned to Pittsburgh and remained in the diaconate until the end of her life (1899). Little is recorded of her actual service; the 1909 *History* covers her work with a bland platitude, "Before her consecration she had been an intelligent and active worker in the congregation and a teacher in the Sunday School, and her later years were full of continued devotion and serious responsibility."[84]

The progress of the diaconate in Pittsburgh did not fulfill its original promise and hope. Two of the four Kaiserswerth sisters were married in 1853, just four years after they arrived in the United States, to Pastor Passavant's great sorrow. Of the four who came first, only one, Elisabeth Hupperts, served until the end. She died in 1895, after serving for sixty years. In thirty-five years only sixteen probationers were consecrated, and all but three of these left the diaconate after a period of one to nine years. The work of the deaconesses in Pittsburgh, Zelienople, Rochester, and other places, especially their service during the Civil War, received recognition, but did not lead others to follow their example. Sister Julie Mergner offers her evaluation of the ultimate failure of the diaconate in Pittsburgh: "The lack of proper oversight and training may have contributed to the failure. Dr. Passavant's many-sided and comprehensive activity left little time for this work. Also, he probably undervalued outward observances, such as systematic training, cultivating the idea of a community, and a uniform dress for the sisters."[85]

Thursday, September 14, 1854, a cholera epidemic broke out in Pittsburgh, the second great calamity which befell the city during Passavant's pastorate. (The first was the devastating fire of 1845.) The morning papers the next day reported forty-six deaths; in two weeks nearly a thousand died. Passavant's Infirmary was taxed to its utmost capacity, caring for sixty cholera victims in addition to thirty or more other patients in the house at the time. The sisters were nearly overcome by their exertions, and a physician, Dr. J. H. Nelson, died during the first week. The number of deaths and the speed with which the victims died paralyzed business and became the overwhelming concern of the whole population. A member of the church council, John Brown, was struck by the disease and barely survived.

Mr. Passavant had an interest in education and was instrumental in founding academies in Zelienople, Leechburg, and Greensburg. He interested young men in the work of the ministry, and in many instances he secured assistance for them in their preparation for it.

He carried on a vast correspondence, and in his home on Ninth Street near the river received visiting clergymen from England, Germany, Sweden, Norway, and elsewhere and many others involved in religious and philanthropic work.

From beginning to end, he had the support of the congregation. His young people were trained to be active workers in the missions, and their elders interested themselves in the Infirmary and the Home. During his eleven years as pastor the church building was the scene of many memorable events. There the Pittsburgh Synod was organized in 1845. There the first collection was taken for the first Protestant hospital in the United States. There in 1850 the first American deaconess was consecrated. There the deaconesses and orphans worshipped. There the first missionary to Texas, through whom the Texas Synod was organized, was commissioned in this church. There also the first missionary to Canada was commissioned, out of whose labors the Canada Synod grew. There in the lecture room the German congregation in Allegheny City was organized. There also the first subscriptions were gathered for the erection of the first Swedish churches of the West.

Even a partial list of the work of William A. Passavant is daunting. He established at least eighteen churches: First, Cincinnati (1842); Grace, South Side Pittsburgh (1852), now disbanded; Calvary Wilkinsburg (1852), now disbanded; Mt. Calvary, McKees Rocks, (1853); Grace, Rochester, Pennsylvania (1856); St. John's Kitanning (1858); Christ, Baden (1858); Trinity, North Side of Pittsburgh (1860); St. Paul's, Glenfield, now Sewickley (1863); St. John's, East Liverpool, Ohio (1863); Redeemer, Monaca (1865); East Liberty (1869); what is now Holy Trinity, Chicago (1874); House of Prayer, Aliquippa (1875); Rehoboth, Freedom,

Pennsylvania (1876); House of Mercy, Freedom, Pennsylvania (1878); Christ, Parker, Pennsylvania (1878), now disbanded; Emanuel, Manchester, now in Bellevue, Pittsburgh (1886). He founded the first institution of Protestant deaconesses in America in 1849 and in the same year the first Protestant hospital in America, now UPMC North Hills Passavant Hospital; in 1852 the Orphans' home and Farm School in Zelienople (now Glade Run Lutheran Services); in 1859 the Lutheran Orphans' Home in the Germantown section of Philadelphia; in 1862 the Lutheran Orphans' Home for Girls in Rochester, Pennsylvania, now disbanded; in 1863 the Lutheran Hospital in Milwaukee (now Aurora Sinai Medical Center); in 1865 the Passavant Memorial Hospital in Chicago; in 1866 the Wartburg Orphans' Farm School in Mount Vernon, New York (now Wartburg Adult Care Community); in 1870 Brook Farm in Concord, Massachusetts, now disbanded; in 1875 the Passavant Memorial Hospital in Jacksonville, Illinois (now Passavant Area Hospital); in 1895 the Protestant Home for Epileptics in Rochester, Pennsylvania (now Passavant Memorial Homes). In 1866 with A. Louis Thiel he founded Thiel Hall, which became Thiel College in 1870; in 1891 he founded the Chicago Lutheran Theological Seminary. Moreover, he assisted in the organization of the Pittsburgh Synod, the Texas Synod, the Canada Synod, the Nova Scotia Synod, the Northwest Synod, and other mid-western synods.

After reviewing all this remarkable activity, the 1909 *History* says frankly, "It was inevitable, however, that burdened by all these enterprises, missionary, educational, editorial, philanthropic . . . that the work of the congregation should suffer and that the pastor should receive widespread criticism from his members." He was not unaware of the situation. He defended his conduct in an eloquent sermon preached in June 1854, on the occasion of his tenth anniversary, but knew the truth of much of the criticism. He realized that his outside interests rendered serious congregational work, pastoral visitation, and proper preparation of sermons, impossible. Consequently, January 8, 1855, he submitted his resignation. The council accepted it and appointed two of its members to prepare an address to the retiring pastor, by far the longest-serving of any the congregation had yet known. It took the form of lengthy and appreciative resolutions, unanimously adopted. Because of the delay in securing a new pastor, Mr.

Passavant continued to serve the congregation for six months and more. Then, free to devote his entire time to his other pursuits, he continued to reside in Pittsburgh. Pennsylvania College (later called Gettysburg College) conferred on him the Doctor of Divinity degree in 1880. He died at his home, 122 Center Avenue, Pittsburgh, on Sunday June 3, 1894, "one of the most forceful and influential personalities in the Lutheran Church. The Church in this country has probably never had another constructive leader who achieved equal success in as many lines of interest—missionary, editorial, educational, and philanthropic."[86]

William Alfred Passavant was added to the calendar of commemorations on November 24 with Justus Falckner in *Evangelical Lutheran Worship* (2006) and on June 6, a date nearer his death, in *The New Book of Festivals and Commemorations: A Proposed Common Calendar of Saints.*[87] That proposal was taken up by the Episcopal Church, and in 2009 he was added to their calendar in *Holy Women, Holy Men: Celebrating the Saints* on January 3 as a "prophetic witness."

William A. Passavant. D. D.

Eliza Walter Passavant

His vast work would not have been possible without the support, counsel, and assistance of his wife, Eliza Walter Passavant. "She encouraged him when he doubted his right to sacrifice all in an unknown venture. She gave him her full cooperation, her counsel, her prayers, and relieved him almost entirely of the care of a large family. The deaconesses found in her a sympathizing friend, a judicious advisor, a practical helper. She served the Pittsburgh Hospital for a long time as matron, when no other could be found. 'She was a true deaconess without a title or habit,' wrote Dr. H. E. Jacobs, possessing 'extraordinary energy, unselfish industry, tenacity of purpose, and administrative gifts.'"[88]

The Reverend Charles Porterfield Krauth (the "au" in his surname is pronounced as in "sauerkraut") of Winchester, Virginia had come to the attention of First Church as a possible successor to William Passavant. Born in Martinsburg, Virginia March 17, 1823, educated at Gettysburg where his father was professor, he had briefly served a mission in Canton, a suburb of Baltimore, in 1842 became pastor of the Lombard Street Church in Baltimore, in 1847 was pastor in Shepherdstown and from 1848 in Winchester, Virginia. George Weyman and Thomas Lane were instructed to invite him to visit the congregation and preach. Mr. Krauth declined the invitation. Thomas Lane, who partook of the persistent and undaunted character of the congregation, was earnest in his determination to secure a strong, conservative pastor, and he was not willing to end the negotiations. He was finally authorized by the church council to visit Winchester and personally to urge upon Mr. Krauth the acceptance of the invitation. He was able to report later that Mr. Krauth had consented to visit Pittsburgh.

The journey of the pastor across the mountains is described in a letter from Greensburg, February 23, 1855, revealing the sensitivity of the pastor as well as the remoteness of Pittsburgh. "I left Harrisburg yesterday about one o'clock and was soon hurrying by the chill river and through the leafless forests to the mountain range of western Pennsylvania. We reached the wildest portions after night, but the moon, about which clouds were drifting, cast her fitful gleam upon them, adding more sublimities than the absence of sunshine concealed. The road is cut through the mountains, and from their sides, where the veins of springs had been touched, there now hung cataracts of ice. The snow lay heavy upon the ground, and in every direction the circles of the mounds, where coal was being burned into coke, cast a lurid light upon it. I enjoyed with a sort of deep, pensive pleasure the rushing into the heart of night and darkness, which seemed to grow thicker and blacker as the hours passed on. The sky lowered more and more with a gathering snow storm, and the wild mountain winds seemed to rush upon the sweeping train as though they would arrest it or hurl it from the track."[89]

He arrived February 24, 1855 and was the guest of Henry Graff, one of the elders of the council. He preached the sermon at the Friday evening service of confession preparatory to the celebration of the Lord's Supper, delivered the principal sermon on Sunday morning, and assisted William Passavant in the administration of Holy Communion in the afternoon. (Such was the usual liturgical pattern of the time.) The congregation was favorably impressed, and on March 5 the council extended a call to Mr. Krauth; the salary was fixed at fifteen hundred dollars a year. Three days later, March 8, the retiring pastor, with his characteristic clear understanding of the opportunities and possibilities the parish offered, its history, and its strategic location, sent a letter to Mr. Krauth pressing the special claims of the Pittsburgh congregation upon him. (He uses the then current spelling of the name of the city.)

"Through the instrumentality of the Church in Pittsburg, the Pittsburg Synod was organized just ten years ago, and during this time seventy-two Lutheran churches within our bounds have been consecrated, and the Gospel has been carried to Canada on the North, and to Texas on the South. So, too, the Church in Pittsburg occupies a central position between the East and the West, and whatsoever is done for religion here tells promptly on the Church in either direction. The position a pastor occupies here gives him access to many minds from different portions of the land, and the seed thus scattered and diffused often springs up again in different parts of the most Western States. After a residence of nearly eleven years in this place, I can safely say that I know of no place in the whole Church where the prospects of an able minister are so encouraging, as the English Lutheran Church in this city."[90]

Thomas Hetich Lane

That same day on which Passavant wrote to Krauth from Pittsburgh, Krauth wrote from Winchester to Thomas Lane with his characteristic sensitivity, charm, and humor. "The very bad cold which has almost laid me up and prevented my writing sooner, if not a remembrance of Pittsburg exactly, is a very unpleasant one of my departure from it. I took it on Tuesday night; the [railroad] cars were first suffocating and then cold. I carefully impress it upon my good people, who would like to think my bad cold a sort of mild judgment, that it was not going *to* Pittsburg but in coming *from* it that I took the cold. The cold I could stand, however, with some philosophy, gently doctoring it with horehound and other time-honored medicaments, but 'the question?' where am I to get horehound for that? The call and your kind note accompanying it have just reached me, and made things look graver than ever. I am pondering and praying and am in huge perplexity."

He then turned to a personal relationship that was to flourish in future years.

"I thank you for the trouble you have given yourself in looking about for a house, and for all the friendly solicitude you have shown in connection with this whole matter. I feel it deeply and shall never forget it. I don't wish to lay myself open to the charge of flattery, but attempting to say how much the prospect of having your friendship and sympathy would do in drawing me to Pittsburg. Whatever may be the issue of the question now pending, you must not refuse to permit me to put your name in the list of my most cherished friends, those to whom congeniality and gratitude bind me with ties that cannot be broken."

He concluded the letter with an amusing summary of the difficult position he was in. "People all up in arms at the bare idea of my leaving them—everybody trying to get me to say I won't go; effort unsuccessful. On Monday night a meeting (the regular monthly one) of the Council took place. Strong speeches, ardent affection; Pittsburg dirty place; coal-smoke, cholera, abolitionists, ruin everything here; might as well take church key along if I ever left here. No place more important than Winchester. Wish some people would let other people alone; wonder why they want *our* minister? *We* are satisfied, why can't they be? Council almost ready to write to your Council and 'give them a bit of their mind.'[91]

Krauth's painful perplexity was so great that he wrote to Thomas Lane on March 12, "I fervently wish that it could have pleased God that the question should not have been raised; a decision either way involves much that is painful." The letter giving the Pittsburgh church "a piece of their mind" was in fact written on March 21 on behalf of the council and congregation at Winchester. March 26 a very long letter from Mr. Krauth declining their call was presented to the Pittsburgh church council. At the same time he had written an even longer letter to Thomas Lane, asking for his continued friendship despite his decision.

The council looked elsewhere for a pastor. Several clergymen suggested by the congregation were invited to preach, but none appeared satisfactory. April 24 George Weyman was delegated on one of his trips to Philadelphia "to call on the Rev. Charles W. Schaeffer of Germantown to ascertain whether he would be willing to take charge of the congregation."

Thomas Lane, however, maintained a constant correspondence with Krauth. For his part, Krauth maintained a lingering interest in the city. After their marriage in May, 1855, Mr. and Mrs. Krauth made their bridal trip to Pittsburgh, and as a result a committee of the congregation addressed his father, Charles Philip Krauth of Gettysburg, asking his intercession on behalf of their people. Mr. Lane reported the declining conditions in the congregation: week by week people were drifting away because of the long interim, the Sunday School was dwindling, the church had even to be closed for lack of a supply pastor. He urged him to reconsider his decision.

August 28, Mr. Krauth wrote to Thomas Lane to tell of his openness to "a renewed and unanimous call." He gave fair warning that he was not to be compared with their previous pastor. "Your people ought to know that my habits are those of a student; that, though I shall, in the fear of God, if I come, try to do all the duties that can reasonably be required of a pastor, I shall not be able to satisfy unreasonable demands. If I am to be tested by Brother Passavant's standard of outdoor and missionary activity, I shall be found wanting. Few men will bear comparison with him, and of those few I am not one."[92]

A renewed call was extended and this time was promptly accepted. Charles Porterfield Krauth and his wife (he had married for a second time, in May 1855, Virginia Baker[93]) arrived in Pittsburgh early in November. He was installed as pastor of the parish by the Reverend Dr. Samuel Sprecher, President of

Wittenberg College in Springfield, Ohio. In those two figures the contrasting sides of the Lutheran Church in America were graphically displayed. Dr. Sprecher was the intellectual leader of "American Lutheranism"; Pastor Krauth was to become a principal advocate of historic and confessional Lutheranism. At this time Dr. Sprecher was impressing upon his brother-in-law, Samuel Simon Schmucker, the need for a clearly defined position, a bold statement of the exact tenets of "American Lutheranism." He had written in 1853, "It is not to be denied that we have departed from the doctrines and customs of our Church in many respects. This we have done in the exercise of our undoubted right, and, I think, under the guidance of divine truth; but our position has never been explicitly enough defined."[94] The Lutheran Church in America was at this time seriously agitated and divided, and that division was apparent at Krauth's installation. Despite sharp voices on either side, the majority were content to tolerate the division and to hope that "truth might win its way without violent conflict."

portrait

Charles Porterfield Krauth

dressed for Liturgy

Adolph Spaeth comments in his biography of his father-in-law that it was a good time to be in Pittsburgh. "Dr. Paxton, afterward at Princeton, was minister of the First Presbyterian Church, Dr. Howard of Second Presbyterian, and Dr. Riddle of Third. Rev. Alfred Cookman became pastor of Christ's Methodist Church; Dr. Lyman, afterward bishop of North Carolina, was rector of Trinity Episcopal Church—all men of influence and ability. In the Presbyterian Seminary, Dr. Jacobus, Dr. Plummer, and Professor Wilson were strong in the pulpit, and preached frequently in the different churches of the city."[95]

Thomas Lane had described the congregation in a letter of September 2, 1855. "I have sometimes feared the social position of our people would contrast unfavorably with that of your present charge. I would not have you infer that we are at all deficient in real respectability, founded upon moral worth. But the idea I wish to convey is, we *are* not, as we *desire* not to be esteemed, fashionable. The congregation is composed principally of active business men and mechanics [perhaps with the archaic meaning of manual laborers]. Many of our congregation are among the leading business men of the city. Many are mechanics, and all are plain and unassuming. It is composed of such men as *I* would prefer associating with. Our influence upon the community in proportion to our age and numerical strength is second to none in the city." Krauth replied, "God save me from a 'fashionable' congregation."[96]

Having begun his work, he wrote to his father on New Year's Day, 1856, "My impressions so far have corresponded with their representations. We have one of the most mixed congregations that I have ever known, mixed as to material, origin, and original religious predilections. This imparts interest to the field, though it increases its difficulties, and makes it harder to fuse into a harmonious mass, the material I have to work upon."[97]

June 2, 1856 the committee on the church debt reported that $6900 had been collected, leaving a deficiency of $600. The members of the council pledged themselves in various amounts to cover this deficiency, Pastor Krauth making the largest pledge of $125; there were two pledges of $100 each, five of $50 (including George Weyman and Thomas Lane), and one for $25.

In 1856 his alma mater, Pennsylvania College, conferred on him the degree of Doctor of Divinity; in 1874 it would award him the LL.D. degree. He wrote a number of essays for Passsavant's paper, the *Missionary,* while he was in Pittsburgh, many of which dealt with the Augsburg Confession. "Being convinced that an acquaintance on the part of our Church with her fundamental creed is essential to her life, her purity, and her peace, and also that there was a growing desire in our Church, in this country, thoroughly to understand her princely Confession, he endeavored to meet this wish in some measure."[98] His principal work during the Pittsburgh years was his translation of *Tholuck's Commentary on the Gospel of St. John,* published by Smith, English & Co., in Philadelphia in 1859. To the end of his life, he always looked with special pleasure on this work, although his father opined that "Charles has better prepare original commentaries than waste his time on translations."

In 1855, at the persistent urging of Samuel Sprecher, Samuel Simon Schmucker published his *Definite Platform*, as a clear statement of the doctrinal basis of American Lutheranism. In the book was included an "American Recension of the Augsburg Confession," which charged the foundational Lutheran confession with five specific errors, among which were baptismal regeneration (the teaching that a new birth is actually effected in Holy Baptism) and the Real Presence of the Body and Blood of Christ in the Holy Communion. Moreover, radical changes were proposed in twelve of the twenty-five doctrinal articles. It was an attempt to refashion Lutheranism to make it like the surrounding Protestant denominations. Schmucker's *Popular Theology* had "exerted a wide influence in propagating his un-Lutheran views and in strengthening opposition to the confessional party in the Church." Thomas Lane, whose loyalty to the confessional cause was always clear, suggested to Dr. Krauth during his pastorate in Pittsburgh that he prepare a book along similar lines to offset the destructive influence of Schmucker's work. The resulting work was *The Conservative Reformation and Its Theology*, not published until 1871, but much of its material had been published as essays in the *Evangelical Review* and the *Lutheran and Missionary*. The expense of publi-

Samuel Simon Schmucker

cation was borne by two devoted Pittsburgh friends, Thomas Lane and George Black.

Dr. Krauth's scholarly interest was reflected in the congregation. For many years the Sunday School had devoted a great deal of attention to its library. In June 1857 it was reorganized and 390 new books were purchased at a cost of $102.08. For many years the needs of the library and the cause of missions occupy a large part of the Sunday School records. Dr. Krauth's own library, already remarkably large, was constantly growing. At his death, it was given to the Philadelphia Seminary.

Membership in the congregation was regarded as a serious responsibility. Many who became careless were admonished for neglect of their church privileges and some were disciplined. Frequent aid was extended to the needy.

Pittsburgh was becoming a noisy city. A committee was appointed by the church council "to confer with neighboring congregations in order to make a concerted effort to prevent the disturbance occasioned by running the omnibuses past the churches on the Sabbath." The committee later reported success.

March 1, 1858, Krauth's sister Julia, wife of the Reverend O. A. Kinsolving of Middleburg, Virginia died. She was very much like her brother, very bright, full of wit and humor, ready with her pen, in constant correspondence with her brother. She left three sons, one of whom, the Reverend G. Herbert Kinsolving, was rector of the Episcopal Church of the Epiphany in Philadelphia and afterward bishop of Texas.

The 1909 congregational history has high praise for their pastor. "Dr. Krauth was in the prime of physical and intellectual life when he came to Pittsburgh, and his great gifts speedily won recognition. He heartily identified himself with his people and confined his labors to their welfare. Although as a speaker he was equal to any demand, he never preached without careful preparation. He used an outline in the pulpit but his delivery was untrammeled and forcible. He was probably at his best as a preacher and speaker while in Pittsburgh, and the influence of his preaching and his personality was most timely and powerful. . . . He advanced the cause of pure Lutheranism, without attacking any special abuses and without exciting any special opposition. He thus accomplished much in the four years of his ministry in strengthening the lines of the conservative forces for the struggle which was immanent in the congregation and the Synod between historic Lutheranism and radicalism."[99]

His time in Pittsburgh, although rewarding to him and encouraging to the congregation, was to be limited. In May of 1858 he rejected inquiries from the venerable St. John's Church in Old Philadelphia, the oldest English-speaking congregation in the world. A year later, July 26, 1859, St. Mark's Church, Thirteenth and Spring Garden Streets in Philadelphia, unanimously elected him their pastor. One of the principal reasons for his accepting the call was the ill health of his wife, who was undergoing medical care in Philadelphia. The Pittsburgh congregation, in an attempt to retain the services of their beloved pastor, generously offered him the liberty to take as much time away from the parish as might be necessary to care for his wife "during the coming year." His acceptance of the call was as painful for him as was his acceptance of the call to Pittsburgh, but at last he relented, and moved to Philadelphia.

He had written to his father in 1858 from Pittsburgh, "If any temptation would try me more sorely than all others, it would be one in which I could devote myself more entirely to thorough and unbroken study."[100] His pastorate of St. Mark's lasted only three years (1859-1861), and he was able to turn his full attention to writing. He was editor of *The Lutheran and Missionary,* a merger of Philadelphia's *Lutheran* and Passavant's *The Missionary,* an influential organ for conservative Lutheran thought. When the Lutheran Theological Seminary at Philadelphia was founded in 1864 he was named Norton Professor of Dogmatic Theology. Four years later, in addition to his work at the seminary, he became Professor of Mental and Moral Philosophy at the University of Pennsylvania and in 1873 Vice Provost of the University. In addition to other duties, he was named Professor of History at the University of Pennsylvania. He died in Philadelphia January 2, 1883, not yet sixty years old.

Charles Porterfield Krauth, like his predecessor at First Church, is included on the calendar in *New Book of Festivals and Commemorations: A Proposed Common Calendar of Saints* (2008).

Although the resignation of Dr. Krauth was a deep wound to the congregation, his people's affection and personal regard remained undiminished throughout his life and still abide as a

Charles Porterfield Krauth, D.D., LL.D.

blessed memory.[101] He frequently visited the congregation upon invitation. His last visit was during a pastoral vacancy when he came to celebrate the Holy Communion on the First Sunday in Advent, 1879. "The services all seemed imbued with an atmosphere of pathos."

In January 1906, Professor Henry Eyster Jacobs, reported to the board of the Lutheran Theological Seminary at Philadelphia that he had received "a communication from a friend of the seminary (who does not desire his name to be known) offering $50,000 for the erection of a library building on the seminary grounds to be known as the Krauth Memorial Library." Dr. Jacobs had noticed a newspaper report that B. Frank Weyman (1842-1919), a manufacturer of tobacco products in Pittsburgh and holder of a patent for Copenhagen snuff, had sold his business for a reported three million dollars. Dr. Jacobs was personally acquainted with Frank Weyman from his time in Western Pennsylvania (1868-1870) when he was principal of Thiel Hall, established by William A. Passavant as a Christian preparatory school in 1866 and knew him to be an active and benevolent member of First English Lutheran Church. Mr. Weyman's first reaction to Jacobs' inquiry was negative. He later offered $10,000 and after further urging increased his offer to $50,000. Three conditions were attached to the gift: that the donor's name not be revealed, that the library should be a memorial to his former pastor, the late C. P. Krauth, and that Luther D. Reed, whom Weyman knew as pastor of Emanuel's Church in the Manchester section of Pittsburgh's North Side, serve as Weyman's representative in the planning of the building. The Dean of the seminary and Dr. Adolph Spaeth served with Dr. Reed as the donor's representatives in planning the building. Professor Spaeth criticized the original plans as too conventional. He wanted, and he convinced the others on the committee, to have something characteristically Lutheran. As finally built, "a handsome specimen of collegiate Gothic architecture, built of local stone with

Indiana limestone tracery and trimmings, in the form of a great cross 132 feet in length and 92 feet in width, with a massive central tower,"[102] the building embodies the idea of "Ein feste Burg" and is also "a symbol in stone of the character of the great and honored man whose name it bears; power and strength combined with a noble and refined elegance."[103] When the scope of the project was enlarged, an additional $50,000 gift was made by the "generous donor," as Weyman was uniformly referred to in board and faculty minutes to shield his identity. "Among ourselves this gentleman was known as 'G.D.' On the 8th of January, 1907, when 'Library Day' was celebrated for the first and last time, Dr. Spaeth alluded to G.D. causing a ripple of excitement and a pricking up of ears in the audience. With a quizzical smile he added, 'Generous Donor,' and the identity of our great unknown was still safe."[104] After the death of B. Frank Weyman in 1919 the identity of G.D. was revealed in an essay by Luther D. Reed in the *Lutheran Church Review* "A Benefactor of the Church: B. Frank Weyman."[105] The Krauth Memorial Library was completed in 1908, twenty-five years after the death of the man it honors. His vast library, given to the seminary, enriched incalculably the holdings of the collection.

The Krauth Library

Despite the pacific pastorate of Dr. Krauth, divisions remained in the congregation of First Church. Upon motion of Thomas Lane, the church council decided by a vote of six to five to call a congregational meeting to consider the Reverend Dr. Emanuel Greenwald (1811-1885) of Easton, at the eastern edge of Pennsylvania, but there is no record of further action. Apparently the close vote of the council doomed his consideration. He was, it would seem, the choice of Mr. Lane as a worthy successor to Pastor Krauth as a leader in conservative and traditional Lutheranism. Dr. Greenwald was born in Frederick, Maryland, and served as pastor in Ohio and Pennsylvania; he was a director of the Lutheran Theological Seminary at Philadelphia 1867-1879, and President of the Ministerium of Pennsylvania 1873-1877.

The council tried to sort out its uncertainties concerning the nomination and election of pastors. After much discussion two rules and eight by-laws were adopted on October 17, 1859. The rules required the church council to nominate for pastor one person "whom they have reason to believe would be useful and acceptable" and to submit his name to a congregational meeting, a two-thirds vote of the council being required for a nomination, although a unanimous recommendation is desirable. The by-laws required two public announcements for congregational meetings; organization of the meeting by election of a president, vice-president, and secretary; voting by ballots marked "For a call" and "Against a call"; a record by the secretary of all the legal voters who cast ballots; electors to be only such as "have paid one year's pew rent or rent for part of a pew sufficient for one person at least and who shall not be in arrears for such rent for more than one year and shall be in full communion with the English Evangelical Lutheran Church"; and a two-thirds vote for an election. One can read in those stipulations indications of the sort of controversies that had troubled the congregation in the past.

On Reformation Day, October 31, 1859, a letter was received from the Reverend Reuben Hill of Hagerstown, Maryland, accepting the council's invitation to preach. He was elected pastor at a meeting of the congregation on November 16. Only twenty-two votes were cast. Nonetheless, Mr. Hill accepted the call. His installation took place on the last Sunday in January 1860, his two predecessors delivering the two customary sermons, William Passavant the "charge to the pastor" and C. P. Krauth the "charge to the congregation." Mr. Hill was born in Hughesville, Pennsylvania July 22, 1826. He graduated from Pennsylvania (Gettysburg) College in 1852 and from the seminary in 1854, after which he served St. James Church in Gettysburg, and St. John's, Hagerstown, Maryland.

A lamentable backward step was taken in the progress of the congregation when a decision was made early in 1860 to reduce the number of communions from six to only four per year: the first Sundays in February, May, August, and November. Those who wanted to be like American Protestants seemed to have gained control.

In April 1860 the attention of the church council centered on the claims of Allegheny City as a mission field. As early as 1846 a Sunday school had been established there by members of First Church, under the direction of William Passavant. After three years it was discontinued for a time, but it was soon revived. In 1854 a church building was secured and in 1859 the school reported 350 scholars. Dr. Passavant was now (1860) Missionary Superintendent of the Synod, and in a long letter to the council of First Church he proposed beginning regular services in Al-

Reuben Hill

legheny every Sunday afternoon at three o'clock. He asked that Reuben Hill preach the first sermon and promised that he and three other pastors would assist in the rotation of the preachers. Allegheny City, he noted, had a population of 40,000 and concluded, "If the Council approves the proposed suggestion I think the way will be gradually prepared for the establishment of a second Church and tho' there is little likelihood that many of the older families of the parent Church would leave it, yet many a wanderer from God would be reached and many a careless family would be gathered into the fold of Christ."

The church council was wary of repeating their experience with Dr. Passavant, who spent much of his time away from the concerns of the parish, and they did not share his expansive view of responsibility and his utter confidence that God would somehow provide for his many and wide-ranging ventures. It put itself strongly on record as opposing such a movement, eleven members signing a reply, dated April 11, 1860. They regarded it as impossible that "another public service should be added to the pastor's duties with justice to himself and the congregation. Nor do we regard the one Church which now represents the interest of our denomination in this city so confirmed in its position that it could be depleted of its membership without jeopardizing its very existence, to say nothing of impairing its influence and diminishing its vitality." The statement concludes with their belief that their first obligations are "to sustain and perpetuate that which has been secured by years of toil and sacrifice and whose welfare demands the devotion of an entire and undivided membership."[106]

Four months later, in August 1860, the Reverend Henry Reck, who had succeeded Dr. Passavant as Missionary Superintendent, again brought the matter before the council. A committee of four conferred with those interested in the project, and reported that "The establishment of a mission separate and apart from the membership of the Church in Pittsburgh seems to us inadvisable, if not entirely impracticable. Aside from the fifty or sixty families who attend the Church on this side, the English Lutheran material is such as to be moulded into faithful members only by time and arduous labor." In the unanimous view of the council, any successful effort would require the transfer of a substantial number of existing families to act as leaven in the new project. "To build at all it must be on the foundation already laid." Their vision did not equal that of their distinguished former pastor, but their thought and language reflected their intimate knowledge of the Bible. The council made three recommendations: preaching services once a month under the supervision of First Church; securing, as soon as the means may be obtained, a second pastor to work at the Allegheny mission; after one year's united work to have the membership on that side of the river form a self-sustaining congregation if they are able "with the hearty approval and sympathy of the parent congregation."

The movement was too strong to be impeded or directed, and October 1, 1860 thirty-two members of First Church asked to be dismissed to organize a new congregation in Allegheny. Their request was granted, and these, together with others who also asked to be dismissed on October 21, organized the First English Evangelical Lutheran Church of Allegheny. (December 6, 1876 the name was changed to Trinity Church, which continues on North Avenue.) The pastor for the first three years of its life was Henry Reck.

Economic depression contributed to the failure of an effort to establish a Sunday school among the Germans on Penn Avenue, but in January 1862 the committee appointed to collect funds to pay the church debt reported that they had fulfilled their duty and that the long-suffering George Weyman had been fully repaid.

The Civil War touched Pittsburgh. A number of young men of the congregation were serving in the Union army. Among them were Henry Balken and B. Frank Weyman, both of whom served with Hampton Battery F of the Independent Pennsylvania Light Artillery. Weyman was wounded at the Battle of Gettysburg and was discharged July 3, 1863. A letter was received in September 1863 from the college and seminary at Gettysburg appealing for funds to repair damage to the buildings and grounds caused by the Battle of Gettysburg in July of that year. One hundred dollars were appropriated.

The congregation never shied away from going into debt for its continuation and health. The church building, just twenty-three years old, was not proving satisfactory. At the meeting in September 1863, the pastor was asked to appoint a committee of twenty members to determine how much money would be required to purchase a lot and build a new church and whether such a sum could be raised.

At the congregational meeting in January 1866, resolutions were passed directing that, since a number of members of the congregation, principally George Black, who recognized that real estate had not yet shared in the general inflation of the period and who advocated a more favorable site for a new church when the congregation would be in a position to build, had purchased a lot at the corner of Penn and Ninth Streets in trust for the congregation, a building committee be appointed to sell the existing church property and to erect a building on the new lot "when in their estimation a sufficient sum be subscribed to insure the success of the enterprise."

The Civil War was tearing the fabric of the nation, and a similarly divisive battle was being waged in the Lutheran Church in America. The "American Lutheranism" of S. S. Schmucker and his allies was being contested more and more vigorously by defenders of confessional Lutheranism, not a few of whom had once been practitioners of the "New Measures." The *Lutheran Observer* of the combative and vitriolic Benjamin Kurtz was answered in Pittsburgh by William Passavant's *The Missionary* and in Philadelphia by *The Lutheran*, both of which were founded to support and maintain the position of the conservatives. In 1864 the Philadelphia Seminary was founded as a protest and protection against what was seen as the radicalism then rampant at Gettysburg. The lines were being sharply drawn. There was growing bitterness and intolerance on every hand. First Church was the scene of some of these conflicts which later divided the congregation as they did the synod and the church at large. The first difficulties arose when the synod recommended a service, one can hardly call it a liturgy, to secure more uniformity in its congregations. November 6, 1865 the council decided by a vote of six to three to submit the recommendation of the synod for a uniform order of service to the next congregational meeting. After that meeting, January 1, 1866, and another two weeks later, the congregation chose by a vote of thirty-eight to fifteen to adopt the recommendation of the synod. It was an "exceedingly simple and moderate" service including little of a liturgical character beyond the recitation of the Apostles' Creed and the Lord's Prayer. Sentiment in favor of such a service had quietly developed in the congregation by the use for many years in the Sunday school of the Creed, the Lord's Prayer, and various responsive readings. "The final adoption of the Synod's Service placed the congregation on the firing line and developed an opposition to conservative usages which had much to do with Mr. Hill's final resignation; and this, notwithstanding the fact that he had not been in the least an agitator and had not evinced any partisan spirit."[107]

Six months after the congregational meetings, June 18, 1866, Pastor Hill, giving as his reason his impaired health and affliction of his throat for which his physician advised him to seek rest and a change of climate, submitted his resignation to take effect July 1. The council accepted his resignation and decided to continue payment of his salary through the rest of the calendar year.

After leaving Pittsburgh, Mr. Hill served a congregation in Rhinebeck, New York, founded the Church of the Reformation in Rochester, New York, and was Pastor of St. John's in Allentown, Pennsylvania for eleven years, during part of which time he was assistant professor of Greek at Muhlenberg College. In 1885 he became financial secretary and business manager of the Lutheran Theological Seminary at Philadelphia. It was largely through his efforts that the site in the Mount Airy section of Philadelphia was bought in 1887 and the dormitory, designed by Pastor Hill, was erected for the students when the seminary moved from its former home on Franklin Street in Old Philadelphia. The new home of the seminary was dedicated October 4, 1889, the twenty-fifth anniversary of the school. Muhlenberg College conferred on him the Doctor of Divinity degree in 1892. He died in Mount Airy March 3, 1895. Thomas H. Lane recorded in his dairy, "1895. March 4. Received a telegraph message from Rev. Dr. Laird announcing the death of Rev. Dr. Reuben Hill, which occurred on Sunday afternoon March 3rd at his home at Mt. Airy, Philadelphia. Dr. Hill had succeeded Dr. Krauth as pastor of our congregation, and had been the predecessor of Dr. Laird." The room in the Gowen Mansion that had been serving as a chapel was in 1898 converted into a classroom and furnished as such by Reuben Hill's wife, the daughter of Dr. Charles F. Schaeffer (1807-1879), in memory of her husband. Her father had been a professor at the seminary from its beginning in 1864 until the close of his life.[108]

It is never easy to predict the response of factions within the church. Both the conservatives and their opponents joined in supporting as a candidate for the pastorate of First Church Dr. Joseph Augustus Seiss,[109] pastor of St. John's Church in Philadelphia, who had preached at the convention of the General Synod in Fort Wayne, May 16, 1866 and upon his return from the synod repeated the sermon in First Church, Pittsburgh. He made a most favorable impression on the entire congregation and, even though he was a conservative, used to far fuller liturgy than the bare outline that caused division in First Church, and was accustomed to wearing the black preaching gown and white bands common to all the Lutheran parishes in Philadelphia, he was unanimously elected pastor at a congregational meeting July 18, 1866, fifty-six votes being cast. "The faction which had opposed the adoption of the Synod's Service and which later withdrew from the congregation was particularly active in urging Dr. Seiss's election and freely expressed its willingness to have him wear the clerical robe and to use the Liturgy, also agreeing to increase the salary if he would come. But he declined the call.

Joseph Augustus Seiss

The surprising unity that emerged during the consideration of Dr. Seiss soon evaporated. The meeting of the General Synod in Fort Wayne precipitated division. Delegates of the Ministerium of Pennsylvania were denied recognition because at the previous meeting of the synod in 1864 the Ministerium, opposing the recognition of the Franckean Synod of New York because of its doubtful subscription to the Lutheran confessions, had withdrawn from the convention. The General Synod viewed that action as severing connection with the Synod. The question at issue was the acceptance of the historic Lutheran Confessions of the sixteenth century. To the Ministerium of Pennsylvania the doctrinal position of the General Synod was unsatisfactory, and it was convinced that another general body should be formed, composed of synods that represented the traditional and historic doctrinal position of the Lutheran Church. The result was the formation of the General Council November 20, 1867.

A very large part of the membership of First Lutheran Church was in sympathy with the position of the General Council, but a small faction favored the General Synod. During the vacancy that followed the pastorate of Reuben Hill, the twelve-man council was evenly divided, six General Council men and six General Synod. Neither side could command a majority. By a vote of seven to five the council defeated a motion to invite eight different pastors to preach on eight successive Sundays and to nominate a pastor from that number.

At a special meeting on September 24, 1866, a motion to propose for election the name of Dr. Samuel Laird, pastor of Trinity Church, Lancaster, Pennsylvania, failed by a tie vote, although it was agreed to invite him to preach to the congregation. When Dr. Laird declined the invitation, it was agreed that two members of the council, one from each side, should go to Lancaster to hear him. Upon their return, both reported in his favor. November 5, 1866, a petition was presented to the council by George Weyman, signed by one hundred twenty-six members, requesting a congregational meeting for the election of the Reverend Samuel Laird. The proposal was defeated by a vote of six to five. The radical faction pointed to a clause in the by-laws of the congregation (section 1, chapter 2) requiring that "no minister shall be eligible to the office of pastor of this Church unless he is a member of some Synod in connection with the General Synod of the Evangelical Lutheran Church in the United States." Mr. Laird and his congregation in Lancaster were members of the Ministerium of Pennsylvania whose connection with the General Synod had been dissolved. The 1909 *History* accurately observes, "In all the unhappy controversy of this time we see that there was no serious opposition to any one person, but simply a bitter factional spirit inflamed against the conservative party in the Church at large."[110]

Nonetheless at a congregational meeting November 21, 1866, it was resolved by a vote of ninety-three to twenty-nine to strike out the troublesome section of the by-laws. Then by a vote of ninety-one to twenty-six, Samuel Laird was elected pastor. A bid to make the vote unanimous failed. The congregation had to meet again two weeks later to act formally upon the striking of the by-law, since the first action had been taken without the required notification.

Such arguments were taken most seriously in those days. After the adjournment of the meeting, in protest against the irregular and to them invalid constitutional action, two members of the minority took the keys to the church from the sexton and nailed down the windows to prevent the use of the building. If they could not have their way, then no one was going to worship. They called a special meeting of the council to exact terms which would place the minority in control. The meeting was held November 24 at 10 o'clock in the morning in the sexton's house, all the council members being present. The minority declared that they had acted under legal advice, and the other side responded, "As you have appealed to Caesar, to Caesar we will go." Nothing was submitted for formal action, and the meeting adjourned.

The church remained barricaded over the following Sunday, although a clergyman had been invited to come to the city to conduct the service and preach. When the members of the congregation who were not aware of the situation arrived and found themselves locked out of their church, "they became very indignant." During the following week the majority appealed to the courts, and a temporary injunction was granted to prevent the minority from retaining possession of the property. Thomas Lane was appointed trustee by the court, and the keys to the church were taken from Jacob Newmeyer, who was a trustee of the church, and placed in the keeping of Mr. Lane, who was a trustee of the court. Services were resumed the following Sunday and the interruption was ended.

This began a protracted legal controversy. The case was taken through the District Court, and when the minority cause lost there, it was appealed to the Supreme Court, where it was finally decided in favor of the majority of the congregation. The church council was equally divided and until another election could be held, every effort to call a pastor or to take any other action involving matters in dispute was futile. An indication of the depth of feeling which prevailed is evident in the action of the council at its meeting on December 3. It was necessary to make nominations for the annual election of church officers at the congregational meeting, and George Weyman's name was submitted for re-nomination as Elder, but the nomination failed by reason of a tie vote. Two days later an adjourned meeting of the congregation was held at which it unanimously decided to reconsider the action of November 21 repealing the by-law requiring the pastor to be a member of the General Synod and also the action relating to the call of Pastor Laird. It was then decided to postpone indefinitely the election of a pastor and to discharge the committee appointed to extend a call and to arrange a salary. It seemed clear to the congregation that the evenly divided council was unable to act on any significant issue.

January 7, 1867 at the annual meeting of the congregation, the council declared that it could not agree on any nominations for the church council. The congregation therefore nominated and unanimously elected the church council for the year. Thomas Lane and William P. Weyman, a son of George Weyman, were appointed to invite a Lutheran pastor to preach the following

Sunday (the minority apparently had no scruples about inviting clergymen of any persuasion to preach in their church) and to install the officers. Thus the majority of the congregation was able to break the deadlock and place the administration of its affairs in the hands of a council that would truly represent it and execute its wishes. Among the members of the new council is the name of Jacob S. Newmeyer, one of the leaders of the minority opposition who had held the keys to the church when it was barricaded. A week later, at the council meeting on January 14, George Hubley, former treasurer and a member of the new council, was requested to turn over to the new treasurer and the trustees all books, accounts, papers, and money in his possession belonging to the church. It was also resolved to call a congregational meeting for January 30 to consider the proposed amendment to the by-laws and to elect a pastor, Samuel Laird being nominated.

The meeting was held. The motion to amend the by-laws carried by a vote of seventy-one to three. Samuel Laird was elected pastor by a vote of seventy-four to two. George Black, Thomas Lane, and William Weyman, by authority of the congregation, visited Lancaster and personally presented the call to Pastor Laird, who, *mirabile dictu* in view of the prolonged turmoil in the congregation, accepted it.

Despite the quarrels that divided the congregation, liturgical progress was being slowly made. Some time before Pastor Laird arrived, a railing had been erected around the chancel and a lectern placed within the rail, as shown in the photograph of the interior of the Seventh Street church, so that the service up to the sermon could be conducted from the chancel. "There was only partial use of the Liturgy, as the people were not accustomed to the full Service." April 1 the council accepted an offer by a group of young men of the congregation to replace the instrument then in use in the church, a harmonium, with a small organ. Subsequently B. Frank Weyman proposed through the pastor to replace the organ with a larger instrument, the church to obtain an interest in the new organ proportionate to the value of the old one, Frank Weyman assuming the additional cost.

Samuel Laird began his ministry at First Church on the first Sunday in May, 1867, the Sunday of the Good Shepherd (the Gospel for the day being St. John 10:11-16). He had been born in New Castle County, Delaware, February 7, 1835, became a member of St. John's [English] Church in Old Philadelphia, graduated from the University of Pennsylvania intending to become a lawyer. Changing course, he was ordained in 1861 and served St. Luke's Church in Philadelphia. In 1864 he became pastor of Holy Trinity Church, Lancaster, from which he was called to First Church.

Samuel Laird

It was a difficult time for the congregation, torn by dissention. George Hubley and Jacob S. Newmeyer, although both members of the church council, were actively engaged in the promotion of the organization of a rival congregation and in securing the services of a minister for it. The council therefore requested Pastor Laird and George Weyman to confer with them concerning the inconsistency of their position. In response, as they had promised, at the next meeting of the council, June 7, 1867, a lengthy letter was read from George Hubley, who had been a member of the council for twenty years, in which he tendered his resignation as an elder of the church; the pastor read a letter to him from Jacob Newmeyer containing his resignation. At the council meeting three months later, the resignation of the third leader of the dissidents, J. H. Lyday, was received.

After the final decision of the supreme count, the forty disaffected members of First Church withdrew from the congregation, bought a property on Hand Street, and secured the services of the Reverend J. W. H. Stuckenberg (a son of First Lutheran Church). The 1909 history, indicating the lingering hard feelings caused by the dissention, concludes the matter with the terse comment, "The venture there was not successful." The new congregation, not dignified by its name in the 1909 First Church history, was called Messiah Church and was a member of the General Synod. The congregation was prosperous at first, the membership reaching 167, and was regarded as a center of General Synod hopes in the Pittsburgh district; then a series of discouragements ensued that caused the congregation to disband in 1884. Most of the remaining members joined Trinity Church on the North Side. Messiah Church was served by four pastors in its sixteen-year history.[111]

Samuel Laird, who began his ministry at First Church on the first Sunday in May, was installed as pastor on the last Sunday in June. The service was conducted by Dr. Passavant; the sermon was preached by Dr. Joseph A. Seiss, pastor of St. John's Church, Philadelphia, where Pastor Laird had grown up.

Liturgical progress was made slowly. The church council decided that the next Communion, to be celebrated on the first Sunday in October, should be in the morning instead of the afternoon as had been the curious practice of the congregation (perhaps in a literalist imitation of the evening meal of the Lord's Supper), and that the preparatory service of confession be held on the preceding Friday evening.

The tension between the Americanizing forces and the confessional forces in the Lutheran Church in North America could not be maintained without causing a break between them. Both sides saw that compromise was impossible, each viewing the other as in error that would lead to the demise of the Lutheran movement in America. When the Ministerium of Pennsylvania withdrew from the General Synod in 1866, it authorized an invitation "to all Evangelical Lutheran Synods, ministers and congregations in the United States and Canada which confess the Unaltered Augsburg Confession" to attend a convention for the organizing of an ecclesiastical body "on a truly Lutheran basis." This convention met in Trinity Church, Reading, Pennsylvania December 12-14, 1866. The Reverend Gottlieb Bassler, of the Pittsburgh Synod, presided. The "Principles of Faith and Church Polity" prepared by Charles Porterfied Krauth were discussed and adopted as the basis of the proposed organization. On October 15 the Pittsburgh Synod adopted, by a vote of sixty-three to twenty-one, the "Fundamental Principles of Faith" proposed for the General Council. In protest, a small faction of ten pastors and seven lay delegates withdrew, and, claiming the name, were afterward recognized by the General Synod as the Pittsburgh Synod. The courts subsequently ruled that such action was illegal. November 20, 1867, the General Council was organized at Fort Wayne, Indiana, in the church in which the General Synod had held its sessions the year before. Prior to that meeting, First English Lutheran

Church in Pittsburgh on November 11, extended a formal invitation to the General Council, presuming that it would in fact be organized less than two weeks later, to hold its second meeting (1868) in First Church in Pittsburgh. The invitation was accepted.

The second convention of the General Council was notable chiefly for an exhaustive discussion of the "four points": (1) chiliasm (belief in the coming of the millennium, the Thousand Year Reign prominent in the emerging fundamentalist movement); (2) secret societies (is it proper for Lutherans to be members of such societies as the Masons?)[112]; (3) pulpit fellowship (should preachers other than Lutherans be welcome in Lutheran pulpits), and (4) altar fellowship (should communicants other than Lutherans be welcome at Lutheran altars?) The General Council defined its position on these disputed questions, and these declarations largely determined the attitude taken subsequently by the Joint Synod of Ohio, the Iowa Synod and the Missouri Synod toward the General Council.

More important for the life of the church was the introduction of the *Church Book*. It had been in the process of formation for several years by the Ministerium of Pennsylvania prior to the organization of the General Council. Now it became their book and formed a solid basis for unity of faith and worship. "It was unquestionably the best liturgy and hymnal which the Lutheran Church in America had yet produced," based on a broad study of the Lutheran liturgies of the sixteenth century. The hymnal "availed itself of the latest developments in England, where as a by-product of the Oxford Movement, a new era in English hymnody had opened."[113] Before the meeting in First Church, on October 15, the treasurer of the congregation was authorized to purchase two hundred copies, which were sold to the members at cost. The *Church Book* was used for services for the first time November 8, a short time after its publication, and when the General Council met on November 12, it found its own book in the pews. For four years the full liturgical order was not used, the council fearing that the people were not prepared for such a step. At the annual meeting of the congregation in January 1872, the congregation by an almost unanimous vote adopted the recommendation of the church council to introduce the full liturgical order. "The pastor gave full explanation of the several parts of the Service and it was then employed in public worship with entire satisfaction."

The introduction of the *Church Book* encouraged the development of music as a significant part of the worship of the congregation. June 25, 1870, the council accepted the proposal by B. Frank Weyman, Charles Baer, and Peter Young that, if the council would appropriate $350 per year, they would serve as organists in the church and Sunday school and at all other services during the week (services were regularly held on Wednesday evenings) and also to engage a soprano to lead the singing at all services and to supply the music. In June, 1871, the services were divided so that Frank Weyman and Charles Baer were to take charge of the music in the church and Peter Young the music in the Sunday school and the Wednesday evening services.

Concern for the needy within and beyond the membership of the congregation was being renewed. In January 1868 the pastor's suggestion was accepted that a schedule of special collections be approved: Beneficiary Education, the second Sunday in February; Home Missions, the second Sunday in May; Synodical Fund, the Sunday preceding the meeting of the Synod; the Orphans' Home, Thanksgiving Day. The next month a request of the Ladies' Relief Society that financial aid be given to assist them in their efforts to relieve the suffering poor of the city. In 1868 the Ladies' Sewing Society was organized with Jane Barclay Black as president. It remained until 2009 as the oldest organization in the congregation. The Reverend W. Berkemeyer was given permission by the council to collect funds on behalf of the Emigrant House in New York City. Pastor Laird on Sunday afternoons began conducting services in the East End of Pittsburgh in the German Lutheran Church of East Liberty. When the Reverend James Q. Waters came to Pittsburgh he was placed in charge of the work and was supported in part by First Church. The congregation was organized June 25, 1869 with twenty-three members.

In May 1870, one hundred dollars was appropriated for Pastor James Q. Waters for his work in East Liberty, where Christ Church had been organized a year before; he was also given the privilege of collecting within the congregation for the mission. October 11, 1871 the distribution of funds collected for the relief of sufferers from the Chicago fire was entrusted to the Ladies' Sewing Society, who were actively engaged in forwarding supplies to be distributed by the pastors of the various Lutheran churches of that city. One hundred dollars were also appropriated from the Indigent Fund for this purpose. A collection was authorized to aid in the mission begun by the former pastor of First Church, Reuben Hill, in Rochester, New York.

During Mr. Hill's pastorate in Pittsburgh, May 6, 1866, St. John's Sunday School was organized in a room on the third floor of a building at the corner of Fifth Avenue and Pride Street. It was the only permanent result of the short-lived City Missionary Society, organized in the lecture room of First Church by members of the Sunday schools of First Church, Second German Church, Trinity Church in Allegheny City, and Grace Church on the South Side. Because the rent for the room was very high, arrangements were finally made with Second St. Paul's German Lutheran Church for the use of their church on Pride Street near Fifth Avenue for $150 per annum. (The church building is now the home of Shepherd's Heart Anglican mission.)

In 1869, the Sunday school prospering, the church council decided to secure a suitable lot for a church building and a chapel for the Sunday school, and sought to obtain the services of a missionary to supervise the enterprise. George Black offered to donate a lot at the corner of Jumonville Street and Forbes Avenue. He died a few weeks after making the offer without having been able to carry it out. His wife, Jane Barclay Black, gave a lot from her own ground, also at the corner of Forbes and Jumonville, and thus fulfilled her husband's wish. A chapel was erected, and in the

George Black and Jane Barclay Black

fall of 1876 the school, led by Pastor Laird, marched in procession from the German church to the new chapel. It was consecrated free from debt the Sunday after Christmas, 1876. At the close of the following year, Jane Barclay Black gave to First Church one thousand dollars, to be held in trust with the interest it accrued, to be applied to the contemplated new building for St. John's congregation.

The organist at the St. John's Sunday school and mission during this period was Annie Childs Shaffer, who later married Henry Phipps, Jr. (1839-1930), business partner of Andrew Carnegie, whose name is preserved in Pittsburgh in the Phipps Conservatory and Botanical Gardens.

At noon on Christmas Day, 1870, George Weyman died. "He had lived to see the congregation, which he was so largely instrumental in founding, and for which he had labored and sacrificed so unsparingly, firmly established, prosperous, active in assisting other struggling congregations, and influential and respected in the councils of the Church at large."[114] Indeed, it is no exaggeration to say that if it had not been for George Weyman, First Lutheran Church would not have survived.

Mr. Weyman was fatherly, firm in his convictions, gentle in his dealings with others, "and was greatly beloved by the congregation that was so much indebted to him. On one occasion, being deeply wounded by remarks publicly made by a member of the radical faction, he would not approach the Communion table until the matter was satisfactorily adjusted. Accompanied by Mr. Laird, his pastor, he waited upon the offender, and came to a brotherly understanding with him, and only then felt free to partake of the Lord's Supper."[115]

Another serious loss was suffered by the congregation on August 5, 1872. George Black died unexpectedly after a brief illness. He was a prominent businessman in Pittsburgh, a Director of the Pennsylvania Railroad, "and largely interested in transportation lines. He was a regular attendant at the services of the First Church, and being possessed of ample means contributed liberally to its support, and to the furtherance of missions and works of mercy."[116] First Church had made an earnest effort to provide for the religious care of the Swedes, who had come in considerable numbers to work in the mills and industries of the city. The Reverend John W. Kindborg, a Swedish student in the

Theological Seminary at Philadelphia, was called as their pastor, and First Church was placed at their disposal, whenever it was not used by the congregation for its own purposes. Pastor Kindborg established congregations in a number of places in New York and eastern Ohio, extending the influence of First Church. George Black arranged for the Reverend Dr. T. N. Hasselquist to go to Sweden and get graduates from higher education institutions there to come to America for theological training at the seminary of the Augustana Synod. All expenses were paid by George Black.

The church building on Seventh Street, after only thirty years of use, was proving unsatisfactory. The location was not prominent, and the construction was shoddy. The roof leaked; the bricks were crumbling. In 1873 a committee of five was appointed to consider the price at which it would be deemed advisable to offer the property for sale, and the time and manner of making such an offer. At the May meeting of the church council, after an extended discussion of a new church building, a committee was appointed to consider the character and cost of a suitable structure on the lot the church had owned for ten years at Ninth Street and Penn Avenue. At a meeting of the congregation on June 10, the congregation approved unanimously a resolution to appoint a committee of the pastor and twelve other members to sell "the present church and property; to collect such additional funds as may be required; to adopt a suitable plan for a new church edifice and to make all contracts required for the building and completion of the same." The committee proceeded at once with the work. James H. Windrim (died 1919) of Philadelphia, who was to be the architect of Trinity Church at 18th and Wolf Streets in South Philadelphia (1889-1890), and afterwards Supervising Architect of the United States Treasury Department 1889-1891 and then Director of Public Works for the City of Philadelphia 1891-1895, was engaged to prepare plans for a building. The plans which he submitted were greatly admired. Two members of the committee traveled East to inspect different churches, the pastor going as far as Hartford, Connecticut, to see a church constructed of Westerly granite, which the architect proposed to use in the new structure.

"A severe money stringency, however, in the community, occasioned by peculiarly depressing financial conditions" compelled the indefinite postponement of all plans for the erection of the new building. After the financial condition of the community improved, the congregation again undertook preparations for building. They were interrupted again, however, by the plans by the United States government to select a new site for a post office. Three places were put under condemnation, one of which was the property of the congregation on Seventh Street between Grant and Smithfield Streets. The property therefore could not be sold, and the purpose of the congregation was again thwarted. The government finally decided to build on Smithfield Street between Third and Fourth Avenues. The Seventh Street property was released from condemnation, but because only a short time intervened before the close of Samuel Laird's pastorate in Pittsburgh, nothing further was done in this direction at that time.

Pittsburgh looking up the Ohio River in 1876

In June 1879 Pastor Laird resigned as pastor of First Church to accept a call he had received from St. Mark's Church in Philadelphia, to which Charles Porterfield Krauth had gone from First Church twenty years before. The council of First Church was unwilling to let its pastor go and went as a body to Pastor Laird to urge him to remain in Pittsburgh. He was not be swayed from his decision, and the longest pastorate in the history of First Church to that time, twelve years and three months, came to a close. He preached his farewell sermon on the last Sunday in July, 1879. In his letter to the council he said, "In all my relations with you, I have received only kindness. I began my work among you almost a stranger. We have lived and labored together as brothers.

While in Philadelphia he served for three years as President of the Ministerium of Pennsylvania (1898-1901),[117] as director of the Theological Seminary (1865-1867, 1883-1911) and its treasurer, a director of the German Hospital (later Lankenau Hospital) and the Mary J. Drexel Home both then located in North Philadelphia. As one interested in the development of the Lutheran liturgy he was one of the representatives of the General Council to the committee that prepared the Common Service of 1888. He was not one of the experts in liturgy (they were G. U. Wenner of the General Synod, Edward Traill Horn of the General Synod South, and B. M. Schmucker and Adolph Spaeth of the General Council), and H. E. Jacobs describes his participation as one of three who "seemed deeply interested but had very little to say in the discussions."[118] Pastor Laird died in 1911.

Samuel Laird

Chapter 5

Building for the Ages: the House of First Lutheran Church

During the vacancy created by the resignation of Pastor Laird, Thomas Lane served as chair of the church council, in the absence of a pastor, and the Reverend Enoch Smith of Greensburg, Pennsylvania, came to the church on alternate Sundays during the interim. While pastor of First Church Greensburg (1872-1881) he continued what was his practice elsewhere and helped out vacant parishes such as St. John's, Bouquet (1876-1877), and Emanuel's, Export (1877). It was a not uncommon practice; Edmund Belfour while at First Church was supply pastor at St. Mark's, Springdale, 1881-1882. After a relatively brief vacancy (First Church was now strong and united and therefore an attractive congregation), the council by a unanimous vote recommended the Reverend Edmund Belfour as pastor, and at a congregational meeting November 19, 1879 he was elected pastor by a vote of ninety-eight to two. The call was made unanimous and the salary fixed at $2800 per annum. He began his work in Pittsburgh February 1.

Edmund Belfour was born in Alstead, a suburb of Copenhagen, Denmark, August 9, 1833. His father, a well-educated Dane, came to America in 1839 and, a common practice of the time, worked to earn money to bring his wife and children to

Edmund Belfour

New York; his family arrived two years later on the ship *Isabella*. Edmund, the youngest of seven children, had to work in order to support the family. He was sixteen before he was able to begin school. A remarkably bright boy, after only nine months of study he was able to pass the entrance examination for the College of the City of New York, from which he graduated in 1854. He graduated from Gettysburg Seminary two years later. He served as pastor of St. Paul's Church in Schoharie, New York, and the associated Lutheran church at Central Bridge for eleven years and as pastor of St. John's Church in Easton, Pennsylvania, for six years.[119] From there he moved to Chicago (1874-1880) to organize the English work of the General Council in that city, especially among the growing number of Scandinavians, establishing Holy Trinity and Wicker Park congregations. In a reversal of the pattern set by Pastors Emanuel Frey and William Smith, who fled the unhealthful atmosphere of Pittsburgh, Pastor Belfour, because the climate of Chicago did not agree with him, left that city and came to Pittsburgh. He was a fine scholar and is reported to have had in his library books written in eight or nine languages[120]

Pastor Belfour's culture and learning were to have a lasting influence on the Pittsburgh congregation and the building it planned as its new house.

The construction of a new church continued to be a matter of concern for the congregation. February 6, 1882, the property at Ninth Street and Penn Avenue on which the congregation had planned to build, was leased for one year to William F. Lang for $1100, the lessee to pay the taxes on the property. At the end of the year, December 28, an offer of $50,000 for the lot was received from Haworth and Dewhurst. Prudently, a committee was appointed to ascertain whether a suitable building could be procured for the use of the congregation in the event of a sale of the church.

The slow progress of plans to build on that lot turned out to be a good thing. The city was changing. During much of the nineteenth century the city was confined to what is now "Downtown," the central business district. Commercial activity had been limited to the riverfronts and the appropriately named Market Square. The rest of the city was largely residential, as is evidenced by the great number of churches there. In 1872, at the height of the post-Civil War economic boom, six churches were located in the Penn-Liberty district, a prime residential neighborhood in the nineteenth century, and seventeen in the area bounded by Grant and Wood Streets between Fifth and Seventh Avenues. As the city's economy continued to grow and industry continued to consolidate, the introduction of the electric street car encouraged the population to spread into the surrounding countryside. During the 1880s and 1890s the construction of office buildings and business blocks and the displacement of the residential population began to transform the "Golden Triangle" (from Grant Street west to the confluence of the Allegheny and Monongahela Rivers) into a central business district.

The astute businessmen of First Church were aware of these trends and were prepared to alter the long-standing plan of the congregation to build a new church on their lot at Ninth and Penn. At the annual congregational meeting in January 1885 Henry Balken, a member of the church council, offered the following resolution:

> "WHEREAS, the Church lot belonging to this congregation at the corner of Penn Avenue and Ninth Street, by changes and encroachments of business traffic and also in the changes of residences of our people, has become unsuitable as a site for the erection of a church; and
>
> WHEREAS, parties have made inquiries after the property for business purposes.
>
> *Resolved,* That this congregation does hereby invest the Church Council with authority to sell and convey said property for a sum of not less than $75,000.00, it being left to the direction of the Church Council whether to sell or not, without further authority from the congregation unless otherwise ordered."

After considerable discussion the meeting was adjourned to meet on Monday January 12. At that meeting the motion prevailed by a vote of twenty-nine to five.

As earnest thought was being given to the matter of securing another and more suitable lot and the building of a new church, the congregation was growing in its understanding of stewardship and the proper place of the offering in the liturgy of the church. The council had long been troubled by the annual deficit in church finances. In January of 1885, because "it is not expedient to have the periods for the collection of that which has been laid aside for the Lord's work placed at long intervals," George W. Geissenhainer proposed "that we return to the early and churchly custom of weekly collections and that such collections be taken as a part of the regular service, according to Lutheran usage, the first weekly offering to be received on Easter Sunday morning of this year." A strong feeling had developed against the "penny collection" as undignified and not a real offering or a proper part of worship, and therefore it had been the long-standing custom of the parish not to receive an offering during the liturgy and to rely on yearly pew rentals, paid at the end of the year, for the support of the church. The pew rents had been supplemented from 1875 by subscriptions by members of the congregation "of such amounts as they may be willing to give towards the support of the Church in addition to the assessments they now pay for pews or sittings."[121] Notable in the proposal to collect offerings weekly is the reference to "Lutheran usage". The congregation was now proud of its Lutheran heritage and eager to follow its practices.

The congregation also, even while preparing for its own future house, was actively engaged in assisting other congregations. An offering was taken to aid in the rebuilding of the Lutheran church in Rochester, Pennsylvania, after it had been destroyed by a fire. The council agreed to pay the interest on the mortgage on a mission church in Alliance, Ohio, served by the Reverend J. Q. Waters, a son of the First Church, which was in danger of losing its property.

A property at the corner of Grant Street and Strawberry Alley had come to the attention of the council. It was apparently the same property that had been considered in 1838 before the lots on Seventh Street were purchased but which the owner would not sell. July 6, 1885 a committee was appointed to learn what price the property commanded. On July 27 a communication was received from M. Seibert and Company, the owners of a part of the property on Grant Street, offering their share, consisting of 100 x 94 feet, for $45,000, the offer to remain open for three weeks. Dr. F. Bese, the owner of twenty feet on the corner of Grant Street and Strawberry Alley, offered to sell his portion for $11,500.

A congregational meeting was called for August 12. The pastor chaired the meeting; Thomas Lane was vice-president, and

B. Frank Weyman secretary. An extensive and detailed communication was considered.

> "The Council of this Church having received an offer of a plot of ground as a site for the new church which we have so long contemplated building, and being convinced of its advantageous character, have deemed it their duty to call this meeting of the congregation and to submit this proposition for consideration and decision; and in order that the material facts in the case may be brought out and a clear understanding of its merits attained, the following statements are submitted:
>
> FIRST: *Geographical Location of the Lot.*—It fronts on Grant Street from Strawberry Alley to a line within a few feet of the Reformed Presbyterian Church, and extends back to Foster Alley [now Garland Way]. It is therefore central, easy of access, and very near our present location.
>
> SECOND: *Surroundings of the Lot.*—In front is Grant Street. On the right [standing on the lot, looking toward Grant Street] is a church separated by a private passageway; on the left is Strawberry Alley, on which a public schoolhouse fronts at a distance of twenty feet from the building line and a like distance from the Grant Street line, bringing the lot into bold relief. At the rear is Foster Alley, which at this point is exceptionally good in the character of its buildings. The lot therefore is open of all four sides, affording ample light, ventilation, and safety against fire. Sewer, water, and gas connections are complete on the premises.
>
> THIRD: *The Size of the Lot.*—It has a frontage of 120 feet on Grant Street and a depth of 94 feet to Foster Alley, being nearly twice as wide as the lot we now occupy and only six feet less in depth. Only on such a large lot, affording room for grass and trees, can an edifice appear to advantage. The expenditure of $50,000.00 would probably make a more pleasing showing than one of $75,000 on a narrow lot, so important is the bearing of the surroundings.

FOURTH: *The Price of the Lot,* $56,500.00 which by common consent is very cheap. More than two years ago, the Council appointed a committee to ascertain whether a suitable church lot could be secured, and although they made diligent inquiry, they found none until the one now under consideration was offered. Owing to the increasing demands of business, good lots are constantly becoming more scarce and more expensive. The present is an exceptional case.

FIFTH: *The Financial Question.*—A mortgage of $18,000.00 rests on the lot offered us and does not mature for several years. Subtracting this amount from the purchase price, $56,500.00, $38,500.00 remains to be provided for. If we sell the Penn Avenue lot for $75,000.00 and to this add the amount of the Church Lot Fund in hand, namely, $12,000.00, we would have $87,000.00 available. Paying $38,500.00 on the lot, we would still have $48,500.00 for building. We might with this in hand finish the new church, continuing in the meanwhile to occupy the present edifice, and the current interest on the $18,000.00 would be no more than rent which we would have to pay for a temporary place of worship if this building were torn down to make way for another. The cost of building is at present very low, about 25 per cent. less than a few years back. We have an instance of this in the fact that four years ago the lowest bid for building a public schoolhouse in a certain part of this city was $43,000.00. The erection was delayed until this summer and now the contract has been let for $31,000.00.

SIXTH: A new church is desired and needed. It is needed to carry out the fundamental purpose of the donors of the Penn Avenue property. It is needed to satisfy the earnest wishes of our people in general according to repeated expressions. It is needed for the comfort of the congregation and especially for the interests of the Sunday School. It is needed to replace the present building, which is falling into decay. It is needed for the honor of the great Lutheran Church which we represent in this city. It is needed above all as a testimonial of our reverence for God and His worship. The serious question which ought to be met and determined is whether the present time and circumstances are not such as should call forth prompt action on the very important matter of deciding on a suitable site for a new church and proceeding to build it without delay. Within two days an answer must be given positively in regard to the offer now before us. Others are awaiting the opportunity to buy the lot."

It was a persuasive and compelling presentation. Upon motion by William B. Wolfe, it was resolved to purchase the site and to build a new church. Upon motion by J. Boyd Duff, it was resolved to pay the price named for the lot, $56,500, or less. Both resolutions passed unanimously. The meeting was adjourned to meet September 9.

At that September meeting it was announced that the purchase had been made and that the deeds were held by the congregation. A $600 reduction in price had been obtained from M. Seibert & Company. The final cost of the property was $55,900: $44,400 to M. Seibert & Co. plus $11,500 to Dr. Bese.

The purchase was a remarkably bold and insightful decision. The leaders of the congregation were convinced, correctly, that Grant Street was to become the principal thoroughfare of downtown Pittsburgh and a new church there would be a clear testimony to the pride the congregation had come to have in its distinctive tradition and to its commitment to use that tradition to enrich the life of the city.

Moreover, the congregation by building the newest church on Grant Street declared its commitment to remain there through whatever changes the future might bring. It chose not to follow its members as they moved to suburban areas as did all of the neighboring churches. An important contribution to that decision was the fact that its members did not generally relocate to one developing area beyond downtown; they moved to all directions of the compass. There was no concentration of members in any one area, and so there was no obvious place for the church to consider going, should it decide to leave downtown.

Before long, the other churches along Grant Street began to depart for other sections of the city. At the very beginning of the twentieth century Henry Clay Frick sought to purchase church properties for his business projects: the Frick Building, the Union Trust Building, and the William Penn Hotel. The Roman Catholic Cathedral of St. Paul at Fifth and Grant was relocated to Fifth and Craig in Oakland. The extraordinarily lovely St. Peter's Episcopal Church on the corner of Grant and Diamond Street (Forbes Avenue) was rebuilt in 1906, stone by stone, at Frick's expense, at Forbes and Craft in Oakland.[122] First Baptist Church (built in 1876, demolished in 1909) moved from Fourth Avenue near Ross Street to Bellefield and Bayard in Oakland; Third Presbyterian Church went from William Penn Way (then called Cherry Street) near Sixth Avenue to Fifth Avenue at Negley Street in Shadyside in 1896. The United Presbyterian Church (a union of the Associate and Associate Reformed churches) on Seventh Street moved to the East End in 1897. St. Andrew's Episcopal Church at Fort Duquesne Boulevard and the Ninth Street bridge removed to Highland Park in 1906. By 1910 all but one of the churches near Penn Avenue had closed and only seven[123] of the seventeen in the Grant Street area remained. Of all the churches that had once lined Grant Street, only First English Lutheran Church, the last to be built, remains. It is an impressive testimony to its continuing commitment to the city where, the congregation understands, God intends it to be.

February 1, 1886 a rough estimate of the cost of building a church according to the plans and specifications already in the possession of the church council, prepared by James Windrim, was secured, but a committee of the pastor and four laymen was appointed "to make inquiries in regard to new plans." The reason for new plans is not recorded. In any case, an accomplished Pittsburgh architect, Andrew Peebles, who had designed St. Peter's Roman Catholic Church at Arch Street and Ridge Avenue on the North Side (1872-1874),[124] submitted plans and at a meeting of the council in May 1886 explained the drawings. He was highly regarded in the city, and his work was eclectic, reflecting a variety of nineteenth-century styles. The council approved the plans for a one-storied church (the Seventh Street church was two-storied with Sunday School meeting rooms on the lower level and the church above) and chapel with certain modifications, but a final vote was postponed until a later meeting. On May 15 the modified plans were approved, although the interior arrangements were left for future decision. Five hundred lithographic prints of the plans were prepared by William G. Armor of the building committee and distributed to members of the congregation, "with special ground plans for each member of the Council." A surviving copy now hangs in the parish house of the First Church.[125]

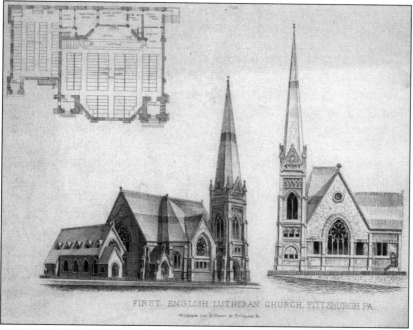

Architect's drawing of First English Lutheran Church

A special meeting of the church council on November 16 considered the offer by John Caldwell to purchase the property on Penn Avenue and Ninth Street for $75,000, cash payment to be $25,000, and the balance payable in two years and secured by a bond and mortgage bearing five per cent interest; possession to be given on December 1. The offer was unanimously accepted. The lot when it was bought for the congregation during Reuben Hill's pastorate had cost $20,000.

At the annual congregational meeting on January 3, 1887 the church council was authorized to sell the church property on Seventh Avenue and Miltenberger Alley [now Montour Way] for such sum as might in their judgment seem adequate. On January 10 Thomas Lane and William F. Lang were appointed to negotiate the sale of the church property. The Union Veteran League inquired concerning the lowest price for which the congregation would sell the old church and the amount of cash required. The price was fixed at $60,000, with $25,000 in cash, the balance in nine equal annual payments bearing five per cent interest. The old church remained in use until the new church on Grant Street was finished. It was not sold until April 1, 1889, and then to the Central District and Printing Telegraph Company for $58,000. The brick building, now AT&T, is on the site of the old church.

Work began on the new building. Considerable difficulty was experienced in making a proper foundation for the new church. In excavating, the workers came upon a strong flow of water at the northeast corner of the lot, where the tower now rises, at a depth of fourteen feet. It was what a 1795 map of Pittsburgh shows as Hogg's Pond, which flowed from Grant Street at Strawberry Way in a southwestward direction to empty into the Monongahela River at Wood Street. To lead the water away and to reinforce the foundation, at an additional cost of five thousand dollars, a drain was constructed, and pilings fitted with iron points made by a blacksmith on site were driven to a depth of thirty feet along a part of the alley side and also along a section of the rear wall.[126]

Sunday, November 6, 1887, at 2:30 p.m. the cornerstone was laid. "The weather was exceptionally fine and the attendance large." The order of service was that provided by the Ministerium of Pennsylvania; the hymns were from the *Church Book*, Agnes Bulmer's "Thou, who hast in Zion laid/The true foundation stone" (no. 291), the hymn appointed in the *Church Book* for the laying of a cornerstone,[127] and "Now thank we all our God" (no. 11), sometimes called "the Lutheran Te Deum." The address was given by the Reverend Dr. John Alleman Kunkleman, President of the Pittsburgh Synod; Pastor Belfour laid the stone with the prescribed words, "I lay the cornerstone of an edifice to be here erected, by the name of the First English Evangelical Lutheran Church, and to be devoted to the service of Almighty God, agreeably to the principles of the Evangelical Lutheran Church in its doctrines, ministry, liturgy, rites and usages." The Grant Street side of the stone bears in inscription "Erected A.D. 1887 Founded A.D.1837"; on the Strawberry Way side is a Greek cross bearing the first three letters of "Jesus" in Greek, "IHS". In a copper box in the southeast corner of the tower were placed copies of the

Bible, the Church Book (which included the Small Catechism and the Augsburg Confession), the Sunday School Book [edited by the daughter of Charles Porterfield Krauth, Harriet Reynolds Krauth Spaeth]; the Fundamental Principles of the General Council, the General Council Constitution for Congregations, printed minutes of the General Council 1886; Minutes of the Pittsburgh Synod 1887; church papers (Krauth's *The Lutheran*, Passavant's *the Workman, The Herald und Zeitschrift,* and a Swedish paper); an autographic list of the names of the pastor, officers of the church, officers and teachers of the two Sunday schools (First Church and St. John's), officers of the Ladies' Society, members of the choir, members of the building committee; a printed program for the laying of the cornerstone, a print of the church building on Seventh Avenue; and an historical sketch of the congregation from its organization compiled by the pastor.

As work on the construction of the new church continued in 1888, farewell services were planned for the old church. There was to be a service of Holy Communion on October 14, the Reverend George Anton Wenzel, former president of the Pittsburgh Synod, preaching the sermon; on the following Sunday, October 21, the morning sermon was to be delivered by the Reverend Dr. William A. Passavant and the evening sermon by the Reverend John Kauforth Melhorn; October 28 the Reverend Reuben Hill was to preach in the morning and Pastor Belfour at the final service to be held in the evening. The concluding hymn at this service was written by Pastor Belfour.[128] This, together with a picture of the old church and a list of the pastors, was printed for distribution. November 4, 1888, was set as the date of the consecration of the new church, the sermon to be preached by the Reverend Dr. Samuel Laird.

The pew cushions of the old church and the benches used in the Sunday school were donated to the East Liberty Lutheran Church. The carpet was given to St. Thomas German Lutheran Church in Allegheny City. The minimal communion table, baptismal font, and reading desk were given to the Lutheran Church in Philipsburg (now called Monaca), Pennsylvania where the Reverend William A. Passavant, Jr. was the pastor. The organ was sold to the Methodist Episcopal Church in Oakland for $1000.

The day of the consecration was "favored with beautiful weather and the church was crowded to its capacity." At that time the church seated more than five hundred. The pastor wore the "clerical robe" for the first time at the first service in the new church. This was a natural continuation of the progress the congregation was making in recovering the traditional uses of the Lutheran Church. Indeed, it is remarkable that until this time the black preaching gown was not worn by the clergy at First Church, not even by the leaders of the conservative movement, Dr. Passavant and Dr. Krauth,[129] who like all their predecessors wore street clothing for the services of the church. At the congregational meeting January 2, 1888, C. A. Gaissenhainer presented a resolution "That, as the complete usages in the Services of the Evangelical Lutheran Church are approved by this congregation, the Council is authorized to procure the clerical robe commonly used in the Lutheran Church, and further that its use shall be introduced at the consecration service of the new church edifice." The resolution "called forth only favorable expressions," but a final decision was postponed for a special meeting. That was not held until October 3, and the resolution was adopted by ballot by a vote of 43 to 14.

On the day of consecration the morning service began with the Order for the Consecration of a Church. The morning service of the Church Book (ante-communion) followed immediately. Dr. Samuel Laird, the eighth pastor of First Church was the preacher. There was a special Sunday school service at 2:30 in the afternoon in the new chapel, inaugurating its use. The President of the Synod, the Reverend J. A. Kunkleman, D.D. preached at the evening service.

In the First Church commission, Andrew Peebles worked with a difficult site, a broad but shallow rectangle which made the traditional long rectangle impossible. The result is notably successful. The church is built of sandstone in the Gothic Revival style but in the form of a Greek cross, the nave being 74 feet deep and 74 feet wide in the transepts. The altar is of necessity at the west end of the building rather than the liturgically traditional east (where it would face the rising sun and look toward Jerusalem). At the northeast corner of the building is a pleasing tower and spire 170 feet high.[130] The chapel, now the parish house, is of the same material and of the same design, its dimensions being 52 by 30 feet, set back from the street to form a courtyard and entry way. The result, in the words of the Pittsburgh History and Landmarks Foundation description (the church was designated a Historic Landmark in 1975), is "a picturesque cluster of steep-roofed Gothic elements and a 170 foot spired tower" that had still "for a brief time, a chance to dominate the immediate area." The graceful dimensions of the church complement Henry Hobson Richardson's massive Allegheny County Court House and Jail down Grant Street, designed in 1883 and 1884, erected contemporaneously with First Lutheran Church and dedicated in the centennial year of Allegheny County, September 24, 1888, six weeks before the consecration of First Church.[131] Details of the church such as the rusticated stonework and the vermillion-tinted mortar echo Richardson's buildings.

The tower did not originally have bells, although space was allowed for their installation. Only in November 1995, were three bells bearing the names *Glaube* (faith), *Hoffnung* (hope), and *Liebe* (love) blessed and hung in the tower, from which they announce daily to the city that First Church is about its work in the city.

In 1888 as the building was being erected, the pastor announced the decision, in which his hand can surely be seen, that an inscription be placed over each of the two entrances of the building. Over the door of the north tower is carved the inscription "God is our refuge and strength" (Psalm 46:1), dear to Lutherans because of its association with Luther's hymn "A mighty fortress is our God." The worn and now barely legible inscription over the south portal exhorts, "Reverence my sanctuary" (Leviticus 19:30). It echoes the phrase of the resolution which gave authority to purchase the Grant Street property as it described the necessity for a new church on a prominent site, "It is needed above all as a testimonial of our reverence for God and His worship." The inscription reminds the congregation of its history and responsibility and invites passersby to join the company of those who revere the place where God has chosen to meet his people.

The building is wonderfully conceived and executed, and it has been cared for by those who appreciate its beauty. The more one looks, the more one sees and discovers and learns. The basic plan of the church, a Greek cross, a cross the arms of which are of equal length, suggests the four directions of the compass to which the Word of God goes forth. The Greek cross is repeated

Exterior of First Church

throughout the decoration of the exterior and interior of the church: in the mosaic panels of the chancel, in the ends of each prie dieu and the high-backed chairs of the chancel, on the hymnboards, on the top of the altar rail, on the tabernacle.

The second organ in the congregation's history (the first was a small instrument purchased when the congregation was thirty years old, 1867, and installed in the Seventh Avenue church), by William A. Johnson and Son of Westfield , Massachusetts, Opus 697, was installed in the present building in 1888. It was a three-manual tracker action instrument of 32 stops with a wind chest driven by a water-powered motor. It "was, for its period, a very satisfactory instrument."[132] The present organ casework, refurbished, originally housed this second organ.

In the following year, 1889, the congregation began planning to rebuild and enlarge the organ. In 1900, Austin Organs of Hartford, Connecticut, was chosen to carry out the work. Twelve new stops were added (two in the great organ, three in the swell, three in the choir, and four in the pedal) giving forty-two stops in all. Many new couplers, piston movements, adjustable non-moving registers and release pistons, pedal movements and releases were built in, greatly increasing the efficiency of the instrument. The original pipes of the Johnson Company were used, revoiced by Philip Wirsching, who made all the new metal pipes. The pitch was lowered to international 435A, which necessitated the addition of a new CC pipe for each stop, the setting up of all stops a semi-tone, and revoicing and retuning at that pitch. The Austin air chest was adopted because of the steadiness of its wind supply, the accessibility of all parts of the mechanism, and other advantages. When the organ was completed in the fall of 1900 it was said to be "one of the finest in the city." A generous gift from B. Frank Weyman underwrote the cost of the extensive project. In 1915 the organ blower was converted from water to DC electric power. The large wheel from the water power remains in the possession of the church and is at this writing kept on the mezzanine of the parish house as an historical artifact. About 1925 a new Tellers (of Erie, Pennsylvania) console was installed and new stops which included chimes and a vox humana. A second update was done in 1948 by M. P. Moeller; a new console was installed and all the reeds were revoiced at the Moeller factory. A third update, which again included a new console, was done by Austin in 1978.

The present organ was built by Casavant Frères Limitée of Ste. Hyacinthe, Quebec, Opus 3709, and was installed in 1992. The specifications are given in Appendix 3.

On December 5, one month after the cornerstone was laid, the pastor announced that B. Frank Weyman had offered to present a marble baptismal font for the new church as a congregational memorial to the Reverend Charles Porterfield Krauth, D.D., LL.D. The font was to be an exact copy of the celebrated angel font carved in 1823 by the Danish sculptor Bertil Thorwaldsen (1770-1844) for the [Lutheran] Vor-Frue Kirke, the Cathedral Church of Our Lady, in Copenhagen. (The pastor of the church, Edmund Belfour, it will be remembered, was born in Copenhagen.) It had been the intent of Weyman's sister, Harriet K. Weyman, to make this gift, but her sudden death a few weeks before had thwarted her plans. Her desire was fulfilled by her brother. The minutes of the church council for January 6, 1890 record that "Mr. [B. Frank] Weyman ordered the Font, made in Florence, Italy, by the American sculptor Park."[133] The font was completed in Italy and shipped to Pittsburgh where it was set in place at the head of the center aisle on the first step of the chancel, inside the altar rail (recalling the location of the font in the Cathedral of Our Lady, before the altar and in the center of the choir, where the angel's arms echo the outstretched arms of the great sculpture of Christ above the altar with its inscription, "Come to me.") It was dedicated in October 1889. The preacher for the occasion was the Reverend Dr. Jacob Fry (1834-1920), professor at the Philadelphia Seminary and a colleague of Dr. Krauth. The immediate biblical reference of the angel, is the occasional Old Testament view that an angel is the visible form of God's presence, a messenger nearly indistinguishable from the sender of the message. "Angel" is sometimes a way of saying "God," as in Isaiah 63:9 (RSV), "the angel of his presence" and Genesis 31:11-13, "The angel of God said to me in a dream . . . I am the God of Bethel. . . ." Luther's morning and evening prayers in the Small Catechism reflect this view, "Let your holy angel have charge of me." The outstretched arms of the angel effectively dramatize Gustav Aulén's description of baptism as "an expression of the open arms of the Father."[134] Because the candidates for Holy Baptism are usually children, other allusions include Matthew 18:10, "Take care that you do not despise one of these little ones; for, I tell you, in heaven their angels continually see the face of my Father in heaven." Other significant allusions are to Psalm 91:11-12, "For he will command his angels concerning you to guard you in all your ways. On their hands they will bear you up, so that you will not dash your foot against a stone," and Luke 15:10, "There is joy in the presence of the angels of God over one sinner who repents."

The scallop shell which the angel holds is a traditional symbol of Holy Baptism, and an actual shell or one made of silver is sometimes used to pour the water over the candidate. The seashell also suggests the hiding place of a pearl, thereby reminding astute congregants that the grace of baptism is the precious pearl that waits to be discovered by the baptized.

The 1909 *History* records the appreciation of the congregation, describing the font as "one of the chief adornments of the church and a beautiful work of art."

There exist several fonts that resemble the one prized by First Church, but none is exactly like it. The others, for example the one in Trinity Episcopal Church in Southport, Connecticut, have a softer, more sentimental and child-like angel. The original and the copy in First Church presents a much more sturdy and impressive figure of massive size and strength with both male and female characteristics. (Angels are described theologically as sexless beings; Jesus remarked that in heaven there will be no marriage but that we will be like the angels [Mark 12:25].) The font in First Church is a convincing statement of the substantial foundation on which the Christian life is built.

In the renovation of the chancel in the mid-1890s, so as not to impede access to the altar, the font was moved from the head of the center aisle. Through the years it has migrated leftward. It was first placed beneath the left hymnboard, facing the congregation; then into the present baptistery area; and then, when the area was remodeled in the centennial year 1937, it was placed in the center of that space

The angel font

and guarded by the rail that was created from the brass of the huge chandelier which once hung in the center of the nave.

The chancel was originally furnished with a small wooden altar (without cross or candles) and a tall Gothic reredos, both painted white. It was appropriate and attractive, perhaps a representation in wood of the marble altar in St. Peter's Church which Andrew Peebles had designed 1872-1874. Entrance to the chancel was had by way of two doors, one through each of the angled walls of the chancel from the rooms behind the chancel wall. The principal door was to the right from the "robing room." Six sedilia, three on each side, were next to the doors on the angled walls. The chancel floor was carpeted. The wood pulpit and lectern were situated at the center of the bank of pews on each side of the center aisle, impeding the view of the altar by worshippers sitting on the sides of the congregation. The altar rail was at the level of the nave; no provision was made for kneeling. The walls of the chancel were heavily stenciled. Above the circular window are the words "Holiness unto the Lord," the inscription worn by the high priest on his forehead (Exodus 28:36; 39:30; see Zechariah 14:20).

The original altar and chancel

The original windows of the church, by J. Marshall & Bro. of Allegheny City, seem to have been designed specifically for once-smoky and still frequently gloomy Pittsburgh. They are seen to best advantage on overcast days and at twilight when the blues in the windows, particularly the pair of lancets and the lesser rose window toward the parish house, appear wonderfully rich. The principal original window is the rose window, so called from its shape, in the east wall on the Grant Street end of the church. The rose is a traditional symbol of the Virgin Mary, as are the lilies which adorn the window. This window, opposite the altar, is set within a Gothic arch. In the center is an open Bible from which emanate several themes. The pair of medallions at the top show the two dominical sacraments: on the left a no longer discernable representation of a baptismal font (it once looked like the one in the window in the south wall) and on the right the Holy Communion shown in the wheat, grapes, and chalice. The next pair of medallions tell of judgment: the scales of justice by which souls are weighed and the two tables of the Decalogue (given in proper Lutheran and Roman Catholic form: the first three commandments dealing with our relationship to God are on the first table[135] and the other seven dealing with our relationship to others are in the second table[136]). The next pair of medallions give the cross, crown, and Bible (the Word of God, death, and life) and on the other a Latin cross with a Bible and banner reading "Faith, hope, and charity" (1 Corinthians 13:13). The lower pair of medallions present a harp, promising heaven ("I heard a voice from heaven [and] the voice I heard was like the sound of harpists playing on their harps, and they sang a new song before the throne," Revelation 14:2-3) and on the right a Bible and a lamp ("Your word is a lamp to my feet and a light to my path," Psalm 119:105). At the top of the Gothic arch is the descending dove of the Holy Spirit with olive leaves of peace, a subtle connection with the rose window: see the words of the angel to the Virgin Mary, Luke 1:35, "The Holy Spirit will come upon you." In the lowest corners of the Gothic design are two angels with harps, echoing the two angels of the reredos lunette.

On either side of the rose window, also original to the building, is a double lancet, each adorned with lilies, associated both with the Resurrection (Easter lilies) and the Virgin Mary (see Song of Solomon 2:1, "I am a rose of Sharon, a lily of the valleys"). To the left at the top is an eight-pointed star suggesting the eighth day of the new creation; below it, the medallion on the left is the dove and a book (the Holy Spirit working through the Bible), while on the right are bundles of harvested sheaves of grain, a reference to the gathering of the faithful at the last day and also a subtle allusion to the Holy Communion. The double lancet window to the right shows at the top a Latin cross with the title of Christ, Alpha and Omega (Revelation 1:8), the first and last letters of the Greek alphabet; below that on the left a crown with flowers of paradise, telling of the rewards of heaven, and on the right a forearm in Victorian dress pouring water, an allusion to Holy Baptism by which one enters paradise. The bit of Victorian costume reminds worshippers today that before this building was erected for First Church the pastors of the congregation simply wore street clothing, not any sort of ecclesiastical vestments.

In the south wall of the nave is a lesser rose window, also original to the building. The lower corners of the Gothic arch suggest the theme of the Last Days: Noah's ark, a symbol of the Church (Genesis 6-8) in which the faithful find safety amid the storms of the world and also, as in 1 Peter 3:20-21, a symbol of Baptism; on the right the hourglass reminds viewers that, in the words of the mid-twelfth century hymn by Bernard of Cluny,

> The world is very evil;
> The times are waxing late;
> Be sober and keep vigil;
> The Judge is at the gate:
> The Judge that comes in mercy,
> The Judge that comes with might,
> To terminate the evil,
> To diadem the right.
>
> *[CSB 526, SBH 586; revised in LBW 322]*

The central medallion of the window is Luther's seal (a black cross on a red heart declaring that faith in the Crucified saves us; set on a white rose, showing that faith gives joy, comfort, and peace; against a sky blue-field showing that such joy is the beginning of heavenly joy grasped through hope; and around the field a golden ring of eternity with no beginning and no end).[137] The top pair of medallions show flowers of paradise; the next pair display the Chi Rho, an abbreviation of "Christ" in Greek, emanating rays of light, and the helmet of salvation (Ephesians 6:17; 1 Thessalonians 5:8). The third pair of medallions are the cross with rays of hope and the Lamb of God sitting on the book with the seven seals (Revelation 5:8-10). The lowest pair of medallions present on the left Holy Baptism shown by a font (identical with the now illegible medallion in the great rose window), and on the right the Holy Communion, shown by the chalice and grapes and wheat. These two Sacraments are our strength and sustenance as we await the end of time and the day of judgment.

The windows in the Sunday School chapel, remodeled in 1999 to become the parish house, are also original. Several medallions repeat those in the nave: the lamp on a Bible on a cushion, the scales of justice, the cross with the banner "Faith, Hope, Charity", the dove with the olive branch. There are two versions of the Agnus Dei, the Lamb of God, one carrying a cross (one may recall Paul Gerhardt's hymn "A Lamb goes uncomplaining forth to save a world of sinners") and the other returning with the banner of victory. Two medallions are of particular interest. In the west wall (now the upper level of the mezzanine) is the first, a pelican on her nest "vulning" herself with her beak to feed her young with her blood. It is a widely-used symbol of Christ's sacrificial redeeming work, especially as mediated in the Holy Communion, which is represented in the larger medallion below it. To the right is the anchor of hope of Hebrews 6:19, "hope, a sure and steadfast anchor of the soul". Such hope is established in Baptism, which is represented in the medallion below the anchor. The other medallion of particular interest is on the Grant Street end of the original chapel. It is a yellow beehive, a symbol of the cooperative interworking of the members of the church.

The three openings in the north narthex, now the Lamb of God Oratory, wall are original. The windows that filled them (no record of them has been preserved), one may imagine, were similar in style and design to the corresponding original windows in the south wall and those on the Grant Street side of the nave. October 27, 1957, three new windows were dedicated in the north narthex in memory of Esther Gunnell Greenslade. The one on the left shows Luther's seal, the one in the center commemorates the founding of the World Council of Churches in Amsterdam in 1948 (the Greek word *oikumine* means the whole inhabited world and is the source of the word "ecumenical"), and the window on the right presents the seal of the National Council of Churches of Christ in America.

The tower is pierced with two courses of stained glass windows that are above the ceiling of the Lamb of God Oratory and are largely lost to viewers because there is no provision for light to shine within them.

Beneath the rose window are three small windows. The 1909 history reports that among the extensive improvements of the early 1890s were "three small windows in the front of the church, representing the Christ, St. John, and St. Matthew."[138] It may be assumed that "the front of the church" here means the wall facing Grant Street. The installation of the glorious lunette provided no place for three small windows in the chancel wall, and in any case that wall did not open on to the outside for light to illumine glass windows. Originally, there had been two openings high up on the chancel wall, one on either side of the altar, with a shape like that of the Good Shepherd window, filled not with glass but with fabric since the openings were not to the outside light but into the darkness of an attic space. These openings were plastered over on the nave side when the lunette was installed. The inside of one of them may still be seen in the financial secretary's office. It seems probable that these three windows on Grant Street were originally filled with unremarkable colored glass and that those who planned the early renovations, ever alert to good churchly practice and adornment, chose to replace them with representations of the Savior and the two evangelists most used at that time in the Church's lectionary, St. Matthew and St. John.

The years in smoky Pittsburgh were surely not kind to these windows near street level. They had probably faded and had become discolored and even illegible as is a medallion high above them. In the nineteen thirties[139] these three small windows were replaced with three windows of the Nativity. Their rich blues are of excellent quality. The window to the left, presented by the family of J. Boyd Duff and his wife, shows three shepherds with their offering of a lamb. The central window, given by Rhonda Hines in memory of Jacob and May Hines, shows the Holy Family with the ox and the ass of the carols "What child is this, who laid to rest" and "Good Christian men [friends] rejoice with heart and soul and voice"; three angels above hold the star, while below the angel announces the holy birth to the shepherds. The window to the right, given by Dr. and Mrs. A. J. Holl in memory of his parents, Martin and Elizabeth Holl, shows the three magi, each with a gift for the Christ Child—gold for a king, frankincense for a God, and myrrh for burial.

The spiritual teaching of stained glass windows is that from the outside they appear dark, but when one enters the building and sees the windows with the light coming through, they are transformed into wonderful works of art. So it is with those who have been brought into the Church by baptism: when the light shines through them, they are transformed into works of beauty.[140] Moreover, the light coming through the colored glass, in an evocative phrase, paints the air.

The completion of the new house of First Lutheran Church was an achievement of wide-ranging import. The congregation rightly rejoiced in their new building. The day following the consecration of the church, November 5, 1888, the church council held its regular meeting for the first time in the new building. At the next meeting, December 5, the council extended "its hearty thanks to the members of the building committee for the faithful and highly satisfactory manner in which they have carried out their difficult and laborious trust in erecting and bringing to completion a church edifice that in all its parts is a joy to every member of the congregation as well as an honor to Him to whose service it has been consecrated." The 1909 history notes, "The pastor, Dr. Belfour, had been untiring in his labors, and his services during the entire undertaking were invaluable and received the especial appreciation of the congregation." The congregation was proud to host the twenty-second convention of the General Council in its impressive building October 10, 1889; a silk banner commemorating the event is preserved in the parish house.

The congregation did not simply luxuriate in its new house. During Reuben Hill's pastorate a Sunday school had been established in the Hill District, known as St. John's Sunday School. In 1869 the council had decided to secure a suitable lot for a church building and a chapel for the Sunday school. Jane Barclay Black gave a lot at the corner of Forbes and Jumonville Streets. The chapel was built in 1876, and its prosperity was such that a year later, on the Sunday after Christmas 1877, the new chapel was consecrated free from debt. In September 1881 Jane Black presented to the congregation a lot adjoining St. John's Chapel and later gave eight thousand dollars toward the Building Fund of St. John's Church. November 7, 1889 a communication was presented to the church council:

"We, the undersigned, agree to pay annually (in quarterly installments) the sums set opposite our names for the purpose of paying the salary of an assistant pastor for the First English Evangelical Lutheran Church of Pittsburgh. The duties of said assistant pastor to be to officiate in the First English Evangelical Lutheran Church of Pittsburgh and in St. John's Mission Church controlled by said First Church, as he may be directed by the vestry and pastor of said First Church. The salary of said assistant pastor not to exceed $1000.00 the first year, and thereafter to be determined by Council."

The names of B. F. Weyman, George P. Black, William H. Black, H. W. Sellers, J. A. Barker, John B. Kaercher, James W. Kim, George A. Watson, Jacob Lang, and E. W. Belfour (son of the pastor) were appended. The council approved the recommendation and "the young men who submitted it" were commended. At the next regular council meeting a committee was appointed to consider a pastor suitable for the position; that the labors of the assistant pastor be devoted chiefly to St. John's Mission in building up the Sunday school, holding public services, and in pastoral visitation with a view to gathering a congregation; that he render such services in the mother Church as the council may direct; and that he give his entire time to the duties assigned to him. At the congregational meeting on January 6, 1890, the proposal was approved and the council was authorized to call an assistant pastor. On March 3, the Reverend Franklin Philip Bossart, a graduate of the Philadelphia Seminary in the class of 1889 and pastor of Mount Zion Church on the North Side, accepted the call to become assistant pastor.

April 14 it was resolved to hold Sunday morning services in St. John's Mission; evening services were to be arranged as soon as deemed expedient. A committee on the affairs of St. John's chapel was appointed; an advisory committee on the mission was also created. It was decided that all monies collected at the mission should be expended under the supervision of these committees for the local purposes of the mission and that reports of such expenditures be made to the treasurer of First Church.

The Hill District was becoming ethnically diverse with an influx of Eastern Europeans. The seldom used but surviving Russian Orthodox Cathedral of St. Michael at 43 Reed Street lingers as a testimony to those who for a time lived there. In 1890 the use of St. John's chapel was granted to the Magyars and the Slavs for service once a month on Sunday afternoons. It was an indication of the future of the area.

October 14, 1890 St. John's Mission requested the privilege of organizing as a congregation, forty-three persons having agreed to become members. The petition was accepted with the following conditions: that the constitution proposed for congregations by the General Council and by-laws in harmony with it, and approved by the council, be adopted; that the pastor shall be *ex officio* a member of and president of the Council; that the pastor shall be the Reverend F. P. Bossart, and that he and his successors shall hold their appointment from the council of the parent church until such time as St. John's shall become self-sustaining; that the organization be a mission of First Church until it becomes self-sustaining; that after such appointment of The Reverend Mr. Bossart, he shall no longer hold the office of assistant pastor in the parent church; that it shall connect with the Pittsburgh Synod of the General Council; and that the council of First Church appoint an advisory committee to act upon minor questions which may arise.

By July 1891 the mission announced that it proposed to pay one-half the pastor's salary and one-half the current expenses. Pastor Belfour submitted a request respecting the building of a church. Contributions amounting to $12,000 had already been promised, and permission was asked, if they could secure enough additional to make the sum $20,000, to solicit further subscriptions for this purpose among the members of First Church. The request was granted with the proviso that the mission incur no debt in carrying out its desires and that all plans, specifications, and contracts be submitted to the council for its approval. In February 1892 the building committee of St. John's church presented preliminary drawings of the new church. The council was pleased with the general plans and promised its approval if the building could be completed without debt.

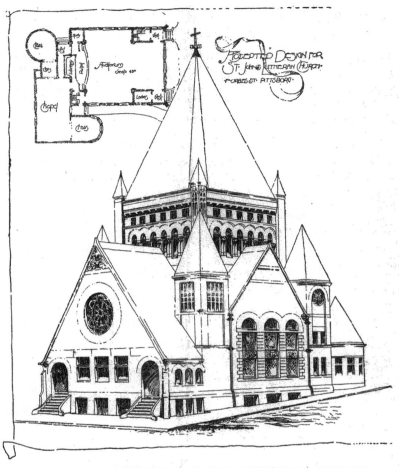

ST. JOHN'S ENGLISH EVANGELICAL LUTHERAN CHURCH.
Corner Forbes and Jumonville Streets, Pittsburgh.

Architect's drawing of St. John's Church

Something in these transactions was not going well. April 4, 1892 Dr. Belfour submitted his resignation to the church council.

"Dear Brethren:--I hereby offer the resignation of my office as pastor of the Church which you represent, the resignation to take effect on the first of July, 1892. Yours truly in Christ, Edmund Belfour."

The curt language of the resignation, submitted not in person but through Thomas Lane, who on February 1, 1892, at his own request, had been "excused from serving on the advisory committee of St. John's Church," indicates seriously injured feelings. The brevity of the resignation is in stark contrast to the florid language of the resignations of previous pastors. The hostile feelings were apparently mutual. The minutes of the church council record baldly, "On motion, the resignation was accepted to take effect July 1, 1892." Previous resignations had been received and accepted with lengthy commendations of the departing pastor. The council after accepting the resignation went on to approve the request of Lilie Wattles Stephenson for a letter of dismissal and to accept the resignation of the church organist Mr. McComsey, "from all musical connection with the church, to take effect immediately." The meeting then adjourned as always with the Lord's Prayer.

Thomas Lane in his sporadic Diary recorded on June 26, 1892, "Dr. Belfour preached his last sermon as Pastor of the Church. He preached a sermon from the text Psalm xci.iv ["He shall cover thee with his feathers, and under his wings shalt thou trust: his truth shall be thy shield and buckler"]. After the sermon he read a statement expressed in very bitter terms as to the cause of his resignation." There are no further details.

Tempers eventually cooled. The 1909 History was able to say of Dr. Belfour, "His scholarly tastes and attainments have been widely recognized and the Church has frequently called him to positions of responsibility and honor. For years he was President of the Pittsburgh Synod and for many years he has been a member of the Board of Trustees of Thiel College and a valuable member of important Synodical and General Council Boards and Committees. His translation from the Danish of 'Pontoppidan's Explanation of Luther's Catechism' has passed through many editions and is widely used. He received the degree of Doctor of Divinity from Thiel College in 1886."

Pastor Belfour did not resign in order to accept another call. After his resignation from First Church, Dr. Belfour supplied Memorial Church in the city of Allegheny for some months. It was far from a plum. The congregation on what is now the North Side of Pittsburgh was organized April 9, 1883 and its building was dedicated November 18 of that year. Four years later the building was raised and a basement was built underneath for the growing Sunday School. The Reverend William John Finck had been pastor from 1888-1893. Dr. Belfour, after supplying the church for several months, accepted a call and served as pastor from June 1, 1893 to November 19, 1919. He at once began to wear "the clerical robe" he had introduced at First Church and to observe all the festival seasons of the church.[141] A new church

Edmund Belfour, D.D.

building was erected in 1951. Twenty years later, in 1971, when the church, located at Hazlett and East Streets, was taken by the Pennsylvania Department of Transportation for the construction of Interstate 279, Memorial Church merged with St. Luke's Church to create St. Luke's Memorial Church. Sharply declining population caused the remaining members of that merged church to merge with Trinity Church on North Avenue March 23, 2008.

Pastor Belfour died July 5, 1923, at the Old Peoples' Home in Zelienople, a month short of his 90th birthday.

B. Frank Weyman had established a tradition of good church music in the First Church. In 1892, with the appointment of Harry G. Archer as organist, the music program moved toward an excellence exceedingly rare in Lutheran churches of the time. He presented in First Church a large number of sacred works not previously heard in the city. He was especially interested in Palestrina's works and the Gregorian chant (Ratisbon version)

During the nine-month interim following the resignation of Pastor Belfour, extensive improvements were made in the church. Thomas Lane notes in his diary, "1892, August 14. Last Sunday, and this one, we have no services at our church, it's undergoing repairing and alterations." It was an understatement. The interior of both the church and the chapel was frescoed, electric lighting was installed replacing the great gas chandelier in the center of the church, hymnboards were installed, and, most of all, the entire chancel was renovated. The work was so extensive that the church was closed for nearly two months. It was reopened for services September 25, 1892. Dr. Laird, who had preached at the dedication of the church in 1888, conducted the services and preached in the morning and in the evening. He also celebrated the Holy Communion in the renovated building November 6.

B. Frank Weyman was a major contributor to the efforts, offering differing levels of financial support in accordance with the extensiveness of the project as a way of encouraging a more ambitious work.

Not all were entirely satisfied with the existing chancel. While Dr. Belfour was pastor, the Ladies Sewing Society had contributed $2400, their savings for twenty years, "toward the erection of a marble altar and the placing of other chancel furnishings." The women had apparently given the original wooden altar, and so they were treading on no one's toes when they decided it should be replaced. ("The immediate improvements which they [the ladies] decided to make included a new marble altar, in place of the one which they had installed in the church at the time of its erection."[142]) A committee of five women was appointed by the pastor and the secretary of the council to have charge of the chancel and altar furnishings. "The ladies received very generous assistance in this work from one of the members of the congregation."[143] The contributor remained anonymous until the work was completed.

Original altar installed in St. John's Church

The marble altar and the marble wainscoting in the chancel to the height of the new altar were the first to be installed. The original wooden altar and reredos that had been removed, as well as the original wooden pulpit, were donated to St.

John's Church that was being constructed on 40th Street in the Lawrenceville section of the city.[144]

When the building was sold in 2001 to be converted into residences, the altar, at the insistence of the buyer, was included as a condition of the sale. One prefers not to imagine the uses to which the holy table on which Pastor Belfour celebrated the Eucharist was to be put. Some of the wooden wainscoting that had lined the chancel walls was moved to what is now the baptistery. The arches in that paneling match those in the wooden base of the pulpit and in the organ case, preserving the original harmony.

The marble altar is adorned with five mosaics of him who gives himself as food on this holy table: the central mosaic is the *Agnus Dei*, the Lamb of God, with the banner of victory; on the left is a *Chi Rho* monogram, the first two Greek letters of the title Christ, meaning Anointed One; on the right is *IHS,* the Greek abbreviation of the Name Jesus, which means Savior; on each end is a Greek cross. Each of the five symbols, recalling the five wounds of Christ (feet, hands, and side) is set in a field of gold surrounded by a glorified crown of thorns. The mensa, the top surface of the altar, is inscribed with the traditional quincunx pattern of five crosses representing the five wounds of Christ. The gradine or retable of the altar presents the three-fold "Holy" of the *Sanctus,* each word separated with Greek Maltese crosses, reminding all who preside and all who commune there of the sacredness of the action and of the presence of the angels in the Holy Mysteries.

These enhancements encouraged the expansion of the renovation of the chancel. By 1897 the chancel had attained its present appearance. Panels in the Italian Renaissance style with mosaics were added above the wainscoting, crowned with the extraordinary lunette[145] of the mother and child, adored by angels. The Holy Virgin, seated on her throne, presents to viewers her infant Son and Lord, whose infant arms are already moving in the shape of a cross while an angel on either side bows in adoration. The angel to the congregation's right is St. Gabriel, the angel of the Annunciation (see Luke 1:26-38), whose word Mary chose to accept. The lilies between him and the Holy Mother are a traditional symbol of virginity. The angel to the left, indicated by his gold vestment and circlet of gold in his hair, is St. Michael the defender of the faithful and the one who receives the dying and presents them to God Most High as many prayers for the dying implore. In him we see the Father's care for his Son and for all who belong to him.

The magnificent mosaic in the lunette holds before the congregation's eyes and hearts far more than "the Christmas story." Here is seen the great mystery of the Incarnation, God taking on human flesh to redeem the fallen world, and also subtle but undeniable indications of the cost of that redemption are apparent. The position of Jesus' arms, the red on the Virgin's dress, the presence of St. Michael the archangel all remind viewers that the crucifixion is not far away. Beyond that, can be seen the glory of the resurrection. The golden cloud called a "nimbus" (in popular language, a "halo") that rests on the head of each figure, Mary on her throne as queen of heaven, the serenity of both mother and child, the adoration of the archangels, all declare that Christ our God who came into the world to live and die as one of us, now reigns in glory everlasting as King of the universe.

The Church of the West, to assert the mystery of the Incarnation often refers to the mother of Christ as *Mater Dei,* Mother of God. In the Byzantine tradition of the Eastern Churches, the Virgin Mary bears the Greek title *Theotokos,* birth-giver of God, and she is never shown by herself but always with her Son. Jesus Christ, as Martin Luther teaches in the *Small Catechism,*[146] is divine because he has God for his Father, and he is human because he has Mary as his mother. All who enter First Church are confronted with that profound mystery that is central to Christianity.

Cyril of Alexandria in a homily to the Council at Ephesus in 431, the Third Ecumenical Council, declared, "Behold then the joy of the whole universe. Let the union of God and man in the Son of the Virgin Mary fill us with awe and adoration. Let us fear and worship the undivided Trinity as we sing the praise of the ever-virgin Mary, the holy temple of God, and of God himself, he Son and spotless Bridegroom. To him be glory for ever and ever. Amen" The lunette in First Church extends the same invitation.

A story reported by Frances Fafata (who died January 16, 2000) is that when the mosaic arrived in crates from Italy and was eagerly unpacked by the congregation, some pieces were missing. When the artisan arrived from Italy to supervise the installation, he was immediately informed of the missing pieces. He replied that he had brought the pieces with him. They were the flesh-toned pieces, and he was afraid that if he were not present, the American congregation, seeing the olive-skinned features, would have replaced them with whiter skin tones.

Immediately below the lunette are seven winged cherub faces, which represent "the seven flaming torches, which are the seven spirits of God" (Revelation 4:5), more commonly symbolized in other churches by seven hanging red lamps. The cherubim (the Hebrew plural of cherub) are the highest of the nine orders of angels and appear in the Hebrew Bible as God's attendants who guard his presence from profanation. Representations of them were set up in Solomon's temple. The mosaic panels of the chancel are each surmounted with a design of angels' wings, recalling the biblical descriptions of God who is "enthroned above [or upon] the cherubim" (2 Kings 19:15; Isaiah 37:16; Psalm 80:1) God the Son, with his mother, is enthroned above the cherub heads. The two pilasters which support the lunette present a feather design which suggests the descent of the angels to the altar during the Holy Mysteries[147] and their ascent bearing the prayers of the holy people to the throne of God.

For those with eyes to see, the lunette also presents a New Testament interpretation of the description in the Hebrew Bible of the God of Israel being enthroned "between the cherubim" (Exodus 25:22; Numbers 7:89) or "above the cherubim" (2 Kings 19:15; Isaiah 37:16) or "upon the cherubim" (Psalm 80:1; 99:1). The ark of the covenant, a chest containing the tablets of the covenant between God and Israel, served as a throne for the Lord of hosts (that is, Lord of the angelic armies). In the lunette, the angels, although not specifically cherubim in the usual Christian hierarchy but rather archangels, bow before their commander. On the cover of the ark were two cherubim, creatures which in the ancient Near East used to flank royal thrones. One of the traditional epithets of the Virgin Mary in Christian devotion, especially in Eastern hymns, is the Ark of God. The Litany of the Virgin Mary, the "Litany of Loreto," calls her "Ark of the covenant" (*foederis arca*), for she contained within her the one who was the fulfillment of the ancient covenant, and it also calls her the "gate of heaven," represented in the lunette by the stream of gold behind her.[148] She and her Son are thus literally enthroned "above the cherubim." The second stanza of John Athelstan Laurie

Riley's hymn, "Ye watchers and ye holy ones" praises her, the "bearer of the eternal Word," in soaring language, "O higher than the cherubim, more glorious than the seraphim."

The pair of gas candelabra which flank the altar were the gift of B. Frank Weyman in the early 1890s. The congregational legend (Dr. Braughler says that he heard it from Mrs. Seiferth, who knew George Weyman) is that while in England Weyman found a candelabrum in a castle chapel, bought it, and had it shipped to the church. His gift was received coolly by the church council because, as they pointed out, it is difficult to use a single candelabrum. The next year Weyman traveled again to Europe and visited another castle, this time on the continent, which was going to be demolished, and discovered there at the foot of a stairway a second candelabrum, identical to the first. He bought it and had it shipped to the church. The pair were then installed in the chancel where they have been ever since.

The brass pulpit replaced the earlier and simpler wooden one, preserving the wood base of the former pulpit. The pulpit is an eight-sided design, symbolizing the eight days of the new creation, with three sides removed for access. The five brass panels present three Greek crosses, each with a crown, interspersed with

The Chancel ca. 1908

two elaborate quatrefoils which are echoed in the four quatrefoils at the base of the altar rail.

The brass lectern, in a common design, shows an eagle holding the globe of the earth. Although the eagle is a symbol of St. John the Evangelist, here it is a powerful symbol of the protecting care of God ("I bore you on eagles' wings and brought you to myself" Exodus 19:4; see also Deuteronomy 32:11-12a) and also the saving power of the Word of God. The design is also perhaps an allusion to Revelation 12:14, "The woman was given the two wings of the great eagle, so that she could fly from the serpent into the wilderness, to her place where she is nourished for a time, and times, and a half time," the woman being understood as the Church which by the Word is preserved from the wiles of Satan and brought to the place of nourishment.

Interior of First Church

The renovations having been completed, the council at last was able to reveal the name of the benefactor who generously contributed to the work begun by the Ladies Sewing Society. It came as no surprise. At the annual congregational meeting January 3, 1898, the pastor reported to the congregation the action of the council, which "received the hearty endorsement of the congregation." All seemed to understand the significance of what had been achieved. "The Church Council having deferred making formal expression of their delight and gratitude for the improvements added to the chancel of the church through the generosity of Mr. B. F. Weyman, preferred to await its completion before making such acknowledgement to him. We do now beg to assure him that we regard the improvement as a most valuable contribution to the adornment of our church, not only as a work of art, but also for its elevating influence, inspiring the hearts of worshippers by presenting to their contemplation that culmination of the Divine Mercy, the Incarnation of our Blessed Saviour. Both in the conception and in the execution of the improvement, our fullest desires have been satisfied and our most grateful thanks are tendered Mr. Weyman, with our sincere wishes and prayer that he may long be spared to share with us and our successors the privileges of our spiritual home."

The impressive adornment, however, was not yet finished. A very great treasure of First Church is the impressive window in the north wall of the nave above what is now the choir space. It was given in memory of George Black, who died August 5, 1872, before the church was erected, and Jane Barclay Black, who died May 7, 1896, by their children, and dedicated appropriately on the Sunday of the Good Shepherd, April 24, 1898. The window is of unusual size, consisting of three lancets and over 500 square feet of Tiffany Favrile glass, designed by Frederick Wilson and fabricated by the Tiffany Studios in New York. The glass, employing a technique developed by Louis Comfort Tiffany, was made in such a way that the colors blend together at the borders of individual pieces of glass, blues melting into lavender or green marbleized with pink. The over-all impression given by the technique is the appearance of painter's canvas. The prevailing colors of the window are blue and purple with the borders worked out in different shades of amber. The theme of the window is the Good Shepherd, described in the twenty-third Psalm and personified in Jesus. The great window is divided into three lancets, the upper portion of which is an arch design that is carried up through the tracery of the window. In the center lancet the Christ the Good Shepherd stands in the midst of his sheep, hands clasped in prayer and eyes looking toward heaven, interceding for his flock. Beneath the image is the beginning of Psalm 23, "The Lord is my shepherd." In the side lancets are two angels; on the left, one holds the torch of faith together with the book of knowledge, beneath which is the beginning of Psalm 23:6, "Surely goodness and mercy shall follow me"; on the right the angel holds a palm of victory in one hand and a crown of stars in the other, beneath which is the continuation of verse 6, "all the days of my life." Unsaid, but surely in the mind of those who know the Bible and look at the window, is the conclusion of the verse and of the psalm, "And I will dwell in the house of the Lord forever."

The Good Shepherd window is flanked by two smaller windows, identical in design, featuring pomegranates, a traditional symbol, not only in Christianity, of life out of death: the fruit opens like a wound, but in the red flesh are seeds of new life.

The council again eloquently expressed their gratitude for the magnificent gift.

"WHEREAS, The children of the late George and Mrs. Jane Barclay Black, in loving memory of their parents, have caused to be placed in the north transept of our church three windows, the large or central one of which is of extraordinary beauty and artistic excellence, therefore,

Resolved, That we hereby, for ourselves and on behalf of the congregation, express our high appreciation of their commendable act. We are especially gratified, since those who are thus affectionately commemorated were held in high esteem by those who knew them, and who for many years were pleasantly associated with them in the services and activities of the congregation. We therefore deem it eminently fitting that the memory of these faithful servants of the Master should thus be perpetuated.

"We regard these windows as a valuable addition to the impressive and instructive decoration of our church. The admirably chosen design strikingly interprets one of the most precious assurances of the Divine Word and will thus be a constant object lesson to all."

In these eloquent and insightful statements of gratitude, the hand of the new pastor is surely to be detected. He was David Harrison Geissinger.

Before going to Chicago and then to Pittsburgh, Dr. Belfour had been pastor of St. John's Church, Easton, Pennsylvania. To find his successor, First Church this time looked directly to St. John's. At a special congregational meeting January 25, 1893, by a vote of 97 to 7, David H. Geissinger was elected pastor of First Church. His salary was set at $3000 per year. The call was made unanimous, and was promptly accepted. He began his pastorate April 23. On the 26th of April a reception in the chapel was given for Pastor and Mrs. Geissinger by the women of the congregation. He was installed May 20 by the Reverend J. Q. A. Waters, President of the Pittsburgh Synod and son of First Church, and the former pastor, William Passavant.

David H. Geissinger

David Harrison Geissinger was born near Grafton, Huntington County, February 12, 1844. After the Civil War began, in 1861 at the age of seventeen he enlisted in the Fifth Reserves, Pennsylvania Volunteers. He was the youngest member of that regiment, and his promotion and the regiment's splendid record throughout the war testified to his bravery and ability. After three years he re-enlisted as a second lieutenant and remained in the service until the end of the war. He was wounded in the four-hour battle of Fort Steadman near Petersburg, Virginia, March 25, 1865. When the war ended he was serving as an officer of the staff of General John Frederick Hartranft (1830-1889). During the famous Surratt trial of alleged conspirators in the assassination of Abraham Lincoln, David Geissinger had charge of the prisoners.

After study at Mercersburg and at Allegheny College in Meadville, Pennsylvania, he studied theology at the Lutheran Seminary at Philadelphia from 1869-1872 and was ordained in Zion Church, Philadelphia in June 1872. For two years he served as assistant pastor of Old Trinity Church in Lancaster, where Samuel Laird had been pastor, and served two mission congregations. In 1874 he organized Grace Church, one of the Lancaster missions, and remained there for five years. In 1880 he took charge of a mission of Holy Trinity Church in New York City, located on 82nd Street. In 1885 he became pastor of St. John's, Easton. While there, he was a leader in the movement to restore the episcopacy to the Lutheran Church in America. He read a paper, "Should We Have the Episcopate in the Lutheran Church in America?" at the convention for the study of Church organization held at St. John's March 27-28, 1883. (His answer to the question he posed was "an unqualified and emphatic affirmative.") In 1896, three years after he became pastor of First Church, Lafayette College (located in Easton) conferred upon him the degree of Doctor of Divinity.

First Church under the guidance of their new pastor continued liturgical development. Pastor Geissinger continued to wear "the clerical robe" which he had introduced in St. John's Church less than three months after he had begun his pastorate there and which was introduced in First Church by his predecessor, Dr. Belfour. The new edition of the *Church Book* which included the 1888 Common Service was introduced on the first Sunday in July, 1893, the books being purchased by the Ladies Sewing Society. December 3, the first full rendering of Vespers was sung, the music being a manuscript arrangement of plain song. It was a significant beginning of a tradition that after several years of use in the congregation was incorporated in the *Choral Service Book* edited by Harry Archer, organist at First Church and Luther D. Reed, pastor of Emanuel Church, then in the Manchester section of the North Side. The influential book was published in 1901.

March 7, 1898 "authority was given the choir to wear vestments on all occasions when the Sunday School worships with the congregation." Why vestments were limited to those occasions and the relationship between vestments and scholars in the Sunday school are not explained. Nonetheless, the progress from a time, just a few years before, when the pastor did not even wear a black gown to the introduction of a vested choir is remarkable. The vestments, one may assume, given the close association of the organist, Harry Archer, with the pastor of Emanuel's Church, Manchester, Luther D. Reed, were at least the cassock. Apparently, surplices would come later, after 1911.

In the chapel of First Church, October 3, 1898, the Lutheran Liturgical Association was founded and continued to hold monthly conventions there for seven years. Three special annual evening services were held in the church, at which addresses, afterwards printed, were delivered by the Reverend Doctors Edward Traill Horn, Jeremiah F. Ohl, and President John A. W. Haas. The lectures and subsequent discussions of this body and the publications which it sent forth from Pittsburgh to members in twenty-two states of the Union and four provinces of Canada, the District of Columbia, and India were of great influence in promoting a knowledge of the principles and the history of Christian Worship in the broadest sense., and helped to develop a desirable uniformity of practice through all branches of the Lutheran Church in North America. The officers of the Association throughout the entire seven years of its active history were President, the Reverend Luther Dotterer Reed; Vice President, the Reverend Elmer F. Krauss, D.D.; Secretary-Treasurer, the Rev. R. Morris Smith, Ph.D.; Archivarius, the Reverend George J. Gongaware, who was to become associate pastor and then pastor of First Church. At the meeting on December 4, 1905, the Association declined to accept the resignation of its President, who was to become the director of the library at the Philadelphia Seminary, but acceded to his urgent request to be relieved of the duties of the office "for the present." The meeting proved to be the last, for it was decided to discontinue the regular meetings and publications "for the present." It was also decided to collect and bind in a single volume the various publications and papers. Two volumes appeared under the title of *Memoirs of the Lutheran Liturgical Association,* both published in 1906, Volumes I-II and Volumes III-VIII. Dr. Belfour was the author of "The History of the Liturgy in the Lutheran Church of Denmark."[149] Dr. Geissinger was the author of "Thematic Harmony of Introit, Collect, Epistle and Gospel"[150] and "Liturgy and Doctrine."[151] Dr. Gongaware was the author of "The Significance of Symbolism and Its Employment in the Service of the Church."[152] Dr. Geissinger's essay on "Liturgy and Doctrine" expounded a truth that later was lost to First Church for many years and was not recovered until the closing decade of the twentieth century: "Liturgy is the form that doctrine takes for the purposes of worship." He said, "As a matter of fact, if the Confessions were lost we could restore their substance from the Liturgy. But on the other hand, if the Liturgy be entirely and permanently abandoned, it will be very difficult to retain the doctrines in their original purity and living power."[153]

An essential ingredient of sound doctrine and liturgical development is a clear and thorough explanation of the traditions of the Church. Dr. Geissinger excelled at this. With the First Sunday in Advent, 1893, Dr. Geissinger began the *Weekly Parish Bulletin,* which continued for many years as a useful contribution to the congregation's life. He "filled its columns with bright, pithy paragraphs of optimistic philosophy, sound instruction, high ideals of churchmanship, and wide conceptions of the Church's mission, as well as local parish items. Sound doctrine and churchly practices were explained and it soon established itself as a positive, helpful factor in developing the congregational intelligence, interest, and unity." For more than four years it appeared weekly, and since September 25, 1898, when it changed its name to the *Parish Bulletin,* it was issued at frequent intervals.

The cornerstone of St. John's English Evangelical Lutheran Church of Pittsburgh at Forbes Avenue and Jumonville Street was laid Sunday afternoon August 7, 1892.[154] The building was completed and it was dedicated October 29. The morning service at First Church, its mother, was omitted, and the members attended the dedication in large numbers, "rejoicing with the young congregation in its possession of its own completed and beautiful building." Pastor Geissinger was the preacher for the dedication.

The handsome church was built of Pompeian brick trimmed with brown stone, with an imposing square tower that crowned a square nave with arched recesses on either side, and a seating capacity of 500. The building also included a chapel, several classrooms, a library, and a sacristy. One of the most generous contributors to the work was Jane Barclay Black, who also left a legacy of $2000 to the congregation at her death. Pastor F. P. Bossart resigned April 24, 1895, to become pastor of Redeemer Church in Buffalo, New York, at which time the congregation had 200 communing members.[155] March 4, 1907, during the pastorate of the third pastor, W. H. Fehr (1901-1908), the congregation became self-supporting and assumed title to the property. In the decades that followed, many changes took place in the community, "thousands of Lithuanians and other foreign-born people taking up the homes of the native Americans. As a consequence parish work has become increasingly difficult, and many have urged the relocation of the church."[156] The attitude inherent in that remark, reflecting the views of those who themselves, only a few generations before, were "foreign-born", is a serious indictment of the perceived mission of that congregation. By 1925 the membership was steady at about 225. Then decline set in, and the congregation disbanded in 1954. The building was demolished, and the forlorn lot remains vacant to this day.

St. John's Church

In 1892 the Pittsburgh Synod had authorized the creation of The Evangelical Lutheran Mission and Church Extension Society of Pittsburgh, Allegheny, and Vicinity. The society was organized January 3, 1893 in the chapel of First Church. The society was incorporated in 1894. The purpose was to establish Sunday schools and congregations, to purchase lots, erect houses of worship, and to assist in the payment of debts.

The missionary concern of First Church, instilled by William Passavant, also came to the assistance of Grace Church in the Spring Garden section of Allegheny (now the North Side). The congregation had been organized in 1888 by the Reverend William J. Finck with thirty-three members. He resigned two years later and his successor because of poor health had to end his pastorate. A long vacancy followed, and the mission came under the care of the newly organized Church Extension Society. The society appealed to First Church for workers to take charge of the Sunday School. Nine members responded, and they "labored with remarkable success, doing their work in a commonplace hall on Spring Garden Avenue, and in the face of a very trying environment, beginning in 1893." Four additional volunteers were added to the original number in 1894. After more than four years of earnest work by the sturdy band who labored with heart and mind and hand, the cornerstone of a church was laid November 1, 1896 and the church building was consecrated January 31, 1897. It continues its precarious existence as St. Michael and All Angels Church.

Pittsburgh in 1892 from Mount Washington

January 17, 1894, a series of Wednesday afternoon organ recitals was begun. These were continued during Lent, and were the beginning of the beautiful Lenten services which were continued for ten years. The service was held at four o'clock. Special organ music, often with violin or cello, was followed by appropriate Passion music by the choir, and hymns and the Litany sung by the congregation.

William Alfred Passavant, who had continued his association with First Church after his resignation as pastor, died June 3, 1894. His funeral was held in the church. "The building was crowded, many clergymen from a great distance being present to honor the memory of one who was recognized as one of the leaders of the Church, a great missionary, an influential editor, and one of the greatest philanthropists of the country." Addresses were given by the Reverend Dr. Henry W. Roth representing the Synod and Thiel College, and by Dr. Geissinger.

The Pittsburgh Synod, founded in the Seventh Street church, observed its fiftieth anniversary by meeting in First Church September 18, 1894.

Small liturgical changes can take a long time. The use of wafers instead of leavened bread in the Sacrament was discussed at the annual meeting in 1895. The question was left undecided. Pastor Geissinger gave a full discussion of the subject in the *Parish Bulletin* of January 20. Two years later a motion to introduce the use of wafers was made, but final action was postponed because of the small attendance at the meeting. The matter was not taken up again until May 3, 1909: "By unanimous resolution of the Council, it was decided to use unleavened bread in the form of wafers at our Communion services."

November 4, 1894, the Altar Society was organized for the purpose of caring for the church vestments, providing flowers for the altar, and arranging the chancel for the liturgies of the church. The organization continues today as the Altar Guild.

First Church was taking its place as an important parish of the national church. June 15 and 16, the Second Convocation of Church Musicians authorized by the General Council held its sessions in the church. The papers read at the convocation were afterwards published. The church invited the Luther Leagues to hold their first national convention in the church October 30-31, 1895. "The convention was a notable one, with representative men and women from all parts of the Lutheran Church in attendance, nearly four hundred delegates from twenty states being enrolled. "The proceedings were dignified and impressive, the addresses were of a high order, and the singing was a noteworthy feature. At this convention a national organization was effected." Sunday evening, December 3, the Jubilee anniversary of the organization of the Protestant Deaconess work in the United States was observed. The Reverend Dr. Henry Eyster Jacobs of Philadelphia Seminary delivered the address.

Beginning December 3, 1900, the Lutheran Choral Society met in the chapel of First Church on Monday evenings for some years. Under the direction of Frank Benbow, who was to become the organist at First Church in 1909, it united the young people of various congregations in an organization which led services and provided special music at many general conventions of the Lutheran Church in the Pittsburgh area.

The Third General Conference of Lutherans was held in First Church April 5-7, 1903, gathering representatives of the General Synod, the General Synod South, and the General Council. One hundred ninety-four clergymen enrolled and many laymen attended the sessions. Papers of permanent value were read and afterward printed. Then conference closed on Thursday evening with Choral Vespers at which representative Lutheran music was sung by the choir and congregation and an address on "The Common Music for the Common Service" was delivered by the Reverend Luther D. Reed. The conference was part of the extensive preparation for the eventual merger of the three bodies into the United Lutheran Church in America.

October 18 and 19, 1903, the Pennsylvania State Luther League held its convention in First Church.

The thorough cleaning, refrescoing, and general renovating so frequently required in a church located in Pittsburgh has always been an item of heavy expense. This was done in the summer of 1900, when the church was only twelve years old. The Seventh Avenue church, built in 1840, was cleaned in 1850 and again in 1869 and again in 1875. The industrial pollution in the air in Pittsburgh, which reached its height during the 1940s, was already intense.

On a rail journey around the country following his inauguration for a second term, President William McKinley at Buffalo to open a Pan-American Exposition on September 6, 1901 was shot in the stomach by an anarchist. Infection set in after surgery, and the President died September 14. After a week of painful anxiety, the news of his death at two o'clock in the morning on Saturday was received. The services the next day in hymns, anthems, prayers, and sermon took note of the national sorrow. President Theodore Roosevelt's proclamation of Thursday September 19 as a national day of mourning and prayer was read followed by a prayer and the announcement of a service in First Church for that day at eleven o'clock in the morning. The church, draped in black, was filled with worshippers, many non-members present with the congregation. "It was a service in which every one was a mourner and where all felt that millions of others sincerely shared the sorrow." The service was read by Pastor Luther Reed of Emanuel's Church, Manchester, and the sermon was preached by Pastor Geissinger.

June 15, 1904, another tragedy deeply affected the Lutheran community. An excursion boat, the *General Slocum,* caught fire in the East River of New York and burned, killing more than a thousand people, members and friends of St. Mark's Lutheran Church in Tompkins Square who had chartered the boat for a Sunday School outing. It was the greatest loss of life in New York until the September 11, 2001 terrorist attack on the World Trade Center towers. July 11 Pastor Geissinger presented an appeal from St. Mark's on behalf of the sufferers from the disaster.

Bad news comes in three, it is said. Wednesday, December 7, 1904, the congregation, the community, and the church at large were shocked to learn that Dr. Geissinger had suffered a paralytic stroke. He was beloved by his people and most highly esteemed throughout the Church. "[T]housands hoped and waited with anxious sympathy for tidings of improvement. But it was the beginning of a long struggle of many months with disease, and never was nobler courage, greater faith, brighter cheer, or more loving consideration for others than that which transfigured his affliction."

At the congregational meeting January 2, 1905, a letter dictated by the pastor from his sickbed was read. ". . . Perhaps my chief concern in my present affliction is for the continued welfare of the congregation and of all our people. But I am fully persuaded that everything possible in this emergency will be done by you to make up, and even more than make up, for my enforced and, I trust, temporary absence. Be assured of my presence in spirit and of my earnest wish for the prosperity of the congregation and for the highest welfare of each one of you. May the New Year bring to each of you richer and sweeter blessings than have ever come to you before." The phrase "richer and sweeter blessings" is characteristic of Dr. Geissinger.

The hoped-for improvement in Pastor Geissinger's condition did not occur, and it became clear that, even should he recover, he would require assistance in his pastoral duties. A special congregation meeting was therefore held on March 1 to consider the nomination by the church council of the Reverend George J. Gongaware of Warren, Pennsylvania, as associate pastor. He was elected unanimously. David H. Geissinger, as president of the council, together with the acting president Thomas Lane and the secretary of the council, signed the formal call letter. It was accepted in a letter of April 10, 1905, and Pastor Gongaware began his work as associate pastor of First Church May 11, 1905.

The President of the Pittsburgh Synod, the Reverend Dr. John A. Kunkleman, served as supply pastor for some months before the arrival of Pastor Gongaware. During this interim, as Dr. Geissinger had hoped, the people of the congregation continued the work of the church. April 26, 1905, the Chapel Guild was organized by the young women of Samuel Hamilton's Sunday School class. Its purpose was caring for the "chapel vestments" (presumably the paraments of the pulpit in the Sunday School chapel), and decorations and assisting mission congregations in securing furnishings and supplies. The concern for the welfare of others beyond the congregation had been deeply embedded in the life and practice even of the young people of First Church. It is a testimony to the ministry of William Passavant.

Dr. Geissinger made slow progress in recovery. On Sunday October 1, 1905, he was able to give one of the addresses at the organization of the Shadyside branch of the main Sunday School at First Church. The project had been under consideration for several years. At the long-awaited organizational meeting in the Alinda School at Fifth Avenue and Clyde Street, addresses were given by Dr. Geissinger, Thomas Lane, J. Harvey Wattles, and Pastor Gongaware.

George Gongaware was installed as associate pastor of First Church on December 3, the First Sunday in Advent, 1905. The Reverend Luther D. Reed was the preacher and Dr. Geissinger was able read the words of installation.

Dr. Geissinger was able to be present and to preside at the annual congregational meeting on New Year's Day, January 1, 1906. He gave his annual report and stated that his progress toward recovery had been slow "and that if the near future did not give assurance of more active usefulness," he would very reluctantly be constrained to relinquish the active ministry.

Another indication of the significant role First Church had begun to assume in the national church is the service held on January 17, 1906, in commemoration of the two-hundredth anniversary of the sailing of Bartolomäus Ziegenbalg and Heinrich Plütchau, the first Lutheran foreign missionaries, from Copenhagen, Denmark, for Tranquebar on the coast of India, where they arrived July 9, 1706.[157] The missionaries sailed November 29, 1705, but the observance of the anniversary was deliberately postponed until the Epiphany season, which in Lutheran circles has long been associated with world missions which spread the light of the Gospel to the nations. Addresses were given by Dr. Jacob Fry of Philadelphia Seminary and by Dr. Luther Kuhlman of Gettysburg Seminary. "The occasion was made the more notable by the presence in large numbers of Lutherans of various Synodical affiliations."

Pastor Geissinger's health was not improving. February 5, 1905, a letter was received by the church council:

"Dear brethren:

"After long and careful consideration, I herewith tender my resignation as pastor. I am persuaded that, under the circumstances, my withdrawal from the active work of the pastorate is a duty that I owe to myself and to the congregation and that it will be for the best interests of both.

"I respectfully beg you to take action in this matter as soon as may be agreeable to your discretion. I shall ever cherish as a most precious possession the delightful remembrance of our association as pastor and people. I especially wish to thank you, one and all, for your considerate and generous treatment of me in my affliction. For many, many years to come, may the Council and congregation of the First Church enjoy that peace, harmony and prosperity which have marked the years that are past.

"Yours in the Christian faith, D. H. Geissinger."

The letter was received and laid over for future consideration. At the meeting the following month, March 5, the resignation was accepted with the deepest regret, to take effect April 1, 1906, from which date, it was declared by unanimous vote, that Dr. Geissinger was to be pastor emeritus (at "the annual appropriation of six hundred dollars") and George Gongaware was to be the pastor of the congregation. In the letter announcing this to Pastor Geissinger, Thomas Lane observed, "The deep-seated affection felt for you personally, and the profound admiration entertained for your pulpit and pastoral ministrations, are so manifest to you, that a certification in words would diminish rather than emphasize their existence." In response, Dr. Geissinger, accepting the title pastor emeritus, said, "This will relieve me from active duties and burdensome responsibilities, and at the same time enable me to feel that I still occupy an important official relation to the congregation." He, however, declined the six hundred dollars offered him: "You have dealt with me very generously during all the years of my pastorate and especially during the protracted period of my illness. Indeed you have done so much for me that I should not feel quite comfortable to accept more, especially in view of the fact that in the future larger demands will be made upon the members in order to maintain effectively the increasing work of the congregation. To allay any disturbing solicitude in regard to the welfare of myself and my family I may be permitted to say that we shall have a sufficient competence to relieve us from anxiety in regard to material necessities."

In reply to the letter announcing his succeeding to the pastorate of First Church, Pastor Gongaware wrote of "the serious responsibility resting upon those who are called to the office of the ministry," and continued, "This impression is deepened by a full realization of the importance of this parish. When I review the illustrious history of this congregation, when I recall the capable, godly men who have ministered to you in holy things and led you to your present exalted position in the Church at large, I shrink from the duties to which you have called me; but when I note your faithful kindness, when I am reminded of the zeal, devotion and loyalty which have constantly characterized your church life, when I fully believe the promise of the great Head of the Church, 'My grace is sufficient,' I am encouraged to accept the office of pastor, fully appreciating the great honor of this position and willingly assuming the responsibilities of this place of trust and opportunity. For the glory of God, and for the extension of Christ's kingdom, I now undertake this work, in the name of the Father, and of the Son, and of the Holy Ghost. Amen."

A profound understanding of the ministry and the Church is apparent in this careful acceptance. First Church was in good hands.

The congregation had sustained a particularly close relation to the Puerto Rican mission of the General Council from the beginning of that work. For years Dr. Geissinger was president and Thomas Lane the treasurer of the board. Moreover, W. Warren Wattles, William Steinmeyer, and J. S. Seaman, among others, represented the congregation on the board. It was therefore appropriate and fitting that in the evening of September 19, 1906, in the chapel of the First Church, Dr. Geissinger's last public service was the commissioning of Mary C. Mellander as missionary to Puerto Rico. In the previous year, April 3, 1905, the strained relations apparently having healed, Dr. Belfour returned to the chapel to commission the Reverend and Mrs. Alfred Ostrum as missionaries. He returned again April 10, 1907, to commission the Reverend A. P. G. Anderson as a missionary to the island. In 1911, a member of the First Church, Margaret Haupt, was commissioned as a General Council missionary to India, and First Church assumed the payment of her salary for the first year.

Friday evening, March 22, 1907, David H. Geissinger died. His funeral was held in the church Monday, March 25. The church was filled with mourners, many of whom were personal friends not connected with the congregation. He was buried "on a beautiful hillside in Allegheny Cemetery, Pittsburgh, as the sun was declining, its warm beams and the evidences of approaching spring giving their comfort to the sorrowing and adding their assurance to the promises of the Gospel concerning the resurrection of the body."[158]

A service in memoriam was held on Sunday morning April 7, the pastor and members of St. John's Church uniting with the congregation of First Church in this last public tribute to a beloved pastor. Pastor Gongaware preached the sermon; the printed order of service contained an extended account of his life and character, and warm expressions of respect and affection prepared by members of the church council. On Sunday, March 21, 1909, a handsome bronze tablet given by the Ladies Society of the congregation was dedicated by Pastor Gongaware. Within a wide border of raised ivy leaves is the inscription,

In loving memory of
Rev. David Harrison Geissinger
Doctor of Divinity
1844+1907
+Soldier and minister of the Gospel+

A faithful pastor of this parish
For fourteen years
Until the close of his life.

This is the victory that overcometh the world even our faith

David Geissinger 's service as a soldier in the Civil War was remembered and joined with his service as a pastor of the Church expanded to include an allusion to 2 Timothy 2:3-4, "Share in suffering like a good soldier of Jesus Christ. . . . The soldier's aim is to please the enlisting officer." "Soldier" also recalls Isaac Watts' hymn, "Am I a soldier of the Cross?" and Charles Wesley's "Soldiers of Christ arise," as well as "Onward Christian soldiers." The concluding verse is 1 John 5:4 in the King James Version. It is the only tablet in the church memorializing an individual pastor.

The original location was the west wall (toward Grant Street) of the south transept (the organ side). It was later moved to the north narthex and then in 2008 to the parish house staircase.

Dr. G. W. Sandt writing in *The Lutheran* March 28, 1907 gave his tribute. "The paralytic stroke, which prostrated him two years ago, had slowly robbed him of his vitality, and the hope of many of his friends that he might still prove useful to the Church has been dissipated. If the disabling of so serviceable a man will tend to teach the larger Synods the lesson, that no conscientious pastor should be expected to serve a parish while he attempts to discharge the multifarious duties that devolve upon the Synod's chief officer, his untimely death will not have been in vain." Dr. Geissinger had been president of the Pittsburgh Synod for several years. The tribute continued, "He wrote far too little. His language was choice and his diction faultless. His thoughts were clear as crystal, and his vision broad and sympathetic. He never appeared to better advantage than when he took up his pen, though absorption in pastoral and other duties made it difficult for him to give much attention to literary work. . . . He was an exceptionally strong representative of the buoyant, hopeful, sunshiny characteristics of the Christian life. There was a childlike naturalness and a manly strength in the quality of his Christianity. . . . To be near him was to catch the radiance of his cheerful spirit."[159]

Further testifying to the esteem in which Pastor Geissinger was held, during 1908 two Sunday schools of the First Church, Grant Street and Shadyside, erected a beautiful art glass memorial window of the Good Shepherd in the new Emanuel's Church, dedicated February 7, 1909, which had moved from Manchester to its present location in Bellevue. The congregation traces its origin to the foresight of William Passavant; its sixth pastor (1895-1902) was the good friend of the First Church, Luther D. Reed. The window may still be seen in Emanuel's Church.

George Justus Gongaware, who had assumed the pastorate at the retirement of Pastor Geissinger April 1, 1906, was born in Adamsburg, Pennsylvania, December 17, 1866. He graduated from Thiel College in 1893 and received his M.A. from there in 1896, the same year in which he graduated from the Lutheran Seminary at Philadelphia. He was pastor of St. Paul's, Uniontown, Pennsylvania from 1896 to 1901, taught at Gettysburg Seminary from 1901 to 1903, was mission superintendent of the Pittsburgh Synod from 1903 to 1904, and pastor of First Lutheran Church in Warren, Pennsylvania from 1904 to 1905 when he was called as associate pastor of the First Church, Pittsburgh.

On Sunday May 27 an offering of $463.20 was received for the sufferers of the San Francisco earthquake and fire which had devastated the city April 18, 1906.

Liturgical appointments continued to be added. A brass missal stand and handsomely bound volumes of the *Church*

George J. Gongaware

Book were given by B. F. Weyman. J. Harvey Wattles and Charles W. Wattles presented the church a private communion set in memory of their mother, Julia Wattles, and their sister, Annie Wattles Horner.

Foreign missions continued to be a concern of the congregation. "To assist in making up the loss sustained by our India mission on account of a bank failure, an offering amounting to $931.37 was forwarded to the Board of Foreign Missions."

Work at home was not neglected. October 2, 1906, the first meeting of the General Council Inner Mission Committee was held in the First Church. In the evening a public meeting was held in the interests of the Inner Mission work in Pittsburgh; the Reverend Dr. C. Armand Miller of New York City delivered the address. This and other preliminary meetings held in the chapel resulted in the organization of the Lutheran Inner Mission Society of Pittsburgh, April 18, 1907, with one hundred sixty members. Two years later the membership had grown to 344 members, and the society had established and maintained the Hospice in the East End of Pittsburgh, 248 Amber Street, the Reverend Dr. Alexander J. D. Haupt superintendent. The society's first annual meeting was held in the chapel, Thursday, April 30, 1908.

December 3, 1906, the church council had appointed a committee consisting of Pastor Gongaware, Thomas Lane, B. F. Weyman, and Henry Balken to arrange for special services in commemoration of the seventieth anniversary of the founding of the congregation. The pastor took special note of the anniversary in a sermon on January 20, 1907 and the committee decided to recommend the publication of a congregational history. The committee's "further and final report" is the 1909 *History of the First English Evangelical Lutheran Church in the Pittsburgh* on which this present account is built.

The existence of the splendid and still new house of First Church was threatened by changes and developments in the neighborhood of the church. In April 1907, J. Harvey Wattles was appointed to represent the congregation and to accompany a delegation to Harrisburg to protest the issuance of a charter for a contemplated elevated road, the proposed route of which would pass near the church. June 3 the Commonwealth Real Estate Company was given an option on the church property for thirty days, subject to the approval of the congregation, at $4000 a foot on

Grant Street with certain reservations. The elevated roadway was not built, crisis was avoided, and the church remained on Grant Street.

May 6, 1907, the charter of the Church Music and Liturgical Art Society was signed in Pittsburgh, and the organization was later incorporated by the Philadelphia courts "to promote interest in and knowledge of Church Music, Liturgics, and the Arts employed in Divine Worship by the printing and publishing of music, literature, etc." The Reverend Luther D. Reed was the president of the board of directors, Pastor George Gongaware the secretary-treasurer, and Harry G. Archer, the organist of the First Church, was also a member of the board.

Thomas Hetich Lane died on the last day of December, 1907, in his eightieth year. He was born in Chambersburg, Pennsylvania, August 21, 1828, the third child of Dr. W. B. Lane and Eliza Hetich Lane. At the age of nine he visited relatives in Pittsburgh, and while in the city he heard the announcement that on the following Sunday a meeting would be held to consider the advisability of organizing an English Lutheran congregation and Sunday school. Four years later he made Pittsburgh his permanent home and in the following year he was confirmed by the Reverend W. H. Smith during his short-lived pastorate. "From that day to the hour of his triumphant death his heart's affection was centered here, and his prayers and labors for her prosperity were unceasing." He had retired a year before his death after sixty-five years of work. His connection with the Sunday school during his life almost paralleled its history. He was a pupil from 1840 to 1844; librarian 1844-1845, secretary 1845-1848; a teacher 1848-1857; assistant superintendent 1857-1866; and superintendent 1866-1902. He was a member of the church council for fifty-seven years. His last service to the church was gathering material for the 1909 History of the congregation. Among his very last words was this testimony: "In the forty years since the organization of the General Council I have seen no occasion for her to retract any point of doctrine or practice then affirmed."

The 1909 *History* gives this tribute to him: "The home life of Mr. Lane was beautiful in its quiet retirement. At his genial fireside his pastors and his chosen friends always found a safe counselor and a sympathizing brother. In his large and carefully chosen library were gathered the writings of the great and wise and good. His house was his refreshing grove, his library his perennial fountain, and his Bible his constant inspiration." He was buried in Chambersburg, the place of his birth, January 3, 1907. The pastor, three members of the church council, and two other members of the congregation accompanied the body from Pittsburgh to Chambersburg. In the Minute Book of the church council Thomas Lane's memorial tribute bears the superscription "Behold a man in whom there was no guile." A photogravure of him was placed in the council room of the church in 1910.

Thomas Lane's lasting contribution is the gathering of material for the 1909 *History of the First English Evangelical Lutheran Church in Pittsburgh.* In gratitude the church council dedicated the volume to his memory. In August 1909 Pastor Gongaware announced to the council that copies of the history "had been sent to theological seminaries, colleges, and other institutions throughout the country of different denominations, and that he had received some highly complimentary letters in regard to it."

The congregation's understanding of its mission continued to be evident in numerous ways. Concern was shown for its own needy members. Dr. L. W. Smith, a member of the congregation, offered his services free of charge to those in need; the treasurer of the Indigent Fund was authorized to pay for any required medicines. Concern was shown for both inner and foreign mission work. The entire Easter offering of the church and the combined Sunday schools for 1908 was distributed to others: City Mission and Church Extension Society of Pittsburgh, Allegheny, and Vicinity $48.66; General Council Slavonic Mission $100; General Council Home Missions $305.82; General Council Church Extension $405.83; Pittsburgh Synod Home Missions $405.83. In 1908 the custom of receiving an offering at the service on Christmas Day was introduced and was given to the Indigent Fund.

In the pastor's annual report to the congregation in 1909 the increasing difficulty of pastoral work was described owing to the development of large businesses and industries in the vicinity of the church and the resulting relocation of families to the residential suburbs. The resulting situation is substantially unchanged a century later. The actual parish boundaries are not less than forty by forty miles, he observed, "and it is unquestionably true that if all the families who live nearer to other General Council churches than they do to the First Church were to unite with those churches the First Church would have fewer than a dozen families left."

Pastor Gongaware continues, "We need to recall the fact, and meditate upon it long enough to realize its physical significance, that in addition to our membership located in almost every part of the older city and on the North Side, we have faithful parishioners living at Ingram, Mt. Washington, Hazelwood, Glenwood, Irwin, Crafton, Carrick, Wilkinsburg, Duquesne Heights, Hulton, Oakmont, Bellevue, Edgewood, West View, Knoxville, Sewickley, Avalon, Tarentum, Duquesne, McKeesport, Gibsonia, Brownsville, Aspinwall, Swissvale, Beechview, West Liberty, Rosslyn Station, Brushton, Belmar, Woodlawn, Confluence, and Indiana. In addition to these there are earnest souls at greater distances from the church who desire and receive the ministrations of our pastoral office; at the same time we endeavor not to forget our young people who are attending schools away from home.

"The utmost that can be done in regular pastoral work is to visit the sick, the aged and prospective members. Much attention is given therefore to parish literature in lieu of direct pastoral visitation. An effort has been made to reach all the families of the parish by mailing *The Parish Bulletin* and other pastoral messages from time to time, together with daily use of the telephone. In this connection grateful acknowledgement is made of the generous gift of an Addressograph which will greatly facilitate our clerical work."

The survey of the vastness of the work (which has not decreased as the decades pass) was not to elicit sympathy for an exhausted pastor but to suggest the services of a parish deaconess. The suggestion was referred to the church council. Nothing further is heard on the matter until May 1910, "The pastor was authorized to make arrangements to have the Deaconess cause presented to the Congregation."

The movement of members away from downtown resulted in decreased attendance at the services of the church. The evening services were the first to suffer. In October 1909, "The pastor was authorized to issue a special letter of appeal for a more general attendance of the congregation at our evening services." In his annual report to the congregation in January 1911, Pastor Gongaware "lamented the preaching to so many empty pews on Sunday nights and Wednesday nights. He stated that something must be done to remedy the deplorable condition."

At the congregational meeting in January 1911, the pastor, pointing out "the well-known fact" that "it is not possible to increase the membership in our present location," laid out a stark choice for the congregation: "remove to a residential part of the city" or else conduct what might be called an "institutional church" for which a large endowment would be necessary. "The decision in this matter will be forced upon us and it is well to be prepared by its careful consideration." In January 1912, he again proposed "that we both publicly and privately strive to increase the attendance at the services of the church."

November 1, 1909 the use of the chapel was granted to the Luther [sic] Choral Union for rehearsals on the second and fourth Monday evenings of each month until the Luther League of America [national convention] in 1910."

February 1, 1909, the church council received the resignation of B. F. Weyman as director of the church's music and of Harry Archer as organist, to take effect May 1. After seventeen years of united service, "during which time the musical services of the congregation have received most noteworthy development and enrichment,"[160] B. F. Weyman earnestly desired to be relieved of the responsibility he had borne for twenty years and Harry Archer was planning an extended trip abroad. At a subsequent meeting Mr. Weyman presented a plan for "the reorganization of the musical interests of the congregation which included an exceedingly liberal subscription [$2500] towards the expense." His plan was to engage four voices at an annual cost of $1600, five voices at $1500, a director at $300, an organist at $300, a "pupil" or organ scholar to play in the Sunday school and possibly on Wednesday evenings at $100, an organ tuner at $150, and water to power the organ estimated at $300. The plan was gratefully accepted by the council and "unanimously approved in all its details." Despite the resignations of Weyman and Archer, the tradition of excellence was to continue.

February 8, 1909, a statement of gratitude and appreciation was adopted by the council. "Appreciating the value and sacredness of the historic in Church Music, and that the musical setting of the services of our Church has been brought to a high standard of excellence by Mr. Weyman, who has for a number of years taken full charge of the music in our congregation, bearing himself the greater part of the expense for the sole purpose of developing a common setting of music to our Common Service throughout the Lutheran Church, which he has also put in printed form and which is now available, and realizing that what he has accomplished has been possible only through a large and constant expenditure of thought, time and money, which can never be requited or adequately recognized, we, the Council of the First Lutheran Church, Pittsburgh, hereby record our heartfelt gratitude for his invaluable services to our congregation as well as to the entire Lutheran Church."

At its meeting May 3, 1909, two days after the resignations had taken effect, the council passed a resolution concerning the work of Harry G. Archer. "Whereas. After a period of seventeen years of faithful service as Organist of this Congregation, Mr. Harry G. Archer has resigned the position in order to pursue his professional studies abroad, be it—

Resolved, that we hereby express our cordial appreciation of the eminent ability and the constant devotion with which he has filled this office, and that we gratefully recognize the distinguished service which he has rendered to the cause of Lutheran Service music."

Harry Archer, described by Luther Reed as "the best-equipped church musician in Pittsburgh at the time" had studied in Berlin with the great Bach cantor Heinrich Reimann (1850-1906). In Berlin he also had studied with Albert Loeschorn (1819-1905), famous for his piano etudes. Harry Archer was described by Dr. Caspar Koch as "Pittsburgh's most successful teacher of piano," and counted many of Pittsburgh's better musicians as his former students. His first student was Dr. William H. Oetting, who became president and director of the Pittsburgh Musical Institute. Another of his students was none other than Luther D. Reed himself, who came to know him through Dr. Geissinger. The two became close friends. Archer also had a number of Roman Catholic organists as his pupils, and through them he learned of Gregorian music and came to appreciate it and adapted much of it for the service at the First Church, attracting the musicians of the city.

He proposed that Pastor Reed join forces with him in the production of *The Psalter and Canticles. Pointed for Chanting to the Gregorian Psalm Tones. With a Plain Song Setting for the Order of Matins and Vespers. Accompanying Harmonies and Tables of Proper Psalms for the Use of Evangelical Lutheran*

Congregations (1897).[161] The Introduction was by David H. Geissinger. Their next cooperative effort was *The Choral Service Book. Containing the Authentic Plain Song Intonations and Responses for the Order of Morning Service, the Orders of Matins and Vespers, the Litany and the Suffrages of the Common Service for the Use of Evangelical Lutheran Congregations with Accompanying Harmonies for Organ* (1901).[162] These two books, along with *Season Vespers Containing the Full Text of the Vesper Service with a Hymn of Invocation, the Authentic Music of the Responses and of the Proper Antiphons, Psalms and Canticles for Every Season of the Church Year, and the Authentic Music of the Litany and the Suffrages with Accompanying Harmonies for Organ* (1905),[163] introduced plainsong to the Lutheran Church in America.

He remained in Europe for five years studying piano with Loechorn, theory with Robert Klein, and organ. He had become interested in the idea of "arm weight" in piano and went to the best masters of Europe to perfect his preparation for teaching it upon his return to America. He bought a Bluthner piano in Leipzig and brought it back with him to America encased in a zinc-lined

Harry Archer and his studio

box to prevent the salt ocean moisture from harming it. His studio was for many years on Sixth Avenue and then the Eichbaum building on Fifth Avenue. As businesses began to take over downtown Pittsburgh, Archer moved his studio to the Denny mansion on Penn Avenue where he lived with his mother.[164]

After the death of his mother, he left Pittsburgh for California, and at his departure, he presented the Breitkopf and Hartel edition of the complete works of Palestrina, thirty-three volumes, to the Carnegie Library of Pittsburgh.

Harry Archer died October 22, 1956 at Los Angeles at the age of 90. The bulk of his $155,000 estate went to Carnegie Institute of Technology "to foster musical art" in Pittsburgh. A confidential report of donors to the Development Program of Carnegie Institute of Technology (now Carnegie Mellon University) from April 8, 1957 to February 1, 1965 records a gift of $171,095 from the estate of Charles K. Archer, Harry's brother, (1869-1955, a prominent photographer) and two gifts, one of $57,074, specifically for development, and another of $17,452 from the estate of Harry G. Archer.[165] The annual Harry G. Archer Award is the largest monetary award given by Carnegie Mellon University.

At the December meeting the council invited the General Council to hold its next biennial convention (1911) in Pittsburgh.

Finances continued to be a concern. The death of generous contributors led to a decline in income for the upkeep of the church, resulting in an annual deficit of about $1500. In March 1910 "It was decided to issue a special letter to the members, asking each one to pledge a stated amount toward our current expenses to be paid regularly by envelope collection, each week or each month, as the subscriber may choose."

In May 1911, the propriety of having a surpliced choir was discussed and was generally approved," but, because of the lack of a proper place where the choir could vest, action was deferred.

October 2, 1911, several of the boys of the congregation sought permission to form an organization such as other churches had "with a view to their moral and spiritual benefit." The constitution of the organization was approved in November.

In November 1911 plans were finalized for the celebration of the seventy-fifth anniversary of the founding of the congregation on January 15, 1837. It was decided to extend the celebration over two Sundays, January 14 and 21 and to have "a service partaking of social features on the intervening Wednesday evening. Two pastors were chosen to represent the sons of the congregation who had entered the ministry: the Reverend Dr. A. F. Siebert was to preach at the morning service on the 14th and the Reverend J. Q. Waters to preach in the evening of the same day. The Ladies Society was given charge of the Wednesday evening celebration. The President of the General Council, the Reverend Theodore E. Schmauk, was invited to preach on January 21 in the morning with a musical program for the afternoon.

Former pastors were not forgotten. Dr. Samuel Laird was sent congratulations upon the occasion of the 50th anniversary of his ordination. All former pastors were invited to send a letter to the congregation on its 75th anniversary.

The celebration was surely hampered by the beginning of the extensive earth-working to change the contour of Grant Street by removing "the hump" in 1912-1913. At the council meeting May 1, 1905, a communication had been received from the city requesting release from claim of damages in connection with the proposed lowering of grades at the church property. What was popularly called "the hump", the remnant of Grant's hill, was to be lowered significantly. There had been two previous attempts in 1836 and in 1849, but this was the most extensive. Grant Street was lowered from the court house to Seventh Avenue. The deepest cut was sixteen feet near the courthouse, lowering the street one story from its original level. The dramatic change may be seen in what is now the ground floor of the court house with its small windows and of the Frick building across the street. Both were built with the provision that should the hill be removed, the entrance to the buildings could be lowered and the then basement level would become the street floor. The cut was about four feet in front of the First Church, accounting in part for the awkwardly steep steps leading from the street into the tower entrance, now the Lamb of God Oratory. It was an enormously disruptive project, but one which made the traversing of Grant Street much less arduous. The completion of the cut enabled the city to expand westward to the Bluff, now the location of Duquesne University.

January 1913 the Shadyside Sunday School was closed after seven years of operation because they were forced to vacate the meeting space.

Grant Street in 1912 before the removal of the hump

A certain measure of frustration may perhaps be found in Dr. Gongaware's reports to the congregation. He also reminded the congregation that momentous decisions would need to be made concerning the ministry of the parish. In the minutes of the council meeting for March 3, 1913, there is this: "Mr. Steinmeyer offered a resolution that inasmuch as inquiries have been received on our Church Property that the Trustees be authorized to say that we consider the Value of the property $400,000.00 but that any bona-fide offer made will be considered by the Council. It is not completely unexpected, therefore, that he requested of the church council a special meeting of the congregation on March 2, 1913 "following the Chief Service" to act upon his resignation as pastor of the parish. His letter of February 23 to the council was read to the congregation.

"My dear parishioners:--

By the evident guiding of God's hand, as I have firmly believed, I was led to the pastorate of your Congregation on May 11, 1905, and now, after serving as your minister in holy things for almost eight years, I am directed by that same Divine hand to another field of labor. On the 22nd of Jan. 1913 there came to me an earnest and unanimous call from St. John's Church, Charleston, S. C. On Feb. 5th that call was repeated. Meanwhile many private appeals have reached me from individuals and societies in that Congregation and also from men prominent in the Councils of the Church at large to accept the call.

"Convinced that a good work is possible for me there by the pledged whole-hearted co-operation of the people and being fully persuaded that in your important field here a very great work is, surely, possible of accomplishment by another pastor, with an increasing measure of lay activity, it becomes my duty to offer to you at this time my resignation as your pastor, which same I hereby do. . . . If it be your pleasure, my pastorate shall close with the Holy Communion on the last Sunday in May 1913."

His churchly piety was evident in his acceptance of the pastorate and also in his leaving it.

Dr. Gongaware married Frances M. Brown. His second wife was Elizabeth Bateman Geissinger, the widow of his predecessor at the First Church. They were married in the spring of 1913. There is no record of the marriage at First Church. The communion record for May 25, 1913, Dr. Gongaware's last service here, lists "New Mrs. Gongaware" as a communicant at that service. On March 23 she had communed as Mrs. D. H. Geissinger.

St. John's Church in Charleston, which dates from a two-day visit by Henry Melchior Muhlenberg in 1742, was and remains a significant parish. The renowned Reverend Dr. John Bachman (1790-1874) was its pastor from 1815 until his death. Within a year of his arrival at St. John's he notified the vestry that he intended to begin a ministry to the black community, and that work proved successful. Dr. Gongaware remained at St. John's until his retirement in 1941. He was a member of the Board of Education of the United Lutheran Church in America from 1918-1926, as he had been a member of the corresponding board of the General Council, 1909-1913. After his retirement he was a member of the Board of Adjudication of the United Lutheran Church in America, 1943-1951. He died June 24, 1951.

St. John's Church memorialized their beloved pastor with a marble tablet describing the man and his work.

TO THE GLORY OF GOD
AND IN LOVING MEMORY OF
THE REV'D GEORGE J. GONGAWARE, D.D., LLD.
BORN DECEMBER 17, 1866
DIED JUNE 24, 1951
THEOLOGIAN, HISTORIAN, AND WRITER
AN AUTHORITY IN CHURCH LITURGICS
BUT ABOVE ALL, A NOBLE MAN OF GOD
DISTINGUISHED FOR HIS PURITY OF CHARACTER
AND HIS DEDICTION TO THE WELFARE OF OTHERS
BELOVED PASTOR OF ST. JOHN'S LUTHERAN CHURCH
JUNE 1913 TO JANUARY 1942
AND PASTOR EMERITUS FOR 10 YEARS THEREAFTER
IN HIM GOD GAVE RICHLY OF HIS GREATNESS.

CHAPTER 6

The Protestant Years

Georg Gongaware had a hand in the search for his successor. In a letter to Dr. Ernst P. Pfatteicher,[166] then pastor of the Church of the Holy Communion in Philadelphia, whom Dr. Gongaware had known since seminary days, Pastor Gongaware wrote:

"My dear friend,

At the request of the Pulpit Committee of the Council of the First Church, Pgh, I address you, and am authorized to say that you are the committee's choice as my successor here, and that you are invited to conduct the services of the congregation on some Sunday convenient for you in the near future. It is their earnest belief, as it is mine, also, that God has thus directed us in answer to our prayers, and we hope, most strongly, that our invitation may be to you a word of Providential significance, and that it may constrain you to come out and see the parish and talk of the possibilities involved. The Committee, Messers W. Warren Wattles, J. S. Seaman, Sr., and William Steinmeyer unanimously await your earliest convenient reply, to their invitation, through me.

"Kindly address me until April 24th at 616 Copeland Street; after that date, until May 26th, Fort Pitt Hotel, Pgh., and after that at 31 Pitt Street, Charleston, S.C.

"With fraternal esteem, and with kindest greetings to Mrs. Pfatteicher, I am

Most cordially yours,

George J. Gongaware"

The undated letter must have been written in April shortly after the church council meeting of April 7 appointing the Elders (the three named in the letter) to act as a pulpit committee.

The call committee introduced this recommendation at a special meeting of the church council May 17, 1913:

"That the Council recommend to the Congregation to authorize a call to Rev. E. P. Pfatteicher, of Philadelphia, to become Pastor of our Church and the Salary be named as $3000. . . . The committee will communicate verbally to the Council all the information in its possession concerning the candidate."

The council met four days later for further consideration of the recommendation. The council received the report and a motion was made to adopt the committee's recommendation. All were not in agreement. "A long discussion was held in which the chairman of the Committee read again the letters recommending Dr. Pfatteicher and no action having been taken on motion it was decided to adjourn to meet at the call of the chairman omitting our regular monthly meeting of June 2nd." There is no record of what the reservations or objections were.[167]

The council met again June 16, and after considering a number of items (bids for cementing the sidewalk and altering the steps to the church caused by the removal of "the hump"; allocation of the Easter offering; approval of a new member of the congregation; report of the representative to the Pittsburgh Synod approving the 25 % reduction of the apportionment which the congregation had asked; acceptance of the resignation of two members; the matter of a court case concerning a will), "The Pulpit Committee report was then taken up for discussion and in view of the inability to obtain an unanimous approval of the candidate, the chairman announced that consideration of the report of the committee would be discontinued." For whatever reasons, Dr. Gongaware's suggestion of his successor was not accepted.

Curiously, at the next meeting of the church council, July 7, 1913, "A letter from Rev. T. O. Keister, D.D., Roanoke, Va. was read in which he offered his services as Pastor for one month. Same was referred to the Pulpit Committee." August 5, 1913, this cryptic entry: "Pulpit Committee reported progress." September 16, "Mr. Steinmeyer reported for the Pulpit Committee and offered the following resolution: 'Final action by Council on the recommendations made by the Pulpit Committee in its report of May 17, 1913, having been considered inexpedient at that time, the committee now withdraws such recommendations and offers the following in lieu thereof: That the Council nominate to the Congregation Rev. T. O. Keister, D.D., of Roanoke, Va. to fill our vacant pastorate.' The above report was unanimously received" The resolutions to present the name of the nominee to the congregation on Sunday, September 28, following the morning service, however, passed only by a 7-4 vote.

Tension was evident at the congregational meeting. William H. Black, one of the four dissenters, introduced a resolution which was duly seconded: "Whereas the Church Council were not unanimous in recommending the selection of Dr. Keister to the Congregation and as the reports received concerning him were not entirely satisfactory, in order that further investigation may be made, I move that this meeting be adjourned till such future time as the Church Council may designate." By a vote of 82-34 the motion was tabled. William Steinmeyer "made some remarks on behalf of the Pulpit Committee in support of the recommendations offered by Council." "Considerable discussion" followed. Ballots were cast, and Dr. Keister was elected pastor by a vote of 75-41. The names of all those voting were recorded in the minutes of the meeting.

A letter of call in the form approved by the General Council was sent October 2, 1913, containing an awesome description of the duties of a pastor of the Church. "In the Name of the Father and of the Son and of the Holy Ghost. . . . That the said Rev. T. O. Keister, D.D. will as our Pastor, teach and preach the Word of God in public and private, pure and incorrupt, according to the rule and guidance of the Holy Scripture, and also according to the Symbolical Books of the Evangelical Lutheran Church. That he will administer the Sacraments as they were instituted by Christ; that he will on Sundays and on the Festivals of the Church preach the forgiveness of sins to the penitent in the Name of Jesus Christ; that he will publish to the impenitent, who continue in their security and ungodliness, the righteous judgment of God; that he will instruct the young and the old in the Catechism; that he will visit the sick with the light and consolation of the Gospel; that he will remember the poor, and that he will fully, freely, and without holding back do everything that properly belongs to an Evangelical Lutheran Pastor, and to the faithful administration of the same."

The call was accepted by Dr. Keister October 28, 1913, to take effect November 15. His salary was $3000 per year.

Thurston Orville Keister (his surname is pronounced KYE-ster) was born May 16, 1860 at Strasburg, Virginia. He married twice, first, Ella R. Lautz, second, Effie M. Lautz; there were four children. He graduated from the Lutheran Theological Seminary at Philadelphia in 1886 and received a D. D. from Newberry College in 1907. He served Muhlenberg Church in Harrisonburg, Virginia, 1886-1890; Grace Church, Prosperity, South Carolina, 1890-1895; Zion Church Greencastle, Pennsylvania, 1895-1905; St. Mark's, Roanoke, Virginia, 1905-1913.

T. O. Keister

After resigning from the First Church, he served as pastor of Christ Church, Staunton, Virginia, 1918-1928, and during that time served also as President of the Southwestern Virginia Synod. He died January 13, 1928.

In December 1913, reflecting a practice that was then making its way into churches of various denominations, the church council explored the matter of having a printed service leaflet. The cost was estimated at about $6.50 per week. The committee was instructed to continue its work.

The Reverend Robert G. Rosenbaum, pastor of Grace Church on Spring Garden Avenue on the North Side, asked for the temporary full time assistance of the teacher Charles W. Fuhr to support the struggling congregation. The request was granted in December 1913. Charles Fuhr's extensive service to the struggling mission is commemorated in the Fuhr Center in the church that now bears the name of St. Michael and All Angels.

The First Church had endured extended financial crises in its long history, all stemming from income not matching expenses. Now it faced a different sort of financial deficit. A special meeting of the church council was held January 2, 1914, after the preparatory service of confession, to consider a serious financial breach. July 7, 1913 the treasurer of the congregation, C. F.

Schaefer "reported collection for May 538.70 and June 332.02. Cash balance today 797.62. Bills and Note owing 1833.24." Written over this report in the minute book of the council is the notice, "False report. See later minutes." On August 4 a shortage of $5863.13 was discovered. At the council meeting the next day, C. F. Schaefer resigned as treasurer, and a three-member auditing committee was appointed to examine the books of the treasurer. At the September meeting, C. F. Schaefer, having resigned as treasurer, resigned from the church council. Albert W. Smith agreed to serve as temporary treasurer until Theodore G. Daub was prevailed upon to become the new treasurer in October. The special committee appointed to investigate the shortfall had employed the services of Atchison & Sterritt, attorneys "and inasmuch as the time limit on Mr. Schaefer's promise to make the shortage good before Congregational meeting has almost expired the Committee on motion was continued and given full power to act. Mr. Steinmeyer reported that he with Mess. Daub and Smith visited the U.S. National Bank and examined our account on their ledger, which showed that Mr. Schaefer has deposited $1248.50 on Jan. 3, 1913 and drew same out Jan. 7th in order to make up Cash Balance when book was closed for audit."

The whole sordid story was brought into the light and its history was reported in detail to the congregation at a special meeting. At that meeting the new treasurer, Theodore Daub, reported a cash balance of $1101.21 and a debt of $4813.34, resulting in a deficit of $3812.13 not counting the Choir Fund. "He also reported that our former Treasurer, Mr. C. F. Schaefer, was short in his accounts $5863.16. Had Mr. Schaefer not taken this money we could have shown all bills paid and a Cash Balance of $2151.03." The report was received and referred to the auditing committee for approval; it was also ordered to be printed and mailed to the congregation.

"In explanation of the manner in which Mr. Schaefer took our money, Mr. Steinmeyer and Mr. Niebaum each read a lengthy report.

"*Mr. Steinmeyer's Report.* In the latter part of 1912 the Church Council learned that certain payments that should have been made by the congregational treasurer, Mr. C. F. Schaefer, had been delayed by him, causing complaint by the persons to whom the money was payable. The treasurer made explanations of these transactions that were fairly plausible, but not entirely satisfactory.

"The auditing committee that examined his accounts on Jan. 6, 1913 made a more than ordinarily careful investigation and found everything in proper shape, the balance due the Church being on deposit with the U. S. Nat. Bank and nothing in the bank pass-book to indicate that the money had been deposited shortly before the audit.

"About the middle of 1913 a Committee of the Council demanded an interview with the Treasurer to discuss the conduct of his office. This conference was held by Mess. Steinmeyer, Smith, and Schaefer in the Director's room of the U. S. Nat. Bank and resulted in a confession by Mr. Schafer that he had appropriated the funds of the Church for his own use. Of this amount a portion pertained to the regular Church Funds in his charge and the balance was a special music fund arising from private sources and not heretofore appearing in any of the Annual financial reports.

"A written statement was obtained from the Treasurer at this time, acknowledging that he had appropriated to his own use the stated amounts of the Church's money. At this time, as well as on numerous occasions thereafter, Mr. Schaefer declared in the most positive terms that he would replace the money before the close of 1913; that he had several deals pending from which he would realize considerable sums and if it came to the worst, he could and would borrow enough to pay what was due the Church. He also said that his father, who was financially 'well-to-do', would see him through rather than have trouble occur.

"All these matters were at once placed before the Council, which has since had full control of everything that has been done.

"The Council members were pledged to secrecy, as it was realized that publicity would take from Mr. Schafer any possibility of earning the money to pay us from his business.

"As Mr. Schaefer has failed to make good his promise to replace his defalcation, it is proper that the Congregation be made acquainted with the facts in order that they may instruct the Council as to their wishes in the future conduct of the case. At this time the Council is acting through a sub-committee, which has been clothed with authority to do everything that seemed necessary in the effort to secure the money of the Church and this Committee is acting under competent legal advice."

"*Mr. Niebaum's Report for Committee.* It has been a custom of the Church Council to hear a report from the Treasurer at each stated monthly meeting.

"The statement has not always been forthcoming owing to the absence of our former Treasurer, Mr. Schaefer.

"In the spring of 1913 he moved to his country place and did not attend a meeting of the Council from May 5th until Aug. 5th 1913.

"In the meantime it developed that a check he had given to Mr. Benbow to pay Choir salaries had been returned unpaid. An investigation was started and it was learned that there were no funds to the credit of the Church.

"Mr. Schaefer was cited and appeared before the Church Council at its next session in August and confessed to having misappropriated the funds of the Church, also the Choir fund and gave a paper over his signature under date of August 6, 1913 acknowledging his delinquency and admitting to a shortage of $5133.32. Since then Mr. Albert W. Smith found an additional item of $495.00 and one of $43.00 and the Trustees also uncovered an item of $191.84 Water Tax unpaid, which Mr. Schaefer had reported as being paid, so that the total known defalcation up to this time amounts to $5863.16.

"At the August meeting Mr. Schaefer offered his note for the amount of the shortage, but the Council declined to settle that way. He then begged consideration on account of his family and his parents and promised and assured the Council that he would raise the money, if given time to do so and positively stated that he had resources or friends to help him and as a last resort, if necessary, he would go to his father, who would help him.

"Owing to our having a new Pastor coming, a number of the members of the Council urged Mr. Schaefer to not wait until the end of the year, but to get busy and pay up before Dr. Keister would arrive and assume his duties, but we got only promises.

"Then at the November meeting a resolution was offered and passed (but kept off the minutes by unanimous consent) that a Committee of three be appointed to push and bring about a settlement. The Committee consisted of John H. Niebaum, W. H. Black, and Theodore G. Daub, Treasurer. Several times a week meetings were held with Mr. Schaefer, but nothing definite developed but promises.

"At the December meeting of the Council, the Committee made a report and asked for further instructions, with the result that Mr. Schaefer was to be notified to settle on or before Dec. 22d, 1913, or take the consequences and the Committee was given full power to act.

"Several meetings were held by the Committee with Mr. Schaefer and he was given the ultimatum to settle by Dec. 22d, but he did not appear before the Committee.

"The Committee then learned that Mr. Schaefer had Mr. Frank Thompson, Attorney to represent him, he having visited our Treasurer Mr. Daub, and offered a note in settlement. This was refused. The Committee then engaged the services of Acheson & Sterrett, Attorneys to represent them and endeavored to reach a settlement according to Mr. Schaefer's oft repeated promises to pay up before the end of the year 1913.

"Payment was not made and this puts it up to the Council to report this very sad and unfortunate condition and loss to the Treasury, to our principals the Congregation at its next annual meeting following the expiration of the date of limitation of promised settlement, and we assure you Brethren that Council and their special Committee have done everything possible to bring about a condition to avoid this scandal and loss of money.

"On the face of conditions and according to our books all this has transpired during the year 1913 and since our last annual meeting, but things have developed that in a recent examination of the Ledger accounts of the church at the U. S. Nat. Bank[168] that just prior to the last audit an unusually large sum for that time of year was put to the credit of the Treasurer, Mr. Schaefer, a few days prior to the audit, and within two days after the annual meeting, this sum was taken out and appropriated by Mr. Schaefer on a Voucher to his own order followed by Vouchers up to the time of his confession at the meeting in August.

"At the August meeting Mr. Schaefer resigned as Treasurer, also as a member of the Council and Mr. Albert W. Smith was elected Treasurer, which he accepted temporarily until a new Treasurer could be selected.

"At the October meeting of the Church Council Mr. Smith resigned as Treasurer and Mr. Theodore G. Daub was elected Treasurer and also a Deacon for Mr. Schaefer's unexpired term."

The question of "Mr. Schaefer's shortage" was taken up later in the meeting and "discussed very freely, although he was present, but the Congregation did not feel justified in issuing instructions, as it was such a sudden shock." The matter was referred back to the church council with full power to act. William Black, because he felt that in such a serious matter the congregation should issue specific instructions to the council, voted No. All others voted in favor of the motion. C. F. Schaefer did not cast a vote.

At a special meeting of the church council January 26, 1914 the treasurer requested a resolution, which was unanimously adopted, "that all checks issued by the Treasurer shall be countersigned by the President or the Secretary of the Church Council and that the Treasurer shall be bonded for $5000." The "committee on the Schaefer shortage" gave a report in which "Messrs

Niebaum, Black, and Daub each related the various clues they had followed down," and a lengthy discussion ensued. On motion, the committee was continued.

At the church council meeting on March 2, 1914, the treasurer, Theodore Daub, reported that his attorney had advised him not to sign the statement of January 1 and that the wording ought to be changed somewhat "regarding the Schaefer shortage." It was decided to print the figures only and to use the term "due from C. F. Schaefer." Quite a lengthy discussion followed as to whether it would be advisable not to send a statement to the congregation that year "on account of Mr. Schaefer's wife and children" [there were two daughters], but it was decided that the congregation was entitled to the statement.

At the same meeting a long and detailed letter was received from the audit committee for January 1, 1913 defending its careful work and showing why it did not uncover any malfeasance in its examination of the books for that year. "Your committee firmly believes that he was shrewd enough, had the facilities and used them in the accomplishment of his crooked work, and also used the members of your committee as tools in defending him against the suspicions pointing toward him, which we considered our Christian duty when his work was so apparently clear." Anger and frustration ran deep. Theodore Daub, the treasurer, moved that C. F. Schaefer be "suspended indefinitely" from his membership in the church and the matter of his spiritual welfare was left in the hands of the pastor "to endeavor to lead him to a true repentance." The Schaefer family (husband, wife, and two daughters) had communed for the last time on May 25, 1913. After that, they disappear from the records until the church council, October 1, 1928, convinced of his repentance, reinstated his membership.

At the congregational meeting January 4, 1914, John Niebaum reported that the Committee appointed to keep in touch with the affairs of C. F. Schaefer "had devoted a great deal of time in this matter and have come to the conclusion that his affairs are so involved that there is not much hope of our realizing anything toward his shortage." Nothing further is heard of the "Schaefer shortage" except that when Thomas L. Sheafer consented to become the treasurer of the congregation October 2, 1916, the secretary of the council inserted a careful clarifying note. "Thos. L. Sheafer is not connected in any way with C. F. Schaefer, our former treasurer, with whom we had trouble and spells his name differently. He is the son of Col. James Sheafer, who formerly served faithfully as treasurer for a number of years."

Another special meeting of the council was held on February 1 following the morning service. This time it was not the financial scandal but the request of the Lutheran Brotherhood to use the church for noonday Lenten services each weekday excepting Saturdays. Seven voted Yes; one, Albert Smith, the secretary of the council, voted No, perhaps because of a not uncommon suspicion at the time of the morality of insurance. It was an admirably ambitious plan: a service in the church for thirty-three of the forty days of Lent. After the financial distraction, the church needed to refocus on its principal activity and source of existence. These daily Lenten services became the established practice of the congregation for a number of years following 1914.

In March 1914 the treasurer was given permission to advertise in the *Dispatch* the times of the church services. In May and June authorization to continue the advertisements of Services in the newspapers was given and broadened beyond the one paper. Thus began a practice that continues to this day.

Ominous signs began again to appear concerning the desirability of moving the congregation to a different part of the city. At the March 2, 1914, meeting of the church council an inquiry was received from a Mr. Rodd asking whether the congregation would consider selling its property, "taking in trade one or two plots of ground at Aiken and Ellsworth Aves., one plot measuring about 140 by 155 ft. which he values at $75,000, and the other a peculiar shape lot about 195 x 330 ft. @ $81,500 with a new house thereon worth $11,000." Since no offer had been made, the matter was referred back to the trustees. August 3, 1914 William Black reported on the proposed "new church lot," and the matter was referred to the trustees for further information. At the October 1914 meeting William Steinmeyer offered a deeply distressing resolution:

"The members of the Church Council believe that the welfare of our Church will be seriously jeopardized if it continues in its present location, because the constant shrinkage of the 'down-town' population will be an important factor in preventing an increase of the membership from that section.

"That this view is generally entertained by others is evidenced by the fact that, with very few exceptions, the down-town churches of all denominations have followed the trend of population and re-located to the Eastward. The few churches still remaining in the down-town section have large endowments[169] or fixed incomes[170] and are expending large sums of money in the erection and operation of Parish Houses, wherein various activities and amusements, not strictly Churchly, even, if otherwise not deserving of censure, are carried on, and used to attract a membership, notably of younger men and women. To follow the example of these Churches, if we wished to do so, would be beyond our means, and if we had the means, there is no room on our present location for such buildings. It is also an open question whether we would be successful in operating along the described lines, if the above described obstacles were removed.

"It is known to the Council that the children of some of our members residing in the East End are sent to Sunday Schools of other denominations in their immediate vicinity, because of the distance from our Church and the time and cost involved in reaching it. These children are almost certain to be lost to us as future members of our Church.

"In view of the stated facts we are regretfully obliged to conclude that we must figure on a re-location of the Church and as this can only be made financially possible by selling our present property, we hereby instruct our Trustees to take such steps, as in their judgment seems proper to bring about a sale of the property, under such instructions as to price and other conditions as the Council may now or hereafter give. It being positively conditioned, however, that negotiations for the sale of the property, shall in all cases stipulate that the sale is subject to the approval of the Congregation, which has the sole authority to ratify the sale of its real estate.

"The Council believes that the opinions herein expressed would be concurred in by practically the entire

Congregation, but that it would be a mistake to bring the matter to Congregational attention at this time, as it would cause harmful publicity and unwise agitation. Every opportunity for full and free expression will be given at the proper time."

Nine members of the council voted in favor of the resolution (Seaman, Steinmeyer, Balken, Niebaum, Graf, Wattles, Bikle, Daub, and Smith); two were opposed (Sellers and Black).

A special meeting further to consider the sale was held on October 19. On a motion by Mr. Sellers, who had opposed the resolution, the trustees were directed to offer the church property for sale at a minimum price of $400,000 in cash or its equivalent, reserving the organ, memorial windows, baptismal font, chancel appointments, Dr. Geissinger's memorial tablet, "and Electrolier."

The forward-looking spirit of William Passavant was gone from the congregation. Few were able to see possibilities in the changing situation of the parish. These were the Protestant years when the leaders of the congregation sought to follow the flight of the other churches from downtown, following their membership wherever they went.

Holy Communion was celebrated only four times a year.

The use of "Rev." with only a surname now becomes the common practice in the minutes, as had become common in Protestant use (e.g. "Rev. Beistel"). In earlier years the careful practice was to say the Rev. Mr. Beistel or The Reverend John Beistel. As early as June 7, 1923 *The Christian Century* had editorialized against the usage of "Rev." with simply a surname on grammatical grounds, underscoring the character of "reverend" as an adjective which can only modify a title (The Reverend Doctor") or a complete name ("The Reverend Horace Smith".) The parallel was made with "honorable" as a title of civic officials: the mayor of Pittsburgh is not addressed as "Honorable Jones" nor is his occupation described as "an honorable."[171]

New members transferring from whatever denomination were received "by the right hand of fellowship." At least half the transfers from the congregation during these decades were to Presbyterian churches. Even though Presbyterianism is the dominant Protestant denomination in Pittsburgh, the statistics show that people saw little difference between the Lutheran and Calvinistic churches.

At the council meeting on April 6, 1919, "The Music of our Church was discussed and the feeling appeared to be that we should confine ourselves more to the old familiar tunes in singing the old familiar hymns." The pastor and the secretary were appointed to request the choir director, Frank Benbow, "to carry out the above idea." The council consistently turned down his yearly requests for increasing the choir to a double quartet.

The work and the spirit that had created and supported the publication of the *Choral Service Book* and *Choral Vespers* was gone from the congregation, supplanted by a renewed resistance to change and to liturgical usage. At the 1920 annual meeting of the congregation a committee was appointed "to make inquiry, consult with Mr. Benbow, and report to the church council with recommendations regarding any changes desired in our music. The council on February 8, 1920, unanimously adopted eight recommendations.

(1) "The Gloria in Excelsis shall be used with the tune used in the past instead of the Canticle in the morning service." The previous tune was known to the congregation from its use in the *Church Book*, and they did not want to change. The phrase "morning service" was the language of the *Church Book;* the 1918 *Common Service Book* called it simply "The Service."

(2) "All hymns shall be played with strong organ lead." Congregational singing, it seems, was weak.

(3) "Hymn shall be sung instead of Responsory in evening Service." This was permitted by the rubrics in Vespers, as the service was called in the new book; the *Church Book* used both names, "Evening Service, or Vespers." The rubric in both books said "After the Lesson a Responsory or a Hymn may be sung." It is regrettable that First Church that had pioneered the use of the full musical resources of the Church now turned away from that heritage and would not tolerate or contemplate even an occasional use of the classic Responsory.

(4) "Antiphones [sic] shall be omitted." The spelling error apart, it is another step away from the rich musical tradition that had been established in the parish.

(5) "Recite Psalm in evening service, singing the Gloria Patri." This marked a further suppression of congregation and or choir song, flattening the service. The contradiction of saying the Psalm but singing its conclusion in the Gloria Patri apparently escaped the congregation. The congregation had learned to sing the Gloria but did not care to exert itself in singing the verses of the Psalm or to have them sung by the choir.

(6) "Nunc Dimittis and Magnificat shall be sung throughout in unison with male and female voices." This is an odd directive. Apparently someone, perhaps Frank Benbow the choir director, had tried an innovation of a male voice singing Simeon's song, Nunc Dimittis, and a female voice singing Mary's song, Magnificat. The congregation wanted things always done in the same way: always in unison, always both male and female voices. Variation was unacceptable.

(7) "Organ shall be used Good Friday morning and evening as in other services." The ancient tradition of the organ keeping silence on the day of the Lord's death, that apparently had been the practice of the First Church, was rejected.

(8) "Hymns in the evening service were to be announced." Informality was to be the style in the evening, despite posting the numbers on the hymn board and listing them in the service leaflet. The contagion of Protestant practice was spreading.

January 3, 1922, the council, owing to financial constraints, declared that the choir budget for the coming musical year beginning May 1, 1922, be limited to $2000. At the same meeting a letter from the Brotherhood of the congregation was read "expressing the desire to have old familiar tunes sung to old familiar hymns in our services." The secretary was unanimously instructed to notify the choir director to comply with the request. (As is always the case when the issue is raised, the identification of old and familiar is not always agreed upon.)

Increasing Protestant practices did not extend to certain areas. At the November 1916 council meeting Dr. Keister read a letter from the Anti-saloon League requesting the use of the church for a service. "It was unanimously decided that the request should not be granted." A similar request in March 1919 was also denied.

William Steinmeyer kept pressing his case. At the November 8, 1915 meeting of the church council he reported that he had learned that the First Congregational Church on Dithridge Street was to be offered at sheriff's sale. The council took no action.

April 3, 1916, William Black reported that an inquiry had been made for the church asking whether $300,000 would be accepted. "No action was taken inasmuch as the Trustees have made an agreement with a Real Estate concern to turn all inquiries over to them until the agreement is cancelled."

Dr. Keister had a talent for organization. May 19, 1914, he called a meeting of the men of the congregation and made four recommendations to them. First, that a corps of ushers composed of young men be organized; second, that a corps of older men to serve as a "Vestibule Committee"[172] to welcome strangers; third, that the congregation be divided into districts and that men be appointed to keep in touch with the members, "especially those who absent themselves from Divine Services"; fourth, that a men's Bible class be organized. It was not thought odd that women were excluded from these organizations and services, despite the remarkably influential work of the Ladies Society, whose lasting memorial is the chancel of First Church.

The work of women went largely unnoticed. The minutes of the regular meeting of the church council for October 1916 record that "Miss Frasch"[173] had resigned as assistant to the treasurer; she was commended for her "efficient services" for a number of years. When men retired, extended notes of praise and thanks were drafted.

The Men's Bible Class arranged a room in the church basement in which to hold its class; smoking was permitted. The class also published the new monthly Parish Bulletin beginning May 1, 1915.

Dr. Keister also drew up regulations governing letters of transfer or dismissal that were approved March 1, 1915:

"I. That letters of honorable dismissal shall be granted
only to those who have faithfully supported the Church
and who have been faithful in their attendance upon

the Holy Communion and the regular services of the sanctuary;

II. That no letters of dismissal to other denominations shall be granted, unless the applicant has complied with the above conditions;

III. Letters of dismissal to other Lutheran Congregations may be granted to members who failed to meet these conditions but the facts must be stated to the pastor and council of the congregation with which the applicant expects to unite."

In December 1914 a committee was appointed to solicit special contributions toward the maintenance of the choir. Slow progress was made. By the following February twenty-one people had contributed $1037, six were yet to be visited, and five had promised to make a contribution, but no more than $100 could reasonably be expected. The drive was ended and the choir was reduced by one voice. The expense of the choir was $3700 per year plus $100 for tuning the organ. February 1, 1914, authorization was given to change from water power to electric power for the organ saving about half the cost of water power. The motor was installed in August 1915 at a cost of $455.

In March 1916 William Black reported for the choir committee that "for a long time there has been a feeling in the Congregation that too much money was being spent on the Church Choir and that we should be satisfied with a quartet. This feeling seems to have attained a majority and while three or four members have expressed themselves as being willing to make special contributions to keep up our present Choir Organization, yet evidently enough money cannot be secured for the purpose. A year ago a special effort was made to get sufficient subscriptions, but only about one-half of the desired amount was realized." By a vote of 8-1 the allocation of the choir for the year was reduced to $2500. The wonderful days of liturgical music and strong congregational song under the leadership of Harry Archer, that were influential in improving the quality of music in Lutheran churches in many parts of the country, were long gone and forgotten.

The discontinuation of the Wednesday evening services because of low attendance was suggested and referred to the pastor. At the annual congregational meeting in January 1914, Dr. Keiser in the course of a long report lamented the decline in membership by ten people during 1913 but was encouraged by keeping careful records of names handed in at communion that 107 people who had not communed in four years had handed in their names in 1913 and by the "earnest" interest in the new Men's Bible Class.

In his report to the congregation in January 1916 (the meeting was not well attended despite good weather), Dr. Keister said that the attendance at the chief service was increasing, which pleased him, "but that the Sunday evening and midweek services were very poorly attended." The declining attendance at evening services was a feature of most congregations across the country at that time. With a deficiency of liturgical understanding, he recommended consideration of changing the time of the morning service to 10 a.m., "having a short sermon, close the service after the morning prayer and merge same into the Sunday School service."

At the July 1916 meeting of the church council there was a lengthy discussion regarding the Sunday School. Horace Bikle announced that he had been elected superintendent "but owing to the discouraging condition of our School he would decline to accept unless he was assured of the co-operation of the members of Council, which assurance was readily given. At the annual congregational meeting in January 1917, Horace W. Bikle "made a very interesting report as Superintendent regarding the work of the Sunday School showing a gain of 44% in membership and 47% in finances, and one of the most interesting features drawn to our attention was the fact that our Primary Department has 20 foreign children drawn from localities near the church." At the same meeting in response to the superintendent's report, the treasurer of the congregation recommended the employment of a deaconess "to work among the children of the neighborhood." The Sunday School was coming to the rescue of the church in its mission to the surrounding area.

In May 1918, the superintendent of the Sunday School, Horace Bikle, reported to the church council "that eight negro children came into our Sunday School and the Executive Committee agreed that we should take them in, but it was difficult to place them in any of our Classes, as it was necessary to start them in the lowest grade. A. W. Smith consented to take a class of 4 negro boys but 4 negro girls on account of age must be placed in the infant class." The minutes record, "It was the sense of Council that we should receive them and show them every attention."

At the annual congregational meeting in January 1919, "Mr. [Horace] Bikle made an interesting report as Superintendent of our Sunday School, which was the most encouraging to which we have listened for years. The School has 125 members and on the last Sunday had 91 in attendance. The spirit displayed by all is fine and all we need is more members [perhaps, rather, teachers]. Chairman [William] Siebert reported that he heard from an outside source that our Sunday School, although not large, is the most active and wide-awake school in the district." During these years, the basement of the church was being finished and prepared for use by the Sunday School classes.

In 1916 the evening services were cancelled from the end of May until the first Sunday in October. It had been the practice of the congregation for many years to close the church during the latter part of August every year for cleaning. Such were the conditions in the smoky city.

The weekday noon services throughout Lent were continued and the Reverend Ambrose Herring was granted the use of the chapel on Thursday evenings during Lent for the Inner Mission Society.

Dr. Keister was invited to preach at the baccalaureate service at Chicago Seminary on the last Sunday in April 1914.

At the January 1916 annual congregation meeting it was decided to move the meeting from the first to the third Monday of January in view of "the difficulties in getting an attendance at our congregational meetings and also of preparing our reports so early in the year." Legal documents were prepared to present to the court to make the change in the charter of the congregation.

World affairs were seldom reflected in the minutes of the congregation, but at the end of the minutes of the February 1917 meeting, the secretary, Albert W. Smith, appended a note, "On Feb. 3d The United States broke off Diplomatic relations with Germany, dispensing with the services of Ambassador Bernsdorff." Above the minutes of the April 2 meeting the secretary inserted a note, "On Apr. 6—Good Friday, also the 14th day of Nisan on the Jewish calendar, Congress of the United States at 3 a.m. declared a State of War existing between the United States and Germany."

In a surge of patriotism at a special meeting of the council April 29, 1917 it was unanimously decided to place the United States flag in front of the church and another inside. At the May meeting it was reported that "the United States Flag had been ordered on the Lectern [presumably the chancel] and that the one outside would be raised in a few days." A committee of three was to arrange for the flag raising. In May the Sunday School addressed a letter to the church council:

> "The Sunday School of your Church has been informed of, and wishes to commend the action of the Church Council in deciding to place the United States Flag within the Auditorium of the Church and upon a pole in the Church yard, where it can remain unfurled and float in the breezes, as it should at this time. . . . [W]e now request permission of your Council to place within the Church Auditorium, above the doors opening into the Sunday School room, a flag of moderate dimensions."

The motion to grant the request was not seconded. (Perhaps it was thought that one flag inside and one outside the church was sufficient, and that two flags in the church would be jingoistic.) The council however, in thanking the Sunday School, allowed them to pay for the flag "on the Lectern" and to participate as a body in the raising of the outdoor flag "on Sunday morning next."

Sunday May 13, 1917 the flag raising took place. A program was printed in red and blue on white paper and is preserved in the minute book of the council, the first such program ever to be so included. Moreover a photograph of the event is preserved in the minute book. The flag pole stood just to the left (south) of where the planter and bronze sign now stand. There was a procession of choir and Sunday school; the patriotic song "My country, 'tis of thee" was sung; an invocation was given by Dr. Keister; William Steinmeyer, Esq. presented the flag; the pledge of allegiance was said; there was an address and acceptance of the flag by G. W. Brawner, Jr.; the flag was raised; the Star Spangled Banner was sung; and a benediction concluded the ceremony.

Patriotic fervor abounded. Mr. Sheafer presented a war resolution for the consideration of the church council:

"*Whereas*—The alleged disloyalty of members of the faculty of a prominent Lutheran College has been given wide publicity in the newspapers of the country and

"*Whereas*—The publication of these articles reflects discredit upon the entire Lutheran Church of our Country and

"*Whereas*—We are convinced that such action is not approved by the great majority of our Lutheran Church members, Therefore

"*Be it Resolved*—That we, the Church Council of the First English Evangelical Lutheran Church of Pittsburgh, do disapprove of the conduct of these persons, if its correctly reported, as disloyal and unscriptural, and contrary to the confessions of our Lutheran Church, which enjoin loyalty and obedience to Government authority.

"That we condemn as unchristian, as well as unpatriotic, any action or expression in this country which is not heartily in support of the Government of the United States in its war against Germany.

"That these resolutions and the newspaper article referred to be spread upon the records of the Council, that the resolutions be read at the chief service next Sunday, and that a copy be sent to the newspapers of this city with the request that they be published in a prominent place at an early date."

Action was postponed until there was a "fuller attendance" at a meeting of the council. At the August meeting the resolution was given "considerable discussion" and then tabled. Perhaps some saw that surely there were many in Germany who could say on their side that Scripture and the Lutheran Confessions enjoin loyalty and obedience to government authority. The narrow, one might say unthinking nationalistic basis of the resolution did not commend itself to the council.

The Red Cross Society and the War Farm Association both asked the church to form branches in the congregation. The matter was referred to the Ladies Sewing Society. The Home Department of the Sunday School was requested to mail literature to any member of the congregation "who enlisted in the services of our government." At the July meeting the pastor was authorized to present a Bible "to any member of our congregation who goes to war." July 16, a Soldiers' Welfare Committee was created "to look after those of our Congregation who go to war." The committee supplied New Testaments and kits containing toilet articles, "and the responses of the soldiers in camp show that they are much appreciated." At the October 1917 meeting of the council the Soldiers' Welfare Committee read several letters "from the soldiers expressing their appreciation of the attention the Committee has given them." The suggestion was made to read these letters from time to time at the chief service of the congregation. (This suggestion, together with the suggestion that the war resolution be read at the chief service, are clear evidence of the decline in understanding of the worship of the Church. The Sunday morning service was seen as a meeting rather than a celebration of the Liturgy of the Church.)

Twenty-five names are listed on the commemorative plaque honoring those who served in the Great War, two women and twenty-three men; the plaque now hangs in the lower hallway of the church.

The minutes of March 4, 1918 report, "A letter from Miss Mary Lane regarding the attitude of the Church Council in the War was read and discussed." Apparently she thought that the War was not being given sufficient attention. A resolution was introduced that "visiting ministers be requested to include in the prayers at our Services a petition for the welfare of our soldiers and the victory of our nation in the present war. A committee of two was appointed to respond to Miss Lane "with instructions to mention the above resolution" and to note that "especially for the past two months such petitions had been the rule in the prayers at our Church services as well as the prayers at the opening of the Council meetings." (The Litany in the service book of the time, *The Common Service Book,* included the petition, "To give to our nation perpetual victory over all its enemies.")

A proclamation by the president of the United States called upon the citizens of the country to "repair to their respective places of worship on Thursday May 30th (Decoration Day) to pray for the forgiveness of our sins, for victory over our enemies, and that we may be guided to do those things only, which are righteous." The First Church set their service at 10:45 a.m. on

May 30 "in accordance with this call." The council, remembering that some of the members of the congregation desired to attend divine service at the cemeteries as had been their custom on that day, decided that "such members would, no doubt, meet with the requirements of the President's Proclamation in carrying out their usual custom." The service at First Church was well attended, Frank Benbow the organist "rendering the Star Spangled Banner" and Dr. J[onathan] Elmer Bittle, Missionary President of the General Synod preaching on Daniel 9:15.[174] "His prayer for victory over our enemies and that we may do only those things which are righteous in the eyes of our Saviour met with the approval of those assembled together in these critical times."

Above the minutes of the church council meeting on December 2, 1918, the secretary, Albert W. Smith, inserted a triumphant note: "At midnight Pittsburgh time Nov. 10—1918 Germany signed the Armistice presented by the United States and our Allies terminating the most terrible War in history and completely obliterating Germany's arrogance. A.W.S." He could not have known at the time, but another terrible war was to follow two decades later. His note makes the excessively patriotic assumption that the Great War was chiefly America's victory. The war began in 1914; the United States did not enter it until 1917.

The intense patriotism inflamed by the war continued even after the armistice. The annual congregational meeting of January 20, 1919 opened with "devotional exercise" which included the congregation singing "Onward, Christian soldiers." The minutes of the meeting declare, "The names of the young men who left their homes and all to fight for our homes are recorded on page 389 of our minute book as a permanent record in order that the following generations may revere their names."[175] Moreover, "Mr. Daub stated that his son, who was in the front trenches in France, appreciated highly the attention paid to him by our Committee and stated that he had no doubt that the same satisfaction was felt by the rest of our Boys." Nothing is said of the two women whose names are on the honor roll. Bertha Pingle was a Red Cross nurse; Lois Singley served at the base hospital library at Camp Beauregard, Louisiana.

October 21, 1917, A "special meeting of the church council was called during Sunday morning service after the sermon" to take action on the resignation read to the congregation by Dr.

Keister. He had accepted a call to Christ Church, Staunton, Virginia. In his letter of resignation, he gave "public expression to my deep and lasting and heartfelt appreciation of the sympathy, kindly courtesies, and co-operation which have been extended to me. These have come oftimes when mind, heart, and spirit were weighed down with the burden of souls committed to my trust, and the responsibilities which come upon every true pastor. They came as sweet and gracious cheer to the weary soul and brought aid and strength when sorely needed. The tender and close personal friendships and the strong ties arising from ministries in the homes of sorrow, trial, and bereavement, I shall never forget." The letter was dated Twentieth Sunday after Trinity, 1917. His resignation was to take effect on the last day of 1917.

The council's resolution accepting the resignation noted "that during his pastorate Dr. Keister has been untiring in his labors and has endeared himself to the members of the congregation. That under his guidance there has been a marked increase in the contributions for the various benevolent purposes of the Church. That his labors have been untiring in visiting members of the Congregation, which, owing to the scattered membership, required much time and great effort. That in the pulpit, and in his pastoral work, Dr. Keister by his eloquence, Christian spirit, and indefatigable work, although laboring under the weight of sickness, has made his Christian presence, as pastor and leader, most strongly felt [by] us, and in the community."

Pastor Keister continued to teach the confirmation class and the men's Bible class until the end of the year. After his departure, the Reverend Ira M. Wallace, Ph.D. taught the class.

The pastor's resignation overshadowed for the congregation the celebration of the four hundredth anniversary of the Reformation, October 31, 1917. Plans for a large celebration in the city had been mentioned from time to time in previous minutes.

The evening service on Sunday December 8 was cancelled in order to attend the installation of the Reverend John Arndt Yount as pastor of St. John's Church on Forbes Avenue, the daughter of the First Church. Pastor Yount came from St. Paul's Uniontown, a parish that had been served by George Gongaware 1896-1901, just before he came to First Church. During the pastoral vacancy it was decided to discontinue ("close" was the language of the time) the evening services.

The Ladies Sewing Society continued to be the guardians of the liturgical traditions of the Church. It was they who renovated the chancel "in keeping with our Lutheran tradition." It was they who provided copies of the *Church Book* for the pews of the church. In 1917 the new *Common Service Book,* prepared by the synods that were merging to form the United Lutheran Church in America, was published. The society was prepared to provide copies for the congregation and in March 1918 telephoned the council "regarding the introduction of the new Church book." The council was hesitant. "After considerable discussion it was the sense of the meeting that we are not yet ready to introduce the new book owing to unsettled conditions. Mr. Graf was appointed [as a] committee [of one] to confer with Miss Spahr and advise her to ask for a delay in the shipment of books ordered until further notice." The men of the council were not ready to take liturgical leadership. After the arrival of Charles MacLaughlin as pastor, on October 6, 1919, the council approved the purchase of copies of the *Common Service Book* to be used beginning the first Sunday in November.

A certain discomfort with change is also evident in the congregation's response to the introduction of Daylight Saving Time. "Owing to the resolution adopted by [the] Congress of the United States and signed by President Wilson enacting into Law the 'Daylight Saving' period from the last Saturday in March to the last Saturday in October the following resolution was offered by Mr. Steinmeyer—

Resolved—That beginning with Easter Sunday morning March 31st our services all start at the same hour as usual after the clocks have been moved forward one hour, and those who do not change their clocks will have to come one hour earlier than usual."

The pulpit committee after a long search was able to present to the council the name of the Reverend Charles Peter Raby MacLaughlin[176], D.D., pastor of First Lutheran Church in Greensburg, Pennsylvania, 1916-1918, where he "was highly esteemed as a forceful preacher,"[177] as their selection for the thirteenth pastor of First Church Pittsburgh. At a special meeting of the congregation July 7, 1918, before putting the resolution before the congregation William Steinmeyer "read a report regarding investigations into Dr. MacLaughlin's fitness to be made our

Pastor and stated that any questions would be answered and that remarks on the motion were in order. No questions or remarks were forthcoming. The congregational vote was unanimous.

The church council announcing the call of Dr. MacLaughlin reported that during the six-month interim, January through June, having been without a pastor "does not mean that our services were discontinued during this period or that we have lacked the means of Grace. It should be a matter for profound congratulation that with the exception of three Sundays during the summer, when the church was undergoing its annual cleaning, we have not omitted the chief Service, and that our communion services were held at the customary times. It should also be a matter for congratulation that the sermons during this period were of an unusually high average order of ability and reflect great credit on the pastors who occupied the pulpit. Lutherans should not only be grateful because the pure word of God is preached to them by this ministry but should also be proud that the ministry exhibits such intellectual equipment."

Charles MacLaughlin

Dr. MacLaughlin was born March 29, 1870. Diligent searches for further details of his life and his education at college and seminary have been unavailing.

July 25 Dr. MacLaughlin requested a special meeting of the church council "regarding the prospects of our Congregation and the nature of the work to be done." August 22, 1918, he accepted the call to what he referred to as "your honored organization," his pastorate in Pittsburgh to begin October 15. At his request, the proposed salary of $4000 per year was reduced to $3500 if the congregation would provide a parsonage. An anonymous member of the congregation (who was Joseph Seaman) offered to pay $5000 toward the purchase of a residence if the balance could be raised to pay cash without borrowing. A house at 336 Amber Street in the East End of Pittsburgh was rented for $75 per month plus $15 for a garage, automobiles now having become common possessions and necessary for the pastor of the First Church with its scattered membership.

September 30 Dr. MacLaughlin requested another special meeting of the council (in Greensburg, he was not far away) to consider the publication of a weekly pamphlet to place in the pews and in hotels, "containing the services, announcements, the names of the Councilmen, Sexton, Choir Director, members of the Choir etc." He also proposed an occasional bulletin called "The Messenger", Dr. Geissinger's useful parish paper having ceased to exist, "giving the Congregation news concerning the various Departments of our work."

It was a difficult time for the nation. In addition to the First World War, an influenza epidemic was sweeping through the country. At the October meeting, the council ordered the church to be closed to all public meetings, including divine service, to conform to the requirements of the State Board of Health. At the November council meeting prayers of thanksgiving were offered that none of the members of First Church had died in the epidemic. The church was reopened November 10 and services were resumed.

In April 1919 the new men's brotherhood placed a sign on front of the church below the rose window, extending over the sidewalk, which was illuminated at night, "with the words thereon, 'First Lutheran Church'." It was not an attractive addition. In 1927 an electric cross was hung on the building above the rose window, also extending over the sidewalk.

At the December 2, 1918, meeting "the adoption of the vested choir" was approved. The vested choir, introduced during Harry Archer's tenure, had apparently at some point been abandoned.

The generous benefactor of First Church and of the Krauth Memorial Library at the Philadelphia Seminary, Benjamin Franklin Weyman died in June 12, 1919. The church council recorded a generous memorial tribute at its meeting on July 7, 1919. "[H]is love for and his interest in the First Church, manifested in such divers ways, were chiefly directed towards beautifying the place of worship, adorning the service with fitting musical settings and appropriate selection of special numbers, and loyally supporting every activity. His modesty, his courteous kindness to all, his successful and honored career in the business world, his unfaltering devotion to the truth, marked him as a genuine Christian Gentleman."

Another generous and cultured member of the church died in 1919, William Holmes Black, who died June 30 at the age of 56. "As a Trustee on the official board, he devoted his time and talents for many years with diligence and zeal to the care of the property and the furtherance of the church's interest spiritually and financially. We note also his interest in Missions, especially his helpful devotion to the progress of St. John's and Spring Garden Congregations in Pittsburgh, Pa., and the beautiful and artistic memorial window in our own church." The window is the Good Shepherd window given in memory of his parents.

November 3, 1919, Joseph Seaman announced that he had bought a lot and house for a parsonage at the corner of Roup and Coral Streets (151 Roup Street) for $28,000 and added improvements costing about $5000. He would give this to the congregation if they would raise $8000 as an endowment toward repairs and taxes. The council readily agreed.

In his first annual report to the congregation Dr. MacLaughlin called attention to the generosity of the membership. "The hearty response that our people have given to every additional call for money has been both remarkable and gratifying. Within the year both the benevolences of Synod, as represented by the apportionment, and the Current Expenses have been largely increased. The required budget for the regular operating cost of our Church, including the synodical apportionment has been increased close to fifty per cent. . . . Over and above these regular requirements, our people have generously contributed nearly $2000 for extraordinary and worthy benevolence."

The devastations caused by the First World War continued to occupy the attention of the Church. The United Lutheran Church in America proposed to raise $1,800,000 from its 1,500,00 members "to relieve the starving Lutherans in Europe." First Church chose to receive a special collection on Sunday May 16 for this purpose. The congregation responded with characteristic generosity, gathering $2246, about five times the quota for the congregation.

Despite the general Protestant influences on the life and practice of the congregation, some basic traditions were steadfastly maintained. At the meeting of the Southwest Conference of the

Pittsburgh Synod at First Church on April 22, 1920, "the Church officers prepared the altar for Communion in the regular way, filling the goblets and tankard with wine in the manner always customary with this church."[178] (Despite the influenza epidemic, individual glasses had not yet been introduced.) The President of the Conference immediately before the beginning of the Service required the removal of the wine from the vessels and the substitution of grape juice "a supply of which was produced by him." Only one of the church officers was present and protested the act, but nevertheless submitted to the action of the president "to avoid an unseemly disturbance." The church council in response to this unauthorized and presumptuous action expressed its displeasure in a forceful resolution unanimously adopted:

"First—This congregation in the exercise of its right of judgment has never used anything but wine in its celebrations of the Lord's Supper,

Second—If the rules of the Southwest Conference require that Grape juice be used in its Communion Service, it surely cannot be unaware of the fact that such is by no means the general custom of the Church.

Third—Common courtesy required that the consent of the Church Council should be obtained before undertaking to set aside a practice that this Congregation has followed and honored for more than eighty years.

Fourth—The Church Council expresses its strong disapproval of the discourtesy referred to and desires to place itself on record in order that no repetition thereof may ever be permitted."

The role of the pastor of the parish in the surprise exchange of elements is unrecorded.

At the December 6, 1920 meeting of the council William Steinmeyer presented to the church a suitcase "for use in carrying the Communion vessels." The purpose is unclear unless the sacred vessels were not kept in the church but in the home of those appointed as their stewards. At the April meeting, the Elders were "unanimously delegated custodians of the Sacred Vessels to be taken care of as they deem proper."

The matter of the sale and re-location of the church surfaced again in a decision made in December and then rescinded in January 1921 to cancel the contract with the Commonwealth Trust Company regarding the option for sale of the church property. In his report to the congregation in January 1921, Dr. MacLaughlin "laid stress on the serious questions confronting us as a downtown church and stated that he felt that the report of the Treasurer reflected the limit of our financial capacity and to his mind we are fast approaching 'the crossing of two roads' which will soon require a decision as to which road we will follow;--viz. either to undertake community work, if we remain downtown, or to move our Church into a residential district. He recommended that a commission be appointed consisting of the chairman and two members of the church council and each of the organizations of our Congregation to seriously consider this question and to make recommendations." Undertaking "community work" was apparently understood to be something other than the basic work of the Church. There is, moreover, a whiff of condescension in the phrase.

In July, 1921 a daily vacation Bible school was conducted. Its success "passed all expectation, having enrolled 162 including Americans, White and Negro, Italians, Syrians, and Jews, the Italians numbering 111. "Considerable discussion was held as to the advisability of having Rev. [Fortunato] Scarpetti, our Italian Missionary Supt. take up the question of establishing an Italian Mission." It is an indication of the narrow outlook of the congregation at that time that, although white and black were included, the name "Americans" was not understood to include Italians, Syrians, and Jews. There was a large Italian population on the Lower Hill to the east of the church; the Italian Roman Catholic Church, now demolished, was directly in front of Epiphany Church. There was also a sizeable Jewish population with many synagogues; the last one was demolished in 2008 to make room for the Consol Energy Center, the new arena.

The pastor's report to the congregation in January 1922 noted "a net loss in membership for the year owing to the extraordinary number of deaths."

At the congregational meeting on February 14, 1922 James A. Armor reported that he had visited all downtown churches at both morning and evening services, making a study of the attendance and the different methods adopted to meet the downtown problem. "His report caused many favorable comments." A committee of three was appointed to study "the downtown problem and to offer recommendations for a solution of same, considering financial or any other subjects."

Unrest with the management of the choir and music of the congregation continued. In October 1922 a description of the responsibilities of the Congregational Music Committee was approved. The committee had broad powers. It was a committee of three elected annually at the yearly congregational meeting. Its duty was "to confer and co-operate with the Choir Director in the selection of singers, hymnal music, anthems, and all other matters pertaining to the musical service of the Church and Sunday School, and to submit to the Choir Director such suggestions and instructions which it deems advisable or necessary for the proper and satisfactory conduct of the service." For his part, the choir director, appointed annually by the church council, was to do what he was told. "It shall be his duty to confer and co-operate with the Congregational Music Committee in the selection of new singers, hymnal music, anthems, and all other matters pertaining to the musical service of the Church and Sunday School and to accept and execute any suggestions or instructions submitted by that Committee."

March 5 the committee reported to the council that it had "experienced considerable difficulty owing to the fact that Mr. Benbow failed to carry out its recommendations. The Committee recommended that Mr. Benbow be placed on probation for a short period." After five deacons met to discuss "the unfortunate physical condition of Mr. Benbow," it was decided to grant him an immediate leave of absence, "his salary to continue until Council determines otherwise." He was paid through April 30, 1924. At the April 2, 1923, meeting of the council, G. Logan McIlvaney, organist since 1917, was appointed both organist and choir director. He was to serve First Church for fifty-four years, until September 1971.

The pastor reported at the annual congregational meeting on January 15, 1923, "great activity on the various organizations and a net gain in membership for the year."

On the 3rd of August 1923, the twenty-ninth President of the United States, Warren Gamaliel Harding, died in San Francisco. His successor, Calvin Coolidge recommended that people gather in the places of worship on Friday, August 10th. Dr. MacLaughlin was out of the city on his vacation. In his absence, the service at the First Church was planned and conducted by the Reverend O. Frederick Nolde,[179] who was conducting the daily vacation Bible school for the congregation that summer.

The importance of the services of worship in the life of the First Church was slowly making itself understood. September 4, 1923, the pastor was authorized to advertise the evening services for the last three months of the year, the cost not to exceed six dollars per week. On the motion of Albert W. Smith, the pastor was authorized to appoint a committee of three to consider the advisability of having noon-day services once a week.

A month later the committee reported that arrangements had been made for a service on each of the last twelve Wednesdays of the year, the service on October 10 to be conducted by Dr. MacLaughlin and the following eleven by six Lutheran pastors and five clergymen from other denominations. The services were from 12:15 to 12:45. "These services proved so successful that it was arranged to continue them with the addition of nine services terminating Feb. 27, 1924. Leading preachers of seven different denominations kindly gave their services without compensation": nine Lutheran, three Methodist, two Baptist, two Episcopalian, two Presbyterian, two United Presbyterian, and one Christian (Disciples of Christ). A special hymn booklet was produced containing twenty-six "old familiar hymns to be sung to old familiar tunes." The weather, except for the last service, was extremely inclement; nonetheless the attendance was remarkably good, averaging approximately 145, the highest being 275. The Ladies Sewing Society provided a cafeteria lunch in the basement after each service.

The value of weekday services at noon for those who work downtown was commending itself to some members of the congregation as an important aspect of its emerging ministry. William Siebert suggested a service at noon on Ascension Day and suggested that the president of the synod, Dr. Ellis Burgess be the preacher. Dr. MacLaughlin sought to make the arrangements, but because Dr. Burgess was not available, the service was not held. It apparently did not occur to the pastor that it would be a good idea for him to preside at the service himself. Commitment to the observance of all the principal festivals of the Church year had not yet established itself in the mind of the congregation.

A small table for the rear of the church was authorized in June, 1923. The mahogany table that remains there to this day, the "ushers' table," was promptly donated by John C. Kohne.

Dr. MacLaughlin in his annual report for the year 1923 said that "the year was the most successful for a number of years from various viewpoints. There was a net gain in membership of 32, 40 accessions, 8 baptisms, 5 deaths and 3 dismissals. The finances showed a marked improvement in that receipts exceeded disbursements and $7700.00 had been paid during the year on Church Debt. The Daily Vacation Bible School conducted by [the] Rev. [O. Fred] Nolde and a number of our members for the third year was very successful. The Boy Scouts consisting of Italian boys conducted by Charles G. Smith for two years has been very successful. The Wednesday noon-day interdenominational services conducted in this church since October have been well attended and are becoming very popular. The Christmas and Easter services were unique, owing to the large number of Italian children in attendance as a result of the Daily Vacation Bible School. Special mention was made of the visit of Rev. F. C. Coleman our Missionary to India accompanied by his wife and three children."

The commission entrusted with dealing with the downtown problem made a series of recommendations: that every effort be made to increase the membership by Easter, that prayer circles be formed, that an assistant pastor be engaged, and that the commission be continued to meet quarterly. At their meeting on March 3, 1924, the church council, while concurring with the reasons the commission outlined for the addition of an assistant pastor, the proposal was deemed not financially feasible, but "the matter was held over for consideration at a future date."

An interesting proposal was received May 5, 1924, but it was quickly dismissed. "A request was received signed by 23 Lutherans, in which they asked our opinion as to leasing the portion of our property on which our chapel stands to be used for a five or six story office building for the general work of the Lutheran Church, part of which could be used for our Sunday School, and on motion of Mr. Steinmeyer the secretary was instructed to reply that it is the sense of the Council that it would be inexpedient for us to consider such a proposition." William Steinmeyer seemed committed to moving the church out of downtown. (At the October 1924 council meeting "Mr. Hamilton reported that the Infant Class of the Sunday School should have more sanitary quarters than its present location in the Basement.")

Nonetheless, the church council continued the careful maintenance of the building. William Siebert presented two sketches showing suggested designs "for redecorating the walls in the auditorium" (that is, the nave). The council agreed that it was imperative that the improvement be made, and contracts were let for redecorating the chapel and nave ($1300), making necessary changes in plumbing ($1400), installing new carpet in the church ($3000), and redecorating the small rooms ($600). The improvements were completed during the summer of 1924, but some unforeseen conditions "such as screens and woodwork connected with [the] large art windows were rotting" would require an additional outlay of between $1500 and $2000. The additional work was done. A special collection was taken on the first Sunday in October toward the expense of repairing the building.

Samuel L. Hamilton, at the June 2, 1924, meeting called the attention of the council to an editorial in the June issue of the *Lutheran Monthly*, the official organ of the Pittsburgh Synod, "in which the editor injected politics." The secretary was unanimously instructed to protest the use of the church papers for political purposes and to demand "a complete retraction in the columns of the *Lutheran Monthly* at an early date." At the October meeting, no reply having been received, the secretary was instructed to write to the president of the synod "for information as to what action has been taken or what action might be taken to have our demand for a complete retraction by the editor of the Lutheran Monthly of an offensive political editorial in the June issue." In November correspondence was read reporting that both the committee on the Lutheran Monthly and the executive committee of the synod ("meeting in our Church") dispensed with the protest "as not of sufficient worth to merit a retraction." The council responded with a letter to the president of the synod, Dr. Ellis Burgess, "expressing our unanimous dissatisfaction at the treatment received at the hands of the Executive Committee of the Pittsburgh Synod, as we consider our complaint a just one and worthy of more consideration than being filed away."

Charles MacLaughlin resigned his pastorate in a brief letter to the church council dated January 2, 1925.

"Brethren:--

In order to accept a call to the Evangelical Lutheran Church in Atlanta, Ga., I herewith tender my resignation as Pastor of the Church, to become effective March 1—1925. Praying that God's richest blessing may ever abide with you and yours,

Very sincerely,

Charles P. MacLaughlin"

The extreme brevity is striking, as is the tone of the council's response. "Inasmuch as the Pastor states that it is his desire to accept a call to the Church in Atlanta, Ga., it is the sense of Council that it cannot do otherwise than receive the Pastor's letter and refer it to the Congregation at its annual meeting to be held January 19—1925 with recommendation that the resignation be accepted." The council's recommendation was ratified 30 to 15. Equally curious is that Dr. MacLaughlin does not provide the proper name of the church to which he was called as pastor; it was the Church of the Redeemer.

In Atlanta, Dr. MacLaughlin found more fertile ground in which to work. He was the fourth pastor of the Church of the Redeemer, founded in 1903, and it was the beginning of an era of growth. During 1926 and 1927 the congregation's vesper services were broadcast over WSB radio once a month, anticipating the radio ministry that was soon to begin in the First Church Pittsburgh. The confirmed membership was 494; the pastor led a successful debt reduction campaign that paid off the mortgage. Pastor MacLaughlin died suddenly November 13, 1928.

The resignation facilitated a proposal made by William Siebert in April 1923, that the parsonage be sold and a smaller one be purchased with a view to making the parsonage fund self-sustaining. The council agreed to the sale "if a reasonable price can be obtained." In January 1925 a definite offer of $21,000 was received from a widow, Helen M. Palmer. Negotiations resulted in an agreed upon sale price of $23,000. The congregation meeting on February 22, 1925, approved the sale.

Because of the interim, the council in April 1925, decided (5 to 3 with one not voting) to dispense with the Daily Vacation Bible School for the coming summer. In May, however, the Sunday School asked and received permission to conduct the vacation Bible school as in the past. Once again, it was the Sunday School that had a clearer sense of mission to the surrounding area than the church council.

The pulpit committee had selected a candidate, the Reverend Orlando Ingoldstad, Ph.D., Dean of the Chicago Lutheran Seminary to be the next pastor of the First Church. July 19 his name was presented to the congregation who voted to extend a call, 58 for and 20 against. Dr. Ingoldstad declined the call.

September 5 the committee tried again. It presented to the council the name of the Reverend Henry Horneman Bagger, pastor of First Lutheran Church of Butler, Pennsylvania. He had the support of the president of the synod. The council secretary, Albert W. Smith, spoke highly of him. The council, however, was unable to agree and postponed action. At a special meeting on September 12 Dr. Burgess, the president of the synod, was present. "Some objections" to Pastor Bagger had been raised since the last meeting. The venerable Henry E. Jacobs, Dean of the Philadelphia Seminary, had sent a letter strongly recommending him. Samuel Hamilton, who was absent, had asked the secretary to announce that he now wanted to change his vote. Others were not satisfied, and as a result of the lack of agreement, Dr. Burgess withdrew Henry Bagger's name. (Dr. Bagger went on to succeed Dr. Burgess as president of the Pittsburgh Synod, 1930-1940, and then to become pastor of Holy Trinity Church in Lancaster for twelve years and then president of the Philadelphia Seminary.) Frustrated in its efforts, the Pulpit Committee on October 5 offered its resignation and asked to be discharged. A new committee of three was appointed, later enlarged by two more members. The committee was asked to confer with the superintendent of the Sunday School "to decide a date and arrange for a special Congregational prayer meeting for the purpose of asking for Divine guidance in selecting a Pastor."

Unhappy tensions were evident. November 2 William Steinmeyer, disappointed perhaps that his plan to re-locate the church was not affirmed, sent a letter of resignation from the council. He began his service as a Deacon in 1902 and as an Elder from 1908 to 1925. The council adopted a statement thanking him for his long and dedicated service.

The new pulpit committee on January 4, 1926 recommended that the name of the Reverend Adam J. Holl, D.D., pastor of First

Lutheran Church in Columbus, Ohio be presented to the congregation at its meeting January 18. The council unanimously agreed and set the salary at $5000 plus parsonage. The congregation voted unanimously to extend the call.

The letter of call was sent on January 19. On February 2 Dr. Holl sent the secretary a letter indicating that he had presented his resignation to his congregation in Columbus. They had made "a united appeal" that he remain with them, but, he wrote, "after earnest prayer, I see my duty, and will come to you in the strength of the Lord to give the best years of my life to a difficult task, but which, under God's blessing and guidance, will indeed be the *First Lutheran Church* not only in name but in reality." He announced

A. J. Holl

that he would begin his ministry at the First Church on Sunday March 21, 1926, but would return to Columbus the following Sunday, which was Palm Sunday, to confirm the class that he had been preparing for confirmation. "We will be with you during Holy Week and for Easter Sunday, when we shall commune together and arise unto newness of life." Ten days later he sent his official acceptance of the call. It was a promising beginning of a pastorate that would last until 1947, the longest in the history of the parish up to that time.

Adam J. Holl[180] was born in New Knoxville, Ohio in 1883. His parents were German immigrants who had come to the rural village in Ohio because some of their relatives from Germany had settled there. Everyone in the village spoke German; Pastor Holl's parents never learned in their more than eighty years to speak English. His father was the village cobbler. When their son was five years old, the parents returned to Germany for several years, and there the son began his formal schooling in a Roman Catholic parochial school. (His mother was Roman Catholic.) When after several years the family returned to Ohio there was no Catholic church, so the small family of three began attending the German Reformed church. A. J. Holl graduated from Northern Ohio University and the Chicago Lutheran Seminary. He was ordained in 1908 and received the Doctor of Divinity degree from Wittenberg University in 1926. He married Lauretta Fisher.

The first six months of his ministry in Pittsburgh were difficult, he told an interviewer from the Pittsburgh Press, July 14, 1945. "If I could have got out, I never would have come back. Now I wouldn't exchange it for any church in the Synod."

During the pastorate of his predecessor, Dr. Holl observed, "the Church began to dwindle. Year after year the Council had to go to the bank to borrow money until they had borrowed $24,000. Shortly before I came an offering was made to wipe out that indebtedness. Went to Chicago with the intention of having a talk about First Church with Dr. MacLaughlin. Dr. Gehr was a member of the Board and Dr. MacLaughlin and Dr. Gehr were talking. I walked up to them and Dr. MacLaughlin said, 'We have just been talking about it.' He was a great big man and he put his big hand on my shoulder and he said, 'Well, boy, I won't say that it can't be done, but I couldn't do it.' Another man said, 'I have told the First Church what they must do if they want to live. Tear down the Church and put up an office building. That's the only way."[181]

Nonetheless, he came to a church whose financial situation was at long last on more secure ground. The Church Debt Committee had announced at the annual congregational meeting on January 18 "that a special effort had been made to cancel the debt by this time and that the effort had been largely successful, as subscriptions have been received leaving only about 1,500 to raise, making a reduction of 20,000 in the three years of the campaign." A vote of thanks was extended to the committee "for this wonderful accomplishment."

His installation as pastor was on April 18th with the president of the synod presiding. A parsonage was rented for the new pastor at 1415[182] North Euclid Avenue at $135 per month.

Twenty-six people, an unusually large number, became members of the First Church on Whitsunday 1926. Fears of a declining membership subsided. William Siebert at the June 7 meeting of the council reported that "in anticipating the needs of a growing congregation it was deemed advisable to increase the size of the rooms being constructed in the basement." Dr. Holl called a special meeting of the church council to suggest that a pastor's secretary be employed, and it was unanimously agreed that Mary Elizabeth Hamilton be engaged at a salary of $100 per month beginning September 1, 1926. The pastor reported on September 13 that "he was well pleased with the services of his new secretary." Among her duties was to serve as the financial secretary of the parish. She was to continue her service until August 1972—forty-six years.

The commitment to the present location of the church was being strengthened. The trustees were authorized to sandblast the exterior of the church on three sides (Grant Street, Strawberry Way, and Garland Way; the fourth side was made of brick and was inaccessible and unseen). The smoke of the mills of Pittsburgh had taken its toll and darkened the sandstone. Even more explicitly, the long-time member of the church council John Kaercher (who had died July 29, 1926 and whose mausoleum may be seen in Allegheny Cemetery) in his will left $10,000 to the First Church as an endowment fund "so long as said Church remains in its present location on Grant Street."

October 17, 1926 "the chief service" began at 11 a.m. instead of 10:45 to give more time for Sunday school instruction.

Not everything was going smoothly. Unhappiness with the music of the church continued. The November 1, 1926 minutes report, "Dissatisfaction was expressed at the services of some of the members of the choir," and "the music committee was unanimously authorized to make any changes in the personnel of the choir and choir director that it may deem necessary." A new soprano, contralto, and tenor were hired beginning January 1, 1927. In May 1932 some members of the congregation had complained because unfamiliar music was being used, and G. Logan McElvany was instructed "to use more familiar tunes for the congregational singing." At the same meeting it was observed that "the organ music during the prayer at the altar be very soft." The "prayer at the altar" was presumably the General Prayer of intercession.[183]

A "magnificent electric cross" (so described in the minutes of January 3, 1927) visible in contemporary photographs of the exterior of the church, extending over Grant Street from the top center of the building, was given to the church by William Siebert in memory of his mother, Mary Zimmerman Siebert. The cross

The church with the electric cross

was dedicated at the Sunday School service on Christmas Eve, 1926. The electric cross, it may be observed nearly a century later, disfigured, cheapened, and detracted from the elegant exterior of the church. It was an unfortunate addition, despite its intended purpose. (It was removed in April 1949.)

In his report to the congregation on January 17, 1927, Dr. Holl noted that the widening of Grant Street had increased the valuation of the church property. The project also involved the change from direct to alternating electric current. He recommended that the Preparatory Service be moved from the Friday night preceding the celebration of Holy Communion to Sunday morning. This change was in line with the emerging practice of the Lutheran Church in America and permitted by a rubric in the *Common Service Book*: "When the Confessional Service immediately precedes The Service, the order shall begin with the words: In the Name of the Father, and of the Son, and of the Holy Ghost. Amen. Then shall follow: The Exhortation, the Confession, the Absolution, and the New Testament Benediction. The Service shall begin with the Introit for the Day."[184]

The second change he proposed was more radical, although again not uncommon in emerging Lutheran practice: "that we adopt the individual Communion Service [i.e. individual glasses], accepting the offer made to the Pastor by a family long connected with First Church to present the service in the form of a memorial to the Congregation." The family was Mr. and Mrs. John C. Kohne, who gave the individual service in memory of their parents. "The Individual Communion Cup" was unanimously approved, fortunately with the provision, "retaining the Common Cup for those who wished to use it."(The use of individual cups had been roundly condemned by a son of the parish, G. H. Gerberding [1847-1927], professor at Chicago Seminary and later at Northwestern Lutheran Seminary, in his book on pastoral practice: "The individual cup has never seriously commended itself among true Lutherans. Thinking people are not affected by the senseless microbe scare. . . . The individual cup is unhistorical and unscriptural. It militates against the idea of a communion."[185])

April 4, 1927 Dr. Holl recommended that Holy Communion be "held" on Good Friday night as well as on Easter morning. Good Friday communion was not uncommon in Lutheran areas that had come under Reformed influence with their emphasis on the memorial aspect of the sacrament. No mention was made of far more traditional celebration of the sacrament on the day of its institution, Maundy Thursday.

Another Reformed influence from Pastor Holl's pre-Lutheran days was his frequent choice of the hymn "Faith of our fathers" at the devotions at the beginning of the annual congregational meeting. That hymn, especially ironic remembering A. J. Holl's Roman Catholic childhood, was originally a hymn for the return of England to the Roman Catholic faith,[186] but it was unaccountably beloved by churches in the Calvinist tradition. It was not included in a Lutheran book until the *Service Book and Hymnal* of 1958. Pastor Holl's other favorite hymn for the congregational meeting was the children's hymn "I love to tell the story," not in the *Common Service Book* but included in its accompanying *Parish School Hymnal* of 1926.

A praiseworthy departure from past practice was the decision to hold Sunday morning services throughout the summer, not closing the church as had been the custom in August, and that the council would meet in July and also in August. (It was nonetheless still necessary to clean the church during the month of August; Pittsburgh was a smoky city.)

April 25, 1927, a reception was held in honor of Dr. Holl's first anniversary as pastor. He "was presented with a $2000 Chandler car in appreciation of his splendid work."[187]

The strength of the church was increasing in many ways. The growth in membership was noteworthy. There were 146 scholars in the Sunday School; the attendance Easter morning was 410; 27 new members were received at the service, 15 more were received on Pentecost. During 1927 seventy-five new members were added to the rolls; fifty-three were received at Easter 1928. The pastor was directed by the council to write a letter of welcome to each of the new members. The synod recognized the importance of the downtown parish, the president, Dr. Burgess, taking the services on August 8, during the pastor's vacation. The organ was rehabilitated, underscoring the commitment of the congregation to remain downtown. It was dedicated on Sunday February 28, 1928 by Dr. Burgess, the president of the synod.

The idea of broadcasting the services of the First Church was considered and approved. The Lutheran Inner Mission Society had begun a broadcast a few months before. The congregation itself bore the cost of "installing broadcasting apparatus in the church and special wire to station WJAS" at a cost of $2715. Broadcasting of the evening services every Sunday beginning at 7:45 began on January 9, 1928. It was the first such broadcasting in the city and one of the first in the nation. It was so well received that the Wednesday noon services during Lent and the Good Friday noon service were broadcast also. In November 1928 the time of Vespers was changed from 8 p.m. to 7:30 "to avail ourselves of the extra time allotted us by WJAS." The broadcast, originally Sunday evenings, was later moved to Sunday mornings for an hour. Toward the end of Dr. Holl's pastorate, network commitments forced that station to reduce the religious program to a half hour. In twenty-five years, the program was off the air only three times: twice because of weather and once because of a power failure. All the broadcasts were direct from First Church.

At the 1928 congregational meeting the advisability of celebrating Holy Communion ("holding communion" was the language of the minutes) on week nights "and possibly on Sunday other than Easter" was discussed. A new sense of mission was arising. The work of the parish was increasing, and the need of a new statistical secretary was considered, to free Mary Elizabeth Hamilton "to make personal calls and do deaconess work." Although the proposal was not approved by the congregation, the recognition of the increasing work is noteworthy. In April the iron fence in front of the church on Grant Street was removed, making the building more welcoming.

A suitable apartment for the pastor was rented at Cathedral Mansions. (April 2, 1928)

A. W. Smith suggested that C. F. Schaefer, who was on the suspension list for a number of years because of his misappropriation of church funds be visited and interviewed by a committee appointed by the pastor. He "expressed contrition for his misdemeanors." His suspension from membership was removed October 1, 1928, and he again became a communicant.

The matter of the location of the church was not yet entirely settled. At the conclusion of the council meeting October 1, 1928, William Siebert suggested "that in view of our increasing congregation and particularly the Sunday School and the noise from traffic of Grant Street, council might properly have in mind a new church building."

As of December 1, 1929 pew rents were abolished, but the council was authorized to assign seats to the membership "based on the present pew holdings." The practice of assigning seats of course led to awkward encounters. In May 1930, "Dr. Rigg reported that everything was going smoothly with the exception of occasional difficulties due to strangers occupying the pews of some of the older members." It was not a welcoming practice, especially for a downtown church that expects visitors.

Grace Church in the Birmingham section of the South Side, founded by William Passavant, had fallen on hard times, its members fled the smoke of the city, and the church closed in 1929. When the congregation disbanded, a memorial plaque honoring those who served in World War I was given to its mother, First Church, and now hangs in the lower hallway.

The calling of an assistant pastor was authorized. After a protracted series of discussions and possible models, a call was extended to the Reverend Otto Ebert. After several conversations, he declined the call in June 1929.

Another model was tried. Dr. Holl, May 9, 1929, had presented to the church council a number of plans for calling an assistant. One of them observed, "Another congregation, known as a downtown congregation, which has had a most unusual growth, is Messiah Lutheran Church, Philadelphia, whose pastor is Dr. Stover. This congregation, too, has a large corps of secretaries, plus an assistant pastor, who is elected for one year only. Each year the congregation calls a senior from the graduating class of the Seminary to this position. Trinity Church, N.S., served by Dr. Turkle, are about to adopt this same plan. A visit to Dr. Stover's congregation for the purpose of studying its method of work would doubtless be helpful, inasmuch as it would enable us to profit by their experience of several years of very successful church work."

Messiah Church was not exactly downtown (not a description used in Philadelphia which speaks of "center city"). It was an urban church in a residential section of North Philadelphia, at 16th and Jefferson Streets. Its pastor, Ross Harrison Stover (1888-1974), "that sunny man of God,"[188] had made a name for himself by downplaying the liturgy, emulating the revival style of some Protestant churches, and assembling 20,000 people at Temple University Stadium for Easter sunrise services. The growing congregation moved from a changing neighborhood and erected a new building in a more prominent location on Roosevelt Boulevard at Broad Street in North Philadelphia. His was a ministry built on his cheerful personality, and when he retired the congregation began its decline. It no longer exists.

The one-year assistant pastor plan commended itself to the First Church, and Edward K. Rogers, upon his graduation from Philadelphia Seminary in 1930 became assistant pastor of First Church at a salary of $1800. Because of continuing financial deficits, the office of assistant pastor was discontinued after June 1, 1931. Indeed it is to be noted that despite the remarkable and steady numerical growth of the membership in these years of the great depression following the stock market crash of 1929, deficits remained a fact of life for the congregation as they had been throughout its history.

The pastorate that had begun in such discouraging conditions now was beginning to show promise and hope and was being noticed. Dr. Holl reports that "a fine compliment" was paid in his third year at the First Church. The "Executive Secretary [Dr. Corbe] came to Pittsburgh for a meeting of the Board, and one of the local ministers met him at the [Pennsylvania Railroad] Station [at Grant Street and Liberty Avenue] and were going to the Wm. Penn and they passed the Church. 'Well, we all predicted failure,'" the local pastor remarked with some surprise. Dr. Corbe told Dr. Holl who regarded it as "the finest compliment." "I am very humble in this," he added. "The work at the beginning was mighty discouraging. . . . We haven't done it, but God, through us, has been able to do something in a field that was so discouraging that some men would not accept the call."[189]

In April 1930, "Dr. Holl suggested an open chapel every day. Considerable discussion was had on this point, none of which, however, led to any final agreement." Nonetheless, the church was opened from 11 to 2 each day for prayer and meditation.

Departures from the best liturgical traditions of the Church continued. At the pastor's suggestion new members were received at the Good Friday evening service. At the May 1930 meeting of the council, William Siebert "asked for an expression regarding the class of music being furnished, and, after considerable discussion, it seemed to be the consensus of opinion that the simpler type of music should predominate." The issue was raised in connection with the expense of buying new music. It "was felt that our present library with minor additions would be sufficient to take care of the needs of the choir."

There was discussion at the May 1930 meeting of the disruption in the Easter Communion service caused by "so many people leaving before the services were over." The solution that was suggested was to discontinue the celebration of Holy Communion on Easter Day. Action was postponed until the following February when it was "thought advisable to hold the services as usual" and that "some mention of this be made in the Church bulletin." In 1932, however, Holy Communion was celebrated on Maundy Thursday and Good Friday evenings and at a special service at 9 a.m. on Easter Day. "No Communion will be held at the chief service except for the Confirmation class."

Dr. Holl's vacation period in the summer of 1930 was extended to six weeks to allow him a trip to Europe. Upon his return he gave a special series of sermons: (1) The Passion Play: is it being commercialized? Pro-Catholic? Anti-Jewish? The greatest thrill in ten years; (2) Meeting a friend in Paris; (3) Over the battlefields of France by air; (4) The Kaiser and the German people; (5) Rome and a new appreciation of Luther; (6) An hour in an upper room in Venice. Special advertising in the newspapers announced the series.

A revised constitution, after long and careful work, was approved by the congregation at a special meeting May 5, 1932.

The congregation was coming to understand ever more clearly that its mission was to the downtown community. Dr. Holl in his seventh annual report to the congregation, January 16, 1933, noted the coming centennial of the founding of the congregation. He said, "It would be interesting to know just how many of the large and thriving commercial organizations, operating in Pittsburgh 96 years ago, are still functioning today. At the time First Church was organized, Pittsburgh had a population of about 35,000, which has since increased to its present population of 669,817. Great changes have taken place in our neighborhood, and most of our then near-by sister congregations have long since moved into residential districts. But First Church still stands, holding aloft the Cross of Christ, although surrounded by tall office buildings, banks, department stores, and hotels. The history of the organization, growth, and development of First Church is a most timely example of what can be done by members who have a firm and living faith in the sure and certain promises of God."

Dr. Holl received permission from the council to "hold Ascension Day services on May 25, 1933, at noon, bringing out the thought of the importance of that event and the recognition we should give it."

A handrail was installed on the steep steps to the north narthex during the summer of 1933.

At the meeting of the church council November 6, 1933, Dr. Holl announced his plan to select a group of about twenty-five members of the congregation each week, taking their names alphabetically from the church roll, and offer prayer at noon each day for that group and on Friday evening of each week these members were to meet with him at the Church "for a heart-to-heart spiritual talk of about an hour." The first of these meetings was held on Friday, November 17. In 1934 the plan was altered so that the pastor would conduct monthly meetings on the third Friday of each month, so that about seventy-five people would be in attendance.

To counter the declining attendance at the Wednesday evening prayer services, Dr. Holl in September 1935 suggested a new plan to be called "First Church Fellowship Circles." He divided the congregation into seventeen circles covering seventeen Wednesday evenings, fifteen to forty-five members at each meeting. The purpose was to afford opportunity to learn about sickness, loss of interest, reasons for absence, prospective members. The meetings began October 2 and concluded February 19.

In October 1935 the Sunday School reported an attendance on September 29, Rally Day, of 253, the largest on any one Sunday in the past ten years. The enrollment was 214. Moreover, a class for newly-married couples was begun.

In March 1936 a flood devastated much of downtown Pittsburgh. The waters crested on March 18. First Church was the only house of worship in the golden triangle to be left untouched by the flood waters. A Red Cross unit was set up in the church to feed the Works Progress Authority workers who were cleaning up the city streets.

January 15, 1937 was the one hundredth anniversary of the founding of the First Lutheran Church in Pittsburgh. A centennial booklet was prepared and a full series of services was scheduled. Sunday January 3, 1937 at the 11 a.m. service Dr. Holl issued "A Call to the Centennial"; Vespers was sung as usual at 8 p.m. Sunday January 10 the preacher in the morning was the only living former pastor, the Reverend Dr. George Gongaware from St. John's Church, Charleston, South Carolina; the preacher in the evening was the President of the Pittsburgh Synod, the Reverend Dr. Henry H. Bagger (who had not been found acceptable as a pastor of First Church in the search that settled on Dr. Holl); Monday, January 11 at 8 p.m. greetings were received from local Lutheran churches by pastors and laypeople; Tuesday January 12 at 8 p.m. the renowned preacher Oscar Blackwelder, D.D. of Washington, D.C. presented "A Message to the Organizations of the Church"; Wednesday January 13 at 8 p.m. the Reverend Dr. F. W. Otterbein of Chicago delivered "A Message from the Church at Large"; Thursday January 14 at 8 p.m. a "message through music" was presented by the choir and guest singers and Dr. Holl spoke of "Worthy Achievements of Our Church"; Friday, January 15 at 6 p.m. there was a congregational birthday dinner and at 8 p.m. a pageant depicting the first council meeting and the one

The church interior in 1937

hundredth congregational meeting. Dr. Holl in his report encouraged the congregation, "The God of our fathers is our God; He heard their prayers; He will hear ours. He blessed their labors; He will bless ours. The future is assured. Looking back from where we stand tonight across the years so rich in faith and good works, who can have any doubt about a glorious future. Onward, brethren, young and old, in the Name of Christ. Onward in faith, in prayer, in service."

The chapel interior in 1937

The congregation made a pilgrimage to Father Heyer's grave in Somerset and laid a wreath at his monument there. The photographs of the event are undated, but it was apparently on Sunday afternoon, May 25, 1941. There is in the parish archives an outline of a Memorial Service for Father Heyer by Members of First English Evangelical Lutheran Church and Sunday School, held on that date. The service began with the invocation, "In the Name of the Father, and of the Son, and of the Holy Ghost. Amen." The versicle, "Blessed are the dead which die in the Lord from henceforth;" and the response, "Yea, saith the Spirit, that they may rest from their labors and their works do follow them." The hymn

"Faith of our fathers" was sung, Revelation 7:9-17 was read, a prayer was offered, the hymn "For all the saints who from their labors rest," an address, "Father Heyer," by Dr. Holl, the placing of a wreath by the superintendent of the Sunday School, A. August Smith, taps, the Lord's Prayer, and the benediction.

Walden Holl, son of the pastor, was ordained May 19, 1937 by the Ohio Synod. He preached at First Church on Rally Day,

Pilgrimage to Father Heyer's grave

September 26. (In the language of the minutes, he "occupied the pulpit.")

Automobiles were becoming the preferred means of transportation. The council minutes for November 1, 1937 report, "Mr. Johnson has been in touch with the management of the parking lot on Grant Street near the church, concerning the use of the lot by our members Sunday mornings and evenings." He was "unable to arrive at a satisfactory agreement with the management of the near-by Eppy Parking Lot. However, through the kindness of Mr. N. F. Arble, one of the church members, the parking lot at Strawberry Way and Telegraph Square has been procured for the free use of our members for Sunday morning and evening alike."

Thomas Sheafer of the finance committee in January 1938 presented a plan to liquidate the church debt by November 1938, the fiftieth anniversary of the dedication of the church. "Paper coin strips" for pennies, nickels, and dimes" were distributed to the membership along with envelopes for this purpose. The slogan "Let's go the whole way" was adopted for the campaign. The idea was to collect a mile of pennies, equal to $844.80, a mile of nickels yielding $3696, and a mile of dimes producing $14,416.80. This would not only liquidate the debt but pay a year's interest besides. The congregation was not taken with the idea, and by June the "Penny a Mile" chart was removed from the chapel. Nothing further is heard of the plan. Finances remained a continuing problem.

In 1938 the Christmas Eve candlelight service was introduced.[190]

During January and February Dr. Holl, who was ill, was in Florida. He returned March 6, 1939.

External forces governed the practice of the church. June 5, 1939 Dr. Holl "announced a curtailment in our radio time on Sunday morning starting next week. Due to arrangements made by station WJAS with the Columbia Broadcasting Co., our time will be from 11:30 until noon. Dr. Holl will arrange our service accordingly to agree with the new radio time allotment." At the congregational meeting January 20, 1941, "Following some discussion as to the order of service which would permit the number by the choir to be broadcast, it was regularly moved, seconded and carried that the matter of re-arranging our order of service be left to the Church Vestry."

September 5, 1939 "Dr. Holl opened the meeting [of the church council] with a very fervent prayer, particularly because of world conditions, war having been declared in Europe just a few days ago." The Second World War had begun, and the United States was to be drawn into it. At the December meeting his prayer especially asked "that Finland be spared in the conflict raging in Europe." A special offering for the Church of Finland was received after the chief service on February 11, 1940.

The United States entered the war when the Japanese attacked Pearl Harbor, December 7, 1941. The nation was shocked and frightened by the attack. The following January it was reported, "As a precaution against fires started by incendiary bombs dropped in the course of air raids over the city in the present war emergency the trustees have announced that the sexton would be instructed to have bags of sand available for extinguishing such fires."

Cryptic minutes make the reader wish for further details. October 2, 1939 reports "the plan of having ushers to assist at the altar on communion Sunday was successfully used on October 1." Perhaps they gathered the individual communion cups. January 2, 1940 again records, "due to the success of the plan to have ushers stationed at the altar on communion Sundays, the same course will be followed next Sunday.

"Mr. Smith's motion that Mr. Hamilton's suggestion be adopted that the congregation sing the entire recessional hymn was lost on vote." Apparently the choir, which was a quartette, would alone sing the final stanza after they had left the church, perhaps singing from the Sunday school chapel. It was a custom employed elsewhere in certain churches.

Dr. Holl presented a plan for the visitation of the congregation. The membership was divided into small groups, and the members of each group were to be visited by a "key-worker." Each member of the church council was responsible for several key-workers. Reports were to be sent regularly to the church office.

Dr. Holl was sick with what appears to have been a heart attack and away from the church during the months of April and May. The council sent him an encouraging and supportive letter, urging him to get his needed rest. "Our one concern at the moment is to have you returned to that measure of health and strength that will permit your usual zealous work among your flock. Please do not think of us a flock without a shepherd, because we feel the presence of the Good Shepherd in abundant measure. Council, to a man, tonight expressed themselves in such a loyal fashion that we feel free to say the one thought uppermost in their minds is your comfort and peace of mind. You may understand from this their affection and regard for you as Pastor and Friend."

At a special meeting of the council on November 28, 1940, the floor of the south narthex was reported to be "rapidly sinking." Repairs were made by the January meeting which required a "re-flooring" of the narthex. The original tile was removed and lost.

January 11, 1942, W. J. Olson "stated that due to certain circumstances that had arisen and to keep peace and harmony in the Church, he would withdraw his name as a nominee to succeed himself for Church Council membership." The circumstances to which he refers are of course not identified.

The Empire of Japan attacked Pearl Harbor on December 7, 1941, drawing the United States into World War II. At the annual meeting of the congregation a month later, January 19, 1942, O. J. Reckard, D.D.S. "referred to the briefness of Dr. Holl's report, calling attention to the seriousness of the time in which we are passing." At the February 2 meeting of the council, the custom of all kneeling in prayer at the beginning of the meeting is noted. Both the war and the urgency of canceling the church debt of $8500 deepened the expressions of piety during this time. A debt cancellation plan was prepared and "prior to presenting the plan to the congregation we would tell God about it first and ask for his Divine approval. Accordingly all knelt in prayer which was led by Dr. Holl." (March 15, 1942). Payment of the debt, as had been the disappointing history of such efforts in the congregation, proceeded slowly over several years. By October 1943 the debt had been reduced from $8500 to $2600. The debt was finally liquidated in January 1944.

The shadow of war was cast over all the work of the church. Note is made at the annual congregational meeting in January 1943 that the Koppers Building served as an air raid shelter for the congregation during air raid alerts. At the April 5, 1943, meeting of the council, Dr. Holl, whose own son Paul was a flight surgeon, "asked Divine guidance in the work of the evening and in the advancement of His Kingdom in our war-stricken world." The pastor's practice was to meet in his study with each of the "boys" of the church in the armed services of the nation, take them to lunch, and have "a helpful talk with them before their departure," write to them on frequent occasions, and send them bulletins, service books, prayer books, and New Testaments.

February 15, 1943, the congregation joined the Ministerial Association in protesting the Sunday collection of tin cans for the war effort as an interference in the life of the churches.

No air raids having been made on Pittsburgh, the question was asked in May 1944 whether the sand buckets and shovels could be removed from the church nave and the chapel.

During Lent of 1942 the choir director, G. Logan McElvany, had augmented the paid quartette with volunteer singers from the congregation, called "the chorus choir," and because of the success of the effort, received permission to continue the practice.

May 4, 1942, "The question as to why the Nicene Creed had been omitted from our Communion services of late was brought up and Dr. Holl gave a very interesting explanation of the historical background and origin of the Nicene Creed, which originated in the year 325 A.D." The omission probably had to do with the radio broadcasting schedule.

In June 1942 Dr. Holl was given a leave of absence and entered the hospital for a three-week series of tests. July 8, 1942 he left for the Mayo Clinic in Rochester, Minnesota. His "return was uncertain." He returned to the parish at the beginning of September. He was again away from the parish because of illness from the end of January through April 1944. In view of the pastor's recurring health problems, the congregation called the Reverend Wallace E. Fischer of Dravosburg as assistant pastor at a salary of $2400 per year. (He was later to become pastor of historic Trinity Church in Lancaster and a nationally-known clergyman.)

In 1943 confirmation was on Pentecost with first Communion on the following Sunday (Trinity Sunday). Dr. Holl explained to the council that he would examine each confirmand privately rather than conduct the traditional public examination.

All Saints' Sunday was observed November 7, 1943, with "a service in honor of our dead."

Beginning in September 1944 the church was open for prayer and meditation from 9 a.m. until 4 p.m. "with altar uncovered, candelabras lighted, and the vestibule doors open." "Suitable notice" was to be made on the outside of the church.

Opportunities expanded. Also in September 1944 approval was given by the council to a "spiritual clinic" suggested by Dr. Holl. The clinic was conducted by the pastor and the assistant pastor "for those who feel the need of pastoral psychiatry." Hours were in the evening and only by appointment.

Curiously, no mention is made in the minutes of the victory in Europe (V-E Day) or in the Pacific (V-J Day) in April and in August 1945 except that Pastor Fischer in his report for September 1945 reports taking part in "2 V-J Day services." [Victory over Japan] In December 1945 "At the request of Dr. Holl, Mr. Armor read a paper he had written on a partial explanation of the atomic bomb. The paper was well received and provoked considerable discussion." Despite the order, "It was regularly moved, seconded, and carried that the paper be made part of these minutes," the paper is absent. At the annual meeting of the congregation in January 1946, Dr. Holl recommended that the people "stand for a few moments in silent prayer, remembering the families of our parish who have lost loved ones during the year, as well as those whose loved ones have made the supreme sacrifice during the war."

June 19-21, 1945, the Common Service Book Committee of the United Lutheran Church in America held a meeting in the First Church that began work on a common book for Lutherans in North America. The work resulted in the *Service Book and Hymnal* in 1958.

In commemoration of his twentieth year as pastor, the congregation presented Pastor Holl with a 1946 Packard automobile.

July 11, 1946 the Luther League held its annual meeting in the First Church where it had been organized a half-century before.

In September 1946 Pastor Fischer presented his resignation as assistant pastor, effective September 30, with a view to accepting a call to English Lutheran Church, Zelienople.

A month later, Dr. Holl offered his resignation. October 21, 1946, he wrote to the church council, "In recent weeks it has again been necessary to take medical treatment. I am experiencing great difficulty in walking, which is, I am told, closely allied to my former illness, and which may be greatly aggravated unless my activities are curtailed. And while one may hesitate to admit it, age too is beginning to tell. [He was 63.] Therefore, for the best interest of the congregation, which has given me such long, sincere, and loyal cooperation, the time has come, I am convinced, when the Pulpit Committee should be instructed to take the necessary steps looking toward the calling of a pastor, able and vigorous, to take up and continue the work which the Lord has permitted me to serve happily these many years. But, since there is no immediate need for the Pulpit Committee to act hastily, I herewith present my resignation to go into effect, with your permission, May 25, 1947." He explained to the congregation at a meeting called to act upon his resignation, November 17, 1946, that he did not intend to retire but to conclude his ministry as he began, in a country church. March 5, 1947 Dr. Holl announced to the church council that he had accepted a call as pastor of Grace Church, Lakeland, Florida, and would take up the work there June 1. He served one term as president of the Florida Synod of the United Lutheran Church in America, 1949-1950. He retired in 1951 and moved to Keystone Heights and was interim pastor of Our Savior's Church in Gainsville. Dr. Holl died in Keystone Heights, Florida, September 15, 1955.

In December the council had identified two requirements of the next pastor: he was to be between 35 and 40 years of age and have a good radio voice. The President of the Pittsburgh Synod, Dr. H. Reed Shepfer, who was present at the meeting had two names to suggest: Harmon J. McGuire of Elgin, Illinois, and Robert W. Stackel, pastor of Emanuel Church, Rochester, New York.

After a search, Dr. Stackel's name was submitted to the congregation April 27, 1947, and by a vote of 288 to 22 a call was extended to him. He accepted the call May 2.

The focus of the ministry of the First Church had at long last become clear and settled, as Pastor Stackel recognized in his letter of acceptance. "The rich tradition of your more than century old past is an inspiration toward the building of an equally glorious future. The strategic position of First English in downtown Pittsburgh, her opportunity to minister not only to her surroundings but to the whole city, the missionary glow in her membership, and the towering talents which her lay people can lay at the feet of Christ—all of these conspire to set your church apart as a chosen instrument of the Lord for service far beyond the average. Especially did the spirit of prayer among you deeply impress me."

A. J. Holl, D.D.

Robert William Stackel [STAKE-el] was born February 23, 1913 at Rochester, New York. He earned his B.A. at Hamilton College in 1935, and graduated from Philadelphia Seminary in

1938. He served as pastor of St. Paul's in Danville, New York 1938-1943 and Emanuel in Rochester from 1943 until his call to the First Church Pittsburgh in 1947. He was married to Virginia M. Gehr; they had four children. Thiel College awarded him the honorary doctor of divinity degree in the spring of 1951, and afterwards he was regularly referred to as Dr. Stackel.

Robert Stackel

The parsonage at that time was at 370 Parker Drive in Mount Lebanon. In April 1952 the congregation approved the sale of that property and the purchase of a new residence at 435 Royce Avenue, also in Mount Lebanon.

Pastor Stackel began his ministry on Sunday, June 22, 1947. Immediately following "the worship service" (ugly language had infiltrated even the council minutes[191]), he met with the council for the first time as pastor and dealt with the request of the organist, G. Logan McElvany, for a salary that would at least match an offer from Sixth Presbyterian Church because of the health expenses of members of his family. The council unanimously agreed to offer $2400 per year and a new contract beginning July 1, 1947.

The new pastor, taking the distinctiveness of the Lutheran Church seriously, (his 1959 book bore the title *Great Doctrines of Our Faith*[192]), instituted an instruction class for new members, each class to have four hours of instruction, one hour per week. No longer was it the custom of the congregation to receive as members any who sought it. The renowned photographer Clyde Haire told the author of this history that when he came to Pittsburgh with his new wife they became interested in the First Lutheran Church. After some discussions, Pastor Stackel told him that he "was not cut out to be a Lutheran." The couple joined the Presbyterian Church.

A frustration for one trying to understand the history of the parish from several perspectives is the note in the minutes of the church council repeated monthly throughout these years that the report of the pastor "is attached." The report is never attached or included in the minute books of the congregation and all have apparently been lost.

Pastor Stackel at the September meeting revived the parish paper as a valuable means of disseminating information and instruction to the congregation and beyond. The first issue (Volume I number 1) appeared in October 1947 with the masthead declaring, "This space will be filled by the best name submitted for our new paper." In the December 1947 issue the name was *First Church Alert.* The name, submitted by Horace W. Bikle, was explained: "During the war [World War II] the alert summoned air raid wardens to their posts. An alert is a summons to action. 'First Church Alert' is a summons to action to us all to support the program and services reported in this paper. The name is also a play on words, claiming that First Church is an alert, wide-awake, progressive church." The name continues to this day, even though memories of the war and air raid sirens have long faded from the minds of most Americans.

The radio ministry continued to shape the order of service. The pastor announced in September that the organist and choir director had worked out a plan by which an anthem by the choir would be broadcast over the radio in place of the hymn before the sermon.

In 1930 First Presbyterian Church began luncheon services for men on Tuesdays under the leadership of their pastor Clarence Edward Macartney. It began with twelve men and twenty-five years later the attendance was 1100. The Methodist Church began a similar program on Wednesdays. In December 1947 the pastor of First Lutheran Church recommended "a weekday noon-time 25-minute informal service for men" begin in the chapel in Lent, "with or without a lunch being served, and, if successful, to be continued permanently." The attendance at the first of these services, held on Thursdays, was fifteen, then dipped to ten, wavered, and then caught on. The congregation recognized that without lunch being served many could not come. Crowded restaurants at noon did not permit time for a church service within the lunch hour. Lunch was therefore served in the church undercroft, and attendance increased. The services were held from October through April.

He proposed a new organization for couples that would "meet monthly on the third Sunday evening of the month for light supper, Bible study led by the pastor or another person, and better Christian fellowship."

He further proposed that each worshipper at the Wednesday evening services during Lent be given a picture "that would illustrate the subject for meditation on that particular evening."

He suggested that the "friendliness toward members and strangers at our church services be furthered by the practice of a husband and wife greeting worshippers each Sunday after service just inside the east church door, this married couple to be chosen by the Ushers Committee for one month at a time."[193]

He proposed that two candles be placed on the altar "just as soon as a donor for the brass candlesticks comes forward." Apparently since the dedication of the church, it had been thought that the two gas candelabra, although, as Dr. Holl recognized, not of liturgical significance,[194] were sufficient.

The position of a parish worker was considered toward the end of 1947. Ruth Zartman was interviewed in November, but then on December 1 the council minutes record that "the question of engaging an assistant pastor in place of a parish worker" was to be brought before the congregation at its annual meeting in January. The council recognized that "the work of spreading the Gospel through the medium of First Church is increasing day by day" and that "it is an impossibility for our pastor to care for the spiritual needs of over 800 members, visit the sick, exert proper leadership over all activities and organizations within the church and at the same time give proper thought and study to continue the fine sermons it has been our privilege to hear since he has been with us."[195] The resolution was unanimously adopted by the congregation. In February it was reported that "letters had been sent to theological seminaries inquiring about students who might be interested in becoming the Assistant Pastor of First Church." At last, in a letter dated November 28, 1949, Paul F. W. Pieper, a 1949 graduate of Hamma Divinity School, presented himself for consideration. He was recommended by the dean of the seminary, the Reverend Elmer E. Flack. At a special meeting of the congregation January 22, 1950, a call was extended to him (by a vote of 318 for and 58 against) at an annual salary of $3000 and $25 per month for automobile expenses; he was allowed two weeks' vacation. Pastor Pieper resigned in March 1952 to become a chaplain in the United States Naval Reserve.

February 2, 1948 an additional celebration of the Holy Communion on the First Sunday in Advent was added to the communion schedule, making six celebrations per year. In that month a carillon was installed in the tower, a gift of Harry G. Samson. Miss Mathilda Ittel agreed that her bequest to the church be used for lighting the stained-glass window at night and for the purchase of two candlesticks for the altar "in the main auditorium" as the nave continued to be called. The use of an Advent wreath was introduced in 1948. In 1951 another communion service was added on the first Sunday in August, since there was a stretch of five months between the Easter communion and "World-wide Communion" on the first Sunday in October. Pastor Stackel received permission to have two celebrations that Sunday, at 8:30 and at 11:00 o'clock.

The Sacrament of Holy Baptism was regularly administered following the 11:00 a.m. Sunday service. Upon the pastor's recommendation January 4, 1949, the council agreed "that a lay communion assistant . . . to collect the empty glasses at each table and re-arrange the glasses in the trays at the altar for the administrating pastor, this lay assistant preferably to be an elder and the same person from communion to communion.

In 1949 the three-hour Good Friday service was introduced, from noon until 3 o'clock, based on "the seven last words of Jesus from the cross." Six invited preachers assisted the pastor, each delivering a fifteen-minute "address," and there was "rich choral music" [February 1, 1949]. Each invited preacher was paid $15. Noonday services were held every day of Holy Week (presumably Monday through Friday).

The congregation was now firmly committed to its ministry on Grant Street. In September 1948 a letter from a real estate broker, Frank Lasner, was received in which he declared that he had a responsible cash purchaser" for the church property. The council promptly responded that it was not interested in selling the church.

Beginning at the October 1948 church council meeting, the members were led in a chapter by chapter discussion of Pastor Stackel's book, *The King's Business.*

In April 1949 the city building inspector having condemned the cross that hung on the outside of the building over Grant Street, the council agreed to remove it. The exterior of the church was thus restored to its original appearance without the distraction of an illuminated cross.

In May 1949 it was proposed that beginning in the fall a lunch and a twenty-five-minute service be offered for business women once a week, the same as had been the custom for business men. The men's service was on Wednesday, the women's service on Thursday. It was thought that the service for women would never draw as many as the service for men. The expectation was mistaken. Nineteen business women came on the first day, and each week the number climbed. Expanding attendance by both men and women moved both services from the chapel to the nave of the church. In 1955, 350 women were worshipping on Wednesday and 300 men on Thursday. Pastor Stackel explained that separating the women from the men at these services made sense, for at that time "Men lunch with men and women with women." Moreover in a small office, the boss and the secretary cannot leave on the same lunch hour." For maximum availability to workers, lunch was offered in two servings: before the 12:25-12:50 service and afterward. Lunch, prepared by the women of the parish under the supervision of a paid supervisor, was always subordinate to the service.

The twenty-five minute service was "lively and well-planned. Attenders are invited to set their watches by the time the service starts and ends. Informality is the mood. There are two hymns, a Scripture reading, a prayer, a 14-minute gospel message, and the benediction. The sermon is designed to be intensely practical. Its purpose is to apply Christianity to the working world. . . . An offering is received once a year near the end of the season."[196]

The appropriation of the Baltic states (Latvia, Lithuania, and Estonia) by the Soviet Union following the Second World War caused many to flee their homelands. A large number of what were called "displaced persons" were resettled in the United States. The Board of American Missions placed such refugee pastors with congregations for a four to six month training period to learn "the American way of Lutheran church life." First Church was asked to undertake the training of Pastor Albert Ozols, who had arrived in the United States with his wife and father-in-law. A stipend of $150 per month was paid by the Board and rent up to $65 per month. There were 70 or 80 Latvians in Pittsburgh, and they held a service of worship in the chapel conducted by Pastor Ozols, followed by a supper. On December 18, 1949, he celebrated the Holy Communion in Latvian in the church nave.

In January 1952, certain changes were made in the constitution of the congregation. Among them was the removal of the requirement that communicants notify the pastor of their intention to commune. It was replaced with the statement that the pastor "shall administer the Lord's Supper to all those who truly repent and desire forgiveness through it."

The June 1952 communion was to be celebrated three times: at 8:30, at 11:00, and at 8:00 p.m.

In the minutes of the November 4, 1952 council meeting, there is a note indicating the discouragingly persistent social conditions of the time. "A letter without date from Mr. Thomas E. Jackson to Dr. Stackel about becoming a member of First Church. The letter from Mr. Jackson (who is a Negro) was turned over to the Membership Committee. At the same meeting, the pastor's recommendation "That we contribute $20 again to the United Negro College Fund" was adopted. At the December meeting the Membership Committee reported that the entire Membership Committee as well as other prominent members of the Church" had been contacted. "All agree that it was the Christian thing to accept his application but were of the opinion that Mr. Jackson should affiliate with some Negro congregation. After general discussion of the problem, it was moved . . . and seconded . . . that the application of Mr. Thomas E. Jackson, for membership, be accepted. Motion carried." Thomas Jackson, who was not married, sang in the choir for many years and was a regular communicant. He is remembered as being remarkably generous, despite his limited resources, giving a $50 dollar bond to each young person of the congregation who graduated from high school. He died December 10, 1986.

The Committee on Church Advertising in encouraging advertisements in the newspapers, observed, "Ours is a downtown, radio broadcasting, congregation with peculiar opportunities to serve the community, transient citizens, and countless unseen friends." [January 19, 1953]

In January 1953 major renovations were authorized to make the church more usable in its various activities. The Sunday School rooms were given folding partitions, the basement was finished and refurbished, new stairways were built from the narthex and from the chapel to the basement, the exterior was cleaned and pointed. The most unfortunate work was the waterproofing of the exterior of the church and chapel. Although it was recommended at the time, it served to trap moisture in the sandstone and hasten its deterioration.

There were difficulties being a downtown church. "Mr. Paul Johnson, of Kansas City, Missouri, a visitor to our church on January 11, 1953, had a valuable overcoat stolen from the vestibule on Grant Street leading to the main auditorium. It was moved by Mr. [Julian] Johnson, seconded by Mr. Koehler, and unanimously carried by council that we reimburse Mr. Paul Johnson $100 for his loss." It was not the only overcoat taken from the coat rack. Eva Marie Pfeiffer told of her husband's loss of an expensive coat at Christmas a few years later.

A brief sentence in the pastor's report for October 6, 1953, noted the death of what had been a promising child of the congregation. "St. John's Lutheran Church on Forbes Street [now Avenue] was being disbanded and the property turned over to the Pittsburgh Synod." The handsome building was demolished, and the forlorn lot remains vacant to this day. The pipe organ from the church was given to Mount Calvary Church in McKees Rocks.[197]

An understanding of the Church year had yet to be inculcated in the life of the congregation. The council minutes of February 3, 1953, report, "Ordinarily communion is administered on Trinity Sunday. Since Trinity Sunday this year falls on May 31st, following a holiday [Memorial Day, May 30], it was moved by Mr. Kester, seconded by Mr. Koehler, and carried by council to have communion on Sunday, June 7, 1953. If Trinity Sunday were not considered to be more important to the church than a national holiday, it apparently did not occur to anyone that the communion would be more appropriately moved to the previous Sunday, Pentecost.

At the annual meeting of the congregation in January 1955 the question of increasing the frequency of the celebration of the

Holy Communion was put to a test vote. "The showing of hands was almost unanimous that the offering of communion as at the present time is adequate."

Another sign of the deficiency of understanding the nature of congregational worship is the request presented by a member of the congregation, Joseph Succop, in January 1954 that at Easter the music be rendered by the paid quartette alone and not by the choir augmented with volunteer singers "which has been the custom for several years in the past." Music was understood to be a performance rather than the work of the congregation. What is now called the "nave" of the building was then referred to as the "auditorium." The request was approved at the February meeting of the council. At that meeting Dr. Stackel suggested that the prelude begin fifteen minutes before the eleven o'clock service, instead of the customary ten minutes, to "reward those who come early."

The pastor at the January meeting made three proposals concerning the worship schedule. (1) "That two identical morning services be inaugurated on a trial basis for Sunday mornings, one at 8:30, the other at 11, beginning with the first Sunday in Lent" ("identical services" was a term then popular in Protestant circles); (2) "That a third Ash Wednesday communion service be added at 2 o'clock in the afternoon to those already customary at 11:30 A.M. and 8 P.M."; (3) "That the processional and recessional of the choir and pastor be down the center aisle." One wonders how the singers and clergy had entered before. The addition of the 8:30 service was understood to be primarily a means by which attendance could be increased. At the November 3, 1954, council meeting, "Discontinuance of the early service on Sunday was discussed. Two services on Sunday will be continued, at least through next Lent, and perhaps until next fall; at which time, if notable growth in attendance shall not have been realized, discontinuance of the early service will again be considered."

An improved liturgical understanding occurred perhaps unwittingly. At the May 1954 meeting the council approved the proposal that "beginning with the year 1955, the communion service heretofore held on Good Friday evening shall be transferred to Wednesday evening during Holy Week, so that communion services will be held on Wednesday evening and Thursday evening, and the regular church service be held on Good Friday evening."

In European Lutheran churches that had come under the influence of the Reformed Church, Holy Communion was celebrated on Good Friday as a memorial of the death of Christ. In the wider tradition of the Church, however, Good Friday was the one day of the year on which the Holy Communion was not celebrated, extending the fast from earthly food to sacramental food as well.

The opening paragraph of the pastor's report for January 1954 is quoted in the minutes of the church council because of its import. "Within a five month period I have been asked by three great churches to consider coming to them. . . . I have never told a church council before of any approaches that came to me, but when three came within half a year, and all three were of immense significance, it seemed as though I should mention them. As I struggled desperately to find God's will, it came to me that He wanted me to continue this ministry in First Church, Pittsburgh. It was necessary for me to study very carefully the present and future of this congregation. I am impressed with its future and with the renaissance of a new spirit surging up within us. . . . I am as one reborn concerning the possibilities of this congregation and our vigor in moving with fresh determination into those possibilities."

At a special meeting of the council held after the Sunday service on March 20, 1955, Dr. Stackel reported to the council that he had received a call from the Church of the Redeemer in Atlanta, Georgia, to become their pastor, and that he had also received a call as director of the two-year Evangelism Program of the United Lutheran Church in America with headquarters in New York City. He told the council that he had not yet made up his mind about either call. Ten days later he announced to the church council that he planned to accept the call to direct the evangelism program of the national church, the resignation to take effect July 31. He said in his letter of resignation, "I am always excited about the promising future of this congregation. Its strength is made up of so many parts, as, for example, its spirit of harmony, its hunger for the sacrament, its missionary interest, its warm friendliness, its radio and noon ministry, its crowded worship services. God will always bless a people of such faith." His description of the congregation remains accurate to this day.

Dr. Stackel, after his two-year term as Director of Evangelism for the United Lutheran Church in America, became pastor of Trinity Church in Akron, Ohio. During his time in Pittsburgh, the congregation completed a $100,000 renovation program inside and outside the building; luncheon services for business men and women were introduced (1948) with an attendance of 700 per week; Pastor Stackel was secretary of the Council of Churches of Christ in Allegheny County, Protestant chaplain of the Pittsburgh chapter of the Fraternal Order of Police; a member of the boards of Passavant Hospital, the Lutheran Service Society of Western Pennsylvania, and Home Missions of the Pittsburgh Synod, and the Board of Education of the United Lutheran Church in America.

A farewell reception for Dr. and Mrs. Stackel was held June 23, 1955 in the social rooms of the church. There was a musical program by the organist, G. Logan McElvany and the church quartette, an address by the Dean of Trinity Cathedral, N. R. H. Moor,[198] and greetings from the President of the Pittsburgh Synod, G. L. Himmelman.

After serving as director of the Evangelism Mission 1955-1958, Dr. Stackel became pastor of Holy Trinity Church in Akron, Ohio, 1958-1972. He was then called as Executive Director of the Lutheran Church in America's Division for World Mission and Ecumenism, 1973-1974, expecting it to be a long-term call, but the Lutheran Church in America in convention decided to give emphasis to alleviating world hunger, and Pastor Stackel became the director of the world hunger emphasis of the Love Compels Action appeal, 1974-1980. He then retired and moved to Charlotte, North Carolina where he was interim pastor of two churches in that city, and then a member of the staff of St. Mark's Church in Charlotte. He died October 19, 1994 of a brain tumor diagnosed just six weeks prior to his death.

CHAPTER 7

A Ministry in and for the City

The pulpit committee promptly found a successor to Pastor Stackel. June 5, 1955, the committee presented the name of the Reverend Dr. Harold Raymond Albert of Columbus, Ohio, as a candidate for pastor of the First Church. Harold Albert was a 1935 graduate of Wittenberg College, which also awarded him the D.D. degree in 1953. He had served as pastor in Springfield, Lorain, and Columbus, Ohio.

Pastor Albert came with firm ideas about the direction he thought the congregation ought to take. He had indicated to the search committee that he did not intend to occupy the parsonage but rather to buy his own home. At the meeting of the congregation that extended the call, Dr. Albert was present and addressed the meeting outlining what he hoped to accomplish in the congregation. He concluded his remarks by saying that if members were not in agreement with these aims and objectives, they should vote against him. After he retired from the meeting, no one chose to speak against his ideas. The vote was 576 for and 6 against a call.

Harold Albert

Harold Albert began his ministry in Pittsburgh September 4 (the attendance that day was 600; the membership was 817), and he was installed as the sixteenth pastor of the First Church September 18, 1955. His father, the Reverend Dr. R. A. Albert of West Carrolton, Ohio, participated in the service.

Pastor Albert suggested, in addition to the two morning Eucharists "a new meditation Communion" at 4:30 on October 2. He had a keen sense of evangelism. He proposed a "loyalty attendance campaign" to begin September 11 and to continue through October 30, emphasizing attendance at the services of the church and planned a series of sermons to encourage continued attendance. The plan was notably successful: the attendance on September 4 was nearly double the average in August, September 11 was 477, September 18 morning services 503, installation 346, September 25 485, October 2 (three communion services) 539. Pastor Albert proposed at the September council meeting that council members be assigned to lead devotions for each meeting. The minutes of the meeting in the following month report, "Mr. Van Cleve leading Council in the usual kneeling prayer." He further proposed that "several men, members of Council and others, join with him before the service in prayers for that service." He also announced that he was "going to ask every Sunday if there are those who want to discuss their faith or spiritual welfare or problems of life with these men in the nature of an evangelism committee. The purpose of the coffee hour is to receive guests and visitors who are in attendance. Strangers should be searched out and brought to the attention of the Pastor immediately." Such immediate attention has been an impressive hallmark of First Church since that time.

Paul A. R. Kurtz and Russell B. Watkins provided two bulletin boards that were installed outside the church in September 1955 and remain to this day.

Pastor Albert and his wife purchased a home of their own at 1430 Navahoe Drive in Mount Lebanon; the congregation, having sold the parsonage at 435 Royce Avenue for $21,000, held the mortgage on the Navahoe Drive property.

The fourteenth pastor of First Church, Dr. A. J. Holl, died September 15, 1955. New radio equipment was dedicated as a memorial to him on January 15, 1956. The radio ministry he began continued to broadcast throughout the greater Pittsburgh area.

Pastor Albert recommended to the Council at its March 6, 1956, meeting that each month, as part of its devotions, the council engage in a ten to fifteen minute study of such topics as "The General Duties of Councilmen," "Our Personal Devotions and

Faith," "The Benevolent Structure," "Elders and Deacons in the New Testament," "The Truth about Tithing." The recommendation was approved, and the series began the following month with a ten-minute talk by the pastor, "What the Church is."

May 1, 1956 reports the council kneeling in prayer "as usual" at the beginning of its regular monthly meetings. The practice is regularly noted again beginning November 7, 1956: "Council knelt in prayer." It had become a figurative expression. The council had not in fact knelt for prayer for many years.

Evangelism was becoming a significant emphasis in the life of the parish. It was noted (February 7, 1956) that "the [Evangelism] Committee makes good use of the Coffee Hour. Visitors are provided with a means of identification, are introduced to all present, and become targets for members of the committee in attendance." The approach sounds, half a century later, as if it would drive people away, but evidently it was successful. Thirty-three new members were received on November 25, 1956, nineteen on February 3, 1957, and thirty-seven on April 7. At the April 1957 council meeting Dr. [Chilton] Prouty reported for the Membership Committee that there would be seventy-five, perhaps one hundred new members during 1957. Dr. Albert reported that in May 1957 there were 143 children in the parish, 73 in the age group 0-5 years and 70 in the age group 6-13; eighty of these were in the Sunday School. Thirty confirmed members of the parish were of high school age; nineteen of these were in the Sunday School.

A plan was devised by which the widely scattered congregation would be divided into seven districts, each under a warden, whereby all members of the church would be visited two or three times per year. "All postal zones of Pittsburgh are represented by our membership except zone 38, Blawnox. At least 20 families live in communities outside of metropolitan Pittsburgh." (April 10, 1956)

Attendance figures were now regularly recorded in the council minutes and are impressive indeed.

February 5, 1956 469
February 12 439
February 19 523
February 22 (Lenten Wednesday evening) . 189

February 26 450
February 29 (Lenten Wednesday evening) . 192
March 4 538
March 7 (Lenten Wednesday evening) 169
March 11 485
March 14 (Lenten Wednesday evening) 187
March 18 (morning) 381
(evening cantata) 228
March 21 (Lenten Wednesday evening) 256
March 25 (Palm Sunday) 672
March 28 (Wednesday in Holy Week) 210
March 30 (Good Friday 3-hour service, estimated) 1634
April 1 (Easter Day) 726
April 8 439
April 15 490
April 22 467
April 29 464
May 6 482
May 13 454
May 20 457
May 27 (Pentecost) 525
June 3(Trinity Sunday) .... 502.

The summer attendance figures were equally impressive, ranging from a low of 87 to a high of 141 at the 8:30 service and from 228 to 304 at the 11:00 service.

The healthy congregation was presented with a significant opportunity in June 1956. A special meeting of the Church Council was called to consider the purchase of a lot next door to the church, at 605 Grant Street, owned by the Philadelphia Company and used as a parking lot by a tenant, Burford Epstein, who had for a number of years allowed church members to park in the lot free of charge on Sunday mornings. The lot was approximately 5589 square feet, 60 feet on Grant Street and 94 feet to Garland Way. The asking price was $185,000. The tenant paid $650 a month rent. His lease was to expire February 1, 1957; he had renewed his lease for five years subject to the property being sold. "The Council discussed in a general way the prospects of recommending to the congregation the purchase of this property. Not only this, but all property to the corner of Sixth and Grant with a view to the future of expanding our facilities in the formation of a center of Lutheranism in the downtown section of Pittsburgh. It was mutually agreed by the Councilmen present that Dr. Albert would write a letter to Lutheran Mutual Life Insurance Company, Waverly, Iowa, to get their reaction to investing in a new downtown church and office building in the City of Pittsburgh, Pennsylvania. It was further agreed that the pastor and Mr. [Lester] Wolf would call on Mr. Park H. Martin, Executive Director of the Pittsburgh Regional Planning Association, to ascertain how they feel about a Church in the location such as ours."

First Church had struggled for many years to determine its mission in downtown Pittsburgh and had resolved to remain where it had been placed and do its ministry there. Not many congregations or church bodies had gone through such a discernment pro-

Eppy's parking lot ca. 1950

cess, and during the decades of the 1950s and 1960s were abandoning the center of cities across the land and following their people into the suburbs and beyond. It was therefore not a propitious time for First Church to look for help or support in seizing the opportunity presented to it for the expansion of its property and ministry not simply for itself but for the larger Lutheran Church. Nothing further is recorded in the church council minutes regarding these negotiations. The opportunity was lost, and the flickering vision failed.

The present bank building, still known by many as the Porter building[199], was erected on this property. The council minutes for February 5, 1957 report: "Referring to the new building to be erected next door to the Church, a request had come from the contractors to encroach on our property during construction work. A written agreement would be in force." A few lines later is the note, "Council was advised that [the] chapel wall damaged by contractor next door would be taken care of." A special meeting of the council February 19 gives the text of the letter the trustees sent to the contractor. The contractor's proposal is given in the minutes of March 5. Damage began to appear in the walls of the chapel and a registered engineer was engaged to look after the interests of the church during the construction process. (April 14, 1957). Concerns continued for several months. (May 7). The chapel and the basement were declared unsafe for use (May 10).

At the annual business meeting of the congregation, January 21, 1957, the pastor "told about a meeting in New York recently with other pastors of down-town churches who have the same problems as we encounter."

At the February 19, 1957 meeting Dr Albert announced that, as had become the custom of the parish, there would be three communion services on Ash Wednesday, at 11:30 a.m., 5:30 p.m., and 8:00 p.m. "Considerable discussion was had as to whether or not an outside ordained minister be brought in to help with these communion services as had been the custom in the past or have councilmen assist the pastor. It was moved by Mr. [Dale] Shaw, seconded by Mr. [John] Reitz and unanimously carried that the Elders help the pastor with the communion services on Ash Wednesday." The pastor apparently had reservations about this action. "Dr. Albert stated that he would confer with Rev. G. Lawrence Himmelman, D.D., President of the Pittsburgh Synod, on this matter." The council had their way, but so did Dr. Albert. "Elders will participate in the distribution of the elements at Holy Communion services on Ash Wednesday. Dr. Stewart W. Herman, Executive Secretary of the Lutheran World Federation, will assist in Holy Week Services—Wednesday through Friday."

The matter of assistants at the communion services continued to be a matter of some dissention. The pastor recommended (May 7, 1957) "that the elders and the pastor hold a meeting to discuss the general conduct of the communions, including frequency of administration, the use of elders in the distribution of elements, and the ushers handling of communicants." May 13: "Interesting discussion was had as to how the ushers should direct worshippers to the Altar rail at the time of Holy Communion." It is a Lutheran peculiarity to make going to and from the altar an exceedingly complex activity.

Further unhappiness is revealed in his suggestion "that the Church Council should decide whether or not Palm leaves should be distributed on Palm Sunday 1958." The council unanimously chose to eliminate the distribution of palms. No reasons for the decision are recorded, but it was apparently beyond the experience of some in the congregation to have even a minimum symbolic participation in the liturgical events of the day. January 27, 1959 what appears a half-century on as self-evident is recorded: "It was moved, seconded, and carried that palms be made part of the Palm Sunday services this year."

The pastor noted the long space between the communion on Trinity Sunday, June 16 and the next scheduled celebration, October 6 ("World-wide Communion Sunday") and suggested another communion at the beginning of August. The council unanimously agreed.

In 1957 consideration was given to a new staff position, a Director of Evangelism and Promotion. The job description defined "our particular situation" this way: (a) "Our central position in the city means that we are a representative Lutheran Church. Our parish is the entire County, and our need is for an active membership of approximately 1,500, who have a strong sense of loyalty and ministry. (b) Our downtown location, in the midst of the office building area, and in the future, the municipal auditorium, brings a quarter of a million people within walking distance of the church daily, as well as out of town business representatives and convention goers, and makes possible a strong weekday ministry." The anticipated "municipal auditorium" was to be the Civic Arena, later named the Mellon Arena, replaced in 2009-2010 by the Consol Energy Center. (Also near the church now is the David L. Lawrence Convention Center.) The Director of Evangelism and Promotion was to be responsible not only for evangelism and advertising, using radio, television, and "public relations techniques as advisable," but for stewardship as well, encouraging giving not only by the members of the congregation but also by "wealthy people who are not members of the congregation but who have an interest in supporting work such as ours."

The position was offered to Richard T. Sutcliffe, Associate Director of the Department of Press, Radio, and Television of the United Lutheran Church in America. Mr. Sutcliffe promised his decision by July 1. He apparently decided to decline the invitation; nothing further is reported in the minutes. The search continued. The Rev. Edward K. Perry, who was later president of the Upstate New York Synod, declined consideration, being obligated to remain where he was for at least two more years. Also considered were Paul Luther Wetzler, D.D. of Minneapolis and the Rev. Carl T. Uehling of Newark, New Jersey. The position was ultimately offered to and accepted by Mr. James J. Morentz of Philadelphia on March 16, 1958. He served until June 30, 1960, when he resigned to join the staff of First Lutheran Church in Los Angeles. He concluded his final report to the church council, "Many of my friends, who should really know, told me two years ago that the downtown is a hopeless situation. This is simply not true. It's a hard road and a long road, but it's worth every bit of it and success is absolutely certain because I now know you have a dedicated congregation and a dedicated pastor, and a God who I am certain wants this church right here."

The congregation clearly understood and valued its location in the heart of the city. Others did also for various reasons. In the fall of 1957, Pastor Albert reported, "Mr. George A. Parkman, of Sewickley, a private investor, has verbally offered, in the presence of one of our members, Mr. George W. Simpkiss, to build a 21-story office building on this site, and to include adequate space for the church and all its facilities in the building, with rent free permanently." The proposal was referred to the development committee, but it was not pursued further.

The congregation's understanding of its ministry on Grant Street continued to develop. In February 1959 the council, in response to the pastor's report agreed that "our one concern should be to provide for the spiritual needs of our people, and further to reach out with the redeeming ministry of Christ to all people who need us at this location." They expressed the hope "that our Sunday attendance can reach a new plateau of around 600 during Lent and that we can regain our full 750 communing members by Trinity Communion."

In April the council and selected laypeople met the Reverend Donald L. Houser, Executive Secretary of the Board of American Missions "to explore the possibility of receiving financial aid from that Board for our urban church work." In June the council unanimously endorsed a request "to the Board of American Missions of the Pittsburgh Synod for classification as an Urban Renewal Congregation and aid from the Board of American Missions Department of Urban Church Planning." In August the council authorized "a one-day Pastors' Urban Institute, to be held as early as possible in the fall, to be operated by the Pittsburgh Synod, with First Church as host and instrument for demonstration of what a vital urban church program can mean to the area churches."

The immediate result of such support was the establishment of the Pastoral Care Center in January 1959. Such centers were in operation in New York City and in Washington, D.C. The committee which was proposed to plan and oversee the operation of the center consisted of a Professor of Social Case Work of the University of Pittsburgh, a representative of the Board of American Missions of the Pittsburgh Synod, the director of the Lutheran Service Society, a psychiatrist, a medical doctor, a representative of the council of First Church, a layperson from First Church, and the pastor of First Church. The pastoral counselor was to become an associate pastor of First Church. Six possible candidates were considered. Dr. H. Reed Shepfer withdrew his name, Dr. Bjorn Nielsen failed to obtain a majority vote of the council, Pastor Donald M. Bravin withdrew from further consideration "because of the small amount of preaching involved in the proposed assistant pastorship." On November 22, 1959, the congregation extended a call to the Rev. George F. Shaffer, Executive Secretary and Chaplain of the Lutheran Service Society of Northern Ohio, in Cleveland, to become its Associate Pastor and Director of its

Pastoral Counseling Center. He began his work January 1, 1960.

In its report of January 3, 1961, the Pastoral Counseling Center, at the conclusion of its first year of operation, summarized its work: troubled individuals have been counseled; classes for specialized problem areas have been offered; two conferences, one for clergy and one for professions dealing with mental health, were sponsored; an intensive consultation program for the work was developed; consultation and referral for area clergy were actualized; relationship with First Lutheran Church and the Pittsburgh community was a primary focus; the director offered his services as preacher, speaker, and workshop leader to the Lutheran Churches. The work was supported by a grant from the Board of American Missions of the United Lutheran Church in America. The merger that created the Lutheran Church in America in 1962 combined with an economic recession made future funding uncertain.

June 9, 1964, Pastor Shaffer resigned as Director of the Counseling Center in order to pursue full-time graduate work at the Western Reserve University in Cleveland. His successor, the Rev. LeRoy Aden, Ph.D., then of the Divinity School at the University of Chicago, was called November 8. He was a member of The American Lutheran Church, a graduate of Wartburg College and Wartburg Seminary and the University of Chicago.

LeRoy Aden

The long search for an assistant pastor concluded on January 29, 1960, with the call of Seminarian David N. Finney, Jr. A graduate of Gettysburg college, he returned to the Marine Corps during the Korean War, taught in public school for four years, served Luther Memorial Church in Erie, Pennsylvania, as director of religious education, and was completing his work at Gettysburg Seminary. He was married with three children. He was ordained in Holy Trinity Church, Greenville, at the annual meeting of the Pittsburgh Synod June 7, 1961. He was called to First Church as Associate Pastor and Director of Education. Pastor Finney struggled to adapt to city life, and in June 1963 he resigned "for the good of the church, myself, and family," and, instead of the specialized ministry in education to which he had been called, sought a general parish ministry.

The service book of the time, the *Common Service Book,* included the texts of the Epistle and Gospel readings in the Authorized King James Version, but its successor, the *Service Book and Hymnal* of 1958 was to allow the use of the Revised Standard Bible for the readings instead of the Authorized Version.[200] In March 1958 permission was given to the pastor to purchase a Revised Standard Bible for the Lectern "if it is possible for him to find someone to purchase same." Preparation was being made for the introduction of the new service book. The *Service Book and Hymnal* was put in the pews on Sunday June 8, the services on that day being shortened to accommodate the playing of a tape recording of the new service following the benediction with explanatory remarks by the organist and choir director G. Logan McIlvaney. The *Common Service Books* were removed from the pews during that week prior to June 15. At its meeting September 2, 1958, the church council authorized the use of the Revised Standard Version of the Bible to begin the following Sunday, September 7.

The frequency of the celebration of Holy Communion slowly increased. At the September meeting the council proposed eight communion services during the year: Advent; Christmas or Epiphany; Ash Wednesday; Holy Week (i.e. Maundy Thursday); Pentecost or Trinity Sunday; July, August, or early September; World-Wide Communion Sunday (the first Sunday in October), and Reformation Sunday. In addition to these eight communion Sundays, there were "Semi-Private Communions each Sunday morning to begin at the end of the regular 8:30 service" and "one communion per month on a Thursday at about 5:30 P.M." In his November 2, 1959 report to the church council, Pastor Albert observed, "The weekly administration of the Communion has now been in practice since Sunday, October 11. Attendances at these weekly Communions have been: 16, 24, 52 and 26. I could give you a dozen individual cases where the need for the Communion, because of personal or private reasons, has made this practice a real source of spiritual power. We believe that the practice will grow in meaning as our people become more accustomed and educated to it."

The charter of the church was revised in December 1958. Pew rents were abolished, a $4000 limit on church income from property was removed, "Church Council" was substituted for what had been called "the Vestry," and the number of council members was increased.

Religious radio programs were losing listeners during this time, and radio station WAMP chose to discontinue the half-hour "Sanctuary" program and to propose two four-minute spots by Dr. Albert each Sunday morning, one between 10:30 and 11:00 and one between 11:30 and noon. The spots were to be "informal, personal, and provocative messages."

Bishop Otto Dibelius of Berlin preached at the 11:00 o'clock service at First Church November 6, 1959 (Dr. J. W. Winterhager preached at the 8:30 service) and also that evening at the Reformation rally at the Syria Mosque sponsored by First Church and the Council of Churches of Pittsburgh and at the noon services at First Church November 7 and 8.

Otto Dibelius
Bishop of Berlin-Brandenburg

December 5, 1960, T. Norman Mansell of Philadelphia, the favored Lutheran church architect of the time, met with the church council to report the results of his study of the church physical plant and to discuss the possibilities for renovation or for rebuilding of the church. Preliminary drawings of a possible new church structure were ordered. The preliminary sketches of the possible new building" were received at the end of 1960, and Pastor Albert arranged a luncheon "with several industrial leaders and see what their reaction is to the possibility of business participation."

Pastor Albert reported December 5, 1961 that he was engaged in discussions with Frank Magee, Executive Secretary of the Allegheny Conference on Community Development, George Main, the president of the Parking Authority, and Merritt Neale, Executive Director of the Parking Authority. "There is a slight ray of hope that the Authority would be interested in the possibility of building an underground parking garage in the vacant area between our building and the Koppers Building, so that we could build a church on the top level."

There was, of course, resistance to replacing the church building. January 2, 1962 Howard Thompson moved, and James Lind seconded a motion that "the church structure is to be kept in its present basic form and maintained in good repair with the use of current funds only until such time as numerical changes indicate

The church in 1960 showing the available lot

the necessity of major revisions." A motion to table the resolution was defeated. Nine voted for the resolution, five against, two abstained. The motion and the voting results were presented to the annual congregational meeting January 15, 1962 for reactions. After discussion, the congregation referred the proposal to the church council for further study. After considerable discussion by the council, its previous decision was rescinded and the Building Committee was directed to "make a complete analysis of the requirements of the congregation and its various activities."

In the summer of 1963 another opportunity presented itself for the church to expand its property. J.J. Gumberg Realtors in a letter to Pastor Albert July 8, 1963 confirmed their previous discussion with the pastor and offered two properties. One, approximately 19,950 square feet, fronting on Grant Street for nearly 150 feet and down Strawberry Way for 133 feet was owned by the Pittsburgh Public School System and leased to Eppy's Parking Company for $54,800 per year. The second, 7,370 square feet of vacant land, was behind it on Strawberry Way to William Penn Way and then owned by the Koppers Company and leased to Eppy's parking company for $20,000 per year. The parcel fronting on Grant street was listed, the letter says, "at $1,000,000,000" (surely a misprint for $1,000,000) but was "open for negotiation." The Koppers Company was asking $35 per square foot for approximately $340,550. "The value, convenience, and strategic location of this property does not need to be stressed to you at this time. If your church is contemplating getting its entire administrative and executive operation centrally located in a larger edifice, what finer spot could be available? Further, there is no costly demolition connected with possession of this property." Once again the congregation chose not to take up the challenge or even consider negotiation. The Bell Telephone building was erected on the property in 1968, and its construction threatened the structural integrity of the old church.

December 5, 1961 is the last note of "the opening kneeling prayer" at the beginning of church council meetings. The phrase had long since ceased to be descriptive of the actual posture of the council members.

Two women (Mrs. F. B. [Eileen S.] Gellert, who was to become the secretary of the council, and Mrs. Gerald [Marguerite] Socher) were elected to the council at the annual meeting of the congregation January 15, 1962

At the beginning of 1962 a "Statement of Policy" was submitted for study and discussion. A preamble noted that "Our church is downtown, at the heart of a great metropolitan area. Ours is the downtown ministry. Our membership is from all parts of the city, from all economic, social, and racial backgrounds. Our task is to gather the fellowship of believers from the entire city and to speak to the entire city, especially to the throngs of people who are concentrated in the downtown area. We are to be alive with the Gospel of our Lord Jesus Christ, and to relate the Gospel to the daily affairs of men." The function of the congregation was described as fourfold. (1) To be an Evangelical Lutheran congregation with the full ministry of Word and Sacraments; (2) to be a "pace setter" in worship, education, social service, with a seven-day-a-week ministry; (3) to minister to downtown workers regardless of their church affiliation or place of residence; and (4) to minister to out of town people who are temporarily in the city. The emphasis of the parish was sixfold. (1) Strong evangelical preaching that will speak to the entire city from the pulpit, radio, and television; (2) the downtown chapel with the church open daily; (3) an educational program that offers full Christian instruction as well as special educational opportunities; (4) lay ministry; (5) the Pastoral Counseling Center; (6) special events to relate the Gospel to the various arts and professions. The purpose was twofold: (1) "to bridge the existing gap between the affairs of the spirit and the affairs of the world"; (2) to offer the ministry to members and non-members alike.

March 13, 1962, Pastor Albert told the council about his "class for young pastors who have been out of seminary from five to ten years. The class is centered in the work of preaching, and the purpose is to help younger pastors in their development of all that relates to communicating the Gospel, including the discipline of time, reading habits, filing, and resource material, construction of the sermon, and delivery." It was a preview of the work he would engage at Philadelphia Seminary at the conclusion of his pastorate at First Church. He conducted a week-long Pastors' Institute at Philadelphia Seminary June 17-22, 1962.

At Christmas 1962, Pastor Albert, with the permission of the church council, introduced "a Christmas morning choral Communion at 10 a.m. This will be held with Eucharistic vestments, the chanting of the service, and special liturgical Christmas features." Pastor Albert asked a knowledgeable pastor, The Rev. Thomas A. Smith, for instruction in the proper celebration of a Christmas tradition that continues to this day. Pastor Albert reported January 8, 1963, "This more formal and liturgical celebration seems to have met with general approval on the part of those who attended. Those who are in any way repelled by liturgical form need not attend. The only criticism I have heard had to do with its length." He then invited discussion of such a choral Eucharist on other weekdays as well, such as Ash Wednesday, Maundy Thursday, Ascension Day, Reformation Day, the Epiphany.

Pastor Albert had a continuing interest in broadening the congregation's experience of the variety of liturgical forms common in the Lutheran Church. Such innovation was not always agreeable to many in the congregation, the years of liturgical leadership having become but a distant memory. He was also a pastor, and he knew when not to push. In his report to the council February 4, 1964, he observed, "In recent years during Lent we have attempted to effect certain liturgical changes for the express purpose of learning more about liturgical usage and of experiencing a bit more flexibility in our use of forms. It would be my personal suggestion that this year we omit such liturgical changes which might result in further unrest and discontent. However, in such matters as the use of forms, I value the judgment of this body."

October 1, 1963, an American flag was placed in the rear of the nave, on the right side of the congregation as it faces the altar. Many members of the congregation were unhappy with this location and insisted that the American and the Christian flags both be returned to where they had been in the chancel. The matter was reconsidered November 5, 1963. Pastor Albert attempted a practical objection to flags in the front of the church: he had from time to time struck the flag with his hand or arm while preaching. He also correctly observed that the "Christian flag" is "in no way universally accepted by the Christian Church." (It had been created at the beginning of the twentieth century for a Methodist church picnic.) The pastor's objections were to no avail, and the council directed the flags to be "put back where they were."

November 21, 1963, the Reverend John G. Gensel, "the Jazz Pastor" from New York City, led a service in First Church and other services at Pittsburgh Theological Seminary, Mount Lebanon Presbyterian Church, and Thiel College.

November 22, 1963 the nation was stunned by the assassination of President John F. Kennedy. A memorial service was held in the church on Monday, November 25.

The convention of the Lutheran Church in America met in Pittsburgh July 2-9, 1964 at the Hilton Hotel. The Rev. Dr. George F. Harkins, assistant to the President of the Lutheran Church in America, attended the annual meeting of the congregation January 20, 1964, and "presented a very fine talk concerning some of the details of the coming convention to be held in Pittsburgh, in July, at the Hilton Hotel, as well as the requirements of a downtown church and the church as a whole." Daily celebrations of the Holy Communion were held each morning in the First Church. July 5 was a Sunday, and on that day three services were held (8:30, 9:45, and 11:00) "Three preachers of Church-wide reputation have consented to be the preachers for that day: Dr. Donald R. Heiges, President of Gettysburg Seminary; Dr. Ralph W. Loew, Pastor of Holy Trinity Lutheran Church, Buffalo, N.Y.; Dr. William H. Lazareth, Professor of [Systematic] Theology at the Lutheran Theological Seminary, Philadelphia."

Under the leadership of Pastor Albert, the First Lutheran Church was discovering the importance of its ministry in and for the city of Pittsburgh. In June 1964 he presented to the church council "a statement of policy for a downtown ministry" to provide "the basic stance from which we will report to the Board of American Missions and to the Church at large for the Pittsburgh Convention. It was a vision and understanding that ran counter to the prevailing mood and actions of most of the church bodies in the United States. The statement began:

"We believe that the resources of the Christian faith must be located and active in the heart of our metropolitan cities, which are the centers of industry and business. First Lutheran Church, located on Grant Street, Downtown Pittsburgh, is in the midst of skyscrapers and hotels.

"We believe that faith and obedience to God are not just for a quiet Sunday morning in the suburbs, and the rest of the week lived in total indifference to the claims of God upon our lives.

"If ever faith in God needs to be available, exercised, and shared, it is in the midst of the world of work, with all its competition, pressure, ambition, success and failure. Here is where life is lived and shared. Here is where the rule of God—and certainly His Grace—needs to be sharply and clearly offered.

"Downtown churches, in our great cities, face a severe dilemma, and have been having a hard time of it. Many have either died or moved out. Yet, this is where people are. More than 150,000 people are within five-minutes' walk of this church building every day, Monday through Friday. Out of town people are in the hotels and lonely people are on the streets.

"Ours is a mission far beyond that of the usual congregation. All regular congregations operate and program their services largely for their own members, with a few visitors now and then. We, comprised of 800 members from all over the County, and from all economic, social, and racial segments of society, are offering our services to people far beyond our own constituency."

The pastor had led the congregation to rediscover the vision of broad service which William Passavant had established.

Worship was understood to be the central feature of the mission of the congregation, and excellence was understood to be the goal. The Music Committee noted in its report of October 13, 1964, "Being a central Lutheran church in this area, we should be responsible for the leadership and be as close to model and mature Lutheran practices as possible. The director [of music] should provide opportunities for the congregation to improve continually their comprehension and expression of the liturgy."

The 1964 convention of the Lutheran Church in America, held in Pittsburgh, adopted a "Statement of Communion Practices" that, among other things, permitted a carefully guarded assistance by laypeople in the distribution of the elements by administering the cup in the Holy Communion. First Church promptly took up the opportunity and permitted the practice, those serving to be approved by the church council and trained by the pastor and participate "from time to time, not necessarily on a strict schedule or limited to times of emergency." Their normal vestments were to be "the cassock and surplice without the stole." These were the common vestments of the time for such lay assistants throughout the Lutheran Church in America.

Moreover, the congregation supported the involvement of its pastor in the emerging civil rights movement. Pastor Albert was seen as the leading Protestant clergyman in the city. June 9, 1964 the council adopted a resolution that declared,

"WHEREAS, the Pastor has, at the request of the Pittsburgh Council of Churches, undertaken, in conjunction with Bishop [later Cardinal] John J. Wright and Rabbi Solomon Freehof, the task of formulating means to bring about social, and particularly racial, equality in our community; be it

RESOLVED, That the Council of First Lutheran Church commend Dr. Harold R. Albert for his personal leadership in this regard and specifically for his endeavors on behalf of the Pittsburgh Inter-Faith Council on Religion and Race; and be it

FURTHER RESOLVED, That the Council, being of the opinion that the issue of social responsibility, as relates to civil rights, is of major importance to every practicing Christian, recommend to the congregation that each member study and attempt to formulate how the individual, and this Church might be more effective and outspoken on behalf of the inherent rights and responsibilities of all men; and be it

FURTHER RESOLVED, That this commendation and recommendation be made known to our members."

The concern of the congregation was wide-ranging. In its report in June 1964 the Evangelism Committee noted that "For some period of time the [First Lutheran] Church has had an informal arrangement with Pastor Charles W. Carlson, Campus Pastor, Lutheran University Center, by which the Center served as an extension of the activities of First Church." Pastor Carlson reported the confirmation of six individuals, and their names were added to the roll of First Church. The arrangement continues to the present day.

The Trustees, August 25, 1964, with one dissenting vote, rescinded its decision of the previous April 16 "to the effect that the gas fixtures in the nave would be removed. It is the present feeling of the majority of the Board that these fixtures should remain in position until more suitable devices can be obtained by gift or by purchase." The pair of gas candelabra continue to be a valued feature of the chancel.

In January 1965 the Board of American Missions announced that it would grant $10,000 to First Church for the Counseling Center (an additional $3,000 was to come from the Synod and another $2,000 from the contributions made by clients of the center, and that the Board would grant to the church for the music and fine arts program $15,000 for the first twelve months of its operation, $6,000 for the second twelve months, and nothing for the third year.

Ecumenical relations were developing in the city. Pastor Albert reported to the council, January 12, 1965, that the Byzantine Catholic Church was planning to sponsor a service of prayer during the Octave of Christian Unity and had invited the Council of Churches to cooperate. "Participants in this service were to be selected from Eastern Catholic, Roman Catholic, Greek Orthodox, and Protestant Churches. I was asked to represent the Protestants in delivering one of three homilies. In other words, to speak for the Protestants."

Dr. William G. Storey, Assistant Professor of History at Duquesne University, later professor of History and Liturgy at the University of Notre Dame,[201] contacted Pastor Albert to invite his participation in an Ecumenical Conference over a five-day period. Each evening of the conference one of the five churches—Greek Orthodox, Lutheran, Presbyterian, Roman Catholic, and Methodist—was asked "to offer its own order of the Eucharistic Liturgy, for in the celebration of the Supper is the heart, the theology, and the worship of the Church." Professor Storey asked Dr. Albert "to be in charge for the Lutherans."

In his report to the council regarding these invitations, the pastor noted, "I am being asked increasingly to serve as Protestant spokesman in the Ecumenical dialog." He added, "The possibilities offered to me are offered also to the congregation. In large measure, the reason is because we are here at the center of the city and at the front line of these developments. It is increasingly impossible for us to see ourselves in the old role of a quiet congregation, serving our people and unchanged by world affairs. On the contrary, we are in the sometimes wild and always moving middle of these issues and developments. . . . . The Ecumenical Movement is more than a possibility; it is a fact, and it is probably the most powerful fact operating in all Christendom today. . . . We cannot escape it. . . ." He understood and was sensitive to the attitude of some in the congregation and he noted this pastoral judgment. "Placing the matter openly before the congregation would almost invite persons with strong anti-Catholic prejudices and little or no information either to control the resultant action or to inflame controversy. I, therefore, ask the Church Council this evening: (1) To recognize the Ecumenical Movement as a fact of the Christian Church, in which we are involved. (2) To recognize the opportunity of our congregation to be the leader of the Lutherans in the area, as well as a prominent voice for the Protestant cause. (3) To offer our physical facilities for ecumenical gatherings where there is wise and joint planning and where such gatherings in no way compromise our faith or our worship. (4) To call upon our people to recognize such opportunity for leadership that falls to us and to attend and support such events and always pray for the unity of the Churches. (5) To endorse the more specialized and particular efforts of individuals who feel called upon to participate in more intensive phases of ecumenicity such as our present Faith to Faith layman's group, or a possible liturgical study group, or the participation in the seminars of the conference being called by Duquesne University."

Not all ecumenical relationships continued to flourish. The Board of Directors of the [Presbyterian] Pittsburgh Theological Seminary had approved the participation of Dr. J. Gordon Chamberlin in the educational work of First Church "for a period in excess of three months, the maximum normally authorized by the Board for service of this nature, because they were attempting to re-define the urban ministry and were seeking to utilize seminary students, for training, in our program." The Board of Directors of the seminary decided not to continue Dr. Chamberlin's service with the church after June 1, 1965.

There were other signs of impending change and challenge for the congregation. Pastor Albert began his report to the annual meeting in January 1965, "The congregation that seeks to exist and minister in the heart of a metropolitan city can expect that the way will be rough and insecure, indeed. The advent and exit of each succeeding year does not make the way smoother or easier. All about us are the swift and unexpected changes in civic, business, social, and religious life. All of these have decisive influences upon us." He noted the announced plan to raze the Penn-Sheraton Hotel across Grant Street from the church and to erect "a huge new US Steel building." Hotel guests interested in worship would be replaced by "new and increasing numbers of people available for ministry during the week and the regular working hours." There were new high-rise apartments in the vicinity of the church, but only "two members have united with us from Washington Plaza, although one or two other persons attend frequently. . . . No members have come to us from Gateway Towers." Chatham Center to the east of the church and Allegheny Center on the North Side were under construction. The "old community pattern of 'door-to-door evangelism'" was impossible in the city: "There you simply don't get by the doorman."

Membership and attendance had passed their peak.[202] Pastor Albert noted, "This [declining] trend has existed over the past three or four years, and there is no way to predict whether the trend will continue or change in favor of net gains rather than losses." He observed further, "An examination of our losses this past year show[s] that they result from three major factors: 1) losses by death, in disproportionate numbers, because of the large number of our members in advanced age; 2) removal from the city; 3) younger families with children who withdraw from us in favor of community or suburban congregations." With the decline in membership, there was a corresponding decline in income. The church council wrote to the congregation in February 1965, "While many individuals and families raised their pledge from the prior year, a greater number who pledged in 1964 either reduced their pledges or declined to pledge at all in 1965. As a result, anticipated income from pledges decreased $12,500 from 1964."

Despite these discouraging reports, the congregation continued its commitment to call an assistant pastor "to assist the pastor in administration and pastoral care and to give leadership to all phases of the educational program." [March 23, 1965]

At the May 11, 1965 meeting of the Church Council, Dr. Albert presented his letter of resignation as pastor of the congregation with a view to accepting the call of the Lutheran Theological Seminary at Philadelphia to be a Professor of Practical Theology with an emphasis on homiletics. The council accepted the resignation to be effective July 1 and called a special meeting for May 17 "for the purpose of discussing the problems created by the resignation of the Pastor." At that meeting Pastor Albert presented the statement of policy which he had drafted several years earlier to guide the congregation in its search for a new pastor. He announced that on Sunday, June 13 his daughter, Janet Albert, was to be married during the regular celebration of the Holy Communion; on June 20 Dr. Aden would be installed as director of the Counseling Center (he was to be ordained by the Synod on June 10); June 27 would be Pastor Albert's final sermon. Pastor Albert also offered to suggest names of pastors to take the services during July and August and would provide "a list of possible candidates to become pastor." Among those names were the Rev. Dr. Franklin Drewes Fry, pastor of Christ Church, York, Pennsylvania, and the Reverend Matthew Winters of Camp Hill.

Dr. Albert retired from the Philadelphia Seminary in 1981. He died in Kissimmee, Florida, October 7, 2002.

August 5, 1965, a special meeting of the church council was called to consider a proposal brought by the Reverend Robert Ruble, Pastor of Berkeley Heights Lutheran Church, that the various facets of the program of the Lutheran Church in America in Pittsburgh be brought together in one structure in the downtown area. The proposal was to use the Grant Street property and replace the present building with "a sanctuary for First Church, offices for its staff, an assembly hall, a cafeteria, parking, educational facilities, a library, music and art facilities, a church supply store, an expanded counseling center, Synod offices, offices of the Lutheran Service Society, and hotel type rooms." The council unanimously agreed to explore the possibility.

In September Pastor Matthew Winters attended the council meeting to present himself to the council. The council was sufficiently impressed as to recommend that a meeting of the congregation be held to issue a call to him as the next pastor. The meeting was not called, but what went wrong is not recorded. Other names were considered, among them the Reverend Arnold Keller of Allentown, Pennsylvania and Dr. Henry Luffberry of Washington, D.C. [203] Progress was slow. The committee reported to the congregation at its annual meeting in January 1966, "Twenty-seven prospective candidates have been suggested to Council; fourteen churches have been visited ["from Allentown, Pa., to Indianapolis, Ind, and from Erie, Pa., to Washington, D.C."]. Nine prospects have been approached about a possible call. One man has talked with the council. Several of the men suggested were changing positions before we contacted them." January 31, 1966, the council voted to recommend Dr. Robert W. Long of the American Lutheran Church to the congregation for a call. He apparently declined. March 15 the Reverend William Downey of Fox Point, Milwaukee, Wisconsin, met with the council. A motion to extend a call to him was defeated. March 20 the council voted (with one dissent and two abstentions) to extend a call to the Reverend Matthew Winters. He had not replied by April 12. April 28 the Reverend Michael C. McDaniel met with the council, and it was recommended that a call be extended to him. After discussing salary, he declined the call. May 11 the Reverend David Richard Gerberding of Milwaukee met with the council. June 2 the Reverend L. William Youngdahl of Omaha, Nebraska met with the council and later declined.

All the while the Reverend D. Dan Bravin had been visiting members of the congregation. He reported to the council on June 14, 1966, "To date, I have visited 214 families of the congregation. Many of them have been visited more than once. When a party is not home on the first visit, I leave some literature in their letter-box or under the door to let them know that I have been there. A day or two later, when I think they have had time to read the literature, I call them over the telephone in the evenings to complete the visit and, if possible, make an appointment for a personal visit. In cases of illness, I visit as often as I think it necessary. I have called on some as many times as they were in need of comfort and succor—3, 4, and 5 times.

"I seek to make all my visits 'pastoral visits'. By that I mean, I seek to keep the conversation on a spiritual level. Before leaving, I read a passage of Scripture appropriate to their needs and pray with them and for them. The faithful are commended for their faithfulness; the unfaithful are urged to re-dedicate their lives to God. Those who are dissatisfied with the way the church is run have things explained to them why it appears to them unsatisfactory and, whenever possible, I seek to put the best construction on their misunderstanding. People who do not know the inner working of the church always think they could do it better. If I do not always succeed in changing their opinions completely, I have, at least, brought emollient to bear on their imaginary hurt wounds.

"On the whole, members of First Church are the same as members of any other congregation: there are the delightfully devout people and the superficial 'joiners'; the well-established and the drifters; those who are attached to the church but not rooted in it, and those who are attached to the Master Who is the Head of the Church.

"It should be noted that whatever impressions I have gained through my visitation are only first impressions. Nevertheless, I am not often wrong in my impressions."

The search continued. June 28 the Reverend Thomas J. Weber of Baltimore met with the council, who voted to extend a call to him. July 8 he wrote to the council specifying certain conditions under which he would consider accepting a call as pastor: salary of $10,000; housing allowance of $5,000; an automobile, leased or purchased be provided him for use in the performance of his duties; that the congregation assume full responsibility for his participation in the church's pension, health, and family protection plan. The council denied his request as exceeding offers made to previous candidates and because the $18,600 package could have an adverse effect on the request for additional funds from the Board of American Missions for the Counseling Center, would immediately give cause for upward adjustments in other salaries, would impair the plan to call an assistant pastor, and would approximate the salaries of "top synod officials, which, if granted, might incur embarrassment and criticism by synod officials."

At long last, August 2, 1966, the council met with the Reverend John T. Braughler, pastor of Good Shepherd Church in Monroeville. A meeting of the congregation was scheduled for Sunday, August 28, 1966, following the 11:00 a.m. service for the purpose of voting to extend a call to Pastor Braughler. The annual salary was to be initially $8500, plus the free use of "a parsonage" or $3250 in lieu of a parsonage and all utilities, and $1800 automobile expense. An exact count of the votes was not recorded. The minutes simply report that more than 75% of the 459 votes cast were in favor of extending a call. What was to prove to be the longest pastorate in the history of the congregation had begun.

CHAPTER 8.

The Longest Pastorate
From Tradition to Mission

John Thomas Braughler (pronounced "BROCK-ler") was born in Cherry Tree, Pennsylvania January 11, 1922. After service in the United States Navy, he graduated from Thiel College in 1947 and from the Lutheran Seminary at Philadelphia in 1950. He married Dorothy Ament, and they had three children. He was pastor of Emmanuel Church in Etna, Pennsylvania from 1950-1954 and was the founding pastor of Good Shepherd Church in Monroeville from 1954 to 1966. Two years after he was called as pastor of First Church, Pastor Braughler was awarded the honorary degree of Doctor of Divinity by his alma mater, Thiel College.

Pastor Braughler had come to the attention of First Church because of the growth of the mission congregation he founded in Monroeville, a growing area east of Pittsburgh. With the arrival of their new pastor, the congregation's understanding of its mission was to change. In an interview in the *Pittsburgh Press* October 19, 1966, Pastor Braughler declared, "Congregations are moving from 'Tradition to Mission' and thriving upon it."

John Braughler

The ecumenical movement of the mid-twentieth century by its dialogue and cooperation caused the Reformation, he said, to fade in importance as a sixteenth-century interlude, and "the First

Century's purpose for the Church begins to assume more prominence for the [present] day." He looked forward to moving into something new and "be reforming still." Now the Church "must accept its present struggle in learning its mission." That uncertain struggle to identify the mission of the parish was to continue throughout his long pastorate.

In his first report to the church council, November 8, 1966, Pastor Braughler submitted his objectives in his ministry: to place highest priority on preaching and teaching, pastoral acts and visitation, administrative duties, "planning of winter and spring program," "to discover the mission and purpose of our Lord for us." That statement guided his next twenty-three years as pastor of the parish. Preaching was understood to be of such a central importance in the work of the congregation that Pastor Braughler proposed that a guest preacher be invited to the church one Sunday each month, and a list of notable figures in the church was drawn up. It was an ecumenical list; the preacher on Reformation Day 1972 was the Roman Catholic Bishop Anthony Bosco. Preaching and pastoral visitation were indeed Pastor Braughler's strengths.

Raised a Presbyterian, he was, however, not fluent in the language of liturgical worship, nor did he have a secure grasp of its centrality in the Lutheran tradition nor of its formative power. "Laymen's Sunday" was observed June 6, 1970 with Caroline Stumpf preaching and Whitey Carlson, Andrew Farley, and Marten Jenkins leading the service. A "Laymen's Sunday" continued to be observed on the first Sunday in June each year. "Laymen's Week" was observed for a time in the mid-1970s with a lay person preaching at the five noon services that week. September 29, 1971 the consensus of the council was to approve "the pastor's plans for a miniature church service each Tuesday, with communion once a month." The plans for 1988 included on Ash Wednesday and Maundy Thursday what was called "communion worship." On Good Friday there was the three-hour service and Holy Communion was "offered following the service." The Easter Vigil was not celebrated in 1988 because of the low attendance the previous year. Reverting to a widespread Protestant practice not uncommon in Lutheran churches in earlier years the pastor suggested using the "three-fold Amen" during Lent, although there was no provision for such an Amen in the *Lutheran Book of Worship*.

Pastor Braughler, who, following the practice of his two immediate predecessors, purchased a home in Mount Lebanon (309 Old Farm Road), was not intimately acquainted with work in the city. In his first report to the congregation, January 16, 1967, he admitted as much. "Serving for the past twelve years in a suburban church, I have not been unaware of the city church. The literature coming to us told us of the struggles with declining membership, change in the parish, and the search for the true mission." He was, as he admitted, groping his way toward understanding the work of the church in the city. In preparation for a meeting of urban pastors to discuss urban strategy, Pastor Braughler asked the church council for suggestions and thoughts. "In our Lord's Church here in the heart of the city what can we do together that we cannot do alone? I want to hear your thinking before I attend a Synodical meeting. . . ." [April 16, 1968] Such a collaborative approach was to be a defining characteristic of Pastor Braughler's ministry.

The whole Church in the United States was groping for ways to address the daunting work in changing urban areas. Many congregations simply abandoned the inner city and relocated where the majority of their members resided. Others sought to identify a ministry in and for the city, as Pastor Albert had begun to do during his ministry at First Church. The distinction between "urban" churches in blighted areas of a city and downtown churches located in the commercial and business center was not often understood. Pastor Braughler in January 1969 made a trip to New York to examine the significant work that was being done in that city. He visited St. Peter's Church at 54th and Lexington in midtown Manhattan, which under the leadership of its pastor Ralph E. Peterson was seeking a way to bring a significant Lutheran Christian witness to New York. In 1970 the congregation authorized the sale of its impressive nineteenth-century Germanic Gothic building and the formation of a condominium with Citicorp to develop a new complex with a church at street level and below, and a landmark bank building rising high above it. The new St. Peter's Church was consecrated in 1977. Pastor Braughler visited the church and its pastors, worshiped there at noonday, at "their evening fellowship communion," the jazz mass, and the Sunday morning Eucharists. He also observed the work of George W. Webber, a faculty member of Union Theological Seminary who had made a name for himself in urban ministry as one of the founding pastors of the East Harlem Protestant Parish in 1948 and as program director of the Metropolitan Urban Service Training Program. He met with Lawrence Lazelle Durgin, pastor (1961-1979) of the Broadway United Church of Christ, a congregation that was preparing to sell its decaying building and to worship on Sundays at the Roman Catholic Church of St. Paul the Apostle at 59th Street and Ninth Avenue. Pastor Braughler also met with the staff of Judson Memorial Church on Washington Square. The purpose of the visit was primarily to gather ideas for the work of

Construction of U.S. Steel tower

a second pastor of First Church whose chief responsibility was to be "to the city."

The frustrations of the work in downtown Pittsburgh were evident in Pastor Braughler's report to the congregational meeting in 1969. "Our membership holds at a level and attendance reflects the national trend" [i.e. downward][204]. "[F]rankly I am at a loss to know how to handle the increasingly difficult problem of getting people to give the time that it takes to come into the city and to sit for the planning, to do the research and to carry out the details involved in any program development."

The immediate vicinity of the church building was changing radically. The first and most obvious challenge to the congregation, after March 1, 1967, had been the loss of the use of the parking lot next door caused by the erection of the Bell Telephone Company's sixteen-story domestic and overseas switching center, completed in 1969. Concern for the integrity of the Tiffany window of the Good Shepherd required that a protective framework be installed by the George A. Fuller Company, which was constructing the building next door. Directly across Grant Street the new headquarters of the United States Steel Corporation was completed in 1970. At sixty-four stories, it was the tallest building between New York and Chicago.[205] First Church, which had briefly been the tallest building on its end of Grant Street, was now to be dwarfed by the surrounding skyscrapers which were closing in around it.

The new dominance of secular buildings was not merely symbolic of the changing city. The construction of the Bell Telephone building next to the church and the U.S. Steel tower across the street threatened the structural integrity of the First Church building. Serious movement was evident in the Grant Street wall of the church. Legal action was begun against the Bell Telephone Company and Fuller Construction Company and against U.S. Steel and Turner Construction Company. This was not the first damage sustained by the building because of neighboring construction. In 1960 a $110,000 settlement had been reached over damages sustained by the church because of the construction of the Porter Building (now the Home Loan Bank building) adjoining the church property to the south. These funds were used to establish a Restoration Fund for the restoration of the chapel or for a major construction program if approved and undertaken. The council minutes of February 18, 1969 report the details of the damage and the state of negotiations.

The suit against the Bell Telephone Company and U.S. Steel was settled in January 1974. Bell Telephone agreed to pay $25,000 and U.S. Steel $49,000. The church in the presentation of its case had offered proof of damages totaling approximately $105,000, but the church's counsel as well as the litigation committee recommended acceptance of the settlement offer totaling $74,000.

In 1979 the city Bureau of Building Inspection required all buildings susceptible to unsound facades that could endanger pedestrian traffic to be examined by a registered engineer. Gustav Stueber, P.E. inspected the building on October 17, 18, and 20 and reported to the congregation on October 27. He referred to the examination made in 1968 that addressed the distresses due to the construction of the Porter Building, the Bell Telephone Building, and the U.S. Steel building and repaired "the main damage to the structure in the north wall of the building, next to the Bell Telephone Building." The 1979 report concluded, "The construction of the Porter Building, Bell Telephone Building, and the United States Steel Building have not caused the stability of the church structure to be impaired. . . . After 11 years, we cannot expect any further vertical or lateral movement. On all century buildings (100 years + or -), bonding of grout between stones and brick is the problem. Most grouting is turned to loose sand and lime. . . . What we have here is a maintenance problem. . . . If maintenance problems are met, the church structure is safe, inside and out."

There were changes in the pastoral staff. Dr. D. Dan Bravin, who had been serving as visitation pastor asked to be relieved of his duties in January 1967. Dr. LeRoy Aden's continued work as pastor and director of the Pastoral Counseling Center was not to last long. In April 1967 the church council received his letter of resignation. He had been appointed associate professor of practical theology at the Lutheran Theological Seminary at Philadelphia, joining his former colleague, Harold Albert, there. The Reverend Hayden Britton, assistant minister of East Liberty Presbyterian Church, agreed to serve as interim Acting Director of the center through the end of 1967. The Reverend John R. Pro, pastor of First Baptist Church in Jeannette and a staff counselor at the center, was appointed interim director while the search for a permanent director continued. Mr. Pro was originally appointed for an interim six-month term, but his work continued for two and a half years.

The continuation of the counseling center was in doubt. The Board of American Missions indicated that it could not continue to provide substantial financial support beyond 1967 and encouraged First Church to make a financial commitment to the continuance of the center. The congregation assigned $5000 for the purpose in the 1968 budget.

A draft prospectus for a Pastoral Counseling Center was prepared as part of the close examination of the work of such a center by the parish and by the Lutheran Service Society of Western Pennsylvania. The need for such a center was affirmed as was its location in a congregational setting. The Lutheran Service Society was turning more and more toward counseling and had relocated its facilities to East Liberty. The prospectus recommended that the director of the Center be called by the synod Executive Board and should maintain his office in First Church. Eventually, after extended discussions, February 12, 1970, the synod proposed and the congregation agreed that the Counseling Center be merged with the Lutheran Service Society with the Society's director overall operation. The Society had a candidate in mind as counselor and director of the Center at First Church. That candidate, the Reverend Lee A. McDaniel, with the approval of the council, was called as director of the Center.

In May 1968, a congregational task force proposed the calling of an assistant pastor to carry major responsibility for the weekday ministry "with special sensitivity to the changing needs for worship experiences and other programs." The person was to be a pastor with four to eight years' experience in an urban setting. The council recognized the need for a second pastor and included such a position in the budget for 1969. In May 1969 a candidate was selected: the Reverend J. Norman Thorson of Cincinnati, Ohio. On May 18, a call was extended to him to become Associate Pastor of First Church. He too found housing in Mount Lebanon (on Magnolia Avenue) and began his work on the second Sunday in June.

His work increasingly focused on young people, especially the alienated, drug addicted, and runaways, and his lasting contribution to the city was the creation of Whale's Tale. The odd name was chosen to recall the story of the resurrection of the runaway Jonah from the belly of the big fish. In 1984 an Ecumenical Runaway Ministry was formed by First Church, Trinity Cathedral, St. Mary of Mercy, and Smithfield United Church and the Pittsburgh Leadership Foundation. Whale's Tale and the Ecumenical Ministry formed a partnership to serve the needs of homeless, runaway young people under 21 years of age in downtown Pittsburgh.

Pastor Thorson resigned in May 1971 to accept a call to a parish in Harrisburg.

The foundation for this ministry was laid in September 1968 when Pastor Conrad W. Weiser of the Lutheran Student Ministry in a letter to the Church Council asked permission to use the church building weekly for an extension of the University Ministry. He requested "a room with access from the alley and the use of a sink and hot plate, where donuts and coffee would be served and where students downtown could be invited to an evening away from their dorms." The coffee house began operation on Thursday, December 5; more than 150 attended and of that number a dozen or more attended Sunday morning services at First Church. The student work was first called "the Crumbling Wall," later simply "The House." In January 1970 it was expanded to three nights each week, Sunday, Monday, and Thursday, from 7:30 until 11 p.m. Each night attracted between 50 and 75 young people. Pastor Thorson's work with the House involved him in counseling with young people with drug addictions, and this led at the beginning of 1970 to the establishment of the Whale's Tale, originally operated out of First Church, for drug addiction treatment and rehabilitation. The center moved into renovated space at 105 Market Street. This work was soon to overshadow and then in 1970 to replace the coffee house and be sponsored by the Catholic Youth Organization and the Western Pennsylvania-West Virginia Synod, as well as First Church. It was a comprehensive program supporting the individual in a decision to withdraw from the use of drugs, supporting that person with appropriate medical and psychiatric assistance, providing the opportunity to live in a half-way house for a period of transition.

In the absence of an overarching plan or vision of what the congregation was to be, experimentation abounded, especially in the weekday services. The goal seemed to be to find something, anything, that worked, something that attracted a significant number of people. There was at least an awareness of the importance of weekday services in the mission of the downtown church. Attendance at the noon services was declining. It was decided in December 1966 to open both the Wednesday and the Thursday services to both men and women, rather than segregating the sexes as had been the practice. Lunch was to be served following each service.

A fuller schedule of noontime weekday activities was proposed in June 1968. Tuesday was to feature lectures, dramatic presentations, and current concerns; Wednesday a service for men and women, followed by a light lunch; Thursday a service for men and women followed by a hot meal. Friday was to follow a varied pattern: the first Friday of each month was to be a celebration of the Holy Communion with a guest preacher; the second Friday was to be ante-communion with a guest preacher; the third Friday an experiment in contemporary worship, a folk mass, being prepared by the student intern, Ray Dice, "to reach some of our young people and the college group," and celebrated in the chapel "as being a more relaxed setting."[206]

The congregation showed its gratitude to Pastor Braughler "for his dedication and love for First Lutheran Church" by presenting him with a Christmas gift of $300 in 1968 and increasing his salary by $900 per year.

What was then popularly called "integration" (primarily of blacks into white congregations to the enrichment of both) was a significant issue for the church of the time. The evangelism committee of First Church understood that a downtown church should be a leader in declaring openness to all people. A statement drafted by the committee was approved by the church council May 9, 1967. "In the light of the immeasurable love and mercy of God, the witness of Holy Scripture, and the stated policy of the Church, we of First English Evangelical Lutheran Church hereby continue to proclaim openly and without apology or reservation that all men, regardless of race or national origin, are welcome to worship our Lord and our God with us, to examine his Word with us, and if they so desire, to unite with us, following proper instruction, as fellow members of the community of believers which is this congregation." The matter was not controversial in the congregation at this time, but had such an inclusive view obtained twenty years earlier, the mission begun by First Church, St. John's Church in the Hill District, might still be a living congregation to this day.

April 4, 1968, Martin Luther King, Jr. was assassinated. His murder set off violent responses in many cities across the land. Pittsburgh was not exempt. In response, to quiet the city, the mayor forbade any large gatherings on the street. First Church offered its space for a peaceful meeting of white citizens. Some at the meeting suggested walking to city hall and marching around it, but Father (later Monsignor) Charles Owen Rice, a Roman Catholic active in the labor movement and other causes, counseled against such a march, and the assembly agreed. Peace was preserved.[207]

The Council of Churches of the Pittsburgh Area, May 10, 1968, addressed a letter to the constituent churches announcing the actions of its executive board to affirm the right of poor people to protest lawfully and non-violently, to urge churches to support the members of the Poor Peoples' March through Pittsburgh to Washington, to declare its support of the goals of the Poor Peoples Campaign.

A year later, the pastor warned the council at its May 20, 1969 meeting, that "an outside group might interrupt a Sunday service to present the 'Black Manifesto.'" The manifesto was an indictment of white society and white churches in particular, disseminated primarily by a group known as the Black Panthers. Their most notable interruption occurred on a Sunday morning at Riverside Church in New York City. The consensus of the council was that in such an event, the pastor should ask the group to make its presentation during the pause for normal announcements, but if the group demanded to speak immediately they should be allowed to do so. "The consensus of Council was clearly that such a visit should not in the first instance be physically resisted."

The role of the church building was not yet secure in the mind of the Board of American Missions. May 14, 1968, Jerry Sandvig and Kent Johnson of the Board met with the church council to make their recommendations. They reported that there were limited available resources for urban work from the Board. New ministries were springing up all across the country based in old facilities. They admired the physical condition of the building, although they found the nave larger than necessary. Three possibilities were discussed concerning the property: redesigning, selling to someone who would build a building on the site with an option on part of it for a church (the model of St. Peter's in Manhattan selling to Citicorp), relocating in downtown Pittsburgh. The board had no definite answers, but it did make the observation that "the use of the building for program will be an ever-changing thing and will need complete flexibility of the space within the building." In retrospect, this was helpful in arguing against

Hemmed in
United States Steel building going up

rebuilding with a specific program in mind. Jerry Sandvig in a follow-up letter dated June 21, 1968, suggested that the congregation continue to use the building as currently designed until the building projects around it reach completion and the area "has stabilized."

What had been originally the Sunday School chapel had become dingy and uninviting, poorly lighted and poorly heated. A brighter and more versatile space was desired for weekday services and for theater in the round and other less structured uses.

A nondenominational Drop-In Center for retired people was proposed by the Social Ministry Committee in September 1969, to be held on Thursdays from 10 to 3. Participants would make handcrafts, engage in recreation, and participate in a devotional period.

Pastor Thorson proposed that the weekday services be reduced to one informal service on Wednesdays and that Thursdays be given to "unstructured events" to serve as "a listening post where the pastors and others could move about and get to know people better." It was not well received and the original two-day pattern was restored. Other proposed changes were accepted. Pastor Braughler suggested the introduction of a third Sunday morning service at 9:45 which would use "new forms of liturgy, etc." and be led by Pastor Thorson. The proposal began in Lent 1970. From June 21 through August 1970 the 8:30 and 11:00 Sunday services were to be merged into a single service at 10 a.m. The "contemporary service" at 9:45 was moved to 5:00 p.m. beginning April 26 "and continuing for the indefinite future." Responsibility for the noonday services was shifted from Pastor Thorson to the City-Social Ministry Committee of the congregation. They proposed "that a single weekly service be conducted each Wednesday" and that the luncheon service be discontinued but that people should be encouraged to bring their lunches.

The Lutheran Church in America under the guidance of the noted church planner Lyle Shaller had identified First Church Pittsburgh as one of thirteen "metropolitan congregations" in the Lutheran Church in America. First Church often referred to this identification as an indication of the distinctiveness of the congregation, although the designation did not help the congregation clarify its mission to the city. The identification, moreover, did not necessarily indicate strength. Some of the thirteen, such

The chapel set up for a service

as Redeemer Church in Atlanta were strong; others were at the time weak, such as St. Mark's in San Francisco.

G. Logan McElvany, after a long and distinguished career as organist and choirmaster at First Church retired from that position in September 1971. The church council in gratitude for his work guaranteed a lifetime pension of $3000 per year, "the use of the organ for teaching except at such times as the regular organist may require use of it," adequate office space in the church, and asked him to continue as the organist for the noonday services. The council by resolution, September 21, 1971, proclaimed Sunday, October 17, 1971, to be "G. Logan McElvany Sunday at First Lutheran Church in honor of the man and his music—preeminently a man of God who worships from his heart through his music—who has devoted his life to the faithful service of Christ and his congregation—who has enriched the lives of all who have known him, be they students, singers, pastors or fellow worshippers, and who now continues his service with us as organist emeritus with our heartfelt gratitude and our prayers."

Three candidates for the position of organist were considered: Mrs. Jamee Graham, Mr. James Chute, and Mr. Robert

Charles McCoy. Mr. McCoy was eliminated from consideration, and Mrs. Graham was appointed for a period of one year. Two months later she resigned, and Robert McCoy was employed as part-time organist for the year 1972.

G. Logan McElvany

Experiments with the liturgy continued. The Worship and Music Committee announced on April 5, 1973, that "Pastor [Roy] Lloyd will sing the liturgy—first setting—at the 11:00 AM Festival Service" on Easter Day. Pastor Lloyd was serving part-time as an assistant to the pastor for the year. His appointment continued the following year. The committee in its report of May 3, 1973, recommended that a new processional cross be purchased because the existing one was homemade, unwieldy, and some seven years old, and that the cross be used at all services throughout the year. The new cross was used on the Day of Pentecost, 1973.

Inter-Lutheran[208] work on what was to become the *Lutheran Book of Worship* began in 1968. The original expectation was that all Lutherans in North America would be able to use the same service book. Moreover, the use of the new book was expected to lead from liturgical renewal encouraged by the revised liturgies and hymnal, to the reinvigoration of the Church. In 1973 *Contemporary Worship 6. The Church Year: Calendar and Lectionary* was published, introducing the three-year lectionary to Lutherans in North America. First Church promptly adopted the new lectionary and began using it in Advent 1973. In 1976 the congregation agreed to participate in trial use of the proposed services of Holy Communion and the Burial of the Dead prepared by the Inter-Lutheran Commission on Worship, but their inquiry asking further information about the project caused their acceptance to be classified as too late for consideration. The emerging liturgy of the Lutheran Church in North America and the opportunity it afforded for teaching about the centrality of liturgical worship and its renewal were not a priority for pastor or congregation.

August 2, 1973 the pastor announced to the worship and music committee that the altar cross had been stolen. It had cost $60 eighty years before and had the name of the church engraved on it. The pastor and the committee believed that the cross would be returned when the thief realized that it could not be pawned. It was, of course, not returned. The old processional cross was cut down and placed temporarily on the altar gradine. In February 1974 the church council (by a vote of 9 for and 6 against) gave permission to the worship and music committee to enter into a contract with the noted Pittsburgh artist Virgil Cantini (1919-2009), Professor of Studio Art at the University of Pittsburgh, with whom they had met, to design a new altar cross. Professor Cantini's sculptures enjoyed prominent places throughout Pittsburgh; one of the most prominent being "Joy of Life" at Baum Boulevard and Whitfield Street, near East Liberty Presbyterian Church. An anonymous donor had given $1000 for the cross. The relatively close vote of approval indicated the mixed reception the cross was to receive. Some were much taken with its striking colors and imposing presence; others found it too harsh, introducing a bright orange which was not otherwise found in the chancel or nave.

The cross itself, 48 inches high, was of wood, edged in brass, bearing enamel inlays with a stylized design of interweaving thorns and lilies, telling of life out of death. At the center of the cross, echoing the central medallion of the marble altar, was an Agnus Dei, whose sacrificial life is the theme of the four evangelists, whose symbols appear at the ends of the cross arms. The color scheme of the cross was designed to reproduce the colors of the stained glass in the rose window at the opposite end of the main axis of the nave. The design was approved July 21, 1974, and its fabrication authorized.

There was unhappiness for some time with the quality and the concept of the paid quartette. It was decided that the quartette be discontinued beginning January 1, 1974 and that it be replaced with a volunteer choir.

During 1973-74 extensive renovations were made to the lower level of the church, especially in the kitchen, an "activities center" was created, and the administrative areas were redesigned. A rededication service was held at 10 a.m., followed by a brunch, June 23, 1974. There was a "festive procession"; Pastor Roy Lloyd and Mr. William Koehler, both of whom regularly assisted in the visitation of the sick, participated in the service.

Experiments with the Sunday service schedule continued. The "Music and Worship Committee" (the erroneous order of names given in the council minutes is significant) proposed that in June, July, and August 1974 Matins be sung at 8:30 and The Service at 10:30. After discussion the proposal was amended so that the service times for July and August be 8:30 and 10 a.m. In September 1974 the church council accepted the Worship and Music Committee's recommendation that on Sundays there be one service only, at 11:00 a.m., for a trial period beginning the first Sunday in October and continuing through the Last Sunday after the Epiphany, January 26, 1975. At the conclusion of the trial period, no clear consensus having developed, the 8:30 service was restored "effective March 2, with Communion an integral part of the service." Thus weekly Eucharist was begun at the First Church.

In May 1974 Caroline Stumpf, the first daughter of the parish to enter the ministry, graduated from seminary and was ordained.

Seminarian Gene Allen Parker was selected as the intern for a year beginning September 1, 1974. He did not want to live on the South Side but rather in Oakland, where, he told Pastor Braughler, "the action is." An apartment rented for him at 705 Ivy Street apparently was not acceptable. September 17, 1974: "Mr. Parker has found an acceptable apartment in Bethel Park and will move in as soon as possible."

Frederick G. Neiderhiser was the intern for the year 1975-76.

In his report to the church council May 21, 1974, Pastor Braughler called "upon the Church Council to do all in its power to serve in strengthening our community and helping it to become the 'family of God' showing concern for one another. Let's remember that we are a mission congregation serving dozens of guests from the city and also meeting crisis situations for those who are referred to us. We need to develop volunteer service and be knitted [sic] together in worship, Bible study, and prayer, and then make available meaningful opportunities for service. I am convinced that First Lutheran Church stands at a crossroad with great opportunity in the future."

On September 25, 1974, the twenty-ninth year of Wednesday services from 12:30-12:50 began. Lunch was served before and after "in our new activities center." Friday was a celebration of the Holy Communion in the chapel. On Thursdays from 12:10-12:50 there was a "Bible study and discussion of great issues." These Bible study sessions continued until 2008.

Thursday April 3, 1975, a strong wind storm moved though downtown Pittsburgh causing the copper cross on the spire of the church to dislodge and "to move back and forth toward Grant Street." The long wooden post which supported the cross had rotted. Alarmed citizens called the church office. Walter Fafata, the chair of the property committee, called a roofer, who worked for three hours but could not do much without scaffolding. Three city building inspectors were on the scene for most of the day; the sidewalk was blocked off. In the early evening, about 7 p.m., the street car wires having been lowered, a crane was in place. About 9:30 Bill Mueller and Walter Fafata were raised on the crane. In driving wind and snow, they cut the ground wire of the cross and brought the cross to the street. The damage to the spire was repaired, and Walter Fafata took the copper cross to his basement where it remained until the renovations to the church basement in 2000. The cross, now polished and fitted with a new trefoil base, adorns the ceiling of what is now called Holy Cross Hall. The spire was capped and remained without a cross until a handsome new one was installed November 2, 1998. The copper cross was the second cross to crown the spire. The original cross, seen on early drawings of the church, came down about 1912 and was unaccountably not replaced until the copper cross was installed in March 1922 when the spire was undergoing repair.

The church organ was in serious disrepair. The original organ was installed by the Johnson Organ Company of Hartford, Connecticut, in 1888. It was powered by water. The controls were partially electrified in 1900, and a new console was purchased. This work was done by the successor of the Johnson Company, Austin Organ. Extensive general refurbishing was carried out in 1924, and in 1948 a Moeller console was installed. Only emergency repairs were performed after that, and these became increasingly frequent. The action of the instrument was sluggish and undependable due to worn parts, air chamber leaks, and accumulated filth. Its range and versatility were reduced to about half its potential because over the years components that ceased to function were simply abandoned if they were not considered vital to the basic operation. "Such handicaps as these try the skill of the most accomplished musician, and it is only because our organist, Mr. Charles McCoy, is exceptionally capable, that the organ's deterioration has not become more obvious to untrained ears. Mr. McCoy struggles weekly to achieve acceptable performance levels from the instrument. He says that the problem of 'ciphers' (notes that sustain sound after release) are a particularly exasperating headache. They happen unexpectedly, and at a moment's notice he must be prepared to accommodate with an alternative combination. He also reports that restoring the out-of-service sections would be most worthwhile." Such frustrations surely contributed to Charles McCoy's resignation as organist. Austin Organs gave as the total cost of these repairs "to restore the organ to first class condition" $40,435. The council chose the LLM [Lutheran Laymen's Movement] Fund Raising and Counseling Service to organize the fund-raising campaign for the organ. When the matter was put to the congregation at a special meeting, of the 269 people at the two services, only 98 chose to participate in the special meeting. Edward C. Menzie, the discouraged chair of the Finance Committee, wrote to the Director of the LLM Fund Raising and Counseling Service (March 7, 1977), reported these facts, and observed, "As you can plainly see, our congregation is not alive with the spirit—as a matter of fact we are currently undergoing a "Parish Renewal Class" hoping to reawaken some feelings. With a vote of 58 in favor and 40 opposed to the assistance that the LLM could provide, I recommend that we not engage you at this time. Perhaps some time in the future before we are forced to close our doors, the congregation will realize the need for a renewed motivated personal commitment in Christian stewardship." The campaign was conducted by a congregational committee chaired by Glen Johnson and raised over $57,000.

The Lutheran Church in America, of which First Church was a part, declared 1977 to be the year of Evangelical Outreach. Pastor Braughler in his annual report to the congregation in 1977 recommended that instead of an intern for the coming year, an ordained assistant be sought "to lead us in the development of a strategy for Evangelism and Parish Renewal"; that the congregation ask Pastor Paul Himmelman, Director of the Pittsburgh Coalition, "to help us with our planning"; and "that we begin to take more seriously our Metropolitan location—to define our parish—look to serving apartment houses—Noonday opportunities—seek more actively new members—be aware of our opportunities to work with students—begin to train and develop our people to become what we are—EVANGELISTS." The Pittsburgh Coalition was an attempt by the Synod to support and encourage work in the Lutheran churches of Pittsburgh, not unlike the work done in Philadelphia by Pastor Robert Neumeyer in the Center City Parish.

Pastor Harry Souders, a doctoral candidate at the University of Pittsburgh and former director of communications for Christian Associates, was engaged in September to assist Pastor Braughler one day a week in planning, promotion, and communication of the ministry of First Church and to assist the pastor at the Sunday services.

The number of communing members held steady as did the Sunday attendance. Nonetheless, discouraging signs were beginning to appear. Seventy-three people who had not communed or contributed for more than two years were removed from the roll of members. There were twice as many funerals (24) in 1976 than in 1975; half as many new members were added in 1976 as in 1975; the Sunday School had declined from 82 to 67 scholars. The situation was not peculiar to First Church. The neighboring churches in downtown Pittsburgh were going through a similar decline.

The church facilities continued to be used by a variety of groups. A lunchtime theater presented dramas in the Grant Street Room (the large room beneath the nave) every day for a week at noon. The National Workshop for Christian Unity, organized by Christian Associates of Southwestern Pennsylvania, was held in the church. The Orthodox Church offered lectures and meditation each Tuesday at noon during Lent in the chapel.

James Hunter, Professor of Music History and Literature and Director of Graduate Studies in the School of Music at Duquesne University, was appointed organist and choirmaster and began his work on All Saints' Sunday, November 6, 1977. A native of Glasgow, Scotland, he earned a B.A. at Carnegie Institute of Technology, and M.A. at Duquesne, and a Ph.D. at Eastman School of Music in Rochester, New York. He studied organ with Arthur Jennings, Marshall Bidwell, Caspar Koch, Charles Pearson, and, in Paris, with Jean Langlais. He studied composition with Bernard Rogers and Alan Hovhaness.

He found that the renovation of the organ had been poorly done and suggested that a representative of the Austin Organ Company come to Pittsburgh to see the shoddy work done in their name. "As things stand, the work is not done, nor, in my view, has value been received for the sum already paid out." (Report to the council September 1978)

Dr. Hunter served with distinction until April 1981 when an irregular heart rhythm interrupted the flow of oxygen to his brain and he lapsed into a coma. Peter Luley served as organist in his absence. Dr. Hunter died April 27, 1981.

The church council at its meeting in April 1978 approved the purchase of the new *Lutheran Book of Worship.* At the December council meeting it was noted that the "Worship and Music Committee did not follow through with implementation of introduction of the Lutheran Book of Worship. A motion was made and seconded that a schedule be implemented. It was approved unanimously." The books were dedicated February 25, 1979. Preparation for the introduction of the book was not a priority nor were its possibilities clearly understood and articulated. There was, therefore, some unhappiness with the new book, especially among the worshippers at the 8:30 service. Most of the discontent, of course, arose from a lack of understanding of the new book and what it sought to do. "Changing the Lord's Prayer" and "changing the creed" (apparently replacing "Christian Church" with "Catholic Church") were mentioned. No one apparently sought to teach that the change was in translation not in meaning and that the Lord's Prayer was given in both the traditional and more contemporary forms and that the word "catholic" means whole and entire, and not simply Roman Catholic; Presbyterians and other Protestants who used the Apostles' Creed did not hesitate to say "catholic Church."

Jazz services "for the business community" were introduced at midday on Tuesdays (12:15-12:45) beginning October 3, 1978. The services were conducted by the Reverend James D. Percy, pastor of North Zion Lutheran Church on Brownsville Road and a former circus chaplain, who wanted to bring to Pittsburgh the jazz ministry begun in New York by Pastor John Garcia Gensel.

After a search through more than twenty names, the Pulpit Committee presented the name of the Reverend Charles R. Stadler, a Pittsburgh native and a pastor of St. John's Church of Highland, as a second pastor for the parish. He "is considered a conservative and traditional minister, whose strengths lie in the programming and organizing capabilities." Pastor Stadler accepted the call March 10, 1979; he was installed April 29. Pastor Braughler was the senior pastor and Pastor Stadler was referred to as the Community Pastor, then the Metropolitan Pastor. (The ecclesiastical meaning of "metropolitan," a bishop exercising provincial, not merely diocesan, powers, was apparently unknown to the pastors or congregation.) He referred to himself in his letter of resignation five years later as "outreach pastor."

He spent a week at the Community of Christ the Servant in Chicago in 1979, discussed with major theologians the problems of Christianity of the time, observed "a non-territorial congregation doing exciting things." He noted, "Central to their life together was the nurture and care which they showed for each other.

I see this as a key to any congregation which wants to grow." (Report November 21, 1979) Accordingly, a program was developed at First Church called Growth on Grant Street, which sought to encourage mutual support and nurture. In his characteristic way, Pastor Braughler reported to the church council September 27, 1982, "We are beginning our 'GOGS' efforts for parish leadership and ask for your cooperation and excitement. As I tried to say in my sermon Sept. 19th, the future of our church in this exciting location demands great efforts of us today. There is no way to achieve results except through hard work. With the Holy Spirit to guide us, our pastors to lead us, and you the members of the congregation all geared to growth, there is no limit to what can be accomplished. Please use your imagination, prayers, and dedication to get on the right track for fall GOGS."

Daily noon services each weekday were begun in September 1979. Monday was a said Eucharist, Tuesday "Worship and the Arts" (jazz services, organ concerts, drama, "worship in mime"); Wednesday was a "traditional preaching service" ("hymns, prayers, brief thought-provoking message"), Thursday "study /discussion while you eat" (Bible studies, theological discussions, special-interest presentations); Friday "Prayer and Praise: singing, sharing faith, prayer, scripture." After a month and a half of experience with these services, the attendance on Monday was 10-12, on Tuesday "anywhere from 10-60", on Wednesday 50-60; on Thursday for the studies 10-18; on Friday about 10. The schedule went from September through April; it was not year-round.

The city of Pittsburgh was planning a renovation of Grant Street to make it a "grand boulevard" by paving the sidewalks with rustic terrazzo, paving the street in brick with granite curbing, and installing planters down the center of the "boulevard." Test borings for the tunneling in preparation for the new light rail transport to the South Hills began in December 1979. The renovation disrupted the work of the city. George L. W. Werner, Dean of Trinity Cathedral wrote to Mayor Caliguiri on behalf of the downtown churches (September 23, 1980). The city's plans called for 550 busses to go down Oliver Avenue each day, past Trinity Cathedral and First Presbyterian Church. "I realize that this protest will do me absolutely no good whatsoever, but I will remind you that 56 years before Pittsburgh ever became a City we were serving people in this area. Downtown churches currently are part of the Convention and Visitors Bureau and are actively seeking to bring conventions to Pittsburgh from their denominations. . . . We are not naïve. We understand the needs of a City in transition and are willing to put up with our fair share of hardship. It does seem obvious, however, to me at least, that the current administration does not believe that the churches are a part of this Renaissance. I realize that I am prejudiced on this subject, but I think any City that wishes to be great needs to keep alive the downtown churches as well as catering to the merchants." It was a point that the downtown churches had to make again and again to the city for many decades.

Because of the disruption, parking for congregants on Sunday became an immediate concern to all the downtown churches. St. Mary's had to eliminate two masses on Sunday. The churches asked the Parking authority for a rate of $1.00 for Sunday parking from 6 a.m. to 4 p.m. and then a four-hour span for 50 cents. A reduced rate continues to be afforded to worshippers.

First Church would be required to resurface its sidewalk as part of the refurbishing of Grant Street. Some forward-looking members of the church, including the architect Wesley Lacock, saw this as an opportunity for the parish to make a significant architectural statement as a contribution to the project. He drew up plans up for a patio area or courtyard in front of what was then still called the chapel. (The area was sometimes referred to by the archaic but inaccurate word "garth," an enclosed yard or garden.) The plans were reviewed by an architect on the Grant Street project, Paul Wolf.

In June 1984 a family, later identified as Glen and LaVonne Johnson, as part of the courtyard renovation announced their intention to give a bronze statue "Resurrection" by Paul Granlund (1925-2003), sculptor in residence at Gustavus Adolphus College in St. Peter, Minnesota from 1971 until his retirement in 1996.[209] The sculptor visited the church and chose the site for the work. The sculpture, he said, "should be life-size or larger and should not be placed on a pedestal. Rather, it should appear to rise from ground level." As the statue was executed, however, the figure emerges from a six-foot tetrahedron mounted on a split square pillar. The sculpture is a representation of John 5:28b-29a, "the hour is coming when all who are in their graves will hear his voice and will come out." The sculpture proclaimed the promise of the Christian faith but most of all celebrated the renewal of Grant Street and of Pittsburgh generally and brought the attention of passers by to the church. Dr. Granlund moreover donated a processional cross with the same figure together with a stand to the church.

The sculpture was dedicated on Sunday October 20, 1985. There was a lecture on Christian art during the Church school time; the dedication took place during the liturgy and at its conclusion the congregation moved into the courtyard where Dr. Granlund and others gave remarks. A reception followed. Attendance at the dedication was described as disappointing. The next day, Monday, at noon the sculpture was presented to the city with the mayor and city and church officials present. A show of some of Granlund's works was set up in One Oxford Center

Pastor Stadler visited Luther Place Church in Washington, D.C. to observe its social outreach. He returned with an idea for a shelter for the homeless. This encouraged the downtown churches to work together to create Bethlehem Haven which began in the basement of Smithfield Church with the support of the Downtown Ministerium.

Following the death of James Hunter, Miles Wallace was named organist and choir director. He was a graduate of Wittenberg University and of the Institute of Sacred Music at Yale Divinity School. He began work, specified as quarter time, in the fall and became a member of the parish December 20, 1981. The following May he presented to the Worship and Music Committee a statement on worship and music in the Lutheran tradition, which was an expansion of his remarks on the subject at his initial audition/interview. He makes observations that had not been articulated so clearly for many decades at First Church and that set in motion ideas and events that were to come to flourish with the next pastorate.

The foundational principle is clear: "Of all the activities in which the church is involved, worship stands at the heart and center of its life and mission. . . . Martin Luther and those who followed him did not see themselves primarily as a new church, but rather as a distinctive confessional movement within a larger Christianity. That understanding is very important as Lutherans approach the matter of worship—how they see themselves in relation to the larger Christian tradition, and how they view music and its role in their corporate praise and prayer." Such an understanding of the centrality of worship was not shared by the pastor, who wrote in a working paper of November 18, 1981, "I am in full approval of the Growth Group Concept that we cannot build a Christian community solely around worship. There is a great hunger for not only hearing and study of the word of God, but for learning what Christian Community and Fellowship means." The remark revealed a rather shallow view of what worship is and does.

"The Lutheran Church," Miles Wallace went on to say, "is a worshipping church. Lutherans concern themselves seriously with all aspects of the church worship life. Particular emphasis, however, is given to corporate, congregational worship, where Christians gather to hear the Word and to share the Sacrament. For Lutherans, corporate worship is not simply a pleasant option; it is the indispensable and central work of the gathered Christian community from which all other facets of the church's life and mission, including one's individual worship life, derive their strength, purpose, and direction."

"The Lutheran Church is a liturgical church. With much of Christianity it shares a concern for ordered worship. Lutheran worship underscores the elements of stability and continuity with worship forms and practices that place them historically in a very long line of worshipers starting in the New Testament. Lutherans worship not in subjective isolation, but '. . . with angels and archangels and with all the company of heaven,' in concert with Christian believers of all times and places.

"Lutheran worship offers a richness and variety of forms and practices that give fullness to the celebration of corporate worship. As Lutherans worship with the recurring cycles of the church year, as they hear the Word proclaimed through ordered readings and preaching that recount the full counsel of God, and as they celebrate the sacraments, Lutherans are united with Christians of other times and places and receive strength for their task in the world.

"Lutherans receive their heritage of worship forms and practices with thanksgiving and appreciation. Lutherans should understand that their heritage is a meaningful source of continuity with their won past as well as with that of the whole church catholic. Yet Lutherans do not deify, ossify, or accept their heritage uncritically. We should view our heritage as a basis for moving toward the future. Thus Lutheran worship is simultaneously conservation yet open and ready for the future.

"As music in Lutheran worship builds on these understandings, as it helps nourish the faith, as it works to the glory of God and the edification of all our Christian brothers, it has always had a welcome and important role among Lutheran Christians. Where it has fallen short of these understandings, when it has substituted other goals, where it has become man-centered rather than God-centered, to that extent it has ceased to be Lutheran in motivation, realization, and most importantly in result.

"Music in Lutheran worship—whether the music of the congregation, choir, pastor, organ, solo voice, or instruments—finds its most natural and comfortable place in the context of the Liturgy, the Work of the People. It is in the liturgy, in all its fullness and completeness, that music in Lutheran worship finds its highest goal and achieves its greatest fulfillment. At its best, Lutheranism can uphold this priority. When Lutheran worship forsakes its roots in the liturgy, as it substitutes other priorities, or it imitates other sectarian practices that surround it, it loses its orientation and blurs the role of music and worship.

". . . . As the implications of these concepts begin to become part of our thoughts, understanding, and eventually our practice, music in Lutheran worship can move closer to a full realization of its potential in the hearts and lives of all worshipers who choose to join with our praise and prayer on Grant Street.

". . . . Because Lutheranism views itself as part of the one holy, catholic, and apostolic church, it looks at the experience of the church at worship throughout its history as an important source of its way of worship. Its use of forms and practices with which the church has prayed and praised for centuries—forms that have been tested, tried, and found nourishing through the experience of countless Christians before us—affirms Lutheranism's continuity with the whole church. In its life of worship Lutheranism gives such forms and practices a central place. Luther's view, which sought to retain from the past all that was useful, rejecting only what could not be retained in good conscience, was no flight into wistful nostalgia; it was rather a pastorally responsible attempt to demonstrate the continuity and unity of Lutheranism with all Christianity.

"... . "It is a Lutheran conviction that the needs of people at worship are most effectively met by forms and structures of prayer which draw on the collective experience of the whole church at worship. For some, such structures and practices—when used the first time—will be new, and, perhaps, disconcerting. Once they become a normal part of the life of worship, however, their richness, strength, diversity, power to nourish faith and life, and their ability to help Christians praise God and enjoy Him forever soon become apparent.

"... [I]t is only when pastors, church musician, and the people work together toward the accomplishment of these goals that a truly living and vital parish worship practice in the Lutheran tradition can result. Each participant plays his own distinctive role, yet each role complements and reinforces the others."

His remarkable statement then moved on to specific suggestions and proposals. The first was "Education: our goal should be to help the laity understand the liturgy and its principles more clearly, to make it more of a joyful event in the life of this congregation in corporate worship. It must be approached from a historical perspective and related to Lutheran worship of the present. This information must come to the congregation from the pulpit and especially the chancel, as what happens there and the manner in which it is done speaks perhaps louder than words of explanation allow. Also classes in Lutheran worship forms and practices should be offered as a regular offering within the Education process of this congregation."

Secondly, concerning the worship space, he suggested that "Acoustic consultants should be contacted to work closely with the organ builder. Ways should be considered by which the worship space itself could present itself in a more positive, brighter, and cheerful manner. Simplicity could well be the best approach."

Thirdly, concerning the organ he observed, "The present instrument has served this congregation for almost 100 years and it not without its technical problems. It is my professional opinion that the investment of any large sum of money for costly repairs would, in effect, be perpetuating a basic error, and rather than continuing numerous 'Band-aid' repairs every year a new instrument should be obtained." He appended a list of proposed organ specifications and suggested builders, four European and four North American.[210] Considerable discussion followed regarding the necessity or advisability of a new organ. In June 1985 the Organ Task Force presented its report which concluded that the existing organ must be replaced, that a Flentrop tracker organ be built, that a balcony be installed as the rear of the nave that would also serve as a choir loft, and that general acoustical improvements be made. In October 1985 the church council authorized the establishment of a fund for the acquisition of a new organ.

Two major commitments were being made at the same time. In addition to the desire of some for a new organ, there was a desire at least to brighten the nave. In the fall of 1985 a Nave Renovation Committee was established. It presented its report February 20, 1986 and made five recommendations: (1) restore the nave and chancel by painting, replacing the carpet, repairing the wainscoting and other woodwork, and the mosaic tiles in the chancel; (2) draw up an extensive ten-year plan to guide the work; (3) resurfacing the walls of the nave ought to have the highest priority; (4) resurfacing the floor ought to have the second priority; (5) replacing the pew cushions and retouching of the pews ought to have the third priority. The committee recognized the reality that the congregation had little money to work with. A few others were more optimistic and foresaw the congregation raising a million dollars in capital finds over the next ten years. In a little more than ten years the congregation in fact generated more than twice that amount.

The lack of understanding of the centrality of worship is evident in the continued observance of "Laymen's Sunday". The laity were sometimes members of the church council, sometimes young people, and on August 12, 1984, the same day as the recognition of Glen Johnson as the leader of a highly successful capital campaign, three seminarians and a deaconess.

Some laypeople were nonetheless showing signs of growth in their understanding of the faith and worship of the Church, encouraged by the adoption of the *Lutheran Book of Worship*. The chair of the Evangelism Committee, Carl Rueter, noting in May that three festivals would fall on Sunday in 1982—St. James the Elder, Mary Mother of our Lord, and Reformation Day, suggested that events be planned on those days. One member volunteered to prepare a bulletin insert on St. James the Apostle. Pastor Braughler took over the other two. "Considerable discussion ensued on a Mary, Mother of Our Lord Festival. Pastor Braughler indicated that he planned to build his sermon around Mary, and felt that, inasmuch as Mary is not a central figure in Lutheran tradition, this should be the extent of the effort." The incongruity of such a remark and of such a sermon with the congregation's splendid mosaic of the virgin mother on her marble throne with her Son looking down upon the worship at the altar below seems not to have made an impression. Also to be noted is Martin Luther's magnificent 1521 essay on the Magnificat in which the Reformer observes, "It needs to be pondered in the heart what it means to be the mother of God."[211] Pastor Braughler further said that "plans were incomplete for Reformation Day and he would keep the committee informed of developments."

It was not the clergy but the Worship and Music committee who in June 1984 expressed the desire to use "other worship settings in the LBW used more often" and "expressed the need for the congregation to be more fluent in these other settings." There are four settings of the Holy Communion in the *Lutheran Book of Worship*: three through-composed musical settings and a chorale service in the manner of Luther's German Mass.

Experiments with the Wednesday noon service continued. To provide variety and "involvement of other people and subjects," the monthly pattern for the fall 1985 was first Wednesday, "Service with Sermon" with the parenthetical note "(Holy Communion will be offered in the Chapel following the service)"; second Wednesday, "Explore and Experience Week (Lay guest speakers, Bible Study, etc.)"; third Wednesday, service with sermon; fourth Wednesday "Service of music with commentary." No provision was made for a fifth Wednesday. Guest preachers were invited during alternate months for the first and third Wednesdays.

In a discussion at the church council meeting March 28, 1983, notice was taken of the protests of a group called Denomination Ministry Strategy, against Mellon Bank because of its foreign investments and the Mesta Machine Company, in support of the unemployed in the area locally known as the Mon [Monongahela River] Valley. DMS, as it called itself, later took the initials DMX to mock the corporate logo of the United States Steel Corporation, USX. The group, under the leadership of Charles Honeywell, became increasingly obstreperous. Mr. Honeywell demanded of what he perceived as "rich" churches a contribution to his work. He was, of course, unsuccessful.

Smithfield United Church had opened a day care center, the Louise Child Care Center, and this encouraged some at First Church to begin a similar project. An ad hoc committee determined that it must be a Christian center with a Christian staff and that its program would be educational, not custodial. About twenty children from six weeks to three years of age could be accommodated. The name selected for the center was the "Strawberry Way Christian Center." The Mellon Bank Foundation offered a grant of $10,400 toward the center.

Pastor Stadler wrote to the Lutheran Service Society of Western Pennsylvania on March 17, 1983, proposing a partnership between LSS and First Church in the operation of a Child Care Center. The congregation would administer the center, provide space, and manage the day-to-day operation. The Lutheran Service Society would provide a start-up advance against future grants and program fees of up to $25,000 and provide business office services. LSS agreed to provide $15,000. The Louise Child Care Center at Smithfield Church agreed to administer and operate the day care program at First Church. The center began operation at First Church in the Grant Street Room in September 1983

January 26, 1983, John D. Reisch, the church building consultant of the Division for Mission in North America of the Lutheran Church in America visited the parish. In his report of February 3 he commented on the proposed renewal of Grant Street and suggested, among other things, "revise the chancel area to a more contemporary setting, and move the communion rail to the nave level." The chancel "contemporary setting" apparently meant a free-standing altar, which had become the style in churches of many denominations following the Second Vatican Council. He suggested working with Carleton Gross of Fortress Ecclesiastical Arts in the renovation.

At the August 1983 meeting of the church council, Pastor Braughler reported concerning the Quilting Society that "new members have not been recruited for this group and that the older members are having increasing difficulty in getting out during the week. The group continued nonetheless until 2009 when the sole remaining member dissolved the venerable organization after one hundred forty-one years.

A capital campaign was planned for 1984 in preparation for the congregation's 150th anniversary in 1987 for renovations to the courtyard, the chancel, structural repairs, and a new organ.

In December 1983 Pastor Stadler's wife, Judy, received her Ph.D. in toxicology from the University of Pittsburgh. Their agreement was that her job would determine where they would next live. He resigned June 12, 1984 so that his wife could take up her work at Dupont in Newark, Delaware. He had been Associate Pastor of First Church for five years.

Pastor Braughler's pastoral style, bright optimism combined with a hesitancy to provide specific direction, is clearly seen in his comments on Pastor Sadler's leaving.[212] "I have been grateful to the special committee for the privilege of interview and input into this first level of study and eventual replacement for Pastor Sadler. I have spoken freely to the committee concerning my observations of our church and my deep feeling that we are now in the renaissance stage of our church and need to be very creative in the use of our staff. I am most optimistic about the future of First Lutheran Church. I believe that the Holy Spirit has been guiding us along our way and I feel keenly at the present that we are under his holy hand. I assure you that I will cooperate with any decision you may want to recommend. I feel we need a new job description and do not have to be bound by the pattern of ministry that Pastor Stadler has so capably performed. I also want you to know that this is a time of reevaluation for me and I want to be flexible to serve our Lord in the best way possible. Thank you for your cooperation, guidance, and prayers."

A decision that turned out to be unfortunate was made July 23, 1984, when the council approved $34,000 for cleaning and waterproofing the exterior of the church. The waterproofing sealed in moisture, did not allow for evaporation, and hastened the crumbling of the sandstone. The lamentable results are seen today.

The call committee, after interviewing a half-dozen candidates, presented the name of Seminarian Larry F. Mort to be associate pastor of First Church. He preached September 22, 1985 and the congregational voted unanimously to extend a call. He was ordained October 12 at St. John's Church in New Florence, Pennsylvania. He began work November 3. His ministry at First Church was short-lived. In his two-page single-spaced report to the church council in February 25, 1987 he indicated that things were not going well. He protested the innate conservatism of the parish, its opposition to new ideas, a climate of suspicion of innovation. Pastor Mort resigned September 27, 1987, effective Reformation Day, and accepted a call as pastor of Alpha Church in Turtle Creek. His frustration is evident in his letter. "As you know, I have been trying to determine the future of my ministry at First Church for some time. . . . . I still see much potential for ministry here that has not been tapped. However, as your Associate Pastor I have been unable to introduce ideas that would more fully utilize that potential. I have accomplished as much as I am able in this ministry."

He was not the only one to experience frustration. Lee Pedersen, who chaired the worship and music committee, resigned from the committee. She had perceived a barrier to worship growth in the congregation that was three-fold. The staff, presumably the pastors, made decisions regarding worship and music and reported to the committee, often after the fact. She was disappointed by what she described as the apathy of the congregation with regard to attendance at the services of the church. Finally she cited the small number of volunteers in the work of the congregation.

Dr. Pedersen was not far off the mark. Social ministry during these years consisted primarily of giving money to a variety of agencies and causes. Actual individual involvement was minimal.

Miles Wallace, who had married Lori Susan Johnson, daughter of Glen and LaVonne Johnson, October 2, 1986 in Heinz Chapel, resigned as director of music effective October 25, 1987.

A number of candidates were interviewed as his successor, all of whom agreed that the condition of the organ was beyond repair and that a new organ was a necessity. The following April, Paul J. Campbell, Jr. was engaged as the director of music. He reported that the concert organist of Thiel College, "after trying to play the organ" at First Church chose instead to give his concert at Smithfield Church.

The year 1987 marked the 150th anniversary of the founding of the First English Evangelical Lutheran Church in the City of Pittsburgh. Considerable notice was given to this anniversary; a year of planning went into the preparation. On January 18, the Sunday following the actual date of the founding, January 15, there was special music and a sermon based on Father Heyer. A display of artifacts was set up in the chapel. On Sunday March 15 during the Sunday School hour between the services there was a presentation on the history of the parish, "Remembering the Past."[213] A weekend event Saturday and Sunday, May 16-17, began with a garden tea party at the home of Glen and Lavonne Johnson. Former pastors Dr. Stackel and Dr. Albert were invited for the weekend. One service was held on Sunday instead of the usual two; Bishop Kenneth May was the preacher. Following the service, a parade with antique cars made its way to the Hyatt Pittsburgh for the anniversary banquet. On June 21 a forum "Honor the Present" took place at a continental breakfast during the Sunday School time. September 27, the third forum urged "Look Forward to the Future." October 25 there was a Bach festival with special music. November 26 there was an ecumenical thanksgiving service with a sermon based on Charles Porterfield Krauth's November 21, 1856 Thanksgiving Sermon, for which Pastor Braughler was "in costume."[214] A memorial plate was made by Wendell August Forge in both bronze and aluminum. James Lind placed flowers on the altar throughout the year in honor of the former pastors. Thursday December 24, the Christmas Eve Eucharist brought the centennial year to a close.

The most lasting contribution during the anniversary year was the renovation of the chancel and nave. Richard Glance was the consulting architect. The replastering and painting of the walls of the nave were done by Ringler Decorating. The walls were a cream color with a stenciled border in a blue design at the top of the restored wainscoting. Protective coverings were removed from the Tiffany window and the great window restored. The chancel was extended to allow for a free standing altar, the communion rail was brought down to the level of the nave to facilitate the distribution of the Sacrament, especially to those with physical limitations, the pulpit and lectern were moved slightly toward the center of the chancel. The work on the flooring of the chancel was completed in October 1988. In celebration of the completion of the work, November 13 at 5 p.m. the director of music, the choir, and guest musicians presented Handel's "Ode to St. Cecelia's Day."

The baptistery was remodeled with the installation of a brass rail made from the old chandelier that had hung in the center of the church. The font was repositioned to the center of the baptistery, squarely facing the congregation. The brass outline of the descending dove was given in memory of Walter Shively and Miss Shively.

A lingering problem was created by the work on the chancel. A United States flag and a Christian flag which had been in the chancel were removed for the renovation and had not been put back. A letter asking that the flags be restored to their accustomed place was answered not by the pastor but by the president of the church council. The recurrent problem did not go away. One of the first responsibilities of the next pastor was to deal with the matter. His letter explaining that the Church's allegiance is to the Cross of Christ put the issue to rest.

By the end of 1986 it was becoming apparent to some in the congregation that Pastor Braughler's ministry was to draw to a close not many years hence. He would be sixty-five years of age in January 1987. In November 1987, a committee was approved "to research the congregation's future pastoral needs." Especially in view of the congregation's sluggish movement on other issues, the committee moved with remarkable speed. Thomas Kessinger, the chairman, announced in December that nine people had agreed to serve on the committee and that four others might also be invited to join. The committee bore the name Research and Assessment Committee and was composed of twelve members, six men and six women: John Harmon, Nancy Headrick, Myer Headrick, Carda Horton, Gayle Jameson, LaVonne Johnson, Sandra Kessinger, Wesley Nelson, Lee Pedersen, Carl Reuter, Karl Voigt, and George Weimer.

In response to the resignation of the associate pastor in the fall of 1987, Pastor Braughler suggested that the congregation not seek a second pastor but rather that a search begin for a new senior pastor. He would continue to serve during the interim. By the annual congregational meeting in January 1988 his intention had clarified: he announced that he planned to retire by November of that year. Tellingly, "he asked for questions and there were none." By April, practical considerations had entered the plan. "My [65th] birthday is January 11, which means that my retirement income centers around that date. November 25, 1988 is, therefore, the earliest reasonable time for my leaving First Lutheran." So as not to rush the call process, he offered to remain in an interim capacity until a new pastor was elected.

March 22, 1988 the Research and Assessment Committee presented its final report to the church council regarding the pastoral vacancy. The committee, created to give representation to virtually all points of view in the congregation, determined that "preaching is of primary importance to our future here. . . . Dynamic preaching is probably the single most important method of outreach and ministry in a downtown congregation. . . . This is to be closely followed by the entire worship experience which is a combination of a number of factors, including quality preaching, quality music, active congregational participation, and many others." The next two areas in terms of priority were Christian education and pastoral care and visitation. The committee also concluded that "it is critical that this congregation make a commitment *at this time* to the eventual hiring of either a second pastor or a lay professional."

In its final report the Research and assessment Committee recommended a call committee, composed of virtually the same people as had served on the Research and Assessment Committee: Sandra Kessinger, chair, John Harmon, Nancy Headrick, Myer Headrick, Carda Horton, Gayle Jameson, LaVonne Johnson, Wesley Nelson, Lee Pedersen, Carl Reuter, Karl Voigt, George Weimer. The council added Sherry Wilson; Paul Pearson, president of the church council, was a member *ex officio*. Most of these same people were to serve on the church council during the first years of the new pastor's tenure. The importance of a committed core of laypeople who understand and care about the work of the Church and who are willing to work unstintingly toward their common goal is to be underscored.

By August the committee had interviewed ten pastors, seven from within the synod, two from elsewhere in Pennsylvania, and one from the Midwest. Since progress was slow, the council asked Pastor Braughler to stay on through Advent and Christmas, until January 15, 1989. The committee, not agreeing on any of the candidates they interviewed, asked Bishop McCoid for additional names. He provided three, one of whom did not match the parish's criteria, one of whom was not open to a call. The third, David Paul Gleason, proved agreeable to every member of the committee (save one). He was asked to preside at the liturgies on the Third Sunday in Advent, December 11, 1988 "with the possibility of a call." Following the services, the congregation voted to extend a call. Pastor Gleason began his ministry at First Church February 1, 1989. Pastor Braughler made it clear to the congregation that he would no longer be pastor of the parish. In his report to the church council December 27, 1988, he said clearly, "Please be clear and let it be known that I cannot and would not break pastoral ethics and be involved in the ministry at the church without the thorough understanding and approval of the pastor." Throughout the next pastorate he honored that pledge.

He and his wife remained members of First Church until 1992 when he became assistant pastor at Zion Church in Brentwood.

CHAPTER 9

Recovering the Tradition

D avid Paul Gleason was born in Pittsburgh, the first pastor of First Church to be a native of the city. A graduate of Indiana University of Pennsylvania and Gettysburg Seminary, ordained June 11, 1972, his intention was not to return to minister in Pittsburgh. He served parishes in East Berlin, Pennsylvania, suburban Washington, D.C., and Palmyra, Pennsylvania. In 1988 he received the Doctor of Ministry degree from the Graduate Theological Foundation of the University of Notre Dame, thus becoming the first pastor of First Church since Father Heyer to possess an earned doctorate. At the insistent urging of Bishop Donald McCoid, he reluctantly agreed to have his name submitted to First Church.

David Gleason

He began his ministry in Pittsburgh on Monday, February 1, 1989. It was not a hopeful time in the life of the parish. The organ was in ill repair. One-third of it did not work; pipes were held together with rags. The roof of the church leaked; the wood underlay was rotting. The Christian Education Committee debated whether or not to close the Sunday School because of a lack of students. The worship committee complained that the Christmas service had been too long: over two hours, and Holy Communion was not celebrated.

His first day in the parish, he observed the noonday service in the chapel conducted by a visiting pastor. After the service in the chapel, a few congregants went into the nave for Holy Communion. The sexton, John Lanyon, asked the new pastor what he thought of the service. He replied, "That's the last time we'll do that." Change was in store for First Church.

Pastor Gleason's undergraduate training had been as a teacher, and careful teaching continued to be a hallmark of his ministry. At Gettysburg Seminary he had been a student and friend of Robert Jenson, professor of systematic theology, who taught him that everything in the Church has a theological dimension. At his first meeting with church council, February 20, 1989, Pastor Gleason announced his intention to use the time allotted to his report as a teaching time as well as a report on his pastoral activities. He wasted no time in beginning the teaching time. He urged consistency in the Wednesday and Sunday liturgies, because, he taught, too many variations lead to confusion. He distributed copies of the Evangelical Lutheran Church in America's Statement on Communion Practices for the council members to read for future discussion. In March his teaching time dealt with ministry, beginning with Baptism, the ELCA having begun a five-year study of the subject intended to define for itself exactly what shape and role ordained ministry should play in what was called "the new church."

The worship and music committee agreed to his suggestion to replace the "Celebrate" Sunday bulletin inserts with a lectionary sheet that provided the prayer of the day and the psalm as well as the lessons from the Revised Standard Version. "Celebrate" used various translations of the Bible, whichever the editor of the series, the Reverend S. Anita Stauffer, thought the best for each passage, and provided texts for intercessions. The intention of the framers of the *Lutheran Book of Worship* was not to provide such texts and thus to encourage congregations to draft locally appropriate prayers. Pastor Gleason understood the new service book.

Some changes were made in the Holy Week schedule in the interest of consistency; other things remained unchanged. The Eucharist was celebrated on the Sunday of the Passion at both services, 8:30 and 11:00, a noonday prayer office was read on Monday and Tuesday from 12:10-12:30, a "noonday liturgy" on Wednesday from 12:10-12:30, the Eucharist on Maundy Thursday at 7 a.m., noon, 5:30, and 7:30. On Good Friday there was the three-hour service from noon until 3 with six guest preachers: two retired pastors, Warren Bieber, and Earl Hively; two parish pastors, John Cochran of Trinity Church on the Northside, and Charlotte Voigt, a daughter of First Church, of First English Church, Sharpsburg; Ruth Becker of Lutheran Campus Ministry, and Robert Newpher from the synod office. Good Friday evening was the historic Liturgy of the Passion and Death of our Lord, which, even though it was in the *Lutheran Book of Worship,* was celebrated in First Church for the first time.

He announced to the worship and music committee his desire eventually to celebrate Holy Communion at both services each Sunday (Holy Communion was being celebrated at one of the two services every week), part of his emphasis on consistency in worship, and that he would begin an education process regarding the subject. He noted his interest in continuing the noonday services throughout the summer. Attendance at these services held steady through the summer, indicating the usefulness of such a service for the downtown community. Holy Communion was celebrated at both Sunday services beginning September 2, 1989. The worship and music committee used Pastor Gleason's own explanatory words in their recommendation: "As believers we must proclaim Christ's Word to the people. When we do not offer the complete liturgy of Word and Sacrament at our principal service on Sunday, we do not offer the fullness of Christ to the congregation."

During April, six "cottage meetings" were held in members' homes in and around the city to afford the new pastor an opportunity to meet more people in an informal setting and to promote discussion of the direction, goals, and concerns for the ministry of the parish. In his report on the work of these meetings, Pastor Gleason noted, "In several groups, discussion centered around the model of a cathedral church. It was felt that our pattern and style of ministry should be exemplary and provide an 'authentically Lutheran' witness in downtown Pittsburgh." The breadth of the discussions led him to suggest the need for a second pastor.

Pastor Gleason began a series he called "Lutheran Basics" May 14; it continued through June 4. The course was to be repeated every few years throughout his ministry at First Church. Such a careful exposition of distinctively Lutheran doctrines and worship had not been heard in First Church for many decades and proved useful not only for new members coming from other traditions and denominations but for long-time Lutherans as well.

Peter Luley, in a letter to the Organ Investigation Committee March 31, 1989, noted that his correspondence on the matter of the condition of the organ went back to 1983. Repair, which he spoke strongly against, would cost $200,000 to $250,000; a new instrument of similar size and design would cost $300,00 to $400,000. "It is my opinion that both the mechanical and tonal qualities of the pipe organ in First Lutheran Church are deficient, and that replacement is the only option which makes both economic and musical sense." This time his opinion convinced the congregation; the council voted unanimously to replace the organ.

An affirmation of the new life that was becoming evident in the parish was the announcement that Theodore R. and Lillian S. Helmbold, long-time and faithful members of the congregation, made the largest addition to the endowment of the congregation in its history. As part of their estate plan, they left the bulk of their estate in perpetual charitable trust to be administered by Mellon Bank as trustee for the Pittsburgh Foundation. First Church was the recipient of 30 per cent of the net payout from the fund decided by the board. The market value of the trust in April 27, 1989, was $1,648,000.

In September, Pastor Gleason prepared a seventeen-page document, "Toward a Vision of the Church" which was distributed to council members, committee chairpersons, and congregational leaders. Upon his arrival, he found the congregation fretting about the definition of its "mission." It had been a continuing concern for many decades, and no clear answer had been arrived at. Pastor Gleason suggested a simple yet profound answer: "our mission is to be the Church." The long document was an expansion of his answer to the congregation's befuddlement, giving clear definition to how a congregation was to "be the Church" in downtown Pittsburgh at the end of the twentieth century. Such a clear articulation of the centrality of worship in the whole work of the Church, solidly grounded in theological understanding, had not been heard at First Church since the time of George Gongaware, perhaps not even since the clear eloquence of Charles Porterfield Krauth. The First Church again had a "theologian in residence."

"Since the entire ministry of the Church is carried out by a partnership of pastor and people, it is vital that the people of the

Church be equipped for their ministry and that a pastor provide an understanding of the Gospel and of its implications for the whole life of the Church that is as clear as possible.

"The process of coming to such a clear understanding is a long and evolving one. It requires constant teaching, study, reflection on the Scriptures and Confessions, an awareness of the heritage of the Church, and insight into the situations to which the Gospel must be addressed."

It was not a static view. "Our God is a living God. His will is made known in always new and surprising ways. It is our task to be open to what he chooses to reveal and to allow our ministry to grow and be shaped by his revelation until our wills are conformed to his."

"The Church is confessionally defined as 'the assembly of all believers among whom the Gospel is preached in its purity and the holy sacraments are administered according to the Gospel.'" (AC VII)[215] "Given our confessional definition of the Church, it is clear that worship is the heart of our life together as the people of God. Indeed, worship is the very life of the Church." A significant step had already been taken without controversy to provide the fullness of the Means of Grace to the people of First Church in the weekly celebration of the Eucharist, Word and Sacrament, at both services each Sunday. Word and Sacraments, at the heart of the congregation's life together, motivate its entire ministry. The tools of growth toward greater spiritual maturity, he taught, exist in the rich liturgical heritage of the Church.

Ten specific suggestions regarding worship followed. (1) More of the contents of the *Lutheran Book of Worship* should gradually be introduced. (2) The role of corporate and of individual prayer needs to be explored, more opportunities for such prayer provided, and the needs for which prayer is to be offered articulated. (3) The downtown community needs to be enabled to see First Church as a place of prayer. (4) Baptisms, weddings, funerals are to be seen not as private but as congregational events. (5) The aesthetic elements of worship, the beauty of holiness, cannot be overlooked. "How things look says much about what we believe." (6) All who assist in the leadership of the services of the Church must be well-prepared and well-trained. (7) Adequate support, both financial support and personal involvement, of the Director of Music is vital. (8) The selection of a new organ "and moving with dispatch to obtain it" is essential in the pursuit of excellence in the music ministry of the parish. (9) Both the corporate and individual forms of The Service of the Word for Healing and the individual and corporate forms of Confession and Forgiveness can be offered as pastoral care to the city. (10) "We need to take some risks and try to offer some new possibilities before we lock ourselves into believing that God can only come to his people on Sunday mornings or on Wednesday at noon."

The second area is Christian Education. "Teaching in the Church is not simply imparting information but teaching a way of life." Nine specific suggestions flowed from this basic position. (1) "The traditional education program of the parish must be maintained and strengthened." (2) Opportunities for learning need to be increased beyond the traditional Sunday and Vacation Church School and could include daytime classes, an adult school in religion, retreats, forums, guest teachers and lecturers, experiential educational activities, and the like. (3) "More emphasis is needed on various ways to involve our members in regular Bible study, whether in formal settings or informal ones." (4) People need to learn about the history, heritage, and life of the whole Church: such subjects as Church history, theology, ethics, contemporary trends in the Church. (5) "Learning for life" should be a concern of the Church. The Gospel should inform the way we live and the decisions we make. (6) "We should provide ample resources for the job of teaching and learning." (7) "Christian learning properly takes place in the home as well as in the Church. Both Church and home need to support one another in providing a total experience in Christian nurture." (8) Educational programs for the general welfare of the community and ecumenical studies to help separated churches know and understand one another and give greater incentive toward Christian unity. (9) "We must carefully identify the gifts of our own members for teaching and broaden our expectations of Christian Education to include some nontraditional topics and teaching methods."

The third area of ministry considered in the pastor's statement is Youth Ministry. Instead of the frequently-heard remark, "Young people are the future of the church," Pastor Gleason says clearly that young people are already "fully members of the Church through Baptism." Ministry to and ministry by young people needs to find expression in the life of the Church. In addition to "the normal educational offerings for young people," the pastor makes six specific considerations. (1) "social activity, while it cannot be the full content of youth ministry, is nevertheless an important element." Young people need to discover that the Church can be enjoyed with classmates and friends. (2) "Any youth program must be diverse and flexible" since the interests and taste of young people vary widely and change quickly. (3) The concerns and questions of the young (human sexuality, drugs, alcohol, relationships to parents and peers) should be welcomed and addressed in an atmosphere of "openness without judgment." (4) The congregation can and should "provide young people with opportunities to serve the Church and its people." (5) "Creativity in planning unique opportunities for youth fellowship along with traditional activities is a priority." (6) "Our young people need to be encouraged to explore the dimensions of the Church beyond our own parish. Involvement in synodical, ecumenical, or church-wide activity and ministry should be encouraged and supported."

Evangelism, "telling the story of Jesus to those who have not heard," is the fourth area of concern. In "the most fundamental task of the outreach of the Church" the importance of congregational life is underscored: "people do not come to faith in isolation from the Christian community. Being a Christian means not simply believing, but also being a part of the believing Family established by Christ." The essential story is told in many ways. "*Everything* we do as a Christian community is a witness to what we believe," and therefore "we need always to examine and evaluate what we communicate to potential believers and prospective members through our life as a parish. Our faith and the joy we find in it should be apparent." Six specific suggestions follow. (1) Each believer needs to be motivated to witness willingly to others. (2) Visitors to the church should find among the members a sense of joy in their relationship to one another. (3) "A process of identifying prospective members, presenting a Gospel witness to them, and informing them about the life of our Family needs to be developed. It should clearly reveal a sense of care for those who come to us without making anyone feel pressed into 'joining the group.'" (4) "Evangelism happens most effectively when believers tell others with enthusiasm and joy about the good things happening in the church and the even better things our life in Christ holds out to us." (5) Being located downtown makes evangelism difficult, but it also affords distinctive opportunities. "Our week-day 'on site' ministries must increase and become more and more visible." (6) We cannot emulate or be in competition with suburban churches. "We need to become increasingly aware of what sort of ministry we can do and do well." Welcoming visitors was already a strength of First Church, and the exercise of such hospitality continues effectively to this day.

The fifth topic is Social Ministry. "We are to love and care for others because Christ loves and cares for us." Social ministry can be carried out in three ways: through money given to agencies and programs, through the direct giving of our time, abilities, and care to individuals and agencies, and through advocacy on behalf of those in need. Specific suggestions are made. (1) The Social Ministry Committee should continue and continually invite members to join it. (2) "The church has a global dimension in its ministry and its people need to be informed about the problems facing fellow children of God in various parts of his world." (3) "Consideration also needs to be focused on social issues in our own society: the breakdown of marriage and family life, domestic hunger, the homeless, civil rights, family violence, child abuse, the threat of terrorism, world peace." (4) "While most social issues are enormous, each of us can initiate some steps toward greater justice through our own ability to think and act justly." (5) Educational programs that place social issues in a theological context are needed. (6) Our ministry to the needy must always increase because the needs are so great. (7) The ministry to those who stop by the church must be done in concert with the entire downtown religious community. (8) Issues which have direct bearing on the quality of life in the city need to be identified and addressed. (9) More of our own members need to be involved in ministry to our own members. He observed later that First Church has a history of taking its ministry beyond the congregation; indeed, the most remarkable thing about the church is what it has done outside the congregation.[216] William Passavant was the great exemplar of such social ministry.

Stewardship is considered sixth. The very word "stewardship" commonly used in the Church "tells us that private property does not exist and that all belongs to God." We are entrusted with something that is not ours. (1) The level of giving in the parish must be increased so that more ministry and more effective ministry can be done. (2) The message of what stewardship is and why it is a vital element of Christian life needs to be taught to the members of the parish. (3) Ways of presenting the many opportunities for people to practice good stewardship need to be considered: special appeals, endowments, wills, memorials. (4) As the blessings from God increase, our response to his goodness should also increase. (5) Making a commitment of support to the church enables the congregation better to plan and direct the ministry. (6) "A clear picture of what our money 'does' helps gain support for ministry." (7) Stewardship is a way of living in response to the goodness of God. Pastor Gleason taught the congregation to call its yearly proposed financial plan not by the secular word "budget" but rather by a more descriptive and theologically accurate title, "proposal for ministry." Ministry, not money, was the key to what it was about. A proposal for ministry "is a theological document which sets forth the church's priorities and the resources allocated to its ministries."[217]

The seventh and related area is Finance. The task of the Finance Committee is to focus on the stewardship of the congregation's financial resources. "In our culture, the price tag placed on anything is important, even on ministry. We want to get the best return possible on our investment in ministry while being sure that adequate funds are provided to do that ministry. (1) In the creation of a yearly budget, the committee needs to consider what the budget says about ministry and how it says it. (2) Money should be allowed to earn money whenever possible. (3) The practice of a yearly audit of the congregation's accounts and transactions should be continued. (4) "Special cooperation should exist among the Finance, Stewardship, and Personnel Committees." (5) Program needs must be communicated to the Finance Committee by each unit so that each can be adequately funded. (6) Policies regarding the handling of bequests and endowment monies must be followed carefully. "Likewise, plans for capital expenditures need to take fully into account all possible approaches to funding and decisions must be based not on financial expedience alone but also on a consideration of the impact which financial decisions will ultimately have on our ministry."

Property is considered eighth. "The beauty of our facilities and the care we give them are signs to the community of the value we give to our life in Christ. They are signs of our faith."

(1) Regular maintenance is essential. (2) Repairs should be handled promptly. (3) "Improvements should be scheduled for completion by priority and be based on the needs of the congregation's program." (4) A thorough inspection of the property should be undertaken twice each year. (5) There needs to be a well-defined and advertised procedure for bringing the need for repairs and improvements to the committee's attention. (6) The appearance of things should not be short-changed. "We should not care grudgingly but lavishly for what God gives us." (7) First impressions given to visitors are important. Cleanliness and orderliness are therefore concerns of the committee. (8) Semi-annual house cleanings could be considered. (9) "The talents and craftsmanship of members should be actively identified and sought out so that people may use such gifts as offerings to the Lord and his Church." (10) "When major repairs and improvements are indicated, they need to be promptly handled. Delay causes members to see such needs as unimportant."

Communications is the ninth area to be examined. The entire ministry and work of the parish centers around communication. (1) Parish publications should be clear, neat, and have esthetic appeal. (2) The efficient gathering of pertinent information is a key ingredient of the work of this committee. (3) Communication can take place in a variety of ways. "Communication by printed and spoken word, by sight and by sound should be creatively developed. (4) Internal communication between committees should be strengthened to present a total picture of the ministry of the parish. (5) Advertising is necessary in the downtown setting. (6) Communication needs its appropriate budgetary support.

The tenth area is Staff Support and Personnel. By providing adequate compensation, the congregation testifies to the value it places on the members of the staff as persons and to the value of their work. (1) Annual reviews of remuneration are essential. (2) When guidelines are provided by the Church at large, they should be carefully considered. (3) How best to compensate is an important consideration. "Varying arrangements of fringe benefits and actual salary figures can be utilized to maximize the benefit to employees. (4) Compensation should always fairly coincide with the level of training required, the amount of responsibility carried in the position, the time involved, and the level of performance. (5) "Under no circumstances should the faith and commitment of employees be used as a rationale for under-paying them." (6) Recommendations for compensation should be made well in advance of the preparation of the budget and should be presented only after conversation with the employee involved. (7) The relationships of staff members to the whole parish and to one another should be a concern of the Staff Support Committee. (8) The Staff Support Committee must be accessible to *all* staff members. An annual conversation with each staff member should be scheduled. (9) Both the Personnel and the Staff Support Committee must maintain confidentiality in their work with staff members. (10) "The needs of a staff member's family are legitimate concerns for the Staff Support Committee."

The Church, Pastor Gleason said in his concluding summary, is a community a believers, a family motivated and upheld by God's love for us all in Christ. "For the Church to truly be a Family in Christ, that love must be manifest in all our plans for ministry, in all our attempts at faithfulness, and in all our relationships to one another."

Throughout his ministry at First Church he patiently taught the congregation that what downtown Pittsburgh needed was not one more general Protestant church, but a church that understood its Lutheran heritage, valued it, and sought to enact it. In his teaching time at the October 16, 1995 meeting of the church council, he spoke of the congregation's history. The Pittsburgh Synod was founded in the former house of First Church on Seventh Avenue. The most cherished heritage of the congregation, he suggested, was the role it played in restoring the orthodox Lutheran tradition and practice, exemplified in William Passavant. He had been a popular revivalist preacher in Maryland, but after his arrival in Pittsburgh he became a staunch advocate for restoring the integrity of the orthodox tradition to the Church. This more orthodox revival centered on what the Church's Christian witness ought to be. First Lutheran Church, especially, had been given a heritage rooted in the Gospel and centered in Word and Sacrament. This tradition, Pastor Gleason declared, should be treasured and celebrated.

With the clear support and encouragement of the pastor, a Major Needs Committee concluded that the two areas needing attention, a new organ and a new slate roof, should be undertaken together. Glen Johnson, who had run three previous successful campaigns for the congregation, observed that the success of a drive is dependent on three actions: inform the congregation of what is to be done and why, keep the congregation informed at all stages of the campaign, set and keep a deadline for the project. He and Myer Headrick agreed that a campaign to raise $400,000 to $450,000 over a three year period could be accomplished. The committee's estimate of the cost of the double project was $350,000 for a new organ, $25,000 for the organ chamber, $25,000 for organ carpentry, and $200,000 for a new slate roof for a total of $600,000. The campaign would raise $400,000 and the remaining $200,000 would be borrowed from the church's own endowment funds.

Relationships with the neighboring Episcopal cathedral were growing. April 24, 1990, a Lutheran-Episcopal celebration of the Holy Eucharist was held in First Church in conjunction with the National Workshop for Christian Unity which was being conducted at the neighboring William Penn Hotel. Bishop Donald McCoid presided at the celebration and the Bishop of the Episcopal Diocese of Pittsburgh, Alden Hathaway, was the preacher.

A call committee had been appointed in October 1989 to search for an Assistant Pastor. The description of the person's primary duties was straightforward: to help the congregation grow and develop in social ministry and evangelism. The language was careful. The new pastor was not to do these things for the congregation but to work with the people in developing these areas. The names of three candidates were given by Bishop McCoid. The committee chose to interview two of the three. April 23, 1990, the committee presented to the church council the name of Lisa Ann Ubbelohde. She was 36 years old, born and raised in Wisconsin, a graduate of the University of Wisconsin at Stout with a dual major in childhood development and family life and in early childhood education. She was a graduate of Wartburg Theological Seminary in Dubuque, Iowa. Her first call was to redevelop Community Lutheran Church in Butler, Pennsylvania from December 1981 through July 1989. She served as interim chaplain at St. John's Care Center in Mars, Pennsylvania and was currently serving as interim pastor of Bethlehem Church in Glenshaw, Pennsylvania. The committee found her "very warm, caring, and kind." The council approved the nomination and set the date of June 3 for Pastor Ubbelohde to preach and assist at the service and be presented to the congregation. The congregation voted (103 to 13) to extend a call to her to be Assistant Pastor of First Church. She began her ministry at First Church July 2 and was installed on September 23. The Reverend Gordon Ray, Dean of the District, presided at the installation; the Reverend Paul Kokenda, pastor of St. Michael and All Angels' Church on the North Side, was the preacher.

In his report to the church council on June 18 Pastor Gleason outlined a procedure to make a staff ministry work effectively: lines of responsibility must be clearly drawn, staff members must know what to expect of each other, committee chairs must know to whom that committee reports, lack of space makes working together difficult. The primary goal is to get more people involved in the ministry of the church.

July 8, 1990 Pastor Gleason and Joyce E. Rowe, a member of the congregation, were married at First Church.

Documents were prepared to codify the practices of the congregation. A statement of Personnel Policies and Benefits was drafted in 1992 for the office and maintenance employees of the church covering vacation, sick days, holidays, leaves of absence, fringe benefits, job guidelines and evaluations, probation periods, and jury duty and the like.

In the same year a series of continuing resolutions was prepared to govern the operation of the standing and special committees of the congregation council. The resolutions begin appropriately with a statement of their theological foundation in Holy Baptism. God gives his people various gifts, and appointment to a committee is therefore to be regarded as a call to serve the Church of Christ.

Several constitutional and by-law amendments were also approved. The principal change was to divide the annual congregational meeting so that a congregational financial meeting would be held in late fall and a congregational organizational meeting be held in late spring.

Pastor Gleason continued to implement the vision he had presented to the congregation when he began his ministry which emphasized the priority of worship in the life of the congregation. He announced in August that "beginning Monday, September 17, there will be a Noonday ministry provided each business day of the week." In addition to the Wednesday Eucharist and the Thursday Bible study, there would be a Service of the Word for Healing on Monday, on Tuesdays and Thursdays "Prayer at Noonday" led by one of the laypeople of the parish, on Friday a simple Service of the Word led by one of the two pastors of the congregation or other pastors in the area, both Lutheran and non-Lutheran.

In August 1991 the consulting firm of Tripp, Umbach, and Associates reported its findings in a study of the weekday worshippers. The weekday population was estimated at about 140,000, 70% under 50 years of age, 25% (the greatest percentage) between 31 and 40, 70% not members of First Lutheran Church. Wednesday had the largest attendance (87%); 85% attended alone; 80% began attending within the past five years; 30% within the past six months; 97% were satisfied with the services. Two-thirds of those attending had encouraged others to attend.

On April 2,1995, Paul Umbach, a member of First Church as well as the consulting firm, gathered a focus group of ten persons who had become members of First Church within the past two years. The greatest attribute of the church was identified as worship, music, and the warm welcome of visitors. Most first impressions were related to the building and its furnishings. The church exceeded the expectations of first-time visitors, making each one feel welcome. The diversity of members who come from all areas impressed the participants in the focus group as did the importance of liturgy and music. The church was seen to be in a stable financial position with an impressive commitment to the downtown community. The consultant summarized the discussion: "First Lutheran Church is a place of worship that welcomes a diverse group of people. While new members rate the church high on key factors such as worship, preaching, warmth, urban ministry and fellowship, most new members first visit the church without being invited by others. Visitors 'just drop by' and are welcomed into a dynamic Christian family. Much can be accomplished in the future by expanding the importance of pro-active person to person evangelism."

A three-page statement of "A Direction for the Music Ministry of First Lutheran Church" was drawn up by a committee consisting of the senior pastor, the director of music, and three laypeople from prior committees (John Harmon, LaVonne Johnson, and Karen Larson). The statement began by acknowledging the central place music holds in Christian worship, standing next to liturgy as a servant of the Gospel. Within Lutheranism "music is always traditional," tied to the past and serving to link the Christian community of today with the Church in all generations, providing stability and continuity. "The Church maintains an active concern for traditional worship that is well-ordered and not shaped by individual whims." Tradition is always evolving. "As a living voice, the Gospel and the music that serves it can always speak in yet new ways."

Seven general goals were identified. (1) Replace the present organ with one that will support and enhance congregational singing, be capable of accompanying choirs and soloists, be capable of playing a wide variety of organ literature, be of technical and artistic quality, be capable of being used as a recital instrument. (2) Continue to employ a director of music who will serve as church organist, direct the choirs, and guide the development of the church music program. (3) Enlarge and develop the choir through recruitment, music education, and development of volunteer soloists. (4) Place greater emphasis on worship planning. (5) Expand opportunities for corporate worship on Sundays and weekdays. (6) Employ variation in corporate worship using the *Lutheran Book of Worship* as the primary resource. (7) Use appropriate resources beyond the Lutheran tradition.

Twelve specific goals were presented. (1) Provide special music at both Sunday services. (2) Expand the program of noonday worship by scheduling services every business day, using a variety of worship formats, making use of resources from Lutheran and ecumenical communities, employing music in some manner each week day, perhaps scheduling one recital per week during certain seasons of the Church year. (3) Develop a regular schedule of late afternoon or evening worship such as a weekly liturgy of Evening Prayer. (4) Develop a regular series of special concerts. (5) Develop a regular series of major organ recitals. (6) Seek to attract and host visiting choirs and musicians. (7) Identify and encourage children in the parish who have special musical ability and use them in instrumental and choral performances and in the development of a children's choir. (8) Graciously host gatherings of the larger church in which music may play a vital role. (9) Develop support for a full-time Director of Music, to be accomplished in stages by annual increases in compensation and in responsibilities and expectations. (10) Consider the employment, if necessary, of paid soloists to provide support and leadership for the choir. (11) Supply a support person to type bulletins, programs, letters, and other correspondence. (12) Supply an assistant organist to assist with extra liturgies and weddings.

September 17, 1991, the organ selection committee (Nancy Headrick, chair, John K. Backus, William Brocious, Carl D. Cassler, Elizabeth Cassler, John C. Harmon, LaVonne Johnson, G. Wesley Lacock, Bonnie Pedersen, Christine Torie; also the presidents of the council 1989-1991 Marjorie N. Backus and Carl C. Reuter; Pastor David Gleason, and the Director of Music Paul J. Campbell; Peter J. Luley organ consultant) made its unanimous recommendation to the church council. The new organ was to be the work of Casavant Frères of Quebec "for the congregation of First English Evangelical Lutheran Church and to the glory of God." The quoted cost was $381,210.

The old organ sounded for the last time in First Church April 26, 1992 and was sold to the Congregational Church of East Hampton, Connecticut. The new Casavant was heard publicly for the first time in First Church on Reformation Sunday, October 25, 1992 at a chorale liturgy, in which hymns replace parts of the ordinary of the service, as outlined in the *Lutheran Book of Worship*.[218] Casavant opus 3709 was formally dedicated November 8, 1992.

The congregation was no longer seeking ways to react to the changes going on around it. Pastor Gleason was leading them from a clear and firm grasp of the fundamentals of the faith to living out those central affirmations. In his teaching time at the council meeting September 17, 1990, in response to a meeting of the downtown Ministerium on the topic "What is the local government's vision for the city of Pittsburgh?" he declared, "Whatever vision emerges for the city, the Church already has a vision and it is the only true vision that will endure." That vision is people living in relationship to God and in relationship to each other. It is therefore the task of Christians to live out that vision both inside the Church and outside it.

In February 1991, a statement of the mission of the congregation appears at the head of a series of job descriptions prepared by the Staff Support Committee. "God has placed us on Grant Street and, through the Holy Spirit, works through us, as Lutherans, to create and sustain Christian faith and fellowship in a downtown and Metropolitan Pittsburgh community; and to creatively reach out in service and witness to the living Christ." The statement puts in clear focus the understanding of the congregation's mission and purpose that had been developed at the beginning of Pastor Gleason's ministry in the parish. It accepts the location of the church as a given, no longer to be questioned or debated, and its work "as Lutherans" in the richness and promise of that distinctive tradition. The scope of the work is not only to the downtown community but to the metropolitan region as a kind of cathedral church.

In spite of the name First English Evangelical Lutheran Church, the congregation moved beyond such restriction to one language (First German Lutheran Church having long since moved from downtown to Oakland). The Reverend Professor Dr. H. Eberhard von Waldo conducted a Good Friday service in the German language for the German community of Pittsburgh. Thus began an expanding ministry to the growing German-speaking community which was increasing by the growth of German companies and industries in Pittsburgh. The attendance on Good Friday 1991 was 67, the largest congregation to that date.

July 24, 1991 Pastor Gleason suffered a heart attack, was hospitalized through August 5, and underwent cardiac rehabilitation at North Hills Passavant Hospital. He returned to work in September. The work of the parish, having been carefully grounded and given clear direction by Pastor Gleason, continued without serious disruption during his convalescence.

At the 1992 annual meeting of the congregation (January 26), the pastor reported that for the first time in very many years there was a net increase in membership and that attendance at worship was also on the increase. The church was turning around. He reminded the church council in February that "crucial times are ahead for the church because the last several years have brought a resolution to various property concerns. Now is the time to use the property improvements as a tool for ministry and to determine how to do it for the downtown community."

When the chancel was extended in 1988 the intention was to provide space for a free-standing altar, but none had been installed. When Pastor Gleason mentioned to Robert Dobson that such an altar would be desirable, he offered to give it as a memorial to his late wife, Ruth Dobson. The altar was designed by the architect William E. Brocious, a member of the congregation, and was consecrated September 27, 1992. It is a graceful work of art, open enough to leave the high altar visible behind it yet a substantial presence in itself. The marble at its base echoes the marble of the high altar; the brass recalls the brass of the pulpit and lectern; the wooden mensa, like the high altar, is inscribed with the traditional five crosses.[219] The altar has received a number of architectural and design awards, among them an Honor Award from the American Institute of Architects which said in its commendation, "The table complements the motions of the priests as well as its surroundings. It blends well with the church and its scale is exact. It is a clever and witty solution."[220]

The Eucharistic table also received a 1995 AIA Religious Art and Architecture Design award. The altar was shown in the February 1996 issue of *Faith and Forum* magazine and was exhibited at the AIA national convention in Minneapolis May 10-13, 1996.

In 1992 Bishop McCoid spoke of the possibility of following the lead of Bishop William Lazareth of the Metropolitan New York Synod and, in the absence of a cathedral, select a congregation that would be the "bishop's church" for that year. First Church proudly offered itself to the bishop for that role in 1993. Their new sense of worth is evident in their long letter to Bishop McCoid, drafted by Thomas Kessinger as Secretary of the church council, detailing the long and distinguished history of the parish. They detailed the founding under the guidance of Father Heyer, the ministry under Doctors Passavant and Krauth, Dr. Holl's radio ministry, Pastor Stackel's initiation of weekday noon services, Pastor Albert's establishing the counseling center and expanding the weekday ministry, Pastor Braughler's role in founding the youth counseling center, Whale's Tale; Bethlehem Haven shelter for homeless women; the Strawberry Way Christian Center. "Today under the leadership of the Reverend Dr. David P. Gleason, First Lutheran Church is striving to extend an authentic Lutheran witness to the downtown working community. Weekday worship has been expanded to fill every day of the week. Our very presence in the center of the busy working world of Pittsburgh speaks to a commitment to ministry. . . . The people of First Lutheran Church are dedicated to their continued presence in downtown Pittsburgh. It is not an easy task, however. Over the past 10 years, this congregation of just over 230 giving units has raised over $750,000 to restore and preserve its century-old building. At the same time it has expanded its staff and its ministry to fulfill its mission. . . ." The bishop, however, recognizing the strength of First Church, chose a congregation that needed his encouragement.

A special meeting of the council was held May 27, 1993 to receive a report of the Staff Support Committee regarding its annual performance review of the director of music. They found that during his seven-year tenure he did not fulfill the goals of the music program, specifically the increase of the size of the adult choir and the development of a children's choir. They found him insensitive to the needs of volunteers, who after working all day, come to the church for choir rehearsal only to find a less than full rehearsal. Spring and fall concerts increased in cost and declined in attendance and had, in the judgment of the committee, become performances rather than services of worship with most of the musicians coming not from within the congregation but from outside. Unhappy with his compensation, he refused to give any additional time to the music ministry of the congregation. The committee recommended and the council approved the immediate termination of his services. He was given the option to resign and sixty days of pay and benefits as specified in his employment agreement.

John W. Becker was engaged as interim director of music, and his presence encouraged a thorough review of the role of music in the ministry of First Church involving a cross-section of the membership of the church.

September 19, 1994, the name of Cynthia A. Pock was presented to the council as the worship and music committee's choice for the position of director of music, which, in recognition of the expanded duties of the position, was renamed, in the German style, Cantor. The council approved the recommendation and a call was extended to her to be the Cantor of First Church.

Cynthia Pock is a native of Pittsburgh, raised in the Lutheran Church—Missouri Synod, and a 1979 graduate of Carnegie Mellon University with a Bachelor of Fine Arts degree in music, with a major in Organ. In 1982 she received the Master of Fine Arts degree from Carnegie Mellon. From 1980-1982 she was assistant organist/choirmaster at Calvary Episcopal Church in Shadyside; 1982-1987 she served as director of music at Zion Lutheran Church in Brentwood; 1987-1994 Minister of Music at Sunset Hills United Presbyterian Church in Mount Lebanon. She also worked for four years as a teacher of general and vocal music in the Pittsburgh public schools, was an instructor in organ, voice, and handbells at the City Music Center of Duquesne University, and instructor of organ in the Carnegie Mellon University College Preparatory Program, and accompanist and organist with the Pittsburgh Oratorio Society. The committee recognized in addition to her obvious musical ability her strong commitment to historic Lutheran liturgy and worship, and her understanding that she was not simply the resident musician but primarily a woman of the Church. She was installed as Cantor of First Church November 27, 1994.

Billy Graham brought his crusade to Three Rivers Stadium in Pittsburgh June 2-6, 1993. Pastor Gleason served on the Executive and Administrative committees for the event and gave the benediction at the Saturday evening gathering.

In his teaching time at the July council meeting, Pastor Gleason raised three questions for the council to consider: what is it that brings people here on Sunday morning? What can we offer that other congregations cannot? What are the expectations of people when they come to a downtown church? The basic answer that was given was excellence in ministry, programming, and worship. Note was taken in the following month that there were forty-three children under the fifth-grade level. "The Council discussed how to keep the older youth active in the congregation."

Questions regarding the Strawberry Way Christian Day Care Center had begun to appear. In November 1994, the council discussed the matter in the light of increasing deficits (in October 1994 the deficit stood at $10,110) and the growth of other day care centers downtown. The Center had become only marginally a ministry of the church. The Center makes great demands on staff time and energy and on the limited space available in the building. "It was generally agreed that the congregation could be proud of the ministry and grateful for the work of the members of the congregation and day care staff who performed their work well and rendered an important service to families." Nonetheless, it was also agreed that it was time for the congregation to begin phasing out this ministry and using the congregation's gifts in other ways to the glory of God. The council voted 13 to 1 with one abstention to close the Center no later than January 31, 1995

The closing of the day care center, the calling of a Cantor, capital campaigns, increase in membership and attendance, the formation of the Evangelical Lutheran Church in America together suggested to Pastor Gleason that the congregation needed to examine itself and ask, Is our vision for ministry in downtown Pittsburgh still clear? Are we doing what is necessary to see that vision happen? A one-day retreat in the spring of 1995 explored these questions.

The tower of First Church was designed to house bells but none had been installed. After searching for many years, John C. Harmon, visiting the Pittsburgh Children's Museum with his two daughters, discovered three church bells on its grounds, still in their yokes. His research revealed that they had been given by William Zoller in 1898 to St. Paul's German United Evangelical Church on East Street on the North Side that was demolished in the early 1970s to make way for the construction of Interstate 279. When the Urban Redevelopment Authority bought the church for demolition, the bells came into the possession of the Pittsburgh History and Landmarks Foundation which placed them in the courtyard of the Allegheny City Post Office on the North Side, which it had rescued from demolition, restored, and was using as its office and museum. After the Foundation moved to Station Square in 1991, the Foundation gave the building and its architectural artifacts, including the bells, to the Pittsburgh Children's Museum. A donation of $1,000 to the Children's Museum obtained the bells for First Church. Verdin Bell Company of Cincinnati figured the cost to restore and hang the bells to be $50,000. A benefactor from outside the congregation, Emma O. Sharp, gave $25,000 toward the cost of restoration by the Verdin Bell Company; her daughter, Susan Sharp Dorrance, gave another $10,000; and the congregation contributed the remainder. The bronze bells were cast in the late nineteenth century at the Fulton Bell Foundry in Lawrenceville and bear the name of their donor, William Zoller, as well as their own German names, Glaube,

Hoffnung, and Liebe (Faith, Hope, and Love).[221] According to ancient tradition bells, whose voice gives them life, were treated as persons, given names and even baptized.

The bells were hung in the tower and were blessed and dedicated on Sunday, November 19, 1995; members of the Zoller family and the generous donors were present for the service. The story of the bells was featured on television and carried by the Associated Press news service. The bells announce the approach and then the beginning of worship each Sunday. A single bell rings daily at 11:55 a.m. to announce the noon Liturgy; three bells ring at 12:10 to announce the beginning of the Liturgy. They ring at 6 p.m. on Saturday night to announce the beginning of the Lord's Day.

The three bells now speak to the city from the tower of First Church, every day of the week, declaring to all who hear them that the church is going about its business on Grant Street.[222]

David Gleason blessing the bells

During the liturgy a bell is rung at the elevations following the consecration of the bread and of the wine, during the praying of the Our Father (the *Vater Unser* bell) to invite those outside the church to join in praying our Lord's Prayer, at the Easter Vigil to announce the glad news of the resurrection. The bells toll for funerals and peal for weddings. They also declare the church's involvement in the life of the city. They have tolled as the funeral procession for three police offers killed in the line of duty in April 2009 passed along Grant Street, and they pealed in celebration in 2009 during the parade of the Super Bowl champion Steelers and again later that year during the parade for the Penguins when they won the Stanley Cup. The bells are the voice of the church.

Ecumenical relationships were beginning to flourish. A Call to Covenant was issued by Donald McCoid, the Lutheran bishop, Donald Wuerl, the Roman Catholic bishop of Pittsburgh, and Alden Hathaway, the Episcopal Bishop of Pittsburgh on February 18, 1995. Significant points included a formal covenantal relationship on a local level; making use of redundant facilities and personnel; participation in one another's educational ministry and offering courses on the unity of the Church; collegial work by the staff members of the churches, sharing special skills and resources.

A master plan was developed presenting the major needs of the congregation and its building and was adopted unanimously by the church council January 20, 1997. Characteristically of the congregation during these years, the recommendation concerning the impending capital appeal was prefaced with a statement of the work of the congregation. "With the guidance of the Holy Spirit, First Lutheran Church has developed a clear vision for its ministry in the heart of Pittsburgh into the 21st century. This vision is embodied in the congregation's commitment to maintain a strong Christian witness that is informed by faithfulness to the Word of Holy Scripture and to the historic Lutheran Confessions. The Congregation recognizes that an authentic Lutheran witness must be shaped by a central focus on worship in Word and Sacraments, by dedication to the educational ministry of Christ's Church as an outgrowth of our baptismal covenant, by efforts to draw unbelievers and the unchurched into the presence of Christ, by compassionate concern for the basic human needs of all God's children, and by wise stewardship of the gifts God has graciously entrusted to us for ministry."

A list of major needs follows: replacement of the slate roof over the chapel, replacement of the flat roof over the offices, replacement of the slate roof of the tower, restoration of a cross to the spire, completion of the renovation of the chancel by the expansion and improvement of the choir loft, improving the lighting of the nave, reconfiguration of the lower level of the church, renovation of the office complex, commitment to benevolent outreach, and support of the church's camps. "Therefore, be it resolved that the Congregation of First Lutheran Church undertake a capital campaign entitled "Celebrate the Vision: 2000," for the purpose of raising $675,000 over a three-year period" beginning February 9, 1997. The season of Lent was "devoted to promoting the campaign and to building an understanding of the vision for the congregation's ministry which necessitates such a campaign." The priorities for expenditure were listed: (1) replacement of the chapel slate roof; (2) replacement of the tower slate roof and cross; (3) repairs to the nave and renovation of the choir loft; (4) renovation of the lower level of the church, including necessary work for the replacement of the church's heating and air conditioning systems; (5) a contribution of at least $12,500 to the capital campaign of Camp Lutherlyn to be paid in three installments during 1997, 1998, and 1999. It was further resolved that the congregation adopt a challenge goal of $280,000 for the renovation of the office complex and chapel as a further phase of the "Celebrate the Vision: 2000" campaign to be achieved by the close of the year 2002.

On Sunday, February 9, the Transfiguration of Our Lord on the Lutheran calendar, the proposal was presented to the congregation, and the campaign began. Ralph Alster of Mount Lebanon was selected as the architect in January 1998. The original estimate of the cost of the work was $955,000. The final estimate was $1,070,000 plus the cost of the chapel roof and the tower, for a total of $1,257,000. Undaunted, with a remarkable display of confidence and faith, the church council authorized Ralph Alster to prepare construction drawings for the whole project.

A retreat for parish leaders was held February 20, 1999 to consider the advisability of moving directly into Phase II of the renovation plan in view of the unexpected necessity of replacing the heating system in the church and chapel and the cost of Phase I work having increased from $675,000 to $950,000. The cost of completing Phase II and of installing an elevator to serve each of the three levels of the building was estimated to be $400,000. The unanimous decision was to continue the work to avoid later increases in cost and to lessen the future disruption of the ministry of the parish. The new spaces were dedicated in the afternoon of May 7, 2000, followed by a festive reception in what was now Holy Cross Hall.

In May 2000 the City of Pittsburgh and the Historic Review Commission gave a Preservation Award to the congregation "for the excellent interior restoration of the First Lutheran Church."

June 11, 1997 was the 25th anniversary of Pastor Gleason's ordination. A celebration was held in the church Sunday afternoon June 15. Pastor Gleason presided at the Eucharist; the preacher was the Reverend Dr. Philip Pfatteicher, then Professor of English and Religious Studies at East Stroudsburg University of Pennsylvania.

The cantor was contributing her abilities and her energy to the expansion of the music program of the congregation. A handbell choir began rehearsals in January 1998.

In April 1998 Pastor Ubbelohde submitted her resignation as Assistant Pastor to accept a call as Pastor of St. Luke's Church in West View. During her eight years at First Church, the work of social ministry expanded in a variety of ways and more members of the congregation became involved in the ministry. Her noteworthy strength was pastoral visitation of the sick and the homebound.

Pastor Ubbelohde's resignation was effective May 31. The next day the council drew up a description of the position of senior pastor, accountable to the council, and of an assistant or associate pastor, accountable to the senior pastor and to the council. At the June 15 meeting of the council Pastor Gleason devoted much of his report to discussing "the Call process and the theology associated with it." Once again, he reminded the council that everything the Church does has a theological dimension.

The search for a second pastor proceeded slowly. At the end of the summer, Pastor Philip Pfatteicher, then living in Madison, Wisconsin, in a conversation with Pastor Gleason indicated that he would be willing to assist the congregation until a second pastor was found. The church council on September 21, 1998 unanimously approved a motion "that The Reverend Dr. Philip H. Pfatteicher be engaged to serve as Interim Associate Pastor of First Lutheran Church for an indefinite period beginning November 1, 1998." December 21, the call committee began talking with him about removing the word "interim" from his title and in January he was presented to the congregation for a call to serve as associate pastor for a term of four years "and that in the event of the Senior Pastor's death, resignation, or retirement, such Call be terminated no later than six months after the termination of the Senior Pastor's Call." His four-year term began March 1, 1999 and was twice renewed.

Philip Pfatteicher, born in Philadelphia, is a graduate of Amherst College (B.A. in English), the Lutheran Theological Seminary at Philadelphia (B.D.), the University of Pennsylvania (M.A., Ph.D. in English Literature), and Union Theological Seminary in New York (S.T.M. in systematic theology). He was assistant pastor of Trinity Church in South Philadelphia (1960-1964), Pastor of Bethany Church in the South Bronx, New York City, (1964-1968) and Professor of English at East Stroudsburg University of Pennsylvania (1968-1998) where he also served as chair of the department and Lutheran campus pastor.

In the fall 1999 semester Pastor Pfatteicher, at the invitation of Professor Ann Labounsky, chair of the Department of Organ and Sacred Music at Duquesne University and a member of First Church, began service as adjunct professor of sacred music at Duquesne in the area of Hymnology and Liturgics, teaching one course each semester.

The State Community Bankers Association in honor of Glen and LaVonne Johnson provided a gift to design and install a Tabernacle for the safe keeping of the Blessed Sacrament. The Tabernacle[223] (also called an aumbry) was designed by William Brocious in conjunction with New Guild Studios of Braddock, who fabricated it. It was installed during the week of October 5, 1998. The closed doors present the traditional symbols of the four Evangelists[224], found also on the Cantini cross in the south narthex. When opened, the doors form a triptych that complements the design of the lunette above the altar. The tabernacle icon portrays the Virgin Mother as the Mater Dolorosa (Mother of Sorrows), seated and grieving over the crucified body of her Son. The adoring angels of the lunette appear in the tabernacle in mourning, holding funeral candles to drive back the darkness of death and to promise the resurrection of him whose sacramental presence is enshrined in the safe behind the central panel. The door of the safe is embellished with the Lamb of God with his banner of victory, recalling the mosaic in the center of the marble high altar, the columbarium, and the center of the Cantini cross. The white presence lamp above it, indicating the reservation of the Sacrament, was given by Ernest and Lois Schindehette.

The spire that rises from the tower is covered in slate, now with a subtle drop-like pattern descending from the cross, suggesting the water of baptism and the blood of the crucified Christ and also the blood and water that flowed from the side of Christ giving birth to the Church. The spire thus lifts the eyes and hearts toward heaven and also proclaims the life that comes down from above.

The spire is crowned with a splendidly-wrought cross, designed by William E. Brocious and given as a combined gift of Irma and Donald Goertzen in memory of their fathers. G. B. Rundstrom and Emil Goertzen, and in honor of their mothers, Alice Rundstrom and Margaret Goertzen; and a gift of Glen and LaVonne Johnson to First Church and to the City of Pittsburgh in memory of the founders of First Lutheran Church who possessed the vision to plant a church in the heart of the city and in honor of the faithful people of God who continue a strong witness to Christ through the ministry of the parish. The cross is fabricated of stainless steel tubing tapered at each end and covered with gold leaf. Polished flat stainless steel bars held in place with quatrefoil fasteners form the petals of a cross flurée (or fleury), a "flowered cross" which, by the open buds at the end of the cross arms, suggests the maturing Christian. The base of the cross, which caps the spire is made of terne-coated stainless steel that ages with time to a slate gray patina.

Blessing the spire cross

At noon on Monday, November 2, 1998, the cross was blessed in the courtyard of the church and raised to the top of the spire. The installation was deliberately timed to coincide with lunch time in the city to attract attention to the new life of the old church.

Raising the spire cross   *The spire and cross*

As the cross was slowly lifted to its location, the tower bells pealed continually. The city of Pittsburgh presented an award for the cross to the congregation, to William Brocious the designer, and to NIKO Contracting Company which installed it.

The cross is best appreciated not by members of the congregation as they enter and leave the church or by passersby at street level but by office workers in the adjoining buildings whose office windows look out directly at the sign of salvation. The splendid cross is thus an example of selfless giving.

Contributions had been received by the congregation for the installation of a columbarium[225] in the north narthex. The Memorial and Fine Arts Committee did not want a standard installation from a catalogue, and so a distinctive design was created by William Brocious and Christine Torie. The Lamb Studios of New York presented a proposal for a 100-niche columbarium with glass panels on a large door. The work languished in their studios, and eventually in May 1999 the congregation negotiated a release from their contract with them and in July engaged New Guild Studios of Braddock to complete the project at a cost of $53,500. There were to be 100 niches, each with space for two urns. An additional $15,325 was later approved to cover enrichments of the original design. The sub-floor of the space had to be rebuilt to support the 3,000 pound weight of the new structure, and the floor tiles, original to the building, most of which had come loose over the years, had to be removed and reset. The new space was given the name the Lamb of God Oratory from the central image on the door of the columbarium and the new use of the space primarily as a place of prayer and secondarily as an entrance to the church. The oratory and columbarium were blessed and dedicated on All Saints' Sunday, November 5, 2000. A red votive lamp was given by Ernest and Lois Schindehette and was dedicated on the Feast of the Nativity of St. John the Baptist, June 24, 2001. Glass doors were fabricated to replace the original oak doors leading into the oratory to make the space visible from the nave. The new entrance, with +Lamb+of+God+Oratory+ in gold letters over the glass doors, is a gift in memory of Daniel Daring Headrick by his family. The doors, made by Wilson and McCracken of Lawrenceville, who had rebuilt the organ case, were dedicated May 20, 2007.

In January 2001 Pastor Gleason reported to the council that an anonymous donor had given $10,000 to install stations of the cross in the church. The bronze stations were made by a Spanish company and set in wood frames designed by New Guild Studios. The fourteen stations were installed in 2002 and dedicated on the First Sunday in Lent, February 17. The stations were used for the first time at Evening Prayer on that Sunday. The remainder of the gift was used to purchase fourteen ceramic stations of the cross for Holy Cross Hall for use by the Sunday School.

Reformation Day, Sunday October 31, 1999, the Most Reverend Donald W. Wuerl, Bishop of the Roman Catholic Diocese of Pittsburgh preached at the 11:00 a.m. Eucharist in recognition of the signing that day in Augsburg, Germany (where the Augsburg Confession was presented to the Holy Roman Emperor in 1530) of the Joint Declaration on Justification by representatives of the Lutheran World Federation and the Roman Catholic Church, declaring substantial agreement on the basic issue that had divided the churches at the time of the Reformation. It was the second time a Roman Catholic bishop had preached in the First Church. On Reformation Sunday 1972, the preacher was Bishop Anthony Bosco, then auxiliary bishop of Pittsburgh and later Bishop of Greensburg. At 4 p.m. that afternoon in 1999 the priests and choir of St. Mary of Mercy Roman Catholic Church at the Point joined the clergy, choir, and congregation of First Church in singing Evening Prayer in First Church.

The accomplishment of full communion between the Episcopal Church and the Evangelical Lutheran Church in America was celebrated in First Church on the first day of the Week of Prayer for Christian Unity, January 18, the Confession of St. Peter, 2001. Bishop Robert Duncan of the Episcopal Diocese of Pittsburgh was the presiding minister at the Eucharist, and Bishop Donald J. McCoid of the Lutheran Synod of Southwestern Pennsylvania was the preacher. Acting on that agreement, First Church, January 16, 2006, called the Reverend Daniel Hall, M.D., a priest of the Episcopal Church, as priest in residence. The non-stipendiary arrangement allows him to exercise his priestly ministry beside his primary work as a physician and surgeon.

In September 2000, a significant change was made in the daily worship schedule at First Church: the Holy Eucharist began to be celebrated every weekday, Monday through Friday. The Monday mass continued to have an emphasis on healing. Music, at least prelude, hymn, and postlude, was a part of each service on at least four days each week to accommodate the Cantor's day off. With the appointment of an organ scholar from Duquesne University music was part of each service Monday through Friday. The liturgies are usually sung. A layperson always serves as assisting minister. The original intention was to include other pastors of churches with whom we are in full communion as well as other Lutheran clergy as presiding ministers at these services. After some months' experience with that plan, it was ultimately decided that, as burdensome as daily celebrating and preaching may sometimes seem to the two pastors, it was best generally to limit the Eucharistic presidency to them. Daily Eucharist has proved to be a significant even indispensable aspect of the ministry of the parish. Those who attend are not many, although attendance usually increases during Lent, but those who attend come from many backgrounds. Not many are members of the congregation; most are not Lutheran. Some are regulars, others come occasionally, and some pass through. Every time the pastors wonder about the stewardship of their time in preparing these services, someone comes along to whom the liturgies are a great comfort or encouragement. One man, who attended nearly every day in Lent and Easter in 2009 and then disappeared, later sent Pastor Gleason an e-mail: "I had the opportunity to attend your noon services for several weeks during a very difficult time. It was through these services I found strength to overcome my difficulties and deal with some hard decisions. The crisis has passed, but I wanted you to know how meaningful those services were to me, especially the Monday healing service. Thank you for the inspiration and prayer." He is but one of many who in one way or another express such sentiments.

In 2003 an attorney from southern California sent his friends and also First Church a seven-page Christmas letter in which he related his experience in Pittsburgh on Presidents' Day, Monday, February 17, 2003. He had arrived in the city the previous night on the last flight before "the biggest blizzard in twenty years" shut down the airport. After he arrived, he learned from his wife, who was "struggling with a chronic illness," that their son had been hospitalized, dangerously ill. Three thousand miles from home, alone, he found the city nearly deserted. In two hours in three department stores he saw only seven other people including sales staff. Trudging through the snow he saw the sign in front of First Church announcing "Holy Eucharist for Healing 12:10." Although unfamiliar with the Lutheran tradition, he entered the church; six men and women were there. "They must really want something to come down here through the unplowed streets," he thought. The homily, he remembered accurately, was drawn from Mark 8:11-12, the Pharisees asking for a sign from heaven. "'They were looking for a sign,' the pastor [it was Philip Pfatteicher] said, 'for the skies to open and fire to come down, or the earth to open up, or something else to dazzle and prove that Jesus was God, and so do we, but we receive no sign of that kind. . . . Perhaps the sign is that in the midst of what we are going through we see Jesus.'" The pastor prayed for each person in turn, anointing them with oil on the forehead. "He laid his hands on my head [and] prayed for me by name. I took the bread of communion . . . and knew that I was not alone, even in gray, slushy Pittsburgh." In time, his son was diagnosed and stabilized; his wife's health improved. "The pastor's admonition was true. We received no dazzling miracle, no signs and wonder of lightning brilliance. But we have recognized Jesus in the midst of our little family, acquainted with our sorrows and afflicted for our sake, and bringing his gifts of love, peace, and hope. Christ lives with us." The grateful communicant concluded his Christmas letter, "The mere fact that the church cleared the snow off its steps and faithfully placed its sign, 'Holy Eucharist for Healing 12:10' proclaims the life that is in Christ. The gathering of the fellowship in spite of the storm and the inclusion of an attorney from California of troubled mind and spirit gives witness to the power of that life. The comfort and peace that I received from Christ in Holy Communion with him and his children in that place and the thankfulness with which I departed that Communion testifies to the truth of his life."

On a cloudless Tuesday, September 11, 2001 two jetliners commandeered by terrorists crashed into the World Trade Center towers in New York demolishing them; another struck the Pentagon; and a fourth, taken over by passengers before it could strike its intended target, crashed in a field in Somerset County, not far from Pittsburgh. Offices in Pittsburgh were evacuated, since it was not known how widespread the terrorist attacks might be. The nation struggled to come to terms with the magnitude of the demonic assault. A day of prayer was proclaimed by the President of the United States for Friday. It was Holy Cross Day, September 14, and First Church celebrated its regularly scheduled noon Eucharist for the feast. Pastor Pfatteicher presided and preached; Pastor Gleason, who took Fridays as his day off, sensing that there might be a large attendance at that service, came in to assist. The church was overwhelmed with worshippers. They crowded into the church, overflowed into the choir loft, spilled over into the chancel, filled the chapel, and stood on the steps of the church. All available standing areas including the aisles were packed. It was the largest crowd the old church had ever seen. It was impossible to count their numbers, but a reasonably responsible estimate was over 700 in a church that seats 300.

September 11, 2002, the one year anniversary of the attacks on New York and Washington, Bishop McCoid preached at a Eucharist celebrated in First Church for the victims and for peace.

A Steinway piano was purchased with a gift from Glen and LaVonne Johnson; it was dedicated September 16, 2001.

The growth of the church was such that there was a need for a director of Christian Education and Youth Ministry. The concern was that, as had been the case in the past, families with young children would transfer their membership to a neighborhood church which had specific programs for children and young people. A full program of Christian education and youth ministry would serve, it was expected, to keep children at First Church and involve them in the congregation's ministry. The search committee presented the name of Elizabeth Caywood, Associate in Ministry, June 1, 2002, and she began her four-year term. She had experience as Director of Christian Education and Youth Ministry at Zion Church in Brentwood, and she and her family had been members of First Church. After the completion of her four-year term, she chose not to renew it in order to pursue other opportunities.

A search began for another Director of Christian Education and Youth Ministry. At length, Cora Lazor Weiland, a graduate of Thiel College and the Lutheran Theological Seminary at Philadelphia, was chosen and began her work June 23, 2008. The beginning of her work coincided with the beginning of Camp Downtown, an innovative approach to vacation Bible school, making use of the opportunities afforded by the city. Mornings were given to the traditional instruction in the Bible; lunch was at one of the five downtown churches; and the afternoon was spent exploring the city—the mayor's office; PNC Park, the Pirates baseball park; Heinz Hall and the cultural district. The Reverend Liddy Barlow, Minister of Education at Smithfield United Church of Christ assisted in planning and leading the program. Volunteers from First Church comprised the staff. Most of the campers were from First Church, but some were from Smithfield and from First Presbyterian churches. The focus of the work of the director of Christian education became the large number of little children (67 from birth through second grade) in the parish.

Cantor Cynthia Pock expanded the opportunities for young people to serve the Church by creating in 2001 the Bel Canto

Choir for those of middle school and high school age. Soon afterward, she formed the Cantate choir for children in grades from kindergarten through sixth grade. Thus the full music program of the congregation consists of the parish choir of high school and adult singers; the Gloria Dei Ringers, high school students and adults who ring a four-octave set of Malmark handbells approximately every six weeks; Bel Canto; Cantate; and various instrumentalists from the congregation who occasionally enrich the Liturgy.

Katherine Hartman, a major financial supporter of First Church, died January 24, 2002 and left her entire estate to the church. The first $20,000 was used to retire the Columbarium debt to the congregation's Good Shepherd Fund; the remainder was used to create the Katherine Hartman Youth Leadership Fund with a broadly-written purpose of supporting youth leadership-building activities for the young people of the parish.

Katherine Hartman in her Romanian confirmation dress

Born in Valchio, Romania, October 26, 1922, and raised during the Nazi occupation of that country, Katherine Hartman was the sole survivor of her Confirmation class; all the other confirmands died in the war. The ethnic dress that she was required to make for her Confirmation is now in the possession of First Church.

Holy Trinity Church, Greenville, Pennsylvania, shares with First Church leadership in the confessional recovery of the nineteenth century. In 2001 a series of celebrations of that shared heritage began. The first one was held in Pittsburgh; John C. Harmon gave a presentation on the interlocking history of First Church and Holy Trinity Church. In 2002 the celebration was in Greenville. Pastor Gleason preached at the morning liturgies at Holy Trinity;

in the afternoon Dr. Paul Baglyos, Thiel College Pastor, gave a presentation on "Lutheranism in North America: Ill Fitting or Fitting In?" After supper choral Evensong was sung by the choir of First Church. In 2003 the celebration returned to First Church. Bishop Ralph Jones of the Northwestern Pennsylvania Synod preached at both morning liturgies and met with the adult Sunday School class. In the afternoon Bishop McCoid spoke on the topic "William A. Passavant: Pioneer of Our Heritage."

In 2003 there were significant transitions in the church office. Beatrice Weimer, after invaluable service of more than twenty-two years, retired as administrative secretary. She had come to First Church as secretary to the associate pastor Charles Stadler two days a week; this was increased to four days a week, and, when Ruth Hitchcock retired, became full time. At the same time as the retirement of the administrative secretary, Sharon Clark retired as financial secretary. Mary Louise Procacina, who had served in a similar capacity at Trinity Cathedral for twenty-nine years and was well known to Beatrice Weimer and Pastor Gleason, was named administrative secretary. Mary Diego, who had an extensive background in financial work and was then employed by the Episcopal Diocese of Pittsburgh, was named financial secretary. Christine Hoffman, who for five years had been working as part-time receptionist, was named parish secretary on a full-time basis.

The long-time Building Manager John Lanyon died suddenly January 8, 2005. A requiem Eucharist was celebrated for him on January 22. His wife, Margaret, continued as Housekeeper. In February 2005, Daniel Scully, an experienced electrician, was hired as building manager.

A relationship with the Sister Parish Organization, a partnership with Roman Catholic parishes in El Salvador, began in 2004. The program was introduced in Pittsburgh by East Liberty Presbyterian Church. First Church's sister parish is San Jose de la Montana.

Air conditioning was installed in the nave in 2004.

In July 2004 the council approved a two-year capital campaign to raise $700,000 for capital debt and improvements. The campaign was given the title "Keeping Our Promise." The most visible improvement was the repainting of the nave which was done in the summer of 2007. (The nave had last been painted twenty years before; some areas had not been done for fifty years.) After extensive discussions and consideration of various ideas, including a deep Victorian color scheme in the manner of Trinity Church, Copley Square, Boston, a brighter scheme was chosen, somewhat similar to the existing cream color, so as to keep the church bright and cheerful. The Victorian color survived in the band above the wainscoting. William Brocious designed a band of blue at the height of the corbels, recalling a design employed early in the building's history. The band gives support to the window on the parish house side which had seemed to need something visually to rest on. The band also separates the treatment of the background yellow gold. It is plain above the band and stippled below it to give it texture and interest and the appearance of wallpaper.

A second project was the refurbishing of the south narthex, which had over the years become the principal entrance to the church. In 2007-2008 it was remodeled as a memorial to Mercy Russell (1917-2007), who had recently died and named the church in her will. The existing flooring was not original and was replaced with English tile compatible with that in the Oratory. The color of the nave was carried out into the narthex to tie the two spaces together. A wooden arch was created on the wall opposite Grant Street to make a frame for the Cantini cross that was then above the altar. The ceiling of the entrance from the courtyard was painted blue with stars arranged in a constellation that reproduces the stars over Pittsburgh on January 15, 1837, the date of the founding of First Church. Thus the south narthex was as inviting from the street as was the north narthex when it became the Lamb of God Oratory with the columbarium. The work was all done by Ringler Restoration, which had painted the nave twenty years before.

The Cantini cross became available for use in the narthex when in June 2007 Glen and LaVonne Johnson gave $25,000 to the church to commission a new altar cross in memory of their daughter, Lori Susan Wallace, the late wife of Miles Wallace, former organist at First Church. The new cross, made by Mark Humenick of Humenik Metal Arts in Santa Fe, New Mexico, arrived at the church just before Ash Wednesday. It was hung and veiled in white for the Last Sunday after the Epiphany (The Transfiguration) and then veiled in violet for Ash Wednesday and Lent.

The cross was unveiled at the Easter Vigil 2009 as the Eucharist began with the singing of the Gloria in Excelsis and the ringing of bells. It was blessed at the Liturgies on Easter Day.

The cross is a portrayal in metal of Christ the King, *Christus Rex,* clothed as a priest and crowned as King, reigning from the throne of his Cross. The technique is marquetry, a specialty of the artist, in which sheet metals are cut in specific shapes and fitted together. The technique reflects the way the chancel mosaics were produced. Copper is used for the flesh tones of Christ's face and hands and feet. His vestments are made of sterling silver, nickel silver, and aluminum; the chasuble is banded by an orphrey of brass, which is also used for the crown. The orphrey and the crown are studded with round cabochon gemstones, smaller garnet cabochons are used to adorn the wounds in Jesus' hands and feet. Gold leaf covers the projecting arms of the cross which is constructed of steel tubing and copper. Then broad color palette, lustrous surfaces, and light and dark effects that add depth and enhance the work are due primarily to the use of the different metals, which have been polished, patinated, or brush finished to give the appearance of texture.[226]

In April 2005 Pastor Gleason asked for a five-week sabbatical to read, reflect, and rest. "Serving First Church," he wrote, "is a great privilege. It can also be exhausting." His request was granted.

André Bierman, tenor soloist, completed twenty years of service to First Church in September 2006. He is the longest-serving member of the staff.

When David Zubik was appointed Bishop of the Catholic Diocese of Pittsburgh in the fall of 2007, the pastors of First Church invited him to visit First Church and preach. He graciously declined that invitation for the fall because of his responsibilities in his new diocese but suggested the Sunday in the Week of Prayer for Christian Unity, January 20, 2008. He impressed the congregation with his humility (he drove himself to the church), his evident piety, his respect for our tradition and our celebration of the Holy Eucharist (kneeling in prayer throughout the distribution of the Blessed Sacrament.)

During these years, the ministry of First English Church to the German community in Pittsburgh was developing. With the increased age of Professor Eberhard von Waldow of Pittsburgh Theological Seminary, who had long been conducting German services at Christmas and on Good Friday, Pastor Horst Bandle, born in Germany and pastor of Good Shepherd Church in Scott Township, assumed responsibility for the German services and began developing a comprehensive ministry to the German community. *Christvesper* was held on the Sunday before Christmas; the Lord's Supper was celebrated on Good Friday as is the custom in places in Germany influenced by the Reformed tradition; *Erntedankfest*, the harvest festival, was introduced in October; *Pfingsten* (Pentecost, a popular German spring festival) was celebrated beginning in 2009. The addition of the Teutonia Männerchor and the Damenchor at the Christmas service enriched the celebration and increased attendance dramatically. They returned at Pentecost and were supplemented by the Posanenchor, a trombone group. This expansion is a sign of the ever-increasing breadth of the ministry of First Church in response to the changing demographic constitution of the Pittsburgh region.

Although Lutherans in North America had adopted the title "bishop," unaccountably they rejected the idea of cathedral churches. First English Evangelical Lutheran Church in Pittsburgh, in the absence of a Lutheran cathedral, saw its responsibility to fulfill that role without the title.

At the celebration of the twentieth anniversary of Pastor Gleason's pastorate at First Church, John C. Harmon spoke for the congregation in commending Pastor Gleason's twenty years.

"Today is about Pastor Gleason and his twenty-year pastorate here at First Church. As you think of those twenty years, perhaps your minds and hearts turn to the major events: the many magnificent services for the high holy days the Church year; baptisms, perhaps the baptisms of your own children; funerals, perhaps funerals of dear friends or long-time faithful members; confirmations of our young people; reception of all those new members—many of you; marriages, perhaps your own marriage; the services of dedication, and how many services we have had: tower roof, tower cross, bells, columbarium, oratory (and that's just the right rear corner of the church). Under Pastor Gleason we have turned this edifice in the center of our city into a testament in glass, stone, bronze, and marble to the verities of the Christian faith.

"I would suggest that you think about this twenty-year pastorate in terms of all the small things that have occurred during these twenty years that are most meaningful to you: perhaps it is the handshake in the receiving line at the end of a very hot summer Sunday and you are so hot that you are about to pass out, and there is Pastor Gleason in all those vestments, and the only accommodation he makes to the heat is the occasional dabbing of his upper lip with his handkerchief; perhaps it is a meaningful Sunday School class down in the basement of the building before the remodeling on a cold, February Sunday; perhaps it is a chat with the Pastor, naturally over one (or more) cups (or pots) of good coffee; perhaps it is working with the pastor on some project (usually behind the scenes) that will bring some solace, help, or benefit to a person or an organization; or maybe it is just that usual Sunday in Ordinary Time, the paraments are green, and you are so grateful to have this parish church to call home.

"I remember our interviews with Pastor Gleason when I was privileged to serve on the call committee that issued him his call to First Church. His conversations with us were very much like his 'teaching time' that he has at the beginning of church council meetings, and those of you who have been fortunate enough to serve on council will know how meaningful those teaching times always are. As he sat there talking to our call committee about the Church, the Sacraments, Scripture, the life of faith, it came washing over us like a tidal wave: here was a man who really gets it. He really gets it! Here sitting before us was the consummate parish pastor.

"So, pastor, let me give you the highest compliment and testimonial that I can on behalf of your parish family (and, I suspect, the tribute you would most like to hear): You are the consummate, faithful parish pastor.

"Jesus said to St. Peter, 'Feed my sheep.' . . . After this he said to him, 'Follow me.'" [St. John 21:17, 19] David Gleason, you have fed us well and thereby demonstrated most surely your love for the Lord. Your grateful congregation says, Thank you, pastor, and may God's blessing rest upon you and your ministry. And let the congregation in unison exclaim, AMEN."

CHAPTER 10

Into the Future

Jesus Christ has promised that his Church will exist forever. "On this rock I will build my church, and the gates
of Hades will not prevail against it." [Matthew 16:18] It
is an interesting picture. The Church is not on the defensive, attacked by enemies but is on the offense, battering down the walls
of sin and death. The Augsburg Confession says still more explicitly, "one holy church will remain forever."[227] That grand promise, however, does not extend to individual parishes.

The current lay and pastoral leadership of the First English
Lutheran Church is aware of the fragility of what has been developed in the past two decades. Presently, the parish is healthy,
strong, and vibrant, with a remarkable number of young families
and children. But as has happened to neighboring congregations
in the past, the situation can quickly change. More than a century
ago the First Church lived through divisive years in the history of
American Lutheranism when "American" became more important than "Lutheran" in the eyes of many. Doctrinal and liturgical
distinctiveness was diluted and sometimes abandoned altogether,
and the Lutherans became nearly indistinguishable from the Protestant groups around them. Confessional orthodoxy won that battle
in the nineteenth century, but the once-dead issues have revived,
and the Church is under attack once more.

The Church has always lived in a certain tension with the
culture in which it finds itself.[228] The persistent question for a
confessional church, one that bases its life and teaching on a co-
herent, defined body of doctrine, is whether there are limits to
which traditional religious teaching and practice can be re-nego-
tiated in response to changes in the cultural landscape. How much
accommodation is acceptable before the essential content is lost?

For First Lutheran Church, these questions became acute
when the national church of which it is a part, the Evangelical

Lutheran Church in America, published a new service book in 2006, *Evangelical Lutheran Worship.* In the past, the congregation had been quick to adopt the new service book of the denomination. When the General Council met in First Church November 12, 1868, it found its *Church Book,* published just months earlier, in the pews.[229] The *Common Service Book* of 1918 was promptly introduced, as was its successor *The Service Book and Hymnal* of 1958 and then the *Lutheran Book of Worship* of 1978. With the publication of *Evangelical Lutheran Worship* the situation changed. After careful study of the preparatory process and the book itself, the pastors, cantor, and leaders of the congregation concluded that, unlike its predecessors, the book did not represent an advance over its predecessor. The general quality of the music was deemed inferior; the language of the liturgy was judged inelegant and sometimes incoherent; the version of the psalms was found to be an unacceptable rewriting of Holy Scripture, departing from the Hebrew texts in order to avoid the use of masculine names, pronouns, and titles for God. The liturgical texts were considered generally unsatisfactory.[230] The congregation therefore chose to retain the *Lutheran Book of Worship* rather than adopt the new book. It was a step taken reluctantly. In the past, one entering a church and finding the previous book of the church still in use took that as evidence of intransigence, a refusal to adapt to new and perhaps improved ways of doing things. First Church did not want to be obstructionist or recalcitrant. Nonetheless, in view of its confessional and liturgical leadership in many periods of its life, the congregation found it necessary to reject the new book. It was not alone in that decision. Some others across the land arrived at a similar judgment, most notably the Society of the Holy Trinity, an organization of confessionally-minded Lutheran clergy in North America. Because it takes worship with the utmost seriousness as the center and source of the Church's life and work, First Church declined to adopt the book.

The confessional identity of Lutheranism in North America was achieved through hard and diligent work as this history has demonstrated. The future for First Lutheran Church would seem to require a continuation of the contribution of the distinctiveness of the Lutheran tradition to Pittsburgh and beyond.

Such adherence to the tradition is not isolationist or reactionary. It is indeed the way forward into the future. It is carried out first of all in the practice of daily, earnest prayer. This is done in the church in two ways. At First Church there is the daily Eucharist, the Church going about its principal work in this place on Grant Street, declaring the forgiveness of sins, the reading of sometimes creatively jolting lessons from the Bible, preaching both law and gospel, praying for the city and the world, feeding hungry people with life-giving Holy Mysteries. Secondly, there is the practice of Daily Prayer, the regular, incessant prayer of the Church in heaven and on earth, evening and morning, centered in the great storehouse of Jewish and Christian prayer, the Psalms. The Welsh priest and poet R. S. Thomas (1913-2000) in "Adjustments" writes of God,

> Patiently with invisible structures
> He builds, and as patently
> We must pray, surrendering the ordering
> Of the ingredients to a wisdom that
> Is beyond our own.

Diligent, faithful, ordered prayer builds the Church.

The congregation of First Church has learned to treasure its lovely building as the center and sign of its mission on Grant Street. The columbarium, an urban cemetery, is there to remind the congregation of those faithful people who have gone before in the Christian pilgrimage in this place. It indicates even to passersby that here continuity and connectedness are important and that the past is not forgotten. Especially for long-time members, the building is the focus of many memories of past clergy of various and varying interests and abilities, of remarkable saints among the laity, of Christians made at the font and fed at the holy table, of life-long promises made by couples standing before the altar, of the blessed dead sent on their final journey from this holy house. The building holds and preserves these past events until the Last Day when all will be perfected in the everlasting kingdom. The Church is people, of course, but buildings "in which prayer has been valid"[231] are "more like people than stone or brick, because of their vibrant association with the folk whom we and others have loved. They are not so much haunted as thin to another world in which past, present, and future converge."[232] The centrality of the building and what happens and has happened within it, rightly understood, impel those who find forgiveness and life within its walls, to go out into the city strengthened to live more faithfully in thanksgiving for the fullness of the tradition enacted daily in the holy house.

The lovely building, now surrounded by the towers of business and commerce, helps those who make use of it to know who they are by giving them some elements of what is past. The building teaches and reminds those who enter it who they are now and who they were in the past. The connectedness through the centuries reminds even casual visitors that we are not alone, left to our own devices, and it comforts and strengthens them with this knowledge.

The future of the First English Evangelical Lutheran Church in the City of Pittsburgh is admittedly fragile, but its purpose remains secure. Because the First Church is the sole survivor of the many churches that once graced the street, the weight of its responsibility has increased. As the congregation has come to understand, the mission is simply to be the Church on Grant Street.

Pastors of First Lutheran Church

John Christian Frederick Heyer	1837-1838
Emanuel Frey	1838
John McCron	1839-1842
William H. Smith	1843-1844
William Alfred Passavant	1844-1855
Charles Porterfield Krauth	1855-1859
Reuben Hill	1860-1866
Samuel Laird	1867-1879
Edmund Belfour	1880-1892
Franklin Philip Bossart, Assistant Pastor	1890-1895
and Pastor St. John's Mission	
David Harrison Geissinger	1893-1907
George Justus Gongaware	
Associate Pastor	1905-1906
Pastor	1906-1913
Thurston Orville Keister	1913-1917
Charles Peter Raby McLaughlin	1918-1925
Adam J. Holl	1926-1947
Edward K. Rogers, Assistant Pastor	1930-1931
Wallace E. Fisher, Assistant Pastor	1944-1946
Robert William Stackel	1947-1955
Paul F. W. Pieper, Assistant Pastor	1950-1952
Harold Raymond Albert	1955-1965
Leroy Aden, Pastoral Counselor	1959-1967
George F. Shaffer, Pastoral Counselor	1959-1964
David N. Finney, Jr., Director of Education	1959-1963
John Thomas Braughler	1966-1989
J. Norman Thorson, Associate Pastor	1969-1971
Charles R. Stadler, Associate Pastor	1979-1984
Larry F. Mort, Associate Pastor	1985-1987
David Paul Gleason	1989-
Lisa A. Ubbelohde, Assistant Pastor	1990-1998
Philip H. Pfatteicher, Associate Pastor	1998-2010

Organists and Choir Directors
at First Lutheran Church

Philip Emmert	?--1844--?
B[enjamin] Frank[lin] Weyman	
with Charles Baer and Peter Young	1870-1875
Mr. McCompsey	1875-1892
Mr. Diehl	1875-1877
Professor McCollum, Voice Teacher	1885-1889
B. Frank Weyman, Organist and Director	1889-1892
Director	1892-1909
Harry G. Archer, Organist	1892-1909
Frank Benbow, Director	1909-1923
Frederick W. Lotz, Organist	1909-1923
G. Logan McElvaney, Organist and Director	1917-1972
Charles Robert McCoy	1972-1976
James Hunter	1977-1981
Miles J. Wallace	1981-1987
Paul J. Campbell, Jr.	1988-1993
John W. Becker, Interim	1993-1994
Cynthia A. Pock, Cantor	1994-

Specification Casavant Opus 3709

			Feet/Pipes	
	Grand Orgue (I)			
1. Bourdon	(Extension of No. 3)		16	12
2. Montre	(70% tin)		8	61
3. Bourdon			8	61
4. Flute harmonique	(1-12 common with No. 3)		8	49
5. Prestant	(70% tin)		4	61
6. Doublette	70 % tin)		2	61
7. Fourniture	(1-1/3', 70 % tin)		IV	244
8. Trompette			8	61
9. Trompette royale	(Positif)		16	--
10. Trompette royale	(Positif)		8	--
11. Trompette royale	(Positif)		4	--
	Recit (III)			
12. Diapason	(50% tin)		8	61
13. Flute majeure			8	61
14. Viole de gambe			8	61
15. Voix céleste	(TC)		8	49
16. Principal	(50 % tin)		4	61
17. Flûte douce			4	61
18. Nazard			2-2/3	61
19. Quarte de nazard			2	61
20. Tierce			1-3/5	61
21. Plein jeu	(1', 50 % tin)		IV	244
22. Contre trompette	(L/2, extension of No. 23)		16	12
23. Trompette			8	61
24. Hautbois			8	61
25. Clairon			4	61
Tremblant				
Récit 16'				
Récit 4'				
	Positif (II)			
26. Principal	(50 % tin)		8	61
27. Bourdon			8	61
28. Octove	(50 % tin)		4	61
29. Flûte à fuseau			4	61
30. Principal	(50 % tin)		2	61
31. Larigot			1-1/3	61
32. Cymbale	(2/3', 50 % tin)		III	183
33. Cromorne			8	61

34. Trompette royale	(Nos. 1-12 from No. 46 Fron No. 35)	16	--
35. Trompette royale	(High pressure, hood)	8	61
36. Trompette royale	(Extension of No. 35)	4	12

Pedale

*37. Contre bourdon	(Electronic ext. of No. 39)	32	--
38. Montre	(Zinc, extension of No. 40)	16	12
39. Bourdon	(Grand Orgue)	16	--
40. Octavebasse	(70 % tin)	8	32
41. Bourdon	(Grand Orgue)	8	--
42. Octave	(50 % tin)	4	32
43. Bourdon	(Grand Orgue)	4	--
44. Mixture	(2-2/3, 50 % tin)	IV	128
*45. Contre bombarde	(L/2, extension of No. 46)	32	--
46. Bombarde	(F/L)	16	32
47. Contre trompette	(Récit)	16	--
48. Trompette	(Extension of No. 46)	8	12
49. Trompette royale	(Positif)	8	--
50. Clairon	(Extension of No. 48)	4	12
51. Cromorne	(Positif)	4	--

* The stops thus marked are prepared in console only with cable connection to the organ coupling-switching junction board.

Analysis

	stops	ranks	pipes
Grand Orgue	7	10	610
Récit	13	16	976
Positif	9	11	683
Pédale	4	7	260
Total	33	44	2569

Couplers (S.S.L)

Grand Orgue	/	Pédale	8
Récit	/	Pédale	8
Positif	/	Pédale	8
Récit	/	Grand Orgue	8
Positif	/	Grand Orgue	8
Récit	/	Positif	8
Grand Orgue/Positif transfer		(Not affected by combinations or cancel)	

Members of First Lutheran Church who have gone into the ministry

One sign of the health of a congregation as well as its influence is the number of its sons and daughters it sends into the holy ministry. First Church enjoys an impressive company by whom it has enriched the Church. They are in chronological order:

John Rugan
George B. Holmes[233]
Asa Waters
James Quigley Waters
John Henry Wilbrandt Stuckenberg
Franklin Richards
Albert Franklin Siebert
George Henry Gerberding
Dettmar Luther Passavant[234]
William Alfred Passavant, Jr.
Oscar V. Holmgrain
John Leonard Fischer
G. Edward Krauth
F. W. Barry

Samuel Rise Frost
Walden M. Holl
G. Warren Rigg, Jr.
H. Ivor Kraft
Caroline Stumpf
Sandra Kessinger
Susan Montgomery
Charlotte Ebert
Barbara Anne Davis
Edward John Robbins, Jr.
Brian Evans
Brian Chaffee
Carl Hendrickson

In addition to these clergy, Elizabeth Caywood serves as an Associate in Ministry of the Evangelical Lutheran Church in America and Sara Luley is entering the diaconal program of the ELCA..

An Historical Time Line

1748 Ministerium of Pennsylvania organized

1758 English take Fort Duquesne from French

General George Forbes renames the territory Pittsburgh after William Pitt, British Secretary of State

1782 Lutheran and Reformed Germans call as their pastor a Reformed minister.

He organizes the First German United Evangelical Protestant Church, the oldest union church in the world.

1787 Descendants of William Penn grant lots to the Presbyterians, the German Lutherans and Reformed, and trustees for an Episcopal church

1788 Allegheny County created, separating from Westmoreland County

1790 Census: Pittsburgh's population 376

1791 German Lutherans and Reformed build a church at Sixth and Smithfield

1800 Pittsburgh's population is 1565

1806 German Lutherans withdraw from the union church

St. John's, Philadelphia, established, the first permanent English Lutheran congregation in America

1810 Pittsburgh's population is 4768

1812 German Lutherans return to the union church

1814 Ministerium of Pennsylvania begins work among Lutherans in Western Pennsylvania by sending traveling missionaries

1816 March 18. Pittsburgh incorporated as a city

1817 . C. F. Heyer preaches the first English sermon in Western Pennsylvania

1818 Darby's *Emigrant Guide,* a travel journal, notes that "the constant volume of smoke preserves the atmosphere is a continued cloud of coal dust"

1820 General Synod organized

Pittsburgh's population is 7248

1821 The German Evangelical Protestant Church incorporated

1822 George Weyman comes to Pittsburgh from Philadelphia

1825 West Pennsylvania Synod organized

1830 Pittsburgh's population is 12,568

1836 West Pennsylvania Synod makes new attempt to organize a Lutheran church in Pittsburgh

1837 January 15. Organization of First English Evangelical Lutheran Church

January 22. Organization of First German Evangelical Lutheran Church

March 26. Easter Day. Holy Communion celebrated for the first time in First English Church.

Late fall. Father Heyer organizes St. John's German Evangelical Lutheran Church in Allegheny City (now the North Side)

November. Congregation begins meeting in Old Court House until April 1839

1838 October 24. Sabbath School Society formed at First Church

November 19. Emanuel Fry becomes pastor of First Church

December 24. Emanuel Frey resigns

1839 March 13. George Weyman purchases three lots on Seventh Street for a church building

May 9. John McCron arrives as "resident missionary"

1840 March 8. contract awarded for the construction of First English Church

March 11. The congregation receives its charter from the Commonwealth of Pennsylvania

April 5. First German Church dedicates its building at 6th and Grant

October 4. the Seventh Street First English Church is dedicated

Pittsburgh's population is 21,115

1842 November. John McCron resigns as pastor

1843 April. William H. Smith called as pastor

July 4. George Washington's tent exhibited at a fund-raising event for First Church

1844 May. William H. Smith resigns as pastor

June. William A. Passavant called as pastor

1845   January 15. The Pittsburgh Synod organized in the church on Seventh Street

April 10. Fire destroys 50,000 acres, more than one-third of Pittsburgh

1848   January. *The Missionary* established by William A. Passavant

1849   January. William Passavant opens the Infirmary, the first Protestant hospital in the United States (later known as Passavant Hospital, now North Hills Pasavant Hospital)

July 17. Theodor Fliedner brings four deaconesses from Germany for work in Pittsburgh at the Passavant Hospital

1850   Consecration of Catherine Louisa Marthens, the first American deaconess, in First Church

1851   Railroad service to Pittsburgh begins with completion of the Ohio and Pennsylvania's line from Cleveland to Allegheny City

1852   April. The Orphans' Home organized in Pittsburgh. Removed to Zelienople in May, 1854

1854   September 14. cholera epidemic in Pittsburgh

1855   January 8. William Passavant resigns as pastor

November. Charles Porterfield Krauth becomes pastor

1859   September 12. Charles Porterfield Krauth resigns

November 16. Reuben Hill elected pastor. Installed January, 1860

1860   Trinity Church, Allegheny (the North Side), organized by members of First Church Pittsburgh's population is 49,221

1861-1864 United States Civil War

Steel and iron production surge

1862   January 8. Final payment made to George Weyman on amount due him by the congregation

1864   The Lutheran Theological Seminary at Philadelphia established

1865   April 14. President Abraham Lincoln assassinated

1866   January. A lot purchased for a new church building on the corner of Penn Avenue and Ninth Street

May 6. St. John's Sunday School organized in the Hill District

June 18. Reuben Hill resigns

November. Controversy with a minority faction in the congregation which sought to secure control of the property

1867   January 30. By-laws of the congregation amended

May. Samuel Laird becomes pastor; installed the fourth Sunday in June

Dissidents leave First Church to form Messiah Church (disbanded 1884)

November 20. General Council organized in Fort Wayne, Indiana

1868   November 8. The *Church Book* introduced in the services of the congregation

November 12. Second Convention of the General Council held in the First Church

The Ladies Sewing Society organized

1869   June 25. Christ German Lutheran Church of East liberty organized with support from the First Church

November 8. George Black gives funds to secure Lutheran pastors from Sweden and Norway to labor among the Scandinavians in the West

1870   December 25. George Weyman dies

1871   Henry Clay Frick forms a company to buy coal

1872   January. Congregation votes to begin using the full liturgical order of the (1868) *Church Book*

Lots given for St. John's Mission on the corner of Forbes Avenue and Jumonville Street by Jane Barclay Black

1873   November 7. Father Heyer dies

1874   A building committee appointed and plans prepared by James Windrim for a church building on the Penn Avenue property. Project later abandoned

1876   Sunday after Christmas. The first Sunday School building of St. John's Church dedicated

1879   June 30. Samuel Laird resigns

1880   February 1. Edmund Belfour begins his pastorate

Pittsburgh's population is 156,389

1883   November 11. Service to commemorate the 400th anniversary of the birth of Martin Luther

1885   August 12. A lot purchased on Grant Street for a new church building ($55,900)

1886   November 16. The Penn Avenue property sold for $75,000 (had been bought 20 years before for $20,000)

1887   January 3. Building Committee appointed

November 6. The cornerstone of the new Grant Street church is laid

1888   January 2. use of "the clerical robe" authorized in the new church

April 20. The Society for Parish and Mission Work organized

October 28. The last service in the Seventh Street church.

November 4. Dedication of the Grant Street church, erected at a cost of $94,000 including furnishings and organ

1889   April 1. The Seventh Street church sold for $58,000

September 10. Convention of the General Council

October 10. Krauth memorial baptismal font placed in the church

November 7. Ten young men of the congregation offer to pay $1000 per year salary for an assistant pastor who would also have charge of St. John's Mission.

1890   January. The Reverend F. P. Bossart called as assistant pastor

1892   April 4. Edmund Belfour resigns

Summer. Grant Street church undergoes extensive improvements: renovation of the Chancel, introduction of electric lighting

August 7. Cornerstone of St. John's church laid

September. Harry G. Archer begins as organist

Andrew Carnegie forms the Carnegie Steel company, at birth the largest steel company in the world

1893   January 3. Evangelical Lutheran Mission and Church Extension Society of Pittsburgh, Allegheny, and Vicinity organized in the chapel

April 23. David Harrison Geissinger begins his pastorate

Introduction of the Common Service of 1888

October 29. dedication of St. John's Church

First Sunday in Advent. First issue of the *Weekly Parish Bulletin*

September 25, 1898 name changed to *Parish Bulletin,* issued at frequent intervals

December 3. First full rendering of the Vesper Service with plain-song melodies

1894   January 17. Wednesday afternoon organ recitals begin, which continued for ten years

June 3. William Alfred Passavant dies

September 18. Fiftieth anniversary of the Pittsburgh Synod held in First Church

December 9. Service commemorating the 300th anniversary of the birth of Gustavus Adolphus

1895   June 2. Convention of Lutheran Church Musicians of the General Council held in First Church

October 30-31. First National Convention of the Luther League held in First Church; nearly 400 delegates from 20 states

November 4. The Altar Society organized

December. Jubilee anniversary of deaconess work in the United States

1896 November 1. The cornerstone of Grace Church, Allegheny, is laid. The church was dedicated January 31, 1897

1897 Chancel renovations completed: marble wainscoting, mosaic reredos and wall panels, lunette of the Mother of God, brass pulpit, eagle lectern

1898 April 24, Good Shepherd Sunday. Formal acceptance of the memorial windows given in memory of George and Jane Barclay Black by their children

July 13. Auxiliary of the Red Cross formed for relief of the suffering in the Spanish-American War

October 3. The Lutheran Liturgical Association organized in the chapel

1899 January 15. Funeral for Sister Louisa Marthens

June 15-16. The Second Convocation of Church Musicians authorized by the General Council met in the church

December 3. The 50th anniversary of Protestant Deaconess work in America. Address by Dr. Henry E. Jacobs

1900 Summer. The organ rebuilt by the Austin Organ Company

October 30. Concert by the Leipzig Quartette for Sacred Music

December 3. Organization of the Lutheran Choral Society, Frank Benbow, Director

1901 September 19. National Day of Mourning for President William McKinley

Publication of the *Choral Service Book* edited by Harry G. Archer and Luther D. Reed. "This book, together with *Psalter and Canticles* and *Season Vespers* by the same editors, contains the historic service music used in the congregation. The choir of the First Church rendered this music in Buffalo, N.Y., October 8 and 9, 1901." [1909 *History* p. 217]

1902 Resignation of Thomas Lane as superintendent of the Sunday School, after having been identified with it since July 1840, a period of sixty-two years, and having served as superintendent since January 28, 1866

1902-1911 Downtown Pittsburgh experiences a building boom: ten skyscrapers built in ten years

1903 April 5-7. Third General Conference of Lutherans (General Synod, General Synod South, General Council representatives)

May 11. *General Slocum* burns in New York; 1100 people, mostly Lutherans, perish)

October 18-19. Convention of the Pennsylvania State Luther League

1904 December 7. David Harrison Geissinger suffers paralytic stroke

1905 March 1. George J. Gongaware elected associate pastor; began May 11; installed December 3

April 3. Alfred Ostrom and his wife commissioned as missionaries to Puerto Rico

April 26. The Chapel Guild organized

October 1. The Shadyside Sunday School organized

1906 January. B. Frank Weyman gives $50,000 to the Philadelphia Seminary for a library in memory of Charles Porterfield Krauth

January 17. Commemoration of the 200th anniversary of the sailing to India of Ziegenbalg and Plütchau, first Lutheran missionaries

February 5. David Harrison Geissinger resigns

April 1. George J. Gongaware becomes pastor; David H. Geissinger named pastor emeritus

October 2. first meetings of the General Council Inner Mission Committee

September 19. Mary C. Mellander commissioned as a missionary to Puerto Rico

1907 January 20. Service commemorating the 70th anniversary of the founding of the congregation

March 22. David H. Geissinger dies. Funeral in the church March 25.

 April 7 memorial service

April 10. A. P. G. Anderson commissioned as a missionary to Puerto Rico

April 18. Lutheran Inner Mission Society of Pittsburgh organized in First Church

May 6. Charter of the Church Music and Liturgical Art Society secured

June 29. Transfer of the title to the property to St. John's Church, which had become self-sustaining

December 31. Thomas Lane dies

1908 Krauth Library at Philadelphia Seminary completed

1909 March 21. Dedication of the bronze tablet in memory of David Harrison Geissinger

Harry G. Archer resigns as organist

1912-1913 Grant Street hill ("the hump") lowered

1913 January. Shadyside Sunday School closed

May. George J. Gongaware resigns

November 15. T. O. Keister begins pastorate

1914 January. Misappropriation of church funds by treasurer discovered

March. First Church begins advertising times of services in newspaper

August. World War I begins

1917 April 6. U.S. Congress declares a state of war with Germany

United States flag displayed in the church and also outside

October. T. O. Keister resigns

1918 November 11. Armistice signed with Germany ending World War I

Influenza epidemic

1919 Charles P. MacLaughlin becomes pastor

House and lot at 151 Roup Street donated by Joseph S. Seaman as a parsonage

November. *Common Service Book* introduced

1920 Pittsburgh's population is 588,343, the ninth largest city in the United States

1921 Daily vacation Bible School begun

G. Logan McElvany becomes organist

1923 G. Logan McElvany named organist and choir director

1925 March. Charles MacLaughlin resigns

Parsonage on Roup Street sold in order to purchase a new property

1927 February. Adam J. Holl becomes pastor

Individual communion glasses introduced

Beginning of the radio broadcasts of the service at First Church (continued until 1965)

1928 Dedication of refurbished organ

1929 Congregation purchased a property on Parker Drive in Mount Lebanon as a parsonage

Pew rents abolished

1930 Edward K. Rogers becomes assistant pastor for a one-year term

1932 May 5. Revised constitution adopted

1933 Handrail installed on steps to north narthex

1936 March. A devastating flood strikes Pittsburgh; First English the only church untouched by the flood waters. Red Cross uses the church in its relief efforts.

1937   Centennial observance of founding of the church

1939   World War II begins

1940   Money, food, clothing, toys collected by families of the parish for distribution to the poor of the city

South narthex floor rebuilt

Pittsburgh's population at its peak: 671,659; the tenth largest city in the United States

1941   The Anna S. Kugler Missionary Society formed

December 7. Japan attacks Pearl Harbor. The United States enters World War II

1944   Wallace E. Fischer called as assistant pastor

1945   August. End of World War II

1946   July 11. Luther League holds its fiftieth anniversary of its organization in First Church

September. Wallace Fischer resigns

1947   April. Renovations made to the organ including the installation of a new console, harp and carillon, and the revoicing of the reed pipes

Organization of couples of the church to meet monthly on Sunday for supper, study, and fellowship

A. J. Holl resigns

Robert W. Stackel called as pastor

First Church Alert begins publication

1948   February 2. memorial carillons dedicated

Candles put on the altar retable

Lent. Weekday service for men begins in the chapel

Use of an Advent wreath introduced

1949   Albert Ozols, a Latvian Pastor, arrives at First Church to acquaint himself with the life of an American Lutheran church

1950   January. Paul F. W. Pieper called as assistant pastor

Allegheny County's smoke control ordinance takes effect

October 15. Construction begins on the first building of Gateway Center, reclaiming the point of confluence of the three rivers

1952   Paul Pieper resigns

The question of moving the location of the church considered.

The congregation resolves to remain on Grant Street and make improvements to its building

Lay communion assistants organized

1953 St. John's Church disbands and is demolished

New entrance to the church added to the south narthex

1954 WQED, the first public television station in the United States, goes on air

1955 January. Two Sunday services, 8:30 and 11:00 inaugurated

July. Robert W. Stackel resigns

September. Harold R. Albert begins his pastorate

September 15. A. J. Holl dies

1956 June. First Church declines opportunity to buy land next to church

October 22. Harry G. Archer dies

1957 February. Construction of the Porter building adjacent to the church damages wall of the chapel

March. James J. Morentz begins as Director of Evangelism and Promotion

1958 June. *Service Book and Hymnal* replaces the *Common Service Book* in the pews

October. Weekly Eucharist begins (after the 8:30 service on Sundays)

December. The name Vestry changed to "church council"; size increased

1959 Counseling Center established at the church

November. George F. Shaffer called as Associate Pastor and Director of the Pastoral Counseling Center

1960 January. David N. Finney, Jr. called as assistant pastor

Pittsburgh's population is 604,322

1961 September 17. Civic (later Mellon) Arena opens

1962 January. Women elected to the church council for the first time

Christmas Day. Choral Eucharist with Eucharistic vestments begins

1963 June. David N. Finney, Jr. resigns

November 22. President John F. Kennedy assassinated

1964 June. George F. Shaffer resigns

November. LeRoy Aden called as Associate Pastor and Director of Counseling Center

1965 May. Harold R. Albert resigns

1966   John T. Braughler begins his pastorate

1967   LeRoy Aden resigns

Ground broken for U.S. Steel tower

1968   April 4. Martin Luther King, Jr. assassinated

December. Lutheran Student Ministry opens coffee house in First Church

1969   June. J. Norman Thorson begins as associate pastor

Bell Telephone building across Strawberry Way completed

1970   Counseling Center closed

U.S. Steel tower completed

1971   May. J. Norman Thorson resigns

September. G. Logan McElvany retires

1972   August. Mary Elizabeth Hamilton, long-time secretary of parish, retires

Reformation Sunday. Roman Catholic Bishop Anthony Bosco preaches

1973   The three-year lectionary adopted

1975   January. The 8:30 service restored as a weekly Eucharist

First Church designated a Pittsburgh Historic Landmark

April. The spire cross dislodged by a violent storm

1977   November. James Hunter begins as organist-choir director

1978   *Lutheran Book of Worship* adopted

1979   April. Charles R. Stadler begins as associate pastor

Category of associate membership instituted

1979-1983 Renovation of Grant Street

1980   Pittsburgh's population is 423,938, the thirtieth largest city in the nation

1981   April. James Hunter dies

December. Miles Wallace begins as organist

1983   August. Strawberry Way Child Care Center opened

1984   Charles R. Stadler resigns

Renovations begin to improve the entrance to the building

1985   July 3. Port Authority Transit subway opens between downtown and the South Hills

September. Larry F. Mort begins as associate pastor

October 20. Resurrection sculpture dedicated

1986   André Bierman begins as tenor soloist

1987   Sesquicentennial of the founding of First Lutheran Church

February. Renovations to the chancel begin

September. Larry F. Mort resigns

October. Miles Wallace resigns as organist-choir director

1988   April. Paul Campbell begins as organist-choir director

1989   January. John T. Braughler retires

February. David P. Gleason begins as senior pastor

A full theological and liturgical expression of the Lutheran Church begins to flourish

1990   July. Lisa A. Ubbelohde begins as assistant pastor

September. A noon service every weekday inaugurated

1992   November 8. Dedication of Casavant opus 3709

January. Net increase in membership reported

1994   September. Cynthia A. Pock named Cantor of First Church

1995   January. Strawberry Way Christian Center closed

Lutheran, Anglican, Roman Catholic covenant signed

November 19. The three tower bells blessed and dedicated

1997   Master plan for the renovation and improvement of the church building approved

1998   April. Lisa A. Ubbelohde resigns as assistant pastor

October. Tabernacle installed

November 1. Philip H. Pfatteicher begins as interim associate pastor

November 2. New cross blessed and installed on spire

1998-1999 Renovation of the parish house and the lower level of the church

1999   February. Philip H. Pfatteicher called as Associate Pastor

October 31. Joint Declaration on Justification signed in Augsburg, Germany, by representatives of the Lutheran World Federation and of the Vatican

Donald Wuerl, Bishop of the Catholic Diocese of Pittsburgh, preaches in First Church in celebration of the Declaration.

2000   May. Dedication of the new spaces

September. Institution of daily Eucharist

November 5. Dedication of the Lamb of God Oratory and the Columbarium

2001   PNC [baseball] Park opens

Heinz [football] Field opens

2002 February. Stations of the Cross installed

June. Elizabeth Caywood, AIM, begins as Director of Christian Education and Youth Ministry

2004 Involvement with Sister Parish begins

Air conditioning installed in nave

2006 Daniel Hall, M.D. called as Episcopal priest in residence

2007 Summer. Repainting of nave

Pittsburgh's population is 311,218, the 59th largest city in the nation

2008 January 20. David Zubik, new Bishop of the Catholic Diocese of Pittsburgh, preaches in First Church on the Sunday in the Week of Prayer for Christian Unity

June. Cora Lazor Weiland begins as Director of Christian Education and Youth Ministry

2009 Installation of Christus Rex above the altar

Installation of Cantini cross in renovated south narthex

2010 June. Philip Pfatteicher retires

The Development of Grant Street

Allegheny County Court House 1888	Frick Building 1902 [replaced St. Peter's Church]

Fifth Avenue

BNY Mellon Center 1983	Union Arcade/Union Trust 1917 [replaced St. Paul's Cathedral] William Penn Hotel 1916, 1929 [replaced Third Presbyterian Church]

Sixth Avenue

U. S. Steel Tower 1970	H. K. Porter Building 1958 FIRST LUTHERAN CHURCH 1888 AT&T Building 1969 Koppers Building 1928

Seventh Avenue

Federal Courts and Post Office 1932	Gulf Tower 1932 Federal Reserve 1932 Federal Building 1962

Pennsylvania Railroad Offices
1900

Bibliography

AIA Pittsburgh. *Columns* 8:8 (October 1994), p. 29.

Archer, Harry G. and Luther D. Reed. *The Choral Service Book.* 2nd ed. Philadelphia: United Lutheran Publication House, 1901.

_____. *The Psalter and Canticles Pointed for Chanting.* 2nd ed. Philadelphia: General Council Publication Board, 1901. Introduction by David H. Geissinger.

_____. *Season Vespers.* Philadelphia: General Council Publication Board, 1905.

Armor, James C. "The First English Evangelical Lutheran Church, Pittsburgh." Typescript recollections, 1954.

Aulén, Gustav. *The Faith of the Church* trans. Eric H. Wahlstrom and G. Everett Arden. Philadelphia: Muhlenberg, 1948.

Bachman, E. Theodore. *They Called Him Father. The Life Story of John Christian Frederick Heyer.* Philadelphia: Muhlenberg, 1942.

Baldwin, Leland D. *Pittsburgh: The Story of a City, 1750-1865* rev. ed. Pittsburgh: University of Pittsburgh Press, 1970 (1937)

Biographical Record of the Lutheran Theological Seminary at Philadelphia 1864-1962 ed. John A. Kaufmann. Philadelphia: Lutheran Theological Seminary, 1964.

The Book of Concord of the Evangelical Lutheran Church ed. Robert Kolb and Timothy J. Wengert. Minneapolis: Fortress, 2000.

Breidenbaugh, E. S. ed. *Pennsylvania College Book.* Philadelphia: Lutheran Publication Society, 1882.

Buck, Solon J. and Elizabeth Hawthorn Buck. *The Planting of Civilization in Western Pennsylvania.* Pittsburgh: University of Pittsburgh Press, 1969 (1939)

Burgess, Ellis B. "The Evangelical Lutheran Church in Western Pennsylvania," *Western Pennsylvania Historical Magazine* 26:1 and 2 (March, June, 1943), 21-46.

_____. *Memorial History of the Pittsburgh Synod of the Evangelical Lutheran Church 1748-1845-1925.* Greenville, Pa.: Beaver Printing Co. for the Pittsburgh Synod, 1925.

Coakley, Sarah. "The Vicar at Prayer," *Christian Century* 125:13 (July 1, 2008), 29.

Couvares, Francis G. *The Remaking of Pittsburgh: Class and Culture in an Industrializing City, 1877-1919.* Albany: State University of New York Press, 1984.

Documentary History of the Evangelical Lutheran Ministerium of Pennsylvania and Adjacent States. Proceedings of the Annual Conventions from 1748 to 1821 Compiled and Translated from Records in the Archives and from Written *Protocols.* Philadelphia: Board of Publication of the General Council of the Evangelical Lutheran Church in North America, 1898.

Eliot, T. S. "Little Gidding," *Four Quartets,* 1942.

Freiert, William K. *Paul Granlund. Spirit of Bronze, Shape of Freedom.* Minneapolis: Primarius, 1991.

Gerberding, G[eorge] H. *The Life and Letters of W. A. Passavant, D.D.* Greenville: Young Lutheran Co., 1906.

————. *The Lutheran Pastor.* Philadelphia: Lutheran Publication Society, 1902.

Grove, Robert Clarke. *The Architecture of Trinity, Pittsburgh.* Pittsburgh, Trinity Cathedral, 1999

Harriss, Helen L. *Trinity and Pittsburgh: The History of Trinity Cathedral.* Pittsburgh: Trinity Cathedral, 1999.

Hays, Clifford E. *Historical Sketch of St. John's Evangelical Lutheran Church.* Philadelphia, 1976.

Hays, Samuel P. ed. *City at the Point: Essays on the Social History of Pittsburgh.* Pittsburgh: University of Pittsburgh Press, 1989.

Heissenbuttel, Ernest G. *Pittsburgh Synod Congregational Histories.* Warren, Ohio: Printcraft, 1959

Heissenbuttel, Ernest G. and Roy H. Johnson. *Pittsburgh Synod History. Its Auxiliaries and Institutions 1845-1962.* Warren, Ohio: Printcraft for the Pittsburgh Synod of the United Lutheran Church, 1963.

Hidy, Ross F. *Ross Stover, That Sunny Man of God: Lutheran Pastor of Philadelphia.* Concord, Calif.: Lutheran Pioneer Press, 1994.

The History of the First English Evangelical Lutheran Church in Pittsburgh 1837-1909. Philadelphia: J. B. Lippincott, 1909.

Jacobs, Henry Eyster. *History of the Evangelical Lutheran Church in the United States.* Vol. IV in the American Church History series. New York, 1893.

————. "The Lutheran Church in Philadelphia," *The Lutheran* October 15, 1908.

Kempton, Barbara Fretz. *A History of St. John's Evangelical Lutheran Congregation of Easton, Pennsylvania, 1740-1940.* Easton: John S. Correll, 1940

Krauth, Charles Porterfield. *Christian Liberty and Its Relation to the Usages of the Evangelical Lutheran Church. The Substance of Two Sermons Delivered in St. Mark's Evangelical Lutheran Church Sunday March 25, 1860.* Decatur, Ill.: Johann Gerhard Institute, 1996.

————. *The Conservative Reformation and Its Theology.* Philadelphia: General Council Publication Board, 1871. Reprinted by Concordia Publishing House, 2007.

Lambert, W. A. "The Life of J. C. F. Heyer, M.D." prepared for the Father Heyer Missionary Society of the Lutheran Seminary at Philadelphia. Philadelphia, 1903.

Lorant, Stefan. *Pittsburgh: The Story of an American City.* 5th ed. Lanham, Md.: Rowman and Littlefield, 1999.

Luther, Martin. "The Magnificat," *Luther's Works* vol. 21. St. Louis: Concordia, 1956.

Memoirs of the Lutheran Liturgical Association. Seven vols. in two. Pittsburgh, 1906.

Mergner, Sister Julie. *The Deaconess and Her Work* trans. Mrs Adolph Spaeth. Philadelphia: General Council Publication House, 1915.

Moeser, Donald H. "Senior Thesis on First Lutheran Church." Gettysburg Seminary, 1962.

The Musical Forecast July 1926, p. 7.

Niebuhr, H. Richard. *Christ and Culture.* New York: Harper, 1951.

Pfatteicher, Philip H. "An Epitaph for St. Peter's," *Christian Century* 107:6 (February 21, 1990), 175-176.

_____.*Dictionary of Liturgical Terms.* Philadelphia: Trinity Press International, 1991.

_____. *New Book of Festivals and Commemorations. A Proposed Common Calendar*

of Saints. Minneapolis: Fortress, 2008.

_____. "Reforming the Daily Office: Examining Two New Lutheran Books," *Cross Accent: Journal of the Association of Lutheran Church Musicians* 15:2 (2007),

32-37; "Reforming the Daily Office in Two New Lutheran Books," *Studia Liturgica* 37:2 (2007), 249-260.

_____. "The Voice of the Church Bell in North American Lutheran Blessings," *Studia Liturgica* 31:2 (2001), 241-252.

Reed, Luther D. "A Benefactor of the Church: B. Frank Weyman," *Lutheran Church Review* 38 (1919), 291-298.

_____. *The Lutheran Liturgy* rev. ed. Philadelphia: Muhlenberg, 1960.

Reiser, Catherine. *Pittsburgh's Commercial Development, 1800-1850.* Harrisburg: Pennsylvania Historical and Museum Commission, 1951.

Ruff, Paul. "John Michael Steck: Central Figure in Early Development of the Lutheran Church in Western Pennsylvania 1791-1830," *Westmoreland History,* September 2003, pp. 506-510.

Smith, Arthur C. *Pittsburgh Then and Now.* Pittsburgh: University of Pittsburgh Press, 1990.

Spaeth, Adolf. *Charles Porterfield Krauth, D.D., LL.D.* 2 vols. New York: The Christian Literature Co., 1898.

Spaeth, Harriet Reynolds Krauth, ed. *The Life of Adolph Spaeth, D.D., LL.D.* Philadelphia: General Council Publication House, 1916.

Stackel, Robert W. "They Have Lunch with God," *The Lutheran* August 17, 1955, pp. 22-25.

Storey, William G., Frank C. Quinn, David F. Wright eds. *Morning Praise and Evensong. A Liturgy of the Hours in Musical Setting.* Notre Dame, Ind.: Fides, 1973.

Stump, Adam and Henry Anstadt eds. *History of the Evangelical Lutheran Synod of West Pennsylvania of the United Lutheran Church in America 1825-1925.* Chambersburg, Pennsylvania, 1925.

Tappert, Theodore G. *History of the Lutheran Theological Seminary at Philadel-*

phia. Philadelphia: Lutheran Theological Seminary, 1964.

Toker, Franklin. *Pittsburgh: An Urban Portrait.* University Park, Pa.: Pennsylvania State University Press, 1986.

Torie, Christine. "He is the King of Glory: First Church's New Altar Cross," *First Church Alert,* Easter 2009, p. 3.

Van Trump, James D. *Life and Architecture in Pittsburgh.* Pittsburgh: Pittsburgh History and Landmarks Foundation, 1983.

————. *The Majesty of the Law: The Court Houses of Allegheny County.* Pittsburgh: Pittsburgh History and Landmarks Foundation, 1988.

Walton, O. M. *The Story of Religion in the Pittsburgh Area.* Pittsburgh Bicentennial Association, 1958.

Wentz, Abdel Ross. *A Basic History of Lutheranism in America.* Rev. ed. Philadelphia: Fortress, 1964.

Wolf, E. J. *The Lutherans in America.* New York: J. A. Hill, 1889.

Zikmund, Barbara Brown ed. *Hidden Histories in the United Church of Christ 2.* New York: United Church Press, 1987.

Endnotes

[1] *The History of the First English Evangelical Lutheran Church in the City of Pittsburgh 1837-1909* (Philadelphia: J. B. Lippincott, 1909), p. 58

[2] *History,* p. 125.

[3] *History,* p. 155.

[4] Luther Reed, the foremost liturgist of the Lutheran Church in North America, was a graduate of Muhlenberg College and the Philadelphia Seminary (1895); pastor of Emanuel Church 1895-1903, pastor of Holy Trinity, Jeannette, 1903-1904; studied in Europe 1904-1906; director of the Krauth Library 1906-1950; instructor 1910-1911, professor 1911-1945, president 1939-1945.

[5] Philip Larkin, "Church Going."

[6] The members were John Harmon, Nancy Headrick, Myer Headrick, Carda Horton, Gayle Jameson, LaVonne Johnson, Sandra Kessinger, Wesley Nelson, Lee Pedersen, Carl Reuter, Karl Voigt, George Weimer: six men and six women.

[7] For the Lutherans, see Ellis B. Burgess, "The Evangelical Lutheran Church in Western Pennsylvania," *Western Pennsylvania Historical Magazine* 26:1 and 2 (March, June 1943), 21-46. See also his *Memorial History of the Pittsburgh Synod of the Evangelical Lutheran Church 1748-1845-1925.* Greenville, Pennsylvania: Beaver Printing Co. for the Pittsburgh Synod, 1925.

[8] Twenty-four lay delegates were present representing the several congregations. The meeting was held in connection with the dedication of St. Michael's Church in Philadelphia.

[9] That is, a member of the Franciscan Recollects, a reformed branch of the Franciscan Observants, founded to renew the strict observance of the Rule of St. Francis of Assisi, begun in France in the sixteenth century.

[10] See Helen L. Harriss, *Trinity and Pittsburgh: The History of Trinity Cathedral.* Pittsburgh: Trinity Cathedral, 1999.

[11] John Henry Hopkins, an Irish immigrant, after working in the iron business, began practicing law in Pittsburgh in 1818 and attending Trinity Church. In 1823 he was chosen as rector even though he was not ordained. After two months study he was ordained a deacon, and five months later he was priested. He moved to Boston and in 1832 was elected bishop of Vermont and served for thirty-six years. As early as 1851 he was calling for a world-wide meeting of all bishops in the Anglican tradition; in 1867 the first Lambeth Conference was held. His son, John Henry Hopkins, Jr. (1820-1891) was the first professor of church music at General Theological Seminary in New York, where he wrote "We three Kings of Orient are."

[12] Burgess, *History,* p. 224.

[13] Quoted in Burgess, p. 224.

[14] See Paul Ruff, "John Michael Steck: Central Figure in Early Development of the Lutheran Church in Western Pennsylvania 1791-1830," *Westmoreland History* (September 2003), 506-510.

[15] "The Evangelical Protestants were an indigenous American denomination, originally German-speaking. In 1925 there were twenty-seven churches, mostly in the Ohio River valley. Dedicated to religious liberty, Evangelical

Protestants stood for freedom of thought, an open mind, and respect for those whose beliefs were different." In 1925 the Evangelical Protestant Church of North America joined the National Council of Congregational Churches. See Curtis Beach, "The German Evangelical Protestants," chapter 2 of *Hidden Histories in the United Church of Christ 2* Barbara Brown Zikmund ed. (New York: United Church Press, 1987), 32-45.

[16] *Documentary History of the Evangelical Lutheran Ministerium of Pennsylvania and Adjacent States. Proceedings of the Annual Conventions from 1748 to 1821 Compiled and Translated from Records in the Archives and from the Written Protocols* (Philadelphia: Board of Publication of the General Council of the Evangelical Lutheran Church in North America, 1898), pp. 506, 510.

[17] In 1925, while the present building was under construction, the congregation received permission from the First Lutheran Council to hold an Easter service, in English, Easter afternoon in the Lutheran Church.

[18] Burgess, *History*, p. 46: "Yah, gook, der Hacke will auch ein Irischer werde."

[19] *Documentary History of the Evangelical Lutheran Ministerium of Pennsylvania*, p. 479

[20] *Documentary History*, p. 483.

[21] Clifford E. Hays, *Historical Sketch of St. John's Evangelical Lutheran Church* (Philadelphia, 1976), p. 16n.

[22] Hays, p. 16n.

[23] Henry Eyster Jacobs, *History of the Evangelical Lutheran Church in the United States* (New York, 1893), p. 319; "The Lutheran Church in Philadelphia," *The Lutheran*, October 15, 1908; *History of First Lutheran Church 1909*, p. 7.

[24] *Documentary History*, pp. 514-515.

[25] Charles Porterfield Krauth, "Christian Liberty and Its Relation to the Usages of the Evangelical Lutheran Church. The substance of two sermons delivered in St. Mark's Evangelical Lutheran Church Sunday March 25, 1860" (Decatur, Illinois, : the Johann Gerhard Institute, 1996), pp. 39-40.

[26] Krauth, "Christian Liberty," pp. 40-41.

[27] 1909 *History*, p. 8. The Schoenberger family were the largest contributors to the construction of Trinity Church (now Trinity Cathedral).

[28] Adam Stump and Henry Anstadt eds. *History of the Evangelical Lutheran Synod of West Pennsylvania of the United Lutheran Church in America 1825-1925* (Chambersburg, Pennsylvania, 1925), p. 95.

[29] *History*, p. 11.

[30] Unaccountably called "Carl Frederik Heyer" in the 1909 First Church *History* and by Abdel Ross Wentz, *A Basic History of Lutheranism in America* rev. ed. (Philadelphia: Fortress, 1964), p. 65, 265, 428. The *Documentary History* refers to him as he himself did, as "C. F. Heyer." Carl Heyer was, in fact, J. C. F.'s elder brother, who like their father was a master furrier in Helmstedt.

[31] J. C. F. Heyer Autobiography ed. The Rev. W. A. Lambert and published in his "Life of Rev. J. C. F. Heyer, M.D." prepared for the Father Heyer Missionary Society of the Lutheran Theological Seminary at Philadelphia. See Burgess, p. 233; E. Theodore Bachman, *They Called Him Father"* (Philadelphia: Muhlenberg, 1942), p. 101.

[32] Autobiography, p. 69.

[33] Similar training was given to lawyers and physicians at the time. Professional schools did not develop until later in the century.

[34] The disappointment is told in Bachmann, p. 30.

[35] Bachman, p. 71.

[36] Bachman, p. 99.

[37] A literary example is Father Mapple, the minister of the Whaleman's Chapel in Herman Melville's novel *Moby Dick*. See Philip H. Pfatteicher, *A Dictionary of Liturgical Terms* (Philadelphia: Trinity Press International, 1991), "Clerical Address."

[38] Snuff is still popular in Denmark and in its former dependency, Iceland.

[39] The 1850 Manufacturers' Census Schedule lists the value of his annual product as $30,198.

[40] He fought in the Civil War as a private in Hampton's Company and was "discharged for wounds received in action" in the Battle of Gettysburg.

[41] *History,* pp. 5-6.

[42] *History,* p. 4.

[43] J. C. F. Heyer, Autobiography, Appendix to April 1906; quoted in 1909 *History,* p. 12.

[44] The curious name derived from the origin of the street at the French fort at the Point, dedicated to the Virgin Mary.

[45] *History,* p. 42.

[46] Bachman, pp. 102-103.

[47] The dramatic appearance of the old man at the synod in Trinity Church, Reading, to declare his readiness to return to India is told in Bachman, p. 303ff. It is also given in Philip H. Pfatteicher, *New Book of Festivals and Commemorations. A Proposed Common Calendar of Saints* (Minneapolis: Fortress, 2008), pp. 550-551.

[48] E. Theodore Bachmann, *They Called Him Father* (Philadelphia: Muhlenberg Press, 1942), p. 104

[49] *History,* p. 26.

[50] J. F. C. Autobiography, pp. 71-72.

[51] *History of the Evangelical Lutheran Synod of West Pennsylvania of the United Lutheran Church in America 1825-1925* ed. Adam Stump and Henry Anstadt (Chambersburg, Pennsylvania: J. R. Kerr, 1925), pp. 127, 135.

[52] *History,* p. 27.

[53] *History,* pp. 44-45.

[54] Francis R. Shunk, later governor of Pennsylvania, is buried beneath a twelve-foot marble shaft in the historic (1742) churchyard of Augustus Lutheran Church in Trappe, Pennsylvania.

[55] *History,* pp. 37-38.

[56] Robert Clarke Grove, *The Architecture of Trinity, Pittsburgh* Pittsburgh: Trinity Cathedral, 1999), pp. 9-10.

[57] *The Life of Adolph Spaeth, D.D., LLD* ed. Harriet Reynolds Krauth Spaeth (Philadelphia: General Council Publication House, 1916) p. 105.

[58] James C. Armor, "The First English Evangelical Lutheran Church, Pittsburgh, Penna." Typescript recollections 1954.

[59] *The Workman* July 24, 1890; quoted in the *History of First English Evangelical Lutheran Church,* p. 38.

[60] Noted by Edwin Liemohn, *The Chorale* (Philadelphia: Muhlenberg, 1953), p. 141.

[61] *History* p. 43.

[62] *History*, p. 43.

[63] *History*, p. 47.

[64] Abdel Ross Wentz, *A Basic History of Lutheranism in America* rev. ed. (Philadelphia: Fortress, 1964), p. 133.

[65] Abdel Ross Wentz (p. 137) notes that Dr. Sprecher "lived to acknowledge the mistake of 'American Lutheranism.'"

[66] *History*, p. 47.

[67] *History*, p. 48.

[68] *History*, p. 48.

[69] *Pennsylvania College Book* ed. E. S. Breidenbaugh (Philadelphia: Lutheran Publication Society, 1882), p. 198.

[70] 1837-1840 Father Heyer; first building, Sixth and Grant, 1840;1840-1842 Frederick Schmidt; 1842-1847 Godfrey [Gottfried] Jensen; 1847-1850 Jacob Vogelbach; second church building Wylie Avenue and High Street 1848; 1850-1856 J. G. Zeumer; 1857-1863 E. A. Brauer; 1863-1871 J. A. F. W. Mueller; third church building on High Street [Sixth Avenue] between Wylie and Fifth Avenue 1868; 1871-1880 J. P. Beyer; 1880-1895 F. A. Ahner; 1895f W. Broecker; fourth church building, Bayard and Neville in Oakland, 1926.

[71] He was born October 9, 1821 at Zelienople, graduated from Jefferson College at the age of 19, studied theology at Gettysburg, was licensed by the Synod of Maryland October 17, 1842, and began his ministry in a small mission church in suburban Baltimore.

[72] George F. Ehrenfeldt of Clarion represented two congregations; Abram Weils of Ginger Hill, two; Elihu Rathbun of Mercer, three; Samuel D. Witt of Shippenville, two; David Earhart of Leechburg, four. The lay delegates were Jacob S. Steck of Greensburg; George Weyman of Pittsburgh; C. S. Passavant of Zelienople; James Griffin of Mercer; Frederick Carsten of Scenery Hill; and Joseph Shoop of Freeport.

[73] *History*, p. 58.

[74] G. H. Gerberding, *The Life and Letters of W. A. Passavant, D.D.* (Greenville, Pennsylvania: Young Lutheran Co., 1906), pp. 145-146. Pastor Fliedner is Theodor Fliedner (1800-1864), commemorated with his two wives on the calendar on October 5. See Philip H. Pfatteicher, *New Book of Festivals and Commemorations: A Proposed Common Calendar of Saints* (Minneapolis: Fortress, 2008), pp.489-493.

[75] Gerberding, *The Life and Letters*, p.154.

[76] Gerberding, *The Life and Letters*, pp. 148-149.

[77] Gerberding, *The Life and Letters*, 159.

[78] *History of First English Evangelical Lutheran Church*, p. 52. The radical professor was Samuel Simon Schmucker, who had preached the sermon at the dedication of the Seventh Avenue Church; the principal radical editor was the fiery Benjamin Kurtz.

[79] Burgess, p. 82.

[80] The paper had been founded in 1831 by J. G. Morris of Baltimore. It later became the organ of less conservative elements of the General Synod.

[81] *History*, p. 59.

[82] See Gerberding, *The Life and Letters,* pp. 137-138.

[83] *History,* p. 61.

[84] *History,* p. 160.

[85] Sister Julie Mergner, *The Deaconess and Her Work* trans. Mrs. Adolph [Harriet Krauth] Spaeth (Philadelphia: General Council Publication House, 1915), p. 71.

[86] *History,* p. 67.

[87] Philip H. Pfatteicher. *New Book of Festivals and Commemorations: A Proposed Common Calendar of Saints.* Minneapolis: Fortress, 2008.

[88] Mergner, *The Deaconess,* p. 70.

[89] Adolph Spaeth, *Charles Porterfield Krauth, D.D., LL.D.* vol. 1, 1823-1859 (New York: the Christian Literature Company, 1898), p. 273.

[90] Adolph Spaeth I, p. 274; quoted in *History,* p. 69.

[91] Adolph Spaeth I, pp. 274-275.

[92] Adolph Spaeth I, p. 284, quoted in the *History,* p. 72. The full text of the letters to and from Krauth make fascinating reading, impressing upon the reader the spiritual depth of all those involved.

[93] His first wife, Susan Reynolds Krauth, whom he married November 12, 1844, had died November 18, 1853.

[94] Adolph Spaeth I, 346.

[95] Adolph Spaeth I, 288.

[96] Adolph Spaeth I, pp. 288-289, 285.

[97] Adolph Spaeth I, p. 289.

[98] Adolph Spaeth I, pp. 302-303.

[99] *History,* p. 75.

[100] Adolph Spaeth I, p. 312.

[101] *History,* p. 79.

[102] Theodore G. Tappert, *History of the Lutheran Theological Seminary at Philadelphia* (Philadelphia: Lutheran Theological Seminary, 1964), p. 61.

[103] *The Life of Adolph Spaeth, D.D., LLD.* ed. by his wife [Harriet Reynolds Krauth Spaeth] (Philadelphia: General Council Publication House), 1916, p. 379.

[104] *The Life of Adolph Spaeth,* p. 378.

[105] Luther D. Reed, "A Benefactor of the Church: B. Frank Weyman," *Lutheran Church Review* 38 (1919), 291-298.

[106] *History,* p. 84.

[107] *History,* pp. 92-93.

[108] Tappert, p. 56.

[109] The pronunciation of his surname had been anglicized to "cease." He was the founding pastor of the Church of the Holy Communion in Philadelphia and its pastor for twenty-nine years, 1875-1904.

[110] *History,* p. 96.

[111] Burgess, pp. 238, 155.

[112] The issue of "lodgery" had divided First German Lutheran Church as well and caused it to withdraw from the Ohio Synod and affiliate with the Missouri Synod July 7, 1856.

[113] Luther D. Reed, *The Lutheran Liturgy* rev. ed (Philadelphia: Muhlenberg, 1960), pp. 179-180.

[114] *History,* p. 105.

115 *History,* p. 106.

116 *History,* p. 108.

117 As President of the Ministerium he signed the ordination certificate of Ernst Philip Heinrich Pfatteicher, grandfather of the author of this history.

118 Quoted in Luther D. Reed, *The Lutheran Liturgy* rev. ed. (Philadelphia: Muhlenberg Press, 1960), p. 186.

119 While at St. John's (1868-1874) he oversaw the peaceful settlement of "the German question" when in 1871 his assistant pastor, Philipp Pfatteicher (great-grandfather of the author of this history), and the German-speaking members separated from St. John's and formed Zion Church.

120 Barbara Fretz Kempton, *A History of St. John's Evangelical Lutheran Congregation of Easton, Pennsylvania, 1740-1940* (Easton: John S. Correll, 1940), pp. 88-89.

121 *History,* pp. 111-112.

122 The rebuilt St. Peter's was demolished in 1990. See Philip H. Pfatteicher, "An Epitaph for St. Peter's" *Christian Century* 107:6 (February 21, 1990), pp. 175-176.

123 First English Lutheran Church, First German Lutheran Church, Reformed Presbyterian Church, First Presbyterian Church, Trinity Episcopal Cathedral, Evangelical Protestant (Smithfield) Church.

124 St. Peter's served briefly as the Cathedral of the Roman Catholic Diocese of Allegheny from its creation in 1896 until the new diocese was suppressed and reunited with the Diocese of Pittsburgh two years later.

125 John Harmon found one of these prints on E-Bay, bought it, and framed it for the church, thinking it had been lost to the church for a century. Subsequently other copies were discovered in the congregation's archives.

126 James C. Armor, "The First English Evangelical Lutheran Church, Pittsburgh, Penna." Typescript recollections 1954.

127 Thou, Who hast in Zion laid
The true Foundation-Stone,
And with those a covenant made
Who build on that alone:
Hear us, Architect divine!
Great Builder of Thy Church below!
Now upon thy servants shine,
Who seek Thy praise to show.

Earth is Thine; her thousand hills
Thy mighty hand sustains;
Heaven Thine awful presence fills;
O'er all Thy glory reigns:
Yet the place of all prepared
By regal David's favored son,
Thy peculiar blessing shared,
And stood Thy chosen throne.

We, like Jesse's son would raise
A temple to the Lord;
Sound throughout its courts His praise,

His saving Name record;
Dedicate a house to Him
Who once, in mortal weakness shrined,
Sorrowed, suffered, to redeem,
To rescue all mankind.

Father, Son, and Spirit, send
The consecrating flame;
Now in majesty descend,
Inscribe the living Name:
That great Name by which we live
Now write on this accepted stone;
Us into Thy hands receive;
Our temple make Thy throne.

[128] O Lord, how clings our hearts' warm love
    To this dear, hallowed place,
Where, in adoring Thee above,
    Our souls have felt Thy grace.

Here, at Thy Font, the babe was blessed
    In Sacrament divine,
In robes of purity was dressed,
    To be forever Thine.

Here, to Thine Altar kindly led,
    Kneeling in faith and love,
Our souls with Bread of heav'n were fed,
    Yearning for Thee above,

In this dear Refuge of our souls,
    How sweet the hours, though fleet,
When with our friends,—some here, some gone,—
    We sat at Jesus' feet.

Here did we learn the life of joy,
    Were drawn by power divine;
Here led to peace without alloy,
    To hopes that ever shine.

The young and old have gathered here,
    Have sought and found Thy grace;
Their joys been made more bright and clear
    Cheered by Thy smiling face.

Dear Old Church of the past, Farewell!
    We move to another home,
And thence may we ascend to dwell
    'Neath heaven's golden dome.

And there we'll praise forevermore
The Holy Three in One,
The God whom heaven and earth adore,
When here our work is done.

[128] C. P. Krauth introduced the use of the gown to St. Mark's in Philadelphia when he became pastor and defended the practice in two sermons in 1860 showing that the practice, universal in Lutheran churches in Philadelphia except for two congregations, was historic Lutheran use and not a step toward Romanism.

[130] The spire of First German Church, a traditional nineteenth-century Gothic building, was 180 feet.

[131] See James Van Trump, *Majesty of the Law. The Court Houses of Allegheny County.* Pittsburgh: Pittsburgh History and Landmarks Foundation, 1988. The opening prayer at the dedication was by R. H. Coster, another by Rabbi L. Mayer, and the benediction by a Baptist minister, B. F. Woodburn. The pastor of First Lutheran Church is notably absent.

[132] *History*, p. 138.

[133] There is a blank space before the surname "Park", but no given name is provided. He was surely Richard Henry Park (1832-1902), born in New York City and active in Chicago and Florence, Italy.

[134] Gustav Aulén, *The Faith of the Christian Church* trans. Eric H. Wahlstrom and G. Everett Arden (Philadelphia: Muhlenberg, 1948), p. 380.

[135] No. 1 You are to have no other gods; 2 You are not to misuse the name of your God; 3 You are to hallow the day of rest.

[136] No. 4 You are to honor your Father and your mother; 5 You are not to kill; 6 You are not to commit adultery; 7 You are not to steal; 8 You are not to bear false witness against your neighbor; 9 You are not to covet your neighbor's house; 10 You are not to covet your neighbor's wife, male or female servant, cattle, or whatever is his.

[137] Martin Luther, letter to Lazarus Spengler 8 July 1530, *Luther's Works* vol. 49 (Philadelphia: Fortress, 1972), pp. 356-359.

[138] *History*, p. 149.

[139] J. Boyd Duff died April 1, 1920; his wife died September 7, 1938; Rhonda Hines joined the congregation April 17, 1927; Martin Holl died in 1930; his wife, Elizabeth Holl, died March 20, 1932.

[140] See George Herbert's poem, "Church Windows."

[141] Ellis Beaver Burgess, *Memorial History of the Pittsburgh Synod* (Greenville: Beaver Printing Co., 1925), p. 261

[142] *History* p. 149.

[143] *History*, p. 149.

[144] The building was dedicated in April 1897.

[145] A semicircular architectural space, often containing a painting, sculpture, or mosaic.

[146] Explanation of the second article of the Apostles' Creed: "I believe that Jesus Christ, true God, begotten of the Father in eternity, and also a true human being, born of the virgin Mary, is my Lord."

[147] See the hymn from the Eastern Liturgy, "Let all mortal flesh keep silence."

[148] Other significant epithets from the Litany are Tower of David, Tower of ivory, House of gold, Morning Star. A principal inspiration for the lunette may found in the Litany of Loreto.

[149] *Memoirs of the Lutheran Liturgical Association* vol. II ,pp. 57ff

[150] *Memoirs* vol. II, pp. 75ff

[151] *Memoirs* vol. IV, pp. 79ff

[152] *Memoirs* vol. V, pp. 31ff.

[153] D. H. Geissinger, "Liturgy and Doctrine," *Memoirs of the Lutheran Liturgical Association* (Pittsburgh, 1906) vol. IV, pp. 79, 83.

[154] The order began with an anthem by the choir followed by a prayer; the hymn "All hail the power of Jesus' Name"; an address by the President of the Pittsburgh Synod, J. Q. Waters; the hymn "Behold the sure Foundation Stone" (the hymn appointed in the *Church Book* for the occasion, the same hymn as was sung at the laying of the cornerstone of the mother church); an address by W. A. Passavant, Jr., the Missionary Superintendent of the synod; another anthem by the choir; the versicles and Gloria Patri appointed for the occasion; Scripture lessons; the laying of the cornerstone; the Lord's Prayer; "A mighty fortress is our God"; and the benediction.

[155] He served Redeemer Church 1895-1899; St. Paul's, Lima, Ohio, 1899-1907; St. Paul's, Pleasant Unity, Pennsylvania, 1907-1916; and Salem Mission in Cleveland from 1916 to his death August 11, 1918. He was not yet 56 years old.

[156] Burgess, p. 284.

[157] See Philip H. Pfatteicher, *New Book of Festivals and Commemorations: A Proposed Calendar of Saints* (Minneapolis, Fortress, 2008), pp. 103ff.

[158] *History*, p. 175.

[159] Quoted in the *History,* pp.177-179.

[160] *History*, p. 191.

[161] New York: The Christian Literature Co., 1897.

[162] Philadelphia: General Council Publication Board, 1901.

[163] Philadelphia: General Council Publication Board, 1905.

[164] *The Musical Forecast* July 1926, p. 7 [magazine published in Pittsburgh 1921-1948].

[165] Archives, University Libraries, Carnegie Mellon University, Pittsburgh, Pennsylvania.

[166] Grandfather of the author of this history.

[167] Although Dr. Pfatteicher did not receive the call that Dr. Gongaware had anticipated, his grandson, the author of this history, did receive a call as associate pastor eighty-five years later.

[168] The United States National Bank "quit business" in the autumn of 1914; council minutes October 5, 1914.

[169] Presumably Trinity Episcopal Cathedral and First Presbyterian Church.

[170] Presumably Smithfield United Church that derives income from the leasing of land it owns adjoining the church.

[171] The original editorial was reprinted March 22, 1961 and followed up April 26, 1961.

[172] Churchly vocabulary, such as "narthex", had not yet made its way into the practice of the congregation.

[173] There were two Frasch sisters who were faithful communicants, Anna and Mary. It is unfortunate that the identity of the one who assisted the treasurer was not specified.

[174] In the King James Version: "And now, O Lord our God, that hast brought thy people forth out of the land of Egypt with a mighty hand, and hast gotten thee renown, as at this day; we have sinned, we have done wickedly." Presumably the last clause was not part of the preaching text.

[175] Capt. Harry J. Armor, Paul H. Armor, J. Boyd Bert, 1st Lt. Walter P. Berg, Thomas P. Beegle, Capt. John J. Daub, Rudolph E. Daub, Maj. Rodney D. Day, Ens. J. Boyd Duff, Sgt. William G. Duff, Edward D. Fuller, Carl A. Frunck, Sgt. Amos U. Harsh, Ralph W. Jackson, Charles W. Jordan, 1st Lt. D. R. Kunkelman, Fred W. Lotz, Frank W. Niemann, Bertha C. Pingle, Cpl. L. Frank Raup, Goss W. Reynolds, Sgt. Frank W. Ritchey, James Sheafer, Edward D. Sheafer, Lois Singley [given as "Miss Louis Singley"], QM Sgt. Howard A. Vierheller, Cpl. T. Lane Watson.

[176] His surname is given in Burgess as "McLaughlin," but First Church consistently in council minutes and printed service folders has "MacLaughlin."

[177] Burgess, p. 655.

[178] The use of secular language is revealing: "goblets" rather than chalices (was more than one in use?) and "tankard" rather than flagon.

[179] Otto Frederick Nolde (1899-1972) was born in Philadelphia, graduated from Muhlenberg College and the Philadelphia Seminary (class of 1923) and remained there as a fellow and then a member of the faculty for the rest of his life. His original interest was Christian education. In 1946 he became Associate General Secretary of the World Council of Churches and was known for his work in international relations.

[180] His original name was simply Adam Holl. He did not like the name "Adam", and found the use of one initial, "A. Holl," odd, so he added the initial "J"; it did not stand for anything.

[181] A. J. Holl, typescript notes for "Lecture on First Church."

[182] This is the address given on p. 68 of the 1922-1929 council minute book; p. 73 gives 1413.

[183] Pp. 19-20 in the *Common Service Book*. Other "pastoral prayers" were often used instead of the text given in The Service or the alternatives on pp. 156-160.

[184] *Common Service Book*, p. 239.

[185] G[eorge] H[enry] Gerberding, *The Lutheran Pastor* (Philadelphia: Lutheran Publication Society, 1902), p. 344. Luther D. Reed and Paul Zeller Strodach in their books on the Lutheran Liturgy agree, but in a concession to popular practice give careful instructions on how such individual cups are to be used. At First Church the bread continued to be placed on the communicant's tongue (a common Lutheran practice) until early in John Braughler's pastorate.

[186] The final stanza begins "Faith of our Fathers, Mary's prayers/Will win our nation back to thee." The author, Frederick William Faber, was a convert from Anglicanism to Roman Catholicism.

[187] Chandler began operations in 1913 with headquarters and factory in Cleveland and concentrated on a good-quality motor-car for middle income drivers. Their peak year, 1927 when 20,000 cars were sold, led to overexpansion and large debt. The company was purchased in 1929 by its Detroit competitor, maker of the Hupmobile, and the Chandler brand was discontinued.

[188] See Ross F. Hidy, *Ross Stover, that Sunny Man of God: Lutheran Pastor of Philadelphia*. Concord, California: Lutheran Pioneer Press, 1994.

189 A.J. Holl notes for "Lecture on First Church."

190 Council minutes November 7, 1938.

191 Careful users of the language avoid the use of such nouns as modifiers and say "the service of worship" or simply "the service."

192 Philadelphia: Muhlenberg Press, 1959.

193 Minutes, January 5, 1948.

194 "They are beautiful but not ecclesiastical," he observed to a reporter July 14, 1945.

195 Minutes, January 5, 1948.

196 Robert W. Stackel, "They Have Lunch with God," *The Lutheran* August 17, 1955, pp. 22-25.

197 The church, built in 1925, is at Dale and Russelwood Streets. In 1968 it merged with St. John's Church, McKees Rocks, to form Good Shepherd Church.

198 Nathaniel Rue High Moor, Dean of Trinity Cathedral 1931-1962, died August 20, 1983 in Falmouth, Massachusetts, at the age of 91.

199 The seventeen-story building was the headquarters of the H. K. Porter Company, once the leading builder of light locomotives in the United States. It built its last locomotive in 1950 and went out of business in 1991. In 1992 the name of the building was changed to the Federal Home Loan Bank Building.

200 The Revised Standard Version of the Bible, which was to become the generally accepted translation in Protestant use, was published in 1952. The New Testament had appeared first in 1946.

201 His *Morning Praise and Evensong. A Liturgy of the Hours in Musical Setting* (Notre Dame, Indiana: Fides Publishers, 1973) was influential in the drafting of Morning and Evening Prayer in the 1978 *Lutheran Book of Worship.*

202 The average Sunday attendance for 1957 was 465, for 1959 was 462, for 1961 was 446, for 1963 was 427, for 1964 was 415. The number of confirmed members at the end of 1963 was 867; at the end of 1964 it was 806; at the end of 1965 it was 785.

203 Further names are recorded in the council minutes for January 11, 1966: Dr. Robert W. Long, recommended by Dr Hankey, President of the Synod, Bruce Weaver of Washington, D.C., "Rev. Bunk of Florida, Dr. Wallace Fisher of Lancaster, Dr. Eric Gustavson, J. Leon Haynes, Thomas Weber, Dr. Shaheen of Silver Spring, Maryland.

204 The average Sunday attendance for 1966 was 312, for 1967 it was 350, for 1968 it was 329.

205 It was later surpassed by buildings in Philadelphia and Cleveland.

206 Minutes of the meeting of the church council, June 11, 1968.

207 The Rev. E. R. Kappeler of the Lutheran Service Society of Western Pennsylvania, letter to council of First Church, April 9, 1968.

208 The cooperating churches were the American Lutheran Church, the Evangelical Lutheran Church in Canada, the Lutheran Church in America, and the Lutheran Church—Missouri Synod.

209 See William K. Freiert, *Paul T. Granlund. Spirit of Bronze, Shape of Freedom.* Minneapolis: Primarius, 1991. Granlund, known for his exuberant human figures and whose work can be found throughout Europe and in India, Hong Kong, and Japan, died of respiratory failure from exposure to the chemicals and dust involved in sculpting bronze.

[210] European: Johannes Klais, Bonn, Germany; Dirk Flentrop, Zaandam, Holland; Rieger Orgelbau, Austria; Rudolph von Beckerath, Hamburg, Germany. North American: Gabriel Kney, Ontario; Casavant Frères, Quebec; Charles Fisk, Gloucester, Massachusetts; Fritz Noack, Georgetown, Massachusetts.

[211] "The Magnificat," *Luther's Works* vol. 21 (St. Louis: Concordia, 1956), p. 326.

[212] Pastor Braughler's report to the Church Council July 23, 1984.

[213] A principal source was Donald H. Moeser, "Senior Thesis on First Lutheran Church," 1962.

[214] The original sermon was thirty-two printed pages in length. To have been historically accurate, Pastor Braughler should have done as the early pastors of First Church, including C. P. Krauth, did and worn no robe or vestments, simply street clothing. His inspiration doubtless came from The Reverend H. Pat Albright, senior pastor of Mount Lebanon United Methodist Church, who in 1976 in Erie and in 1978 in Mount Lebanon would appear in costume several times a year and deliver a monologue giving an account of the life of a selected hero.

[215] The Augsburg Confession (1530) Article VII, *The Book of Concord. The Confessions of the Evangelical Lutheran Church* ed. Robert Kolb and Timothy J. Wengert (Minneapolis: Fortress, 2000), pp. 42-43.

[216] Council minutes, November 15, 1993

[217] Council minutes, November 15, 1993.

[218] *Lutheran Book of Worship*, p. 120.

[219] The five crosses, in a quincunx pattern, represent the five wounds of Christ (hands, feet, and side), the crucified victim who offers himself to his people at the table.

[220] AIA Pittsburgh, *Columns* 8:8 (October 1994), p. 29.

[221] *Glaube* is the largest of the three, weighing 2332 pounds; *Liebe* weighs 1188; and *Hoffnung* is the smallest at 704 pounds.

[222] See Philip H. Pfatteicher, "The Voice of the Church Bell in North American Lutheran Blessings," *Studia Liturgica* 31:2 (2001), 241-252.

[223] "Tabernacle" recalls the tent in the wilderness during the Hebrews' exodus and also John 1:14 "the Word . . . lived among us" sometimes accurately translated "tabernacled among us." The Greek verb derives from "tent." "Aumbry" or "ambry," from the Middle English for cupboard, is a wall cabinet or safe in which the consecrated elements of the Eucharist are reserved for distribution to the sick.

[224] An angel for St. Matthew, a lion for St. Mark, an ox for St. Luke, and an eagle for St. John.

[225] A columbarium is an urban church's answer to the rural churchyard: a place within the church where the faithful departed await the resurrection. The name derives from the Latin, "dove cote," because its standard design resembles pigeon holes.

[226] The description borrows the words of Christine Torie, "He is the King of Glory: First Church's New Altar Cross," *First Church Alert* Easter 2009, p. 3.

[227] Article VII in the Latin version. *The Book of Concord. The Confessions of the Evangelical Lutheran Church* ed. Robert Kolb and Timothy J. Wengert (Minneapolis: Fortress Press, 2000), p. 43.

[228] A classic study is H. Richard Niebuhr, *Christ and Culture. 1951.*

[229] *History*, p. 103.
[230] See, for example, Philip H. Pfatteicher, "Reforming the Daily Office: Examining Two New Lutheran Books," *Cross Accent. Journal of the Association of Lutheran Church Musicians* 15:2 (2007), 32-37; "Reforming the Daily Office in Two New Lutheran Books," *Studia Liturgica* 37:2 (2007), 249-260.
[231] T. S. Eliot, "Little Gidding," *Four Quartets.*
[232] Sarah Coakley, "The Vicar at Prayer," *The Christian Century* 125:13 (July 1, 2008), 29. The odd adjective "thin" is an echo of Evelyn Underhill's report (in *Collected Papers,* 1945) of a gardener on Iona who called the island "a thin place." Asked what he meant by that, he explained, "Well, on Iona, there's very little between you and God."
[233] Licensed 1846-1847; license withdrawn 1848.
[234] Office editor, *The Workman,* 1889-1899; withdrew from clerical roll; antiquarian book dealer.

Index